# THE LIFE AND THE KINGDOM OF JESUS

## IN

## CHRISTIAN SOULS

# THE SELECTED WORKS OF ST. JOHN EUDES

*Comprising the following six titles and Biography*

THE LIFE AND KINGDOM OF JESUS IN CHRISTIAN SOULS

THE SACRED HEART OF JESUS

THE ADMIRABLE HEART OF MARY

THE PRIEST: HIS DIGNITY AND OBLIGATIONS

MEDITATIONS

LETTERS AND SHORTER WORKS

*Edited under the supervision of*

REVEREND WILFRID E. MYATT, C.J.M.

AND

REVEREND PATRICK J. SKINNER, C.J.M.

SAINT JOHN EUDES
*Father, Doctor and Apostle of the Devotion
to the Sacred Heart of Jesus*

# The Life and the Kingdom of Jesus in Christian Souls

### A TREATISE ON CHRISTIAN PERFECTION
#### FOR USE BY CLERGY OR LAITY

BY

## SAINT JOHN EUDES

*Translated from the French by*
*A Trappist Father in*
*The Abbey of Our Lady of Gethsemani*

*With an Introduction by*
### THE RIGHT REVEREND
### MONSIGNOR FULTON J. SHEEN

1826

*NEW YORK*
### P. J. KENEDY & SONS

**Imprimi Potest:**

ALBERT D'AMOURS, C.J.M.
*Praepositus Provincialis*

Laval-des-Rapides, P.Q.,
die 14ª decembris 1944.

**Nihil Obstat:**

ARTHUR J. SCANLAN, S.T.D.
*Censor Librorum*

**Imprimatur:**

✠ FRANCIS J. SPELLMAN, D.D.
*Archbishop, New York*

*September 26, 1945*

# GENERAL PREFACE

St. John Eudes has been called "the wonder of his age." Orator, founder, reformer of the clergy, he crowded into a life of seventy-nine years so many and such varied accomplishments that one marvels how a single man could achieve so much. In addition to the activities of an incessant and many-sided apostolate, he wrote a number of valuable books, which rank him as one of the most prolific ascetic writers of the seventeenth century.

For many years the devotional writings of St. John Eudes were practically unknown. Occasionally a volume was discovered in the library of some seminary or religious house. Many others preserved in manuscript form were lost in the chaos of the French Revolution. At the beginning of the present century the sons of St. John Eudes united in a tribute of filial piety to bring out a complete edition of the works of their spiritual father, seeking for them in public and private libraries throughout the world. About twenty volumes were found and edited in 1905 by the late Fathers Charles Lebrun, C.J.M., and Joseph Dauphin, C.J.M. This first edition in French, *Oeuvres Complètes du Vénérable Jean Eudes,* ran into twelve octavo volumes with introductions, explanatory notes, analytic and alphabetic indexes of great value. These writings constitute a complete summa of ascetic and pastoral theology. The list is as follows:

*Volume I. The Life and the Kingdom of Jesus in Christian Souls.* In this work the Saint develops his spiritual teaching on the Christian life, namely, that the Christian life is simply the life of Jesus extended and continued in each one of us.

*Volume II.* This volume contains six short treatises on subjects relating to the Christian life:

1. *A Treatise on the Respect Due to Holy Places,* which is an echo of the fiery denunciations he pronounced during his missions against profaners of the temple of God.

2. *Meditations on Humility,* a series of meditations on the profession of humility as used daily in his order of priests, the Congregation of Jesus and Mary.

3. *Interior Colloquies of the Soul with God,* meditations on creation, the end of man and the grace of Baptism.

4. *Man's Contract with God in Baptism,* a summary of the teachings of Sacred Scripture and Tradition on the Sacrament of Baptism.

v

5. *The Practice of Piety*, a brief explanation of what is necessary in order to live a Christian life.

6. *Catechism of the Mission*, an outline of the catechetical instructions given during the mission.

*Volume III*. It contains two important works on sacerdotal perfection:

1. *The Memorial of the Ecclesiastical Life*, an explanation of the dignity and duties of the priesthood.

2. *A Manual of Piety for use in an Ecclesiastical Community*, in which the author explains how the means of sanctification he recommended to his priests should be practically applied in their daily lives.

*Volume IV*. It comprises significant works on the priestly ministry.

1. *The Apostolic Preacher* is one of the first treatises written on the ministry of the Word of God and is even yet one of the most practical.

2. *The Good Confessor* explains the qualities and obligations of the minister of the Sacrament of Penance.

3. *Counsels for Mission Confessors* suggests practical means of assisting penitents to make their examination of conscience and excite themselves to contrition.

4. *The Manner of Serving Mass* explains the dignity and holiness of this service and what one must do to perform it devoutly and worthily.

*Volume V. The Admirable Childhood of the Most Holy Mother of God.* This book treats of the holy childhood of Mary and the practical means of honoring the mysteries and virtues of her early life.

*Volumes VI, VII, VIII* contain the entire writings of the Saint on the Sacred Hearts of Jesus and Mary. This work is entitled: *The Admirable Heart of the Mother of God.* It comprises twelve books covering the complete theology of the devotion to the Sacred Hearts. Eleven books discuss the theory, history and practice of the devotion to the Immaculate Heart of Mary. The last book deals with the devotion to the Sacred Heart of Jesus. It is this work, together with the Offices of the Sacred Hearts, that merits for him the title of Father, Doctor and Apostle of the Devotion to the Sacred Hearts.

*Volume IX. The Rules and Constitutions of the Congregation of Jesus and Mary.*

*Volume X* contains *The Rules and Constitutions of the Order of Our Lady of Charity*, the *Directory* of the Order, and a collection of two hundred and forty letters.

*Volumes XI* and *XII* embrace the Saint's *Liturgical Works*, comprising twenty-five Offices and Masses for feasts to which he urged special devotion, the *Memorial of God's Blessings* and several minor works.

The second French edition appeared in 1935, *Oeuvres Choisies de Saint Jean Eudes,* prepared under the direction of Father Lebrun, the leading authority on Eudistic research. It comprises nine volumes: *The Life and the Kingdom of Jesus, Meditations on Various Subjects, Regulae Vitae Christianae et Sacerdotalis, Man's Contract with God in Baptism, Letters and Minor Works, Writings on the Priesthood, The Sacred Heart of Jesus, The Admirable Heart of Mary,* and *The Admirable Childhood of the Mother of God.* The format of these volumes is compact and more convenient than the 1905 edition, which is now out of print.

The publication of the works of St. John Eudes revealed the extent and depth of their spiritual doctrine. Cardinal Pitra, who directed the Process of Beatification of the Saint in 1909, discovered in his writings a remarkable depth of thought and purity of doctrine. Cardinal Vives has more recently expressed his admiration:

I was acquainted with the Doctors of the Order of St. Francis; I was acquainted with Saint Teresa and Saint John of the Cross, the mystical writers of my own country, Spain; but I was completely ignorant of the writings of Father Eudes. As a member of the Sacred Congregation of Rites it was my duty to study his life and his works, and I am in admiration. Blessed John Eudes must be ranked with the great lights of the Church. His spiritual doctrine is profound and of wonderful exactitude. He is one of the writers who best expounded the doctrine of the Gospel.[1]

The late Father Ange Le Doré, for fifty years Superior General of the Congregation of Jesus and Mary, wrote:

The works of Blessed John Eudes, although they do not bear the scientific touch of the professional theologian, are nevertheless proof of his remarkable theological, ascetic and scriptural knowledge. . . . He is not a Doctor after the fashion of the scholastics of the thirteenth century or of the great theologians of the sixteenth and seventeenth centuries. As they, he might have built up theses and composed books didactic in form; but he was before all a saver of souls. For him the science of theology found its chief field of usefulness in the practice of virtue and in the acquisition of sanctity of which it is the principle. . . . He was a Doctor after the manner of the Apostles, the Fathers of the Church, St. Francis de Sales and St. Alphonsus de Liguori. The science which shines in his works not only emits light; it engenders piety and sanctity.[2]

[1] Quoted by Bray, *Saint John Eudes* (Halifax, 1925), p. 116.     [2] *Ibid.,* p. 117.

The doctrine expounded by St. John Eudes follows the school of Cardinal Pierre de Bérulle and Father Charles de Condren, prominent seventeenth-century ascetic writers. He applies this doctrine to the devotion to the Sacred Hearts of Jesus and Mary, developing and rendering it more precise and practical. He has the rare gift of expressing the most sublime truths in simple, familiar language. He also excels in condensing into a few pages a complete scheme of Christian life and perfection.

The wish was repeatedly expressed that these inspirational writings could be made available to English-speaking readers. Excellent abridged editions of certain books were published in England and in Canada, but they did not do justice to the literary value of the Saint. Consequently, the Eudist Fathers commemorating their tercentenary in 1943 resolved to publish a complete translation of the principal works of their founder. Competent translators were secured and much time and effort were expended to produce readable volumes in modern English, faithful to the spirit and style of the original.

The first English edition, *Selected Works of Saint John Eudes,* is the result. In presenting it to the public the Eudist Fathers and the Religious of Our Lady of Charity of the Refuge, and of the Good Shepherd, wish to thank all those who contributed to the success of this comprehensive undertaking. They are especially grateful to the distinguished churchmen who have so graciously accepted to introduce these volumes to Catholic readers, because they consider that the works of St. John Eudes should be more widely known. The Saint in his apostolic work and in his writings ranks with the eminent figures who belong not to one country and to one religious order but to the universal Church. Three centuries have passed since he wrote the works now being printed in the new world, a striking illustration of the truth that he wrote for all time. He still speaks in accents that penetrate the mind and heart of the reader to enlighten, purify and sanctify so that Jesus Christ may live and reign in the Christian soul.

WILFRID E. MYATT, C.J.M.
PATRICK J. SKINNER, C.J.M.
*Editors*

*Holy Heart Seminary*
*Halifax, N. S.*
*Feast of St. John Eudes, 1945*

# CONTENTS

## PART ONE

### NATURE OF THE CHRISTIAN LIFE

### FOUNDATIONS OF THE CHRISTIAN LIFE AND SANCTITY

ix

## PART TWO

## PART THREE

### SANCTIFICATION OF YOUR DAILY ACTIONS

## PART FIVE

## PART SIX

### SPIRITUAL EXERCISE FOR THE BEGINNING OF THE YEAR

### DEVOTION TO THE MYSTERIES OF THE LIFE OF
### OUR LORD JESUS CHRIST

# INTRODUCTION

THERE ARE only two philosophies of life: one begins with the fast and ends with the feast; the other begins with the feast and ends with the headache. The first is Christian, the second is pagan. Those who compromise and accept a little of each generally find that they have just enough religion to spoil the feast and still not enough religion to accept the headache.

Saints are made by the unreserved acceptance of the Christian philosophy: to save one's life one must lose it. Among these spiritual giants towers the figure of St. John Eudes who in 1637 wrote a spiritual treatise on "The Life and Kingdom of Jesus in Christian Souls," which is now so ably translated into English.

Although it was written just a little later than the Elizabethan era of history, it has the same timelessness as any classic, for eternal truths are not subject either to moods or calendars. There is a certain relevance of the spiritual doctrines of St. John Eudes for our times. First of all, he stresses the value of human nature for these days of de-humanization. It is human nature today that is under attack. The individualism of the last century distorted it by isolating man from his fellow-men, from history and from God. Totalitarianism in the twentieth century destroyed it by absorbing man into collectivities such as the state, race, nation and class. The result was that in war the least rationed and cheapest commodity was human life.

How shall man recover his dignity and become something other than a "hand" under Capitalism, an "ant" under Collectivism, or an "animal" in Psychology, except by the vision of our Pattern Man revealed to us in the Person of our Lord and Saviour Jesus Christ? This is the method of St. John Eudes. The poet would hold the "mirror up to nature," but this saint holds the "mirror up to Jesus." To the modern man who is lost, St. John Eudes gives him Jesus the Way of Life; to the modern man who is confused, the saint offers Jesus the Exemplar; and to the modern man who is frustrated, the saint offers Jesus the Prototype of the sons of God and the First-born of creatures.

But in this work of rehabilitation we hit upon the second great quality of John Eudes: he does not take man who would be re-born back 1900 years to Galilee, but he brings Jesus up to the modern man. The imitation of Christ is the essence of the spiritual life, but it does not mean slavish copying, nor repetition of the same actions under similar conditions. Otherwise we ought to be carpenters, because our Lord was a carpenter.

Much modern Christianity is of this type. It takes a purely emotional and sentimental outlook on Christ, as a humanitarian and nothing more. It bids us look back nineteen hundred years to Galilee; it repeats His words, interprets His actions, as it might those of Caesar or Aurelius—and because it does *only this,* it has lost its hold on the modern man. No reason so explains the decay of Christianity among sects, as this tendency to regard it only as a memory of a man who taught and lived. Indeed, if Christianity is only a memory of the teaching and example of a man, then it *should die*—and the sooner it dies the sooner we can welcome a religion which will put Divine Life into our veins.

Christianity, fortunately, is something more than a memory, because our Lord is something more than a man. He is true God and true man. Being God, He can perpetuate Himself not only by His teaching and His example, but also in a third way, which belongs to Him alone as God, namely by His continuing Life. Others may leave their titles, their wealth, their stocks and their bonds, their doctrines and their biographies, but only our Lord can make a last will and testament bequeathing to posterity that which no one else on dying could ever leave: His Life for the Life of the World. He brought Divine Life to earth at the crib, but He willed not that this Life should be only a temporary visitation of a score and ten years and a localized experience confined to a few hundred square miles. He willed to diffuse it in time until time should be no more, and in space until all the thirsty hearts of earth had drunk of its refreshing draughts.

God is too good to circumscribe the gift of Divine Life to a brief human existence stretching between a crib and a Cross. Did He not explicitly state: "Behold I am with you all days even to the consummation of the world"? And Saint John, speaking of the Divine Life prolonged and diffused in all men, says: "Of whose fulness we have all received." It is the fulness of that Christ-Life, beating and throbbing at this very hour in millions of souls, which gives flesh and blood to His teaching and His example. Because He lives today, His teaching is *not* a cold record written only on the pages of history, but a teaching bound up with life in a living mind; His example is not something that *has* happened, but something that *is* happening, not an antiquated historical phenomenon, but a living force active before our very eyes.

If our Lord had remained on earth, He would have been only a model to be copied, but having left the earth and sent His Spirit, He made it possible to become a veritable life to be lived. Seizing upon this sublime truth, St. John Eudes makes the Christian life a fulfilment, in each and every one of us, of the life of Jesus.

The great tragedy of history is not that men should fall, but that they should fail to rise to the full realization of their vocation as children of God, in other words, that they should miss so much.

All about us we see vast multitudes of men and women of refinement and culture, endowed with intelligence and possessed of every natural virtue and every now and then swept by noble emotions and ideals, but who are living second-rate, superficial, unimportant and morally insignificant lives, because they have never had their nature enkindled into flame by the Spirit of Christ. They may do much for the world in the material order, they may build bridges, harness waterfalls, accomplish great pieces of research, but they never sound the depths of their souls which can be filled only by God. The world of the supernatural has no more appeal to them than heroism has appeal for a coward. They have become so used to the dense atmosphere of the material, that they stifle in the more rarefied atmosphere of the supernatural.

And in this lies the danger of our whole civilization, which is gradually turning away from God. Nothing great, nothing really good was ever done in this world by any human life that had not a baptism of God's Holy Spirit. There is no escape from the words of

Him who presided at Creation as the Word, and at the re-creation on the Cross as the Word-made flesh: "Without Me you can do nothing."

How differently do they live for whom our Lord is not just a figure in the past, but the very Spirit of their lives. The great facts of His earthly Life are re-lived not only in His Mystical Body which is the Church, but in every soul incorporated into that Body by Baptism of the Holy Ghost. The details of His earthly Life do not belong to distant history separated from us by nineteen hundred years. For the Catholic these centuries do not exist at all; the Gospel facts are perpetuated independently of their setting in time and space; His Life is not something which *was* lived; it is something which is *being lived* in us *now*.

Nor is it just a mere copy in us of something lived before; rather is the Gospel Life the model of the new Catholic life; it is not a repetition but rather a prolonged Incarnation, for did He not say, speaking of His new way of living in us by His Spirit: "I will not leave you orphans: I will come to you. Yet a little while, and the world seeth Me no more. But you see Me: because I live and you shall live. In that day you shall know that I am in My Father, and you in Me, and I in you" (John 14, 18-20).

The Incarnation, Passion, Death, Resurrection, Ascension, are not mere recorded events of history, they are acts in an enduring drama which is being acted *socially* in the Church and *individually* in every soul vivified by the Spirit of Christ. Christ is in us as the Spirit of our lives, and not outside us as an external example. Hence St. Paul recommends: "Let this mind be in you, which was also in Christ Jesus" (Phil. 2, 5). Thanks to His possessing us by His Spirit we are sons of God. Bethlehem is not merely an historical event of a God "emptying Himself, taking the form of a servant"; it is also that great mystery by which we become by grace, what He is by nature, namely, the sons of God. The first filiation of a human nature in Christ is the beginning of a long line of progressive filiation which will endure until the end of time.

What Jesus did in His own human nature in Galilee He is doing today in other human natures in New York, London, Paris and every city and hamlet of the world where there are souls vivified by His

Spirit. He is still being born in other Bethlehems of the world out-casts; still coming into His own and His own receive Him not; still instructing the learned doctors of the law and answering their questions; still labouring at a carpenter's bench; still "going about doing good"; still preaching, governing, sanctifying, climbing other Calvarys and entering into the glory of His Father.

There are poor people today in our bread queues, there are innocent men in our prisons, there are half-clothed families in our tenements who are as ragged and destitute on the outside as they are rich with the Spirit of Christ on the inside. Externally they appear to most of us like the ordinary poor who attack the rich, like the common captives who harangue against authority, like the selfishly needy who curse their lot, but the resemblance is only on the outside, and thus many are deceived. Some eyes are so filled with the dust of the world's traffic, that they cannot see the Divine grace in men's souls.

The world classifies them in its social surveys as the poor, the dependent, the captive, but in the eyes of the Father in heaven, they are other Christs in other deserts, thirsty at other wells of Jacob, suffering on other crosses and captive in other praetoriums. The world sees them as so many economic problems; the heavenly Father sees them as beloved sons in whom He is well pleased.

In this spiritual classic the reader will find the answer to the question: What does it mean to be a Christian? Christianity is not a system of ethics, it is a life. It is not good advice, it is Divine adoption. Being a Christian does not consist in being kind to the poor, going to church, reading the Bible, singing hymns, being generous to relief agencies, just to employees, gentle to cripples, serving on Church committees, though it includes all of these. It is first and foremost a *love relationship,* and as you can never become a member of a family by doing generous deeds but only by being born into it out of love, so you can never become a Christian by doing good things, but only by being born to it through Divine Love. *Doing* good things to a man does not make you his son, but *being* a son does make you do good things.

Christianity begins with *being,* not with doing, with life and not with action. If you have the life of a plant, you will bloom like a plant; if you have the life of a monkey, you will act like a monkey.

If you have the life of a man, you will do the things a man does, but if you have the Life of Christ in you, you will act like a Christian. You are like your parents because you partake of their nature; you are like God if you partake of His Nature. What a man *does* is the externalization of what he *is*.

There is a world of difference between the two. Most people have their actions governed by their background: for instance, they think a certain way in order to defend their class or their wealth or their want of it; they even build a philosophy to suit the way they live; they do certain things because they are profitable or pleasant to them; they hate certain people because they are a reproach to their conscience or because they challenge their egotism. Their psycho-physical disposition is the center of their lives and therefore of their actions. They are, in a word, self-determined.

To be a Christian means to discard self as the supreme determinant of actions; it means to put on the mind of Christ so as to be governed by Christ's truths; to surrender the will to His Will, and to do all things that are pleasing to Him, not to self.

If we were forced to summarize the spiritual teaching of St. John Eudes in one sentence, it would be this: Cease to be self-determined; begin to be Jesus-determined.

FULTON J. SHEEN

The Catholic University of America,
Washington, D. C.,
June 20, 1945

## DEDICATION

### TO

### JESUS AND MARY

O JESUS, my Lord and my God, reduced to the depths of my own nothingness, I fall on my face before Thy supreme Majesty. I cast at Thy feet my own will, my self love, everything that is mine; I surrender myself utterly to the power of Thy Divine Spirit and Thy holy love. In the infinite immensity of Thy Spirit, in the vast extent of Thy boundless love, in all the virtues and powers of Thy Divinity made man and Thy deified Humanity, in all Thy states and mysteries, in all Thy qualities and virtues, in everything that Thou art in the sight of the Eternal Father, Thy Divine Self, Thy Holy Spirit, Thy Sacred Humanity, Thy most Blessed Mother, all the angels and all the saints, on earth and in heaven, and in the sight of all creatures in the universe, I adore Thee, I love Thee, and I give Thee glory!

But more especially do I revere and adore Thee as the One Who is Life, our only true Life, as the King of kings, the Saint of saints, as our Sanctifier, and, still more, our very Sanctification.

I adore Thy desire and Thy design, both ardent and great, of reigning in my soul and in all Christian souls. I most humbly implore Thy gracious pardon for all the hindrances I have, so far, put in Thy way, both in myself and in other men. In reparation for my faults, and henceforward to contribute in some small measure to the accomplishment of Thy desire, I give myself and I sacrifice myself to Thee, O most great Jesus, making the solemn avowal before heaven and earth that I no longer seek to live, except to work ceaselessly to form Thee, sanctify and make Thee live and reign in my soul, and in all the souls it shall please Thee to bring to me for that purpose. I beg Thee with my whole heart to cause all my cares, thoughts, words, works and labors to be directed and consecrated to that end.

Most particularly, however, do I beg Thee that all these things may be true of this little book, which I have composed, that it may help the souls who belong to Thee to establish, within themselves, the Life and the Kingdom of Thy Love. The book is written about Thee, O good Jesus, and Thou art its source and its true author, since, with all my might, I renounce everything in it that might be only mine, not Thine. I desire also, if it please Thee, that it may be all Thine, and that Thou mayest be its last and single end, just as Thou art its first and only principle, together with the Eternal Father and the Holy Spirit. That is why I give it back to Thee, in honor of and in union with the love by which it first came forth from Thee, and by which Thou hast given it to me. I put it into Thy hands, as an offering, a dedication, a consecration of homage to Thy adorable life, Thy love and all that Thou art. And, in the same way, in honor of and in union with the same love by which Thou didst give Thyself to us, Thou Who art the true Book of Life and of Love, I desire to give and dedicate this book to all the souls who wish to love Thee—especially to those of whom it is Thy holy will that I should have particular care in Thy sight.

And because I can not look upon Thee, O my Lord Jesus, without beholding her who sits at Thy right hand, who formed Thee, and sanctified and made Thee reign within herself in so admirable a manner, and in whom Thou hast always been living and reigning so perfectly, I salute her, and, after Thee, I honor her in every possible way, as Thy most honorable Mother, Mother of Life and Love, as well as my sovereign Lady, and my most dear Mother, to whom I belong by an infinite number of ties. To begin with, I was born and brought up in a place that belongs especially to Our Lady [1] and it was by her intercession and by her prayers that Thou didst give me being and life. Because my mother, having been childless

---

[1] Saint John Eudes was born on November 14, 1601, at Ri, in the diocese of Séez, in the French province of Normandy. The parish was under the protection of the Blessed Virgin Mary.

for a number of years,[2] made a vow to Thee in honor of Thy holy
Mother. In consequence, knowing her prayer to have been heard, and
beholding the accomplishment of her desire, in fulfilment of her
vow she and my father brought me to the shrine of Thy most holy
Mother,[3] to thank her, and to consecrate me to her, and through her
to Thee. Thou didst also give me being and life on the Feast of the
Annunciation, the day on which Thou didst begin to be and to live
in that Mother of Life. Thou didst give me the grace of making my
vow of perpetual service to Thee and Thy most holy Mother on
that blessed Feast and Thou hast given me several other signal favors
on the same day. Thy bounty is full well acquainted with these special favors, and for them I will forever bless Thee.[4] It was also on
the Feast of the Seven Dolours of Our Lady that, by Thy very great
mercy, I put on Thy livery, the holy ecclesiastical habit which I now
wear.[5] Yet more, by a signal favor of that same mercy, I celebrated
for the first time, or rather for the first three times, the most august
Sacrifice of Holy Mass, on the day on which the most Blessed Virgin
and Mother brought Thee into the world: and this I offered upon
an altar especially dedicated to her honor.[6] By reason of all this, not
to mention numberless considerations which entirely consecrate me
to Thee and to her, I have other most particular obligations to consecrate myself, and all that is mine, with all my will to Thee and
to her.

That is why I implore Thee, O my Saviour, that, after having
offered this my work to Thee, I may also consecrate it to Thy blessed
Mother, in homage to the life of love Thou didst perfect in her, and
she in Thee.

So I offer my book to Thee, O Mother of life and love, and I
dedicate it to Thee with all the affections of my heart. O Mother
of all blessings, may it please thee to bless both the work and the

---

[2] His parents, Isaac Eudes and Martha Corbin, had been married for three years.

[3] Our Lady of Recovery, a shrine in the parish of Tourailles, about six miles from Ri.

[4] One of the special favors was his admission into the Oratory of Jesus, a religious
Congregation of priests, founded by Cardinal Peter de Bérulle in 1611.

[5] St. John Eudes received the ecclesiastical habit at the Oratory on Friday of Passion
Week, 1623.

[6] He was ordained to the priesthood in Paris on December 20, 1625, and celebrated
his first Mass on Christmas Day, at an altar dedicated to the Mother of God.

workman, and all who shall make use of it. Offer them to thy Son Jesus, the wellspring of all benediction. Implore Him to bless them and perfectly consecrate them to His own glory and pure love.

O good Jesus, this book is filled with various acts and exercises of praise, love, contrition, humility and other Christian virtues; engrave them deeply on my heart and on the hearts of those who are to read them. For my part, I offer Thee all these acts and exercises with the intention of actually making them for Thee without ceasing, in my heart and spirit, just as I do incessantly by this book, in which they shall always remain printed. And I beg this not only for myself, but for all the men in the world, especially for those over whom I have particular charge in Thy sight. Fulfil this my desire, O my dear Jesus, out of Thy great goodness, out of Thy love for Thy most lovable Mother, and hers for Thee. Graciously regard and accept, by virtue of my present intention granted by Thy holy grace, all these acts and exercises as if I were continually making them with an actual application of mind and heart, just as they remain ever printed upon this paper.

Finally, O God of all blessings, take this book under Thy holy protection. Defend it against Thine enemies and its own; bless it, sanctify it, fill it with Thy mighty spirit and Thy divine virtue. Do Thou Thyself abide within it, so that by it, or rather, by Thy own Self, Thou mayest be blessed, hallowed, loved and glorified in all those who shall read it. Destroy in it all that is mine, and let there remain nothing except what is Thine. Bless each word, so that each may be an act of benediction, love and praise to Thee, and for its readers an arrow and a holy fire, piercing their hearts, setting them ablaze sacredly and for ever, with heavenly wounds and divine ardor of Thy holy love.

## EPISTLE DEDICATORY

To her Most Illustrious and Virtuous Ladyship

MADAME LAURENCE DE BUDOS

Abbess of the Royal Monastery of the Holy Trinity of Caen

My Lady:

I have cast myself at the feet of our Lord Jesus Christ and His most holy Mother, to consecrate this book to Them before all others, because to Them my whole being, all my life and my works belong by countless claims. I now take the liberty of appearing in your presence, in order to dedicate my book to your charitable zeal, to which it is due for several reasons.

First, because its author is bound to your service by obligations too numerous to be mentioned in this place.

Secondly, because its name conveys and expresses the principal employment and occupation of your life, which has been entirely spent, from childhood, in exercises of Christian and religious piety and devotion, of the kind designed to form and hallow Jesus in a Christian and religious soul.

In the third place, its purpose is to make Jesus live and reign in the souls of its readers and to establish His Spirit and His love in their hearts. Now this is the one end to which you also aspire, and it has been your principal work for several years, in the souls entrusted to your wise direction—and in this your progress has been so remarkable as to be seen at a glance. Besides, the divine Goodness of our Lord has chosen you in a special manner from among thousands, that He might be glorified particularly in you, and through you in many devout souls. His divine Spirit is singularly close to you, for your guidance and for the guidance of many others through you, along the paths of His grace and His love. Finally, His blessing rests upon you most abundantly, in the happy success of those religious projects you have undertaken for His glory.

May it therefore please you, My Lady, to receive this little book, as a small token of gratitude for the many obligations by which I am indebted to your bounty, as a testimony of the intense desire I cherish of seeing the Holy Ghost and the Divine Love of Jesus reign ever more and more in your soul, as well as in the souls of your pious daughters, to whom I likewise dedicate this work, at the same time as to their devout and esteemed Mother Abbess. I beg Jesus, with my whole heart, that He may bless both the mother and her daughters with the most holy treasures of His sacred love, and that He may transform them entirely into love and eternal benediction of Himself. Such is the desire and the prayer uttered each day at the altar by one who will always be, my Lady, in Jesus and Mary,

Your humble and obedient servant,

JOHN EUDES,

*Priest of the Congregation
of Jesus and Mary*

# PREFACE

(To be read carefully to ensure a holy use of this book
and a proper understanding of its name and purpose)

JESUS CHRIST, at the same time God and man, is all in all things, according to the inspired words of St. Paul: *Omnia in omnibus Christus* (Col. 3, 11). He must be in all Christians in a special manner, as the Head is in all the members and the spirit in its body; therefore your particular care and preoccupation must be to work at this formation and establishment of Christ within you, that He may live and reign there, so that He may be your life, your sanctification, your strength, your wealth, your glory and your all: or rather, that He may live in you, and in you be hallowed and glorified, and establish the Kingdom of His Spirit, of His Love and of His other virtues.

Some years ago I published a small book called *Exercises of Piety,* devoted to this purpose. It was well received by many, who found it to their taste, and made a holy use of it. For this reason, being about to republish it, I have gone over it more carefully than before, changing the title, and making a few additions, no less useful than necessary to all true Christians who desire to serve God in spirit and in truth.

I repeat: to all Christians, for you must not think that this book is written only for members of Religious Institutes. It is intended for every person who desires to live a holy and Christian life. And this is something to which all Christians are bound, no matter what may be their state of life or their circumstances. After all, according to the words of Heaven, to be a Christian and to be a saint is but one and the same thing, since God has declared that it is His will that all Christians, and not only those who have retired within cloisters, should labor for their sanctification (1 Thess. 4, 3); that they should pursue sanctity, without which no man shall ever see God (Heb. 12, 14); that they should serve in holiness and in justice before Him all the days of their life (Luke 1, 75); that they should be holy in all their conversation (1 Peter 1, 15), which is to say in all their acts and conduct; that they should be holy, unspotted and blameless before Him (Col. 1, 22); that they may be holy and perfect (Matt. 5, 48); that His Name be sanctified in them (Matt. 6, 9); and that they sanctify Jesus Christ in their hearts (1 Peter 3, 15).

The title I have given to this book embodies its two great subjects, namely: *The Life and the Kingdom of Jesus in Christian Souls.*

I have called it the *Life of Jesus in Christian Souls* because its first and principal aim is to show how Jesus Christ must live in all Christians, since Christians are on earth only to perpetuate the most holy life that Christ led here below. Likewise, the most important business and chief occupation of a Christian should be to endeavor to form Jesus within himself, according to the great Apostle's wish: *Formetur Christus in vobis* (Gal. 4, 19). This means that you are obliged to cause Him to live in your spirit and in your heart, and establish the sanctity of His life and behavior in your soul and body, which is what St. Paul calls carrying and glorifying "God in your body" (1 Cor. 6, 20), and St. Peter, sanctifying "the Lord Christ in your hearts" (1 Peter 3, 15). Jesus Christ is your Head and you are His members. By reason of this fact, everything that is His is yours, and everything that is yours is His. So it follows that, since He sanctified Himself for you—as He Himself says, speaking to His Father: "And for them do I sanctify myself that they also may be sanctified in truth" (John 17, 19), that is, "in Myself, Who am eternal Truth," as St. Augustine explains, and as He Himself is your sanctification (1 Cor. 1, 30), so also, when you sanctify yourself, you sanctify yourself for Him so that He may be sanctified in you. And your sanctification is the sanctification of Jesus within you, as you accomplish what St. Peter speaks of in these words: "Sanctify the Lord Christ in your hearts" (1 Peter 3, 15). Now the way to accomplish all this, is to develop the habit of seeing, loving and glorifying Jesus Christ in all things, and performing all your actions in His sanctity. This is what is taught in this book by a method and by means that are very easy, very pleasant and very effective.

In the second place I have called it *The Kingdom of Jesus in Chris-*

*tian Souls* because the aim of the book is not only to explain certain very inspiring and efficacious means of forming Christ and making Him live within you, but also to make Him reign there, in full possession of your heart. Therefore, if you apply yourself with diligence and fidelity to the holy use of these exercises, you will learn the truth of the words of the Son of God when He said: "The Kingdom of God is within you" (Luke 17, 21). You will possess what you ask every day when you say *Adveniat regnum tuum*: "Thy Kingdom come." And whereas the wretched Jews called Him king in mockery, and said of Him: *Nolumus hunc regnare super nos,* "We will not have this man to reign over us" (Luke 19, 14), you will be able to call Him King in all truth and say to Him, in return, *Volumus, Domine Jesu, te regnare super nos:* "Lord Jesus, we do desire Thee to reign over us."

I have divided the book into seven parts, which include everything that should be done by a Christian and even a religious, to live a Christian and saintly life, as well as what is necessary to form and sanctify Jesus and make Him reign in the faithful soul.

Part One outlines what you should do during the whole course of your life to make Jesus live and reign within you.

Part Two contains a few devotional exercises most necessary to achieve this.

Part Three outlines what should be done each day. Here you will find a very satisfactory and easy method of performing all your actions with genuine holiness in the spirit of Jesus, which is the true spirit of Christianity and of all religious Orders which are in the Church of Christ.

Part Four, what should be done each week.

Part Five, what should be done each month.

Part Six, what should be done each year.

Part Seven of the book contains the first and last duties of all Christians towards God, their Creator, in connection with the beginning and the end of their life, on the occasions of their birth, baptism, and death. In this part are given some exercises of piety to render to Almighty God the lawful veneration and homage you ought to have given Him at birth, if you had been endowed with the use of reason. Others aim at reviving and renewing in yourself the grace of holy

Baptism. Finally, there are exercises to prepare yourself for a holy and Christian death.

Most of these exercises take the form of prayers, so that all types of persons may use them. For there are many worthy souls who, when they present themselves before God in prayer, have no facility in adapting to their own special needs the plain and unvarnished Christian truths they have learned by simple catechism. Yet this form of exercise will not prevent those who prefer these truths taught in terms of simple propositions, from drawing forth such points and truths as will give them material to occupy their minds concerning God and the various other subjects in this book, according as they are led by the grace of His spirit in themselves.

If at first you come upon certain exercises which impress you as to being too elevated and difficult to understand and to practise, do not be dismayed. If you will have the patience to read the whole book, if you approach it with a pure and sincere intention and a real desire to profit by it, I am confident that the Lord in His most great goodness will give you light to understand these things and the grace to put them into practice. I am sure that something you may not understand in one place will become clear to you in another, as you read on, and you will come to practise it with great facility and much consolation of soul.

I have said the same things over and over again in many places, but I have done so on purpose, both to give you a clearer understanding and to impress more deeply upon your soul certain fundamentals that are most important. Thus I hope to spare you the trouble of turning back to what has gone before: for this book contains a few important truths and practices that demand many explanations and exercises. For this reason I have seen fit to discuss them in several places, so that if you should happen to read or use one of the exercises or explanations to which they apply, and yet be unable or unwilling to read the others, you may not be deprived of the knowledge of these truths, nor the use of these practices. In any case you will thus be spared the trouble of looking for them in the other places where they are also found.

For the rest, if you desire to make holy use of this book, and glorify God by the exercises it sets forth, I would urge you to read it and use it, not hastily and cursorily, but with careful attention and intelligent application of your mind and heart to what you are reading, especially to the exercises of prayer. Take time to weigh, to savor and to assimilate the meaning and substance of the words which you will pronounce either vocally or silently in your heart, according to the dispositions our Lord will inspire in your soul, once you have given yourself to Him by opening this book with the intention of using what you are about to read in whatever way He may desire.

As a reward for my slight labors I ask you, in the name of the One who is all love for us, that as often as you open this book you may give yourself to Jesus with a renowned resolution to love Him perfectly. I ask you to make three acts of love to Him, on behalf of the one who has given you this book, who has received from His Heart and His Hand all the good there is in it. For my own part, I renew my supplications to our Lord Jesus Christ that He may impart His most holy blessings to this little book, and to you too, my dear reader, and I pray that through Him, it may accomplish in you all the work He desires it to do there; that He may give you grace to make such use of it, on all occasions, as He would have you do; that He may establish in you, forever, the kingdom of His glory and of His pure love; and that He may form and establish Himself in you, to live in you and reign there perfectly, to love and glorify Himself in you forever.

## PART ONE

*What Must Be Done in the Course of Your
Whole Life to Live a Christian and
Saintly Life and to Make Jesus
Reign in Your Soul*

# Part One

## WHAT MUST BE DONE IN THE COURSE OF YOUR WHOLE LIFE TO LIVE A CHRISTIAN AND SAINTLY LIFE AND TO MAKE JESUS REIGN IN YOUR SOUL

### NATURE OF THE CHRISTIAN LIFE

I. The Christian Life Must be a Continuation of the Most Holy Life Which Jesus Led on Earth.

Jesus, Son of God and Son of Man, King of angels and of men, is not only your God, your Saviour and your Sovereign Lord, but is also your head and you are "members of his body," as St. Paul says: "of his flesh and of his bones" (Eph. 5, 30). You are consequently united with Him in the most intimate union possible, that is, the union of members with their head. You are united with Him spiritually by faith and by the grace He gave you in Holy Baptism. You are united with Him corporally in the union of His Most Sacred Body with yours in the Blessed Eucharist. It necessarily follows that, just as the members are animated by the spirit of the head, and live the same life, so you must also be animated by the spirit of Jesus, live His life, walk in His ways, be clothed with His sentiments and inclinations, and perform all your actions in the dispositions and intentions that actuated His. In a word, you must carry on and perpetuate the life, religion and devotion which He exercised upon earth.

This doctrine rests upon a very solid foundation, for it receives confirmation repeatedly from the sacred words of Him Who is Truth Itself. Do you not hear Him saying in several places in His Gospel: "I am the Life" (John 14, 6); "I am come that they may have life" (John 10, 10)? "You will not come to Me that you may have life" (John 5, 40). "I live, and you shall live. In that day you shall know

3

that I am in my Father: and you in me, and I in you" (John 14, 19-20). That is to say, just as Jesus is in His Father, living His life, which the Father communicates to Him, so also you are in Jesus, living by His life, and He is in you, giving you this same life. And thus He lives in you and you live in and with Him.

St. John, the beloved disciple, explains that God has given to man the gift of eternal life, which life is in His Son, and he who has in himself the Son of God has life; and, on the contrary, he who has not the Son has not life (I John 5, 11-12). God sent His Only Begotten Son into the world that you may have life, and you are in this world even as Jesus is, that is, you have taken His place here, and ought to live as He lived (I John 4, 9; 17).

Again in the Apocalypse he says that the well-beloved Spouse of your souls, Jesus Christ, cries out incessantly: "Come. And he that heareth, let him say: Come and he that thirsteth, let him come; and he that will, let him take the water of life freely" (Apoc. 22, 17), meaning, let him draw from Christ, the fountain-head, the waters of true life. Furthermore, it is written in the Holy Gospel that one day the Son of God stood up among a great multitude of people, and cried out with a loud voice: "If any man thirst, let him come to me, and drink" (John 7, 37).

What does the holy Apostle St. Paul constantly preach to you, if not that "you are dead and your life is hid with Christ in God" (Col. 3, 3), and that the Eternal Father has given you life with Jesus Christ and in Jesus Christ (Eph. 2, 5)? This means that He makes you live not only with His Divine Son, but also in His Son and by the life of His Son. Does he not also tell you that you must manifest and show forth the life of Jesus in your bodies (II Cor. 4, 10-11), and that Jesus Christ is your life (Col. 3, 4), and that He is in you, and abides in you? "I live," he says, "now not I; but Christ liveth in me" (Gal. 2, 20). For if you study well the rest of the chapter containing these words, you will find that St. Paul is speaking not only of himself, in his own name, but also in the person and in the name of every Christian. Finally, in another passage, addressing the followers of Christ, he says that he prays God to make them worthy of their calling, and to accomplish powerfully in them all the desires of His goodness and the work of faith, so that the name of our Lord Jesus Christ may be glorified in them and they in Him (II Thess. 1, 11-12).

All these sacred texts show quite clearly that Jesus Christ must live in you; that you must not live except in Him; that His life must be your life, and your life must be a continuation and expression of His. Also you have no right to live on earth except in order to bear, show forth, sanctify, glorify and cause to live and reign in you the name, the life, the qualities and perfections, the dispositions and inclinations, the virtues and actions of Jesus.

## II. CONFIRMATION OF THE FOREGOING TRUTH.

To understand more clearly this fundamental truth of Christian life, and to establish it more solidly in your soul, bear in mind that our Lord Jesus Christ has not simply one body and one life, but two. First, there is His own personal body, which He received from the Blessed Virgin, and the personal life which He lived in human form in this world. There is also His mystical body, namely, the Church, which St. Paul calls *Corpus Christi,* "the body of Jesus Christ" (I Cor. 12, 27). And His second life is the life by which He dwells in this mystical body, and in all true Christians who are the members of the Church. The passable and temporal life of His natural body was ended at the moment of His death. But the life of His mystical body He wills to continue until the end of time, in order to glorify His Father by the acts and sufferings of a mortal, suffering and laborious life, not only for the space of thirty-three years, but until the end of the world. Thus the passable and temporal life of Jesus in His mystical body, that is, in all Christians, has not yet reached its accomplishment, but develops itself from day to day in each true Christian and will not be perfectly complete until the end of time.

This is why St. Paul writes: "I fill up those things that are wanting of the sufferings of Christ, in my flesh, for his body, which is the church" (Col. 1, 24). And what the Apostle says of himself may be said of every true Christian, when he suffers anything in a spirit of love and submission to God. It may also be said of all the other actions performed by a Christian on earth. As St. Paul assures us that he fills up the sufferings of Jesus Christ, so also every true Christian, who is a member of Jesus Christ, and united to Him by grace, continues and accomplishes, by every act he does in the spirit of Jesus Christ, the actions which Christ Himself performed during His earthly life. Thus, when a Christian prays, he continues and accomplishes the prayers of Jesus Christ. When he works, he continues and accomplishes Christ's laborious life. When his relations with his neighbor are inspired by charity, he continues and accomplishes Christ's public life. When he takes his meals or his rest in a Christian fashion, he continues and accomplishes the subjection to these necessities that Christ willed to have in Himself. It is the same for all the other acts he performs in a Christian manner. For this reason St. Paul declares that the Church is the fulness of Christ (Eph. 1, 22-23), and that you are all tending to the perfection and the fulness of His maturity (Eph. 4, 11-13), that is, to His mystical age in His Church, which will not be completed until the Day of Judgment.

You can understand from this the nature of the Christian life. You see that it is a continuation and fulfilment of the life of Jesus, and that all your actions must be a continuation of the actions of Christ. You have to be so many other Christs upon the earth, in order to perpetuate here His life and works, and to do and suffer everything in a saintly and divine manner, in the Spirit of Christ, that is, with the holy and divine dispositions and intentions which Jesus Himself showed in all His acts and sufferings. As this divine Jesus is your head and you are His members, and as you are bound to Him by this union, incomparably closer, nobler and more elevated union than the union between the head and the members of the natural body, it necessarily follows that you must be animated by His spirit and live by His life more perfectly than the members of a natural body.

These truths are very great, very important, and call for intent consideration. They oblige you to do great things, and should be well thought out by those who desire to live a Christian life. Therefore, study them frequently and attentively, and so learn that Christian life, religion, devotion and piety truly and properly consist in continuing the life, religion and devotion of Jesus on the earth. Consequently, not only religious but also all Christians are bound to live a completely holy and divine life and to perform all their actions in a holy and divine spirit. This is not impossible, nor is it even so difficult as many imagine. On the contrary, it is very pleasant and easy for those who remember to lift up their mind and heart frequently to Jesus, and to unite themselves to Him in all that they do, following the practices of the exercises which will be presented further on.

# FOUNDATIONS OF CHRISTIAN LIFE AND SANCTITY

Your only right to live on earth is to continue the holy and perfect life of your Head, Christ. Now there are four things which you must frequently consider and adore in Christ's earthly life, four things which you must try, as far as possible, with the help of His grace, to express and carry on in your life, because they are the four foundations of Christian piety and sanctity. Without them it is not possible to be a true Christian. Hence it becomes necessary to discuss, at this point, each one in particular.

### III. First Foundation of Christian Life and Sanctity: Faith.

The first foundation of the Christian life is faith. St. Paul declares that if you would go to God and have access to His divine majesty, the first step you must take is to believe; for "without faith it is impossible to please God" (Heb. 11, 6). Faith is the substance and foundation of the things hoped for (Heb. 11, 1). It is the cornerstone of the Kingdom of Christ. It is a divine and celestial light, a participation in the eternal, inaccessible light, a beam radiating from the face of God. To speak in accordance with Scripture, faith is, as it were, a divine character by which the light of the countenance of God is imprinted upon the soul (Ps. 4, 7). It is a communication and a kind of projection of the divine light and knowledge which were infused into the holy soul of Jesus at the moment of His Incarnation. It is the science of salvation, the science of the saints, the science of God, which Jesus Christ drew forth from the bosom of His Father and brought down to you on earth, to dispel your shadows, to enlighten your heart, to give you the knowledge necessary for the perfect love and service of God, to submit and subject your mind to His truths which He still teaches you both through Himself and by Holy Mother Church. By faith you can express, continue and fulfil in yourself the submission, docility, the voluntary and undarkened subjection, with which His human mind regarded the lights imparted and the truths taught to Him by His Heavenly Father. Faith, then, being

8

given to you by God, is a continuation and fulfilment of the loving and most perfect submission of the human mind of Jesus Christ to the truths revealed to Him by His Eternal Father.

It is by this light and this divine science that you possess perfect knowledge, so far as it is possible in this life, of all things whether in God or not in God. Reason and human science often lead you into error because they are too weak and limited to penetrate to the knowledge of the things of God, which are infinite and incomprehensible. Human intelligence and knowledge also deceive you, because they are too full of the darkness and obscurity of sin to attain to a genuine knowledge even of things outside of God. But the light of faith, being a participation in the truth and light of God, can not possibly deceive you; indeed, it shows you things as God sees them, that is, in their truth, and just as they exist in the eyes of God.

Consequently, if you contemplate God with the eyes of faith, you will see Him just as He is and, in a certain manner, face to face. Although it is true that faith is accompanied by obscurity and permits you to behold God, not clearly as He is seen in heaven but as through a cloud, darkly, nevertheless, faith does not debase His supreme greatness to fit the capacity of your minds, as does science. Faith penetrates His shadows and His darkness, and goes straight to the infinity of His perfections, making you know Him as He is, infinite in His Being and in all His divine perfections. Faith lets you know that everything that is in God and in Jesus Christ, God and Man, is infinitely great and admirable, infinitely adorable and lovable, infinitely worthy of adoration, glory and love for His own sake. Faith shows you that God is true in His words and unfailing in His promises; that He is all goodness and gentleness and love towards those who seek Him and put their trust in Him, but that He is nothing but terror and severity towards those who abandon Him, and that it is frightful to fall into the hands of His justice. Faith gives a most certain knowledge that Divine Providence directs and guides all things that happen in the universe, with great holiness and wisdom, in fact, in the best way possible. His disposal of all things deserves to be infinitely adored and loved by all creatures that are subject to His order, whether in justice or in mercy, in heaven, on earth or in hell.

If you look at God's Church in the light of faith, you will see that as Jesus Christ is her Head and the Holy Ghost her Guide, it is not possible for her to wander from the truth in anything, nor to stray away into falsehoods. So too, all the ceremonies, customs and functions of the Church are instituted in a most holy manner, and everything she forbids or commands is legitimately forbidden or commanded. Also everything she teaches is infallibly true, and you must be ready to die a thousand times rather than to diverge, even in the slightest degree, from her inspired truth. Finally, you are obliged to pay singular homage and reverence to all the things that exist in the Church, as holy and sacred objects.

If you look at yourselves and all the things in the world by the light of faith, you will see most clearly that you are, of yourself, only nothingness, sin and abomination, and that everything in the world is nothing but smoke, vanity and illusion.

This is the way to look at everything: not in the vanity of the senses, nor with the eyes of flesh and blood, nor with the short-sighted and deceptive view of reason and human science, but in the truth of God and with the eyes of Jesus Christ, that is, with that divine light which He drew forth from His Father's bosom, by which He beholds and knows all things, the light He has communicated to you that you might see and know all things as He sees and knows them.

## IV. FAITH SHOULD BE YOUR GUIDE IN ALL YOUR ACTIONS.

Just as you must consider all things in the light of faith if you would truly know them, so also you must perform all your acts under the guidance of that same light, if you would do them in a holy manner. As God is led by His divine wisdom, and the angels by their angelic intelligence, and men deprived of the light of faith by reason, and men of the world by worldly maxims, and voluptuaries by their senses, so Christians must direct themselves by the same light that directs their head, Jesus Christ, that is, by faith, which is a participation in the knowledge and the light of Christ.

So you must try, by every means, to study the divine science of faith and never to undertake anything except under its guidance. To that end, at the inception of your every act, especially your more important actions, place yourself at the feet of the Son of God and adore Him as the author of faith and its fulfilment, as the One who is the true light, enlightening every man that comes into this world.

Admit that of yourself you are but darkness, and that all the light of reason, science and even of human experience is often but obscurity and illusion, in which you can place no confidence. Renounce the prudence of the flesh and the wisdom of the world. Ask Jesus to destroy them in you, as His enemies, and not to let you obey their laws, their views or their maxims, but that He may enlighten you with His heavenly light and guide you by His divine wisdom. Beg Him to make known what is most pleasing to Him, and to give you grace and strength to cling firmly to His words and promises, and to close your ears resolutely to all opinions and persuasions of human prudence; that you may courageously prefer the maxims of faith which He taught you by His Gospel and His Church, rather than the reasoning and arguments of men who base their conduct on the standards of the world.

To this end, it would be a very good thing to read each day on your knees, either in Latin or in English, a chapter of the life of Jesus Christ in the New Testament, so as to learn the life your Father led, and, through the consideration of His acts, His virtues, and His words, to become familiar with the rules and maxims upon which He based His conduct, and upon which He wishes you to base yours. Christian prudence consists in renouncing the maxims of the world, in calling upon the spirit of Christ to enlighten you, to guide you by His maxims, and to lead you in accordance with His truths, His actions and His virtues. This is what is meant by basing one's conduct upon the spirit of faith.

V. SECOND FOUNDATION OF CHRISTIAN LIFE AND SANCTITY: HATRED OF SIN.

Since you are under obligation to continue on earth the holy and divine life of Jesus, you must be animated by the sentiments and inclinations of Christ Himself, according to St. Paul the Apostle, who says: *Hoc sentite in vobis, quod et in Christo Jesu*: "Let this mind be in you, which was also in Christ Jesus" (Phil. 2, 5). Now Jesus

Christ entertained in Himself two widely opposed sentiments: one of infinite love for His Father and for you, the other of extreme hatred for everything opposed to His Father's glory and our salvation, namely, for sin. Since He loves His Father and you with an infinite love, He hates sin with an infinite hatred. He so loved His Father, and so loves you, that He performed great miracles, suffered sorrowful torments, and gave up a precious life for His Father's glory and your love. On the other hand, He holds sin in so great horror that He came down from heaven, taking the form of a servant, and for thirty-three years He lived on earth a life of labor, of humiliation and of suffering; He shed His Blood even to the last drop; He died the most shameful and most cruel of all deaths, all for His hatred of sin, because of His intense desire to destroy all sin in you.

Now you must see to it that these same sentiments of Christ with regard to His Father and to sin continue in yourself. You have to carry on the war He waged against sin while He was on earth. You are obliged to love God perfectly and with all your might, and you are also bound to hate sin infinitely with all your strength.

In order to dispose yourself to do this, you should henceforth look at sin, not as it is seen by men, with their carnal and blinded vision, but as God sees it, with eyes enlightened by His divine light; in other words, you should see it with the eyes of faith.

By this light you will see that sin, in so far as it is in a certain sense infinitely contrary and opposed to God, and is a privation of an infinite good, which is God, contains in itself a malice, madness, ugliness and horror that are just as great, in their own way, as God's infinite goodness, wisdom, beauty and holiness (St. Thomas, *Summa*, $3^a$, Q. 1, a. 2, ad $2^{um}$). Consequently sin deserves to be hated and fought to the same degree in which God deserves to be sought and loved. You will see that sin is so horrible a thing that it can be obliterated only by the blood of a God, so detestable that it can be destroyed only by the death of a God-Man, so abominable that it can be worthily repaired only by the labors, agonies and death, and infinite merits of a God.

You will see that sin is a cruel murder, a frightful act of deicide, a ghastly annihilation of all things. It is murder because it is the only cause of death, both of the body and of the soul of man. It is deicide, because sin and the sinner caused Christ to die on the Cross and the sinner continues this crucifixion of Jesus, day by day, within himself. Then it is an annihilation of nature, of grace, of glory and of all things. Since, as far as it can, it destroys their divine Author, it consequently destroys nature, grace and glory.

Again you will see that sin is so detestable before God that when the first, most noble and dearest of His creatures, namely, the angels, fell into one single sin, a sin of thought only, a sin of no more than a moment, He cast them down from the height of heaven into the depths of hell, without allowing them even a moment to do penance, since they were unworthy and even incapable of this (St. Thomas, *Ibid.*, 1ª, Q. 64, a. 2). When God finds one mortal sin upon a soul, at the hour of death, even though He is all goodness and love for His creature, and has an extreme desire to save all mankind, and even though He has shed His blood and given His life in order to save humanity, He is nevertheless forced by His justice to pass a sentence of eternal damnation upon that wretched soul. Another thing, even more surprising than this, is that when the Eternal Father saw His own Son, His only well-beloved Son, most holy and most innocent, laden with the sins of others, He did not spare Him, as St. Paul says, but delivered Him up for us to the Cross and to death (Rom. 8, 32), so abominable and execrable is sin in His sight.

You will also see that sin is so full of malignity that it transforms the servants of God into slaves of the devil, the members of Jesus Christ into the members of Satan, and even changes men who are by grace and participation gods, into devils by likeness and imitation, according to the words of Christ Himself who, speaking of Judas, called him a devil: *Unus ex vobis diabolus est* (John 6, 71).

And you will finally come to know that sin is the evil of evils, and the greatest of all misfortunes. It is the source of all the evils and all the misfortunes that cover the earth and fill hell to overflowing. Indeed, this evil is the only one in the world that really deserves to be called an evil. Of all the frightful and appalling things that exist, sin is the most frightful and the most appalling. It is more to be dreaded than death, more fearsome than the devil, and more terrify-

ing than hell, because all that is horrible, appalling and terrifying
about death, the devil and hell proceeds from sin. O Sin, how detestable thou art! Oh, if men only knew thee! Yes, sin, there is something in thee infinitely more horrible than anything that may be
spoken or conceived, since the soul that is befouled with thy rottenness
can not be cleaned nor purged except by the blood of God Himself,
and thou canst not be destroyed and annihilated save only by the
death and annihilation of a God-Man!

O God, no wonder Thou dost hate this hellish monster so, and that
Thou dost pursue it with so hard a punishment! Let those be aston-
ished by this who know Thee not, and who know not what an insult
is offered to Thee by sin. Indeed, O my God, Thou wouldst not be
God, if Thou didst not hate iniquity with an infinite hatred. As it is
Thy joy to be bound by necessity to love Thyself infinitely, since
Thou art infinite goodness, so also art Thou bound by a holy obligation, to hold in infinite abhorrence that which is, in some sense, infinitely contrary to Thee. O you, Christians who read these words, all
of which are based upon the utterance of eternal Truth, if there remain in you some little spark of love and zeal for the God whom you
adore, learn to have horror for what He so abhors, and for what is so
contrary to Him. Fear sin, and fly from it more than from pestilence,
or from death, or from all the other evils that can be imagined. Keep
always alive within you the unshakable resolution to suffer a thousand
deaths, together with every kind of torture, rather than ever to become separated from God by a mortal sin.

And that God may preserve you from this misfortune, be careful
also to avoid venial sin, as far as possible. For you must keep in mind
that the shedding of Our Lord's blood and the sacrifice of His life
were just as necessary to wipe out venial sin as to deliver you from
mortal sin. Remember that anyone who attaches little importance
to venial sin will soon fall into mortal sin. If you do not find these
resolutions in your own soul, pray to Our Lord to put them there,
and do not rest until you possess these dispositions. For you ought
to know that as long as you do not have the will to die or suffer
every kind of disgrace and torture rather than commit any sin,
you are not a true Christian. But if by some misfortune you should

happen to fall into sin, be sure to rise up again at once by means of contrition and confession, and return to your previous dispositions.

## VI. THIRD FOUNDATION OF CHRISTIAN LIFE AND SANCTITY: DETACHMENT FROM THE WORLD AND FROM WORLDLY THINGS.

It is not enough for a Christian to be free from vice and to abhor every kind of sin. Beyond that, it is necessary to work with diligence and resolution at the task of becoming perfectly detached from the world and from the things of the world. When I say "the world," I mean the corrupt and disordered life led in the world, the damnable spirit that reigns over the world, the perverse sentiments and inclinations which men of the world follow, and the pernicious laws and maxims by which they govern their behavior. By the things of the world I mean everything that the world so highly values and loves and strives after, namely, the honors and praises of men, vain pleasures and satisfactions, wealth and temporal comforts, friendships and affections based on flesh and blood, on self-love and selfish interests.

Consider the life of our Lord Jesus Christ, and you will see that He lived on earth in most perfect detachment, stripped of all things. Read His holy Gospel, listen to His words, and you will learn that "everyone of you that doth not renounce all that he possesseth, cannot be my disciple" (Luke 14, 33). So, if you really desire to be a Christian and a disciple of Jesus Christ, and if you wish to continue and express in yourself His holy life of detachment from everything, you must strive to achieve an absolute and universal detachment from the world and from worldly things.

To do this, you should frequently reflect how the world always has been and always will be opposed to Christ, whom it has persecuted and crucified, and will persecute and crucify, even to the end of time. Consider that the sentiments and inclinations, the rules and maxims, the life and spirit of the world are so opposed to the sentiments and inclinations, rules and maxims, life and spirit of Jesus that it is impossible for them to subsist together. Christ's sentiments and inclinations lead entirely to the glory of His Father and our sanctification, while those of the world lead only to sin and perdition.

The laws and maxims of Jesus are very mild and holy and reasonable. The standards of the world are laws and maxims of hell, and are diabolical, tyrannical and finally unbearable.

The life of Jesus is a holy life made beautiful by all kinds of virtues; the life of the world is a depraved life, full of disorder and of all sorts of vice.

The spirit of Jesus is a spirit of light, of truth, of piety, of love, confidence, zeal and reverence for God and for all that belongs to God; the spirit of the world is a spirit of error, of unbelief, of darkness, of suspicion, of dissatisfaction, of impiety, of irreverence and hardness of heart towards God and all the things of God.

The spirit of Jesus is a spirit of humility, of modesty, of self-distrust, of mortification and abnegation, of constancy and of firmness. But the spirit of the world is, by contrast, a spirit of pride, presumption, disordered self-love, fickleness and inconstancy.

The spirit of Jesus is a spirit of mercy, charity, patience, gentleness and of unity with others. But the spirit of the world is a spirit of vengeance, envy, impatience, anger, slander and disunion.

Finally, the spirit of Jesus is the spirit of God, a holy and divine spirit, filled with every grace, virtue, and blessing. It is a spirit of peace and tranquillity, which seeks nothing but the interests of God and of His greater glory. The spirit of the world, on the contrary, is the spirit of Satan, for it necessarily follows that, since Satan is the prince of this world, the world is animated and governed by his spirit—an earthly, carnal and animal Spirit; a spirit motivating all kinds of sin and accursedness; a spirit of unrest and anxiety, of storms and tempests—*spiritus procellarum* (Ps. 10, 7), a spirit seeking only its own convenience, satisfaction and interests. Judge then, if it be possible for the life and spirit of the world to be reconciled with the life and spirit of Christianity, which is none other than the life and spirit of Christ.

If, therefore, you desire to be a true Christian, that is, if you desire to belong perfectly to Jesus Christ, to live His life, to be animated by His spirit and conduct yourself according to His maxims, it is absolutely necessary for you to make up your mind to renounce the world entirely and bid it farewell forever. I do not mean that it is necessary for you to leave the world and shut yourself up between four walls, unless God calls you to do so. But I do say that you must try to live in the world as though you were not of the world, that is, you must make a public, generous and unwavering profession of living otherwise than as the world lives, and of rejecting its laws and maxims. And I tell you not to be ashamed but to enjoy holy pride in being a Christian, in belonging to Jesus Christ, in preferring the saintly maxims and truths that He left you in His holy Gospel, to the pernicious maxims and falsehoods by which the world deceives its disciples.

I urge you at least to have enough courage and resolution to make a clean break with the standards, sentiments and inclinations of the world, and to despise all its empty speeches and deceptive opinions, just as the world makes a show of impious temerity in despising the laws and maxims of Christianity. It is in this alone that true courage and perfect generosity consist: for what the world calls courage and power of character are nothing but cowardice and pusillanimity. This, then, is what I mean by detachment from the world: renouncing the world, and living in the world as though not of it.

## VII. Continuation of the Same Subject.

If you would more firmly establish this detachment from the world in your soul, it is not only necessary for you to strive to break away from the world, but you should even develop a horror for it, like the repugnance in which Christ held it. Now Christ had such a horror of the world that He not only exhorted you through His beloved Disciple: "Love not the world, nor the things which are in the world" (I John 2, 15), but He also tells us, through His Apostle St. James, "that the friendship of this world is the enemy of God" (James 4, 4), that is, He considers as His enemies all those who love the world. He assures you that His Kingdom is not of this world (John 18, 36) any more than He is of this world, and that those whom His Father has given Him are not of this world, just as He is not of it (John 17, 12-16). And another thing—more terrifying still—is that He solemnly protested, on the very day when He wrought the greatest miracle of His goodness, namely, the eve of

His death, when He was about to pour forth His Precious Blood and give up His life for the salvation of men, "I pray not for the world" (John 17, 9). And in these words He thundered a most frightful anathema, a curse and an excommunication upon the world, declaring it to be unworthy of any share in His prayers or in His mercy.

Finally, He assures us that "now is the judgment of the world" and "now shall the prince of this world be cast out" (John 12, 31). And, in fact, the very moment the world fell into the corruption of sin, it was judged by divine justice and condemned to be burnt and consumed by fire. And although the effect of the sentence was deferred, it will none the less be carried out at the end of time. Consequently, Christ looks upon the world as the object of His hatred and His curse, and as something He plans and desires to burn in the day of His wrath.

Enter, then, into the feelings of Christ towards the world, and towards all things that are in the world. From now on, view the world as Jesus Christ does, that is, as the object of His hatred and malediction. Look upon it as something He forbids you to love, under pain of incurring His enmity. See it as a thing He has excommunicated and cursed with His own lips, with which you may not, consequently, communicate without participating in the same malediction. See the world as something He desires to burn and reduce to ashes. Look at all those things which the world most values and loves, like pleasures, honors, riches, worldly friendship and affections, and all other things of this kind, as things which simply pass away, according to this divine utterance: *Mundus transit, et concupiscentia ejus* (I John 2, 17). See all these things as nothing but smoke, deceit and illusion, as vanity and affliction of spirit. Read these truths and reflect upon them often, and each day pray Our Lord to impress them upon your mind.

To arrive at these dispositions, take a little time each day to adore Jesus in His perfect detachment from the world, begging Him to detach you from it entirely and to impress upon your heart hatred, horror and abomination for the things of the world. For your own part, see that you do not indulge in the useless visits and conversation that are customary in the world. If you are taken up with these idle occupations, in the name of God leave them at all costs and fly as you would from a plague, from all the places and persons and from any company where the talk is only of the world and worldly things. Since such things are discussed with esteem and affection, it is very difficult to avoid carrying away some harmful impression from these conversations. Besides, you will gain nothing from them but a dangerous loss of time; you will find in them nothing but unhappy dissipation of mind and affliction of spirit, and all you will bring away will be bitterness of heart, coldness in piety, separation from God, and a thousand faults that you may have committed.

As long as you seek out and love the company of men of the world, Jesus Christ whose delight it is to be with the children of men will not take His delight in you and will not give you any taste of the consolations with which He refreshes those who find all their joy in conversing with Him. Fly then, from the world, I say to you again, fly from it, abhor its life, its spirit and its maxims. Do not make friends with any persons except those whom you can help, or those who can help you and animate you, by word and example, to love Jesus and live in His spirit.

## VIII. SELF-DETACHMENT.

It is no small accomplishment to renounce the world in the manner just described. Yet even this is not enough to give you that perfect detachment which is one of the primary foundations of Christian life. Our Lord cries out to us in a loud voice: "If any man will come after me, let him deny himself, and take up his cross, and follow me" (Matt. 16, 24). So, then, if you want to be among the followers of Christ and belong to Him, you have to renounce yourself, that is, your own mind, your own ideas, your own will, desires, inclinations and your self-love, because it is your self-love that leads you to hate and avoid anything that might cause pain or mortification to your spirit or your flesh and makes you love and seek out everything that may give them pleasure and contentment.

Two reasons oblige you to practise self-abnegation.

First, everything in you is so disordered and depraved, as a result of the corruption of sin, that there is nothing in you that is not contrary to God, and that does not put some obstacle in the way of His plans, or oppose itself to the love and glory you owe Him. Therefore, if you desire to belong to God, you must necessarily renounce yourself and forget and hate and persecute and destroy and annihilate your own self.

Secondly, Jesus Christ, your head and your model, in whom there is nothing that is not all holy and divine, nevertheless lived in so great detachment from Himself and kept His human spirit, His own will and love of Himself so subordinated that He never did anything according to His own human light or spirit, but all according to His Father's spirit. He behaved like a person having no love for Himself of infinite glory and felicity in this world, and of all human pleasures and satisfactions, and sought out and welcomed everything that might cause Him to suffer in His body or in His soul. Now if you are truly His members, you ought, therefore, to share His sentiments and dispositions, and make a firm resolution to live in future in complete detachment, forgetfulness, and hatred of your own selves.

To do this, make sure that you often adore Jesus in this detachment from Himself and give yourself to Him, begging Him to detach you entirely from yourself, from your own spirit, your own will and your self-love so that He may unite you perfectly to Himself, and govern you in all things according to His spirit, His love and His pure will.

Lift up your heart to Him, at the beginning of every action, somewhat like this: "O Jesus, with all my power I renounce myself, my own mind, my own will and my self-love and I give myself all to Thee and to Thy holy spirit and Thy divine love. Draw me out of myself and direct me in this action according to Thy holy will."

Whenever an occasion of disagreement arises because of natural differences of opinion, no matter how sure you may be that you are right, be glad to give up your own opinion and yield to that of someone else, provided the glory of God be not concerned in the matter.

When you feel some desire or inclination for one thing or another, lay it at once at the feet of Jesus, assuring Him that you do not wish to have any other will or inclination but His.

The moment you perceive yourself to have some sensible weakness or affection for any earthly object, immediately turn your heart and affections to Christ, in this way: "O dear Jesus, I give Thee all my heart and my affections. O Thou only object of my love, make me never love anything except in Thee and for Thee."

When someone gives you a word of praise, refer it to Him who is alone worthy of all honor saying: "O my glory, I desire no other glory but Thine forever. To Thee alone is due all praise, honor and glory, and to me all abjection, shame and humiliation."

When something occurs that mortifies your body or spirit, or when you see an occasion to deprive yourself of some satisfaction (such occasions present themselves hourly), accept it with a ready welcome, for the love of Our Lord, and bless Him for giving you an opportunity to mortify your self-love, in honor of His mortifications and privations on earth.

Whenever you feel any joy or consolation, refer it to the sublime Source of all consolation, and say to Him: "O Jesus, I desire never to have any contentment but Thine. Ah, my Lord, it is joy enough for me to know that Thou art God, and that Thou art my God! O Jesus, be always Jesus, that is, always full of glory, greatness and joy, and I shall always be satisfied. O my Jesus, never permit me to find my contentment in anything in the world, but in Thee alone. But rather grant that I may say like Queen Esther of old: "Thou knowest, O Lord, that thy handmaid hath never rejoiced, but in thee" (Esth. 14, 18).

## IX. PERFECTION OF CHRISTIAN DETACHMENT.

The perfection of Christian detachment does not consist only in being detached from the world and from oneself. It obliges the soul to be, in a certain sense, detached even from God. Do you not know that when Our Lord was still on earth, He assured His apostles that it was expedient for Him to depart from them to go to the Father and send them His Holy Spirit? Why was this, if not because they were attached to the sensible consolation of the visible presence of His sacred humanity? Now this was an obstacle to the coming of the Holy Spirit, so necessary is it to be detached from all things, no matter how holy and divine they may be, if you would be animated by the spirit of Jesus, which is the spirit of Christianity.

That is why I say you must be detached, in a certain sense, even from God, that is, from the delights and consolation that ordinarily accompany God's grace and His love. You must be detached from the pious plans you have made for God's glory, from the desires you have for greater perfection and love for God, and even from the desire to be delivered from the prison of this body, to see God and to be united with Him perfectly, and to love Him purely, without interruption. When God allows you to feel the sweetness of His kindness in your devotions, you must be careful not to become attached to this consolation. You must humble yourself at once, considering yourself most unworthy of any consolation, and ready to be stripped of it, to assure Him that you desire to serve and love Him, not for the consolation that He gives, either in this world or in the next, but for love of Himself and merely to please Him.

When you have undertaken a holy task or are doing some good work for the glory of God, you must exert every effort to ensure its accomplishment. Nevertheless, you must take care not to become attached to it, so that if, by accident, you are obliged to interrupt this good work, or even leave it altogether, you will not lose your peace and repose of spirit, but remain content in view of the will and permission of God, who directs all things and is to be equally loved in all.

Similarly, although you must exert all your energy in trying to conquer your passions, vices and imperfections, and to became master of every kind of virtue, you must, nevertheless, work at this without being carried away by your zeal. So that when you do not perceive in yourself as many virtues, or as much love of God as you would like to see, you may remain at peace and undisturbed, humiliating yourself because of the obstacles you yourself have placed in the path of virtue. You must try to love your own abjection, remaining satisfied with what it pleases God to give you, ever persevering in your desire to make progress, having confidence that Our Lord, in His goodness, will give you the graces you need to serve Him with the perfection He requires of you.

So, also, however much you ought to be always eager for the happy hour which will entirely take you away from the earth, from sin and from imperfection, and unite you perfectly with God and His pure love, and however much you ought to exert all your power to accomplish God's work in you so that, His work being finished, He may quickly call you back to Him, you must, nevertheless, desire this without attachment and without anxiety. If it be Our Lord's good pleasure for you to remain several more years separated from the most sweet vision of His divine face, you must remain satisfied with His most adorable will, even if He were to make you bear this bitter privation until the Day of Judgment.

This is what is called detachment from God. In this consists the perfect detachment from the world, from themselves, and from all things which all Christians should possess. Oh, how sweet it is to be thus free and detached from all things!

Some may think that it is very difficult to arrive at such perfection. But it would be easy for you if you gave yourself entirely and unreservedly to the Son of God, and if you placed your reliance and confidence, not in your own powers and resolutions, but in the greatness of His goodness and in the power of His grace and of His love. For wherever this divine love is to be found, all is done with extreme sweetness. True, you must do violence to yourself in certain things, and go through many trials and sufferings, much darkness and mortification; nevertheless, in the ways of holy love, there is more honey than gall, and more sweetness than rigor.

Ah, my Saviour, what glory Thou hast, what joy Thou takest and what great things dost Thou accomplish in one who walks bravely in these ways, abandoning everything, becoming detached from everything, even in a way from Thee, to give himself more perfectly to Thee! How strongly dost Thou then unite the soul with Thee! With what power dost Thou gain possession of it! How divinely dost Thou plunge it into the abyss of Thy love! How admirably dost Thou transform it into Thyself, clothing it with Thy qualities, Thy spirit, and Thy love!

What eminent satisfaction, what delightful sweetness it is for a soul to be able to say with truth: "My God, here I am free and detached from everything! Who will stop me now from loving Thee perfectly? Now I no longer cling to anything. Draw me after Thee, O Jesus. *Trahe me post te, curremus in odorem unguentorum tuorum* (Cant. 1, 3). What a consolation it is for a soul to be able to say with the holy Spouse: "My beloved to me, and I to him" (Cant. 2, 16), and with Jesus, *Omnia mea tua sunt, et tua mea sunt,* "All my things are thine, and thine are mine" (John 17, 10).

Cultivate an earnest desire for this holy detachment. Give yourself entirely and unreservedly to Jesus. Beg Him to break your bonds with the strength of His all-powerful arm, to detach you completely from the world, from yourself, and from all things, so that He may work in you, without any obstacle, all that He desires to accomplish for His glory.

## X. Fourth Foundation of Christian Life and Sanctity: Prayer.

The holy exercise of prayer must be considered one of the chief foundations of Christian life and sanctity, since the whole life of Jesus Christ was nothing but a perpetual prayer, which you must continue and express in your life. This is so necessary that the earth on which you live, the air you breathe, the bread that sustains you, the heart that beats in your breast, are none of them so necessary to man for his bodily life as prayer is to a Christian if he is to live as a Christian. This is because:

(1) The Christian life, called by the Son of God eternal life, consists in knowing and loving God. This divine knowledge is acquired by praying.

(2) Of yourself you are nothing, can do nothing and possess nothing but poverty and nothingness. Hence, you have a very great need of going to God for help, at all hours, by means of prayer, so that you may obtain and receive from Him all that you lack.

Prayer is a respectful and loving elevation of your mind and heart to God. It is a joyous meeting, a holy communication, a divine conversation between God and the Christian. In it the soul considers and contemplates its Creator in His divine perfections, in His mysteries and in His works; it adores and blesses Him, loves and glorifies Him, gives itself to Him, is abased before Him at the sight of its sins and ingratitude. It implores Him to be merciful, and learns to become like Him by imitating His divine virtues and perfections, and finally asks for all the things necessary to serve and love Him.

Prayer is a participation in the life of the angels and saints, in the life of Jesus Christ and of His most holy Mother, even of the life of God and of the Three Divine Persons. For the life of the angels and saints, of Christ, and of His most holy Mother is nothing else but a continual practice of prayer and contemplation, in which their uninterrupted occupation is to look upon God, to praise and love Him, to ask Him, on your behalf, for the things you need. And the existence of the Three Divine Persons is a perpetual contemplation, praise and love of one another, which is accomplished first and foremost by prayer.

Prayer is perfect delight, supreme happiness, a true earthly paradise. It is by this divine exercise of prayer that the Christian soul is united to God, who is the centre of its being, its goal and its supreme good. It is in prayer that God belongs to the soul and the soul to God. It is by praying that the soul pays Him rightful service, homage, adoration and love, and receives from Him His lights, His blessings and a thousand tokens of His exceeding great love. It is during your prayers that God takes His delight in you, according to this word of His: "My delights are to be with the children of men" (Prov. 8, 31), and gives us an experimental knowledge of the fact that our true joy and perfect satisfaction are to be found in God, and that a hundred, or even a thousand years of the false pleasures of this world are not worth one moment of the true delights which God allows those souls to taste, who seek all their contentment only in conversing with Him in holy prayer.

Finally, prayer is the most worthy, the noblest, the loftiest, greatest and most important act in which you can engage your efforts, for it is the ceaseless occupation of the angels and saints, of the Blessed Virgin, of Jesus and of the Most Holy Trinity throughout all the vastness of eternity. It is also destined to be our own unending activity in heaven. Indeed, this is the one true and proper function of a man and of a Christian, since man is created for God and to be with

God, and the Christian is on earth only for the purpose of continuing what Jesus Christ did during His life.

Therefore, with all my power, I urge every one of you who read these words, and in God's name I adjure you, since our Dear Jesus condescends to take His delight in being with you and speaking to you through prayer, do not deprive Him of His satisfaction, but learn by your own experience that like holy wisdom His conversation has no bitterness, nor His company any tediousness, but joy and gladness (Wis. 8, 16). Look upon prayer as the first, the principal, most necessary, most urgent and most important business of your life, and as far as possible, free yourself from all less necessary duties, to give as much time as you can to prayer, especially in the morning and evening, and a little before dinner, and in one or another of the ways I shall set forth.

## XI. VARIOUS KINDS OF PRAYER.

There are several ways of praying and I shall here set down the five most important methods of prayer.

1. *Mental Prayer:* The first is called mental or interior prayer, in which the soul communes with God, taking as the subject of conversation one of His divine perfections, or some mystery, virtue or word of His Divine Son, whether something He accomplished in the past, or is doing now, in the order of glory, grace or nature, in His Mother, His saints, His Church or in the world.

You begin the conversation of prayer by applying your understanding to consider with a determined, yet unstrained, attention and effort the truths to be found in the subjects chosen, truths which can arouse the soul to love God and hate sin. Then make your heart and will produce a few fervent acts of adoration, praise, love, humility, contrition and oblation, with the resolution to avoid evil and do good, according to the prompting of the Spirit of God.

This kind of prayer is more holy, more useful and more filled with blessings than words can convey. For this reason, if God draws you to mental prayer and gives you the grace to practise it, you should indeed thank Him for this very great gift. If He has not yet given you this grace, pray that He may do so, and for your own part exert all your efforts to correspond with His grace and cultivate this holy practice. God Himself will instruct you in the ways of this prayer better than all the books and all the teachers in the world, if you cast yourself down at His feet with humility, confidence and purity of heart, in the way I am about to explain.

2. *Vocal Prayer:* The second method of prayer is called vocal prayer. It consists in speaking to God, either by the recitation of the Divine Office, or the rosary or any other vocal prayer. This is almost as valuable as mental prayer, provided that when you speak to God with your lips you also speak to Him with your heart and with an attentive mind. In this way your prayer will be both vocal and mental. If, however, you get into the habit of reciting many vocal prayers mechanically and inattentively, you will leave God's presence more distracted, colder and less generous in His love than you were when you entered. For this reason I advise you to confine yourself to relatively few vocal prayers, apart from those you are obliged to say, and to develop the habit of saying them devoutly, with great attention and application of the mind to God. During vocal prayers you should occupy your mind and heart with holy thoughts while your tongue is uttering the words, remembering constantly that you are supposed to continue the prayers which Christ said on earth. Give yourself to Him for this purpose. Unite yourself with the love, humility, purity, holiness and most perfect attention characteristic of His prayers, and beg Him to impress upon your soul the holy and divine dispositions and intentions with which He used to pray.

You may also offer your prayers in union with all the holy prayers and divine supplications that have ever been, in heaven and on earth, by the most Holy Virgin, the angels and the saints, uniting yourself with the love and devotion and attention with which they perform this holy function.

3. *Spirit of Prayer:* The third method of prayer is to perform all your acts, even the smallest, in a Christian and holy spirit, offering them to Our Lord as you begin, and then, from time to time, lifting up your heart to Him while you perform them, in the way that will be once more set forth in more detail in "Part Three" of this book. To do your actions thus is to perform them with a spirit of prayer and to

practise prayer continually, in accordance with the commandment of Our Lord, who desires that you should always pray without ceasing. This prayer by action is a most excellent, as well as a very easy way to remain always in the presence of God.

4. *Spiritual Reading:* The fourth method of prayer is to read good books, reading them, however, not in haste, but taking your time, and applying your mind to what you are reading, stopping to consider and turning over in your thoughts the truths that strike you most forcefully, in order to impress them on your mind so as to derive specific acts of virtue and profitable resolutions. Therefore, one thing I recommend to you with singular insistence is that you never let a day go by without reading some spiritual book for half an hour.

The books best suited for spiritual reading are the New Testament, the *Imitation of Christ,* the Lives of the Saints, the works of Luis de Granada, especially his great *Guide for Sinners* and the *Memorial of the Christian Life,* the writings of St. Francis de Sales and of Cardinal de Bérulle, founder of the Oratory of France, and Father Quarré's *Spiritual Treasure.*[1] But remember, at the beginning of your reading, to give your mind and heart to Our Lord and to beg Him to give you the grace to derive the fruit He chooses for you, and that by this He may work His holy will in your soul for His glory.

5. *Conversing About God:* It is also a most useful and devout practice, which usually enflames hearts with divine love, to speak and converse with one another about God and holy things. Christians should indeed spend part of their time this way. God should be the principal subject of their conversation, and it is in this that they ought to seek their recreation and their delight.

You are encouraged to do this by the Apostle St. Peter saying, "If any man speak, let him speak as the words of God" (I Pet. 4, 11).

After all, you are God's children, so you ought to enjoy speaking the language of your Father, a language that is all holy, celestial and divine. And since you are made for Heaven, you ought to begin, even on earth, to speak a heavenly language. Oh, how sweet it is, to a soul who loves God above all things, to speak of what is most

---

[1] Father John Hugh Quarré entered the Oratory of France in 1618 and later became provincial of the Belgium Oratory.

lovable in the world and to hear sweet words about Him! How pleasing are these holy conversations to the One who has said: "Where there are two or three gathered together in my name, there am I in the midst of them" (Matt. 18, 20)! Oh, how different are such precious words from the ordinary chatter of this world! What a holy and profitable way to spend your time, provided you do it in the proper dispositions!

For this end you should follow the rule laid down by St. Paul on this subject: *Sicut ex Deo, coram Deo, in Christo loquimur.* "From God, before God, in Christ we speak" (II Cor. 2, 17). These words indicate the three things you must observe, if you are to speak of God devoutly and inspiringly.

First, you must speak *from God,* that is, you must draw upon God for your topics and your words, offering yourself to the Son of God at the beginning of your spiritual conversation, in order that He may inspire your mind and place on your lips the words and things you are to say, and that you may thus say what He said to His Father: "The words which Thou gavest me, I have given to them" (John 17, 8).

Secondly, you must speak *in the presence of God,* in a spirit of prayer and recollection, remembering attentively that God is everywhere present, and giving yourself to God, so that He may cause to fructify in you the things that you may say or hear said, and that you may make use of them according to His holy will.

Thirdly, you must speak *in Jesus Christ,* that is, with the intentions and dispositions of Christ, even as He spoke so nobly and beautifully on earth, or else as He would speak if He were in your place. To do this, you should give yourself to Him, uniting yourself with His intentions as He discoursed in the world, having no other aim but the glory of His Father alone. You should also share his dispositions of humility, of gentleness and charity towards those to whom He spoke, and of love and attention towards His Father. If you do this, your conversations will be most pleasing to Him. He will be in the midst of you, to take His delight among you and the time spent in these spiritual conversations will be time spent in prayer.

## XII. Qualities of Prayer.

The holy Apostle St. Paul teaches that if you would perform all your actions devoutly, you must act in the name of Jesus Christ. And Christ Himself assures you that whatever you ask His Father, in His name, He will grant you. Therefore, to pray worthily and to obtain from God all that you ask, you must pray in the name of Jesus Christ. But what does it mean, to pray in the name of Christ? I have already mentioned what it means, but it is a point that can not be stressed too often, a truth which must become well impressed upon your minds as of great importance and most useful in everything you do. To pray in the name of Christ means to continue the prayers which Christ said while on earth.

Since all Christians are members of Jesus Christ and constitute His Mystical Body, as St. Paul says, they represent His Person, and must consequently do everything in His name, that is, in His spirit, with His dispositions and intentions, just as He Himself did on earth, and just as He would do now, in their place. In the same way, an ambassador, who represents the ruler of a country, is obliged to act and speak in his name, that is, in his spirit, just as the ruler himself would act and speak if he were present. Therefore, I repeat that to pray in the name of Christ is to continue Christ's own prayers and supplications, to pray in His spirit, with the feelings, thoughts and sacred intentions that animated His Heart as He prayed. All Christians ought to pray as He did, in His name.

To this end, when you begin your prayers, remember that you are going to continue the prayers of Jesus Christ, and that you must also continue to pray as He would, namely, with the dispositions of His earthly petitions as well as His eternal prayer now in heaven and upon our altars, where He is present in a ceaseless act of supplication to His Heavenly Father. Unite yourself with the love, humility, purity, holiness, attention, and with all the holy dispositions and intentions of His infinite prayer.

Now, among these dispositions there are four in particular, with which you should pray if you desire to give God glory by your prayers and to obtain from Him what you ask.

1. *Humility:* The first disposition for prayer is that you should present yourself before God with deep humility, recognizing that you are most unworthy to appear in His august presence to contemplate Him, or to be heard by Him. Of yourself, you cannot entertain a single holy thought, nor perform a single act that is pleasing to Him. Therefore, you must annihilate yourself at His feet, offering yourself to our Lord Jesus Christ, that He may establish Himself in you, that it may be He Himself who prays within you, since He alone is worthy to appear before God's face to glorify and love Him, and to obtain from Him the answer to all petitions. Then, you may approach in full confidence to ask of the Eternal Father all that you ask of Him in the name of His Son, by the merits of His Divine Son, Jesus Christ, who dwells within you.

2. *Confidence:* The second disposition is a loving and respectful confidence, believing most firmly that everything you ask, if it is for God's glory and your salvation, will infallibly be granted, and often with a generosity surpassing your request, provided that you do not ask it relying upon your merits, or upon the virtue of your prayer, but in the name of Jesus Christ, by His merits and prayers, and for Christ Himself, trusting purely in His goodness and His sacred promise: "Ask and it shall be given you" (Luke 11, 9). "If you ask the Father any thing in my name, He will give it you" (John 16, 23); and, "whatsoever you ask when ye pray, believe that you shall receive; and they shall come unto you" (Mark 11, 24). If God treated you according to your merits, He would drive you out of His sight, and destroy you when you presented yourself before Him. Therefore, when He gives you grace, you must not think that He gives it to you in answer to your prayers, but rather that He gives it to His Son Jesus Christ by virtue of His prayers and merits.

3. *Purity of Intention:* The third disposition of prayer is purity of intention, assuring Our Lord that you renounce all curiosity of mind, all self-love, and that you wish to pray not for your own satisfaction and consolation, but purely for His glory and to please Him alone. He deigns to take delight in your company and converse with you in prayer. So ask Him to grant that you may pray solely for His glory and contentment.

4. *Perseverance:* The fourth disposition to accompany prayer should be perseverance. If you desire to glorify God in prayer, and to obtain from His goodness the favors you ask, you must faithfully persevere in this divine exercise. There are some favors that Almighty God does not grant either the first, or the second, or the third time you ask Him, because He wishes you to pray for a long time and often He wills this delay to keep you in a state of humility and self-contempt and to make you realize the value of His graces. He sometimes takes pleasure in putting you off for some time, in matters which oblige you to come frequently to Him, so that, by this means, you may often be with Him, and He with you; so great is His love for you, and so true it is that He delights in being with you.

Finally, to make all the other holy dispositions complete, at the beginning of your prayer, fervently give your mind and heart to Jesus and to His divine spirit, praying Him to inspire in your heart such thoughts and affections as He may desire. Abandon yourself entirely to His holy guidance, that He may guide you as He pleases in this divine activity. Trust in His great goodness to lead you in the most fitting manner, and to give you all that you shall ask, not perhaps in the way that you wish, but in some other way much better for you.

# THE CHRISTIAN VIRTUES

ONCE you have laid down in your soul the chief foundations of Christian life and sanctity, which are faith, hatred of sin, detachment from all things, and, finally, prayer, if you would live a Christian life and make Jesus Christ live and reign in your heart, it is necessary also to work diligently at the practice of the Christian virtues which Our Lord exercised on earth. Since you must continue to fulfil Christ's holy life on earth, you must also continue to cultivate His virtues. Therefore, I urge you to fervent imitation of His virtues by first setting down, at this point, some general remarks on the excellence of the Christian virtues most important and necessary to the perfection and sanctity of Christian life.

## XIII. EXCELLENCE OF THE CHRISTIAN VIRTUES.

There are many people who appreciate virtue, who desire it, seek it and spend much diligence and time to acquire it, yet you see very few who can claim your respect by their true and solid Christian virtues. One of the main reasons is that they follow the paths of virtue not so much in the spirit of Christianity as in the spirit of the pagan philosophers, of heretics, or of those who cultivate virtue for human and social ends. In other words, they act not so much in the spirit of Jesus Christ and His divine grace, purchased for us by His blood, as in the spirit of nature and of human reason.

Would you like to know the difference between these two spirits in this matter of practising virtue? You may detect it in the following way:

1. Those who seek virtue in the fashion of the pagans, the agnostic philosophers, or the politically-minded, look at it through the eyes of human reason alone, and value it as a thing most excellent in itself, most reasonable and necessary for the perfection of man, to distinguish him from animals guided by sense alone. Their desire and

33

quest for virtue is based on humanitarian considerations, not on Christian ideas.

2. They are also persuaded that they can acquire virtue by their own efforts, by dint of care, vigilance and self-analysis with resolutions and exercises. In this they are very much mistaken, because without divine grace it is impossible for us to perform even the smallest act of Christian virtue.

3. They love virtue, and strive after it, not for the glory of God, but for themselves, for their own interest and satisfaction, to render themselves more excellent and accomplished and also to avoid unpleasantness and embarrassment. This is the way pagan philosophers, heretics or sociologists desire virtue and seek it. Indeed, the very devils themselves desire virtue this way because, being full of pride, they want anything that may make them more excellent, and advance their status. They are interested in the cultivation of virtue, because it is a most noble and excellent thing for themselves; they strive after it not to become more pleasing to God, but out of a spirit of pride and self-perfection.

On the other hand, there are those who follow the spirit and grace of Jesus Christ in the exercise of virtue.

1. They look upon virtue not only in itself, but in its principle and source, namely, in Christ, the source of all grace, who eminently and sovereignly embodies every virtue, and in whom virtue attains infinite excellence. Since all that is in Jesus is holy, divine and adorable, virtue is sanctified and divinely exalted in Him, and is consequently made worthy of infinite honor and adoration. Therefore, if you consider virtue as in Christ, your view of it will be infinitely more efficacious in leading you to esteem and love and seek it, much more so than if you regarded it merely because of its own excellence, or because of the esteem accorded to it by reason and the human mind.

2. Those who are led by the spirit of Christianity in the practice of virtue know full well that they can not perform the smallest act of virtue by themselves. They realize that if God were to withdraw Himself from them, they would, at that very moment, fall into the abyss of vice; they know, too, that virtue is purely and simply a gift

of God's infinite mercy; therefore, it is necessary to ask Him for it, with confidence and perseverance. Earnest Christians persistently and continually ask God for the virtues they need, without ever growing weary of asking Him for them, and at the same time they are careful not to rely in any way on their own efforts and vigilance, or on their own exercises and practices, desires and resolutions, but instead they look to God's goodness alone for everything, and do not grow anxious when they do not find in themselves the virtues they desire. Instead of becoming disturbed and discouraged they remain at peace in humility before God, recognizing that this is due to their own infidelity; and that, if He were to treat them as they deserve, He would not only give them nothing that they ask for, but would strip them of all the graces He ever granted. And He would still be show-ing them too great a favor if He did not then cast them out and abandon them entirely. This enkindles in Christian souls a fresh flame of love and new confidence, in the presence of this infinite goodness, and inspires a most ardent desire to pursue, by every possible means, the virtues they need to serve and glorify Him.

3. They desire virtue, and make a point of frequently performing exterior and interior acts of love of God, of charity, of patience, obedience, humility, mortification and the other Christian virtues, not for themselves, or for their own satisfaction or reward, but for the good pleasure and interests of God, in order to .model their lives after the pattern of their Divine Head, Jesus Christ, to glorify Him and to continue the exercise of the virtues He practised on earth.

It is in this that Christian virtue properly consists. As Christian life is nothing but a continuation of the life of Christ, so also the Christ-ian virtues are a continuation and fulfilment of the virtues of Christ. To practise the virtues like Christians, you must practise them in the very spirit of Christ as He practised them, that is, with the same motives and intentions that inspired His admirable and majestic vir-tues. In this way then, Christian humility is a continuation of Christ's humility, Christian charity a continuation of Christ's charity, and so on with all the other virtues.

Thus you may easily see how far the Christian and supernatural virtues exceed, in holiness and excellence, those we call natural virtues, the virtues proper to pagans, heretics and false Catholics. For such persons natural virtues are nothing more than human virtues, feigned virtues, with only the appearance, having no depth and no solidarity, since they rest upon the frailty of the human mind and reason, and upon the shifting sands of self-love and vanity. But the Christian virtues are true and solid virtues, being divine and supernatural. In a word, they are Christ's own virtues, with which you yourself have to be clothed, which He imparts to those who adhere to Him, and who ask Him for them with humility and confidence, and strive to practise them as He did.

### XIV. Manner of Practising the Christian Virtues.

From what has just been said, you may see how devoutly you must practise Christian virtues, since you are to practise them as Christ did. When you desire to advance in the perfection of some virtue, make use of the following acts:

1. Adore in Christ the virtue you have chosen and reflect how eminent He was in it, and how perfectly He practised it during His whole life.

2. Humble yourself before Him, when you see yourself so very far from this perfection. Beg His forgiveness for all the faults you have ever committed against this virtue, recognizing that, of yourself, you are powerless to perform the least act of it, and that you are most unworthy of the grace to do so. Yet implore Him, nonetheless, that in His great mercy He may give you this grace, that you may practise this virtue, whenever the opportunity offers itself.

3. Frequently give yourself to Jesus, with a great desire to practise this virtue with all the perfection He asks of you. Beg Him to destroy in you all that is opposed to this virtue, that He may imprint and establish it within you, purely for His glory.

4. Be faithful in putting the virtue into practice by inward acts and outward results, uniting yourself with the dispositions and intentions of Christ, the perfect example of this virtue.

5. When you happen to commit some fault against the virtue, do not be upset or discouraged, but humble yourself before God, asking his forgiveness and offering Him all the honor rendered Him by His

Beloved Son and His most holy Mother, in their exercise of this virtue, as satisfaction for your fault.

Then give yourself again to Jesus, with a renewed desire to be faithful to him in future, in the practice of this virtue. Beg Him by His great mercy to repair the damage caused by your faults, and to give you fresh grace to be more faithful and effective when similar occasions next present themselves.

## XV. An Example: Practice of Meekness and Humility of Heart.

In order that my readers may acquire some facility in the use of the preceding exercise, and to make it accessible to persons of every type, I should like to show you its complete practical application to a particular virtue. Take, for example, meekness and humility, which were so strongly emphasized by Jesus. If you wish to become well established in these two virtues, take a little time every day, to place yourself at the feet of our Blessed Lord and put yourself in the dispositions outlined in the following prayer:

O Most Meek and Humble Jesus, I adore in Thee Thy most divine and adorable meekness and humility. I glorify Thee in all Thy many acts and exercises of meekness and humility, both inward and outward. How admirable art Thou in these two virtues, as well as in all the others! When I consider the whole span of Thy life upon earth, O Good Jesus, I see that it was one continuous exercise of meekness and humility in Thy thoughts, words, actions and sufferings. Oh, what glory Thou didst give Thy Father! But also, how He exalted Thee, after Thou hadst so humbled Thyself for His glory and our love! May this Heavenly Father be forever blessed, and Thou also, O Good Jesus! May He be blessed because He so glorified Thee after Thy humiliations; mayest Thou be blessed because Thou didst so honor Him by Thy meekness and humility!

O Jesus, Thou art my Head and I am one of Thy members; Thou art my Father and I am one of Thy children; Thou art my Master and Teacher and I am one of Thy disciples. I must, therefore, strive to imitate and resemble Thee. And yet, how far I am from doing so! On the contrary, how full I am of pride and vanity, bad temper and impatience! How often have I offended, in my whole life, against meekness and humility, by thoughts and sentiments, words and actions! Forgive me, O my Saviour, forgive me; I long to imitate Thee in Thy meekness and humility. But alas, I admit that I have no strength of myself to perform the least act of humility, and that I am most unworthy that Thou shouldst give me the grace to do so. Nevertheless, I beg Thee, by Thy great mercy, to grant this precious grace.

O Jesus, I adore Thee as Thou sayest these divine words: "Learn of me because I am meek, and humble of heart: and you shall find rest to your souls" (Matt. 11, 29). I adore the thoughts, the plans and the love Thou didst have for me because when Thou didst utter these sacred words, O Good Jesus, Thou wast thinking of me, in particular; Thou didst utter them with exceeding great love for me, with special designs in mind concerning me. O my Most Amiable Jesus, I give myself all to Thee for the accomplishment of Thy will and the fulfilment of Thy words. Never permit me again to place obstacles in their way. Destroy in me all that is opposed to meekness and humility. Establish and glorify in me Thy meekness and humility for love of Thyself!

When some opportunity of being meek or humble offers itself, lift up your heart to Jesus as follows:

O Jesus, I give myself to Thee to practise meekness, patience and humility in honor of Thy meekness, patience and humility, and in union with Thy blessed dispositions and intentions.

When you lapse into some fault against these virtues, strive to make up for it at once, casting yourself at the feet of the Son of God, and addressing Him thus:

O Most Merciful Jesus, with my whole heart I beg Thy forgiveness for the offense I have committed against Thy divine majesty. O Father of Jesus, I offer Thee all the honor which Thy well-beloved Son and His most holy Mother ever gave Thee by their meekness and humility, to atone for the dishonor I have afforded Thee by the fault I have committed against these virtues. O Jesus, O Mother of Jesus, may it please you to repair my defect, offering your sweet meekness and infinite humility to the Eternal Father, in reparation for my pride and impatience. O Good Jesus, I give myself to Thee with a renewed desire to be more meek and humble in future; destroy arrogance and impatience, and give me the grace to practise patience and humility faithfully at all opportunities, for Thy glory and good pleasure.

You can apply these same practices to charity, to obedience, and to the other virtues.

## XVI. DIGNITY, NECESSITY AND IMPORTANCE OF CHRISTIAN HUMILITY.

If you truly and fully intend to live in a Christian and holy manner, one of your foremost endeavors ought to be to gain a thorough and conscious mastery of Christian humility, which is the most necessary and important virtue. Our Lord most emphatically and insistently recommended it to us in these divine and lovable words of His, which you should keep always in your minds and on your lips with love and respect for Him: *"Learn of Me because I am meek, and humble of heart: and you shall find rest to your souls"* (Matt. 11, 29). This is the virtue which St. Paul says is the most characteristic of Christ. It is the proper and specific virtue of Christians, without which it is impossible to be a true Christian. It is the foundation of all Christian life and sanctity, the guardian of every other grace and virtue. It is one which draws down upon our souls all blessings, for it is in humble souls that the most great and most humble Jesus takes His repose and His delight, according to His words: *"To whom shall I have respect but to him that is poor and little. . . ?"* (Isa. 66, 2).

This virtue, together with burning love, makes saints and great saints. For the true measure of sanctity is humility. Give me a truly humble person and I shall say that he is truly saintly; if that person is humble in great things, I shall pronounce him saintly in great things; and if he is very humble indeed, I shall avow that he is very saintly and adorned with all kinds of virtues. I shall say that God is greatly glorified in such a soul, wherein Jesus Christ dwells and finds in it His treasure and His paradise of delights. That soul will be very great and occupy a most exalted position in the Kingdom of God, since Eternal Truth has said: *"He that shall humble himself shall be exalted"* (Matt. 23, 12). On the other hand, a soul without humility is a soul without virtue; it is a hell of pride, the abode of arrogant demons, an abyss of conceit and vice.

One may finally say that humility, in a sense, is the Mother of Jesus, because it was by humility that the Blessed Virgin Mary was made worthy to bear Him within herself. It is by this virtue, also, that you will be made worthy to form Him in your souls, and to make Him live and reign in your hearts. So you ought, then, to love and seek this virtue with all your might. For this reason I shall devote somewhat more space to this subject than to the others.

## XVII. HUMILITY OF MIND.

There are two kinds of humility, namely, humility of mind and humility of heart. When the two are united, they make up the perfection of Christian humility.

Humility of mind is a profound knowledge of what we really are in the sight of God. If we are to know ourselves well, we must see ourselves, not as we appear in the esteem and deceptive judgments of men, not in the vanity and presumption of our own opinion, but as we are in the eyes and in the judgment of God. To do this, we should view ourselves in the light and truth of God, through the medium of faith.

Now, if we consider ourselves in this heavenly light, with divine insight, we shall see that:

1. As men we are nothing but dust, corruption and nothingness. We are nothing and can do nothing of ourselves. Every creature has come forth from nothingness, therefore it is nothing, has nothing, and can do nothing of itself, without the sustaining power of its Creator.

2. As children of Adam we were born in original sin, enemies of God, subjects of the devil, powerless to do any good or avoid any evil by our own virtue. We have no other way of being saved except to renounce Adam and our fallen heritage, to surrender our own mind and our own powers to Christ and enter into His spirit and His power. We shall also see how true it is that we cannot be free from the servitude of sin if He does not deliver us, that without Him we can do nothing and that, even when we have done many things, we can and must say with truth that we are but useless servants. Add to that what St. Paul says: "We are not sufficient to think anything of ourselves, as of ourselves: but our sufficiency is from God" (II Cor.

3, 5), and that we would be unable to pronounce the Holy Name of Jesus without the help of the Holy Ghost (I Cor. 12, 3).

All this results not only from the nothingness of creatures, which are nothing, and can do nothing of themselves, but also from the subjection to sin, because we are born of Adam, who truly begot us in his own condemnation. He transmitted to us our nature and our life, but only under the domination and captivity of sin. He was not even able to beget us as free men, being himself a slave, nor to give us the grace and friendship of God which he had lost. So that, by a most equitable judgment of God, we all bear this yoke of iniquity which Holy Scripture calls the kingdom of death; this yoke does not allow us to perform the works of true freedom and true life, which belong to the children of God, but only the works of death and captivity, works too degraded for God's grace, justice and sanctity. Oh, how great is our wretchedness and indignity, since it was necessary that the Son of God should purchase for us, by His blood, our very slightest thought of serving God or, indeed, the very permission to present ourselves before Him! Yet this is not all.

If we look at ourselves in the light of God, we shall see that as children of Adam and as sinners we do not deserve to exist, nor to walk on the earth, nor that God should think of us, nor even that He should take the trouble to exercise His justice upon us. Job had, therefore, good reason to be surprised that God should deign to open His eyes to look at him, or be concerned enough to judge him: *Et dignum ducis hujuscemodi aperire oculos tuos, et adducere eum tecum in judicium* (Job 14, 3). He does us too great a favor, tolerating us in His presence, and allowing the earth to bear our weight, and but for a miracle on His part, all things would contribute to our ruin and perdition. We see, too, that sin deprives us of all our rights by withdrawing us from obedience to God. Consequently our being, our life, our bodies, our souls and all their faculties, no longer belong to us under the yoke of sin. The sun no longer owes us its light, nor the stars their shining guidance, nor the earth its support, nor fire its warmth, nor water its refreshment, nor the plants their fruits, nor the animals their services. But all creatures ought rather to wage war against us, and turn all their powers against us, when we turn ours against God, so that they might thus avenge our insult against their Creator. The vengeance which the whole world will visit upon sinners at the end of time ought to be visited upon us every day, when we continue to commit fresh sins; and it would be most just, if God were to punish a single sin by stripping us of life and of all the temporal and spiritual graces which He has given us, letting fall upon us every kind of punishment.

We also see that of ourselves, in so far as we are sinners, we are all so many incarnate demons, Lucifers, antichrists, since everything in us is contrary to Christ. We carry about, within ourselves, a devil, a Lucifer, and an antichrist, which is our own will, pride and self love; and they, indeed, are worse than all the demons, than Lucifer and antichrist, for all the malice of the demons, Lucifer and antichrist is derived from self-will, pride, and self-love. Of ourselves we are a hell full of horror, accursedness, sin and abomination. We have, within us, the principle, and seeds of all the sins of earth and hell, for the corruption left in us by original sin is the root and spring of every kind of sin, according to the words of David, the prophet king: "Behold I was conceived in iniquities; and in sins did my mother conceive me" (Ps. 50, 7). As a result of this, if God did not continually hold us up in the arms of His mercy, and if He did not work, as it were, a perpetual miracle to keep us from falling into sin, we should plunge at every moment into a chasm of every kind of sin.

Finally, we see that we are so horrible and repulsive that, if we were able to see ourselves as God sees us, we would find the sight impossible to bear. And in this connection, it is said that a saint once asked God to give her full knowledge of herself. When God answered her prayer, she saw such a horrible sight that she cried out: "Lord, not so much! Otherwise I shall lose courage!" And that master of the spiritual life, Father Avila, says that he knew a person who made this same request of God and beheld himself to be so loathsome, that he began to cry out in a loud voice: "Lord, I adjure Thee by Thy mercy, take away this mirror out of my sight; I am no longer curious to see my image."

After this, how can one have a high opinion of himself, or think that he is important or possesses any merit? How can anyone love

fame or seek to satisfy vanity, or enjoy the esteem or praise of men?
Oh, how strange it is to see trivial and insignificant creatures like ourselves trying to be important and proud of themselves! Oh, how
right is the Holy Spirit in avowing to us in the Ecclesiasticus, that he
detests and abhors a poor man who is proud (Eccli. 25, 3-4). If pride
is unbearable no matter in what subject it may be found, what must
it be in one upon whom poverty imposes an extreme humility? This
is a vice common to all men who, no matter how great their worth
may appear to be in the eyes of the world, bear upon themselves the
marks of their infamy, namely, the quality of sinners, which ought
to keep them in a state of great abjection before God and all creatures. Yet, what a terrible disaster is ours! Sin has made us so vile
and infamous that we refuse to recognize our misery. This refusal
renders us comparable to Satan who, by reason of the sin that holds
sway over him, is the lowest of all creatures, but is so proud that
he will not acknowledge his ignominy. That is what gives God such
a horror of pride and vanity. As He knows our lowliness and worth-
lessness, it is unbearable to Him to see so low and unworthy a thing
trying to exalt itself, especially when He remembers that He, who
is greatness itself, abased Himself even to nothingness. But even after
His infinite example of humility, nothingness still wants to be exalted,
and then, indeed, He finds this more than unendurable.

So, then, if you want to please God and serve Him perfectly, make
a deep and thorough study of this divine science of self-knowledge.
Firmly implant in your mind the truths I have just outlined and frequently consider them in God's presence; and each day ask Our Lord
to root them deeply in your soul.

Take note, however, that although as a man, a child of Adam and
a sinner you are what I have just described, nevertheless as a child
of God and a member of Christ, if you are in the state of grace, you
bear within you a most noble and sublime life and you possess an
infinitely rich and precious treasure. Notice also that, while humility
of spirit ought to show you what you are of yourself and in Adam,
yet it should not hide from you what you are in Christ and by His
merits. Nor does it oblige you to ignore the graces God has given you
through His Divine Son; otherwise it would be false humility.

Rather, it obliges you to admit that all the good in you comes purely from God's mercy, without merit on your part. This, then, is what constitutes humility of spirit.

## XVIII. HUMILITY OF HEART.

It is not enough to have humility of mind, which shows you your wretchedness and unworthiness. Humility of mind without humility of heart is diabolical. After all, the devils, who have no humility of heart, possess humility of spirit because they are well aware of their disgrace and accursedness. Hence you must learn from Jesus, the divine teacher, to be humble not only in mind but also in heart.

Humility of heart consists in loving your lowliness and abject state, in being content that you are little and abject and insignificant. When you are alone with yourself, you must love to treat yourself as insignificant and rejoice in being judged and belittled by others. Nor must you excuse or justify yourself, except when there is a grave necessity. You should not complain of anybody, remembering that since you have in yourself the source of all evil, you deserve all kinds of condemnation and harsh treatment. You must love to be despised and humiliated and you should even seek opportunity of being reviled and belittled in every way. There are two reasons for this:

1. Every kind of scorn and contempt is merely your due, and all creatures would be justified in persecuting and trampling you under foot. In fact, you are not even important enough for them to take the trouble of doing so.

2. You ought to love what was loved by the Son of God, seeking to base your whole life and find all your joy in the things He chose to give glory to His Father—namely, the contempt and humiliation with which His whole life was filled.

Furthermore, humility of heart is a matter not only of loving humiliations, but of hating and detesting all greatness and vanity, according to the maxim uttered by the sacred lips of the Son of God, which I beg you to consider well and deeply engrave upon your mind: "that which is high to men, is an abomination before God" (Luke 16, 15). I say all greatness, because it is not enough to despise temporal eminence and to abhor the vanity of human respect and praise. You must also have an even greater horror of the vanity that may spring from spiritual things. You should fear and avoid everything that attracts attention and appears extraordinary in your exercises of piety, such as visions, ecstasies, revelations, the gift of miracles and other such manifestations. You should not desire them nor ask God to give you these extraordinary graces. Even if a soul were to realize that God was offering one or another of these singular favors, it should draw back into the depths of its nothingness, considering itself far too unworthy, and implore Him to grant some other grace instead, something less striking, less conspicuous, something which would be more conformable with the hidden and despised life of Christ on earth. Since Our Lord takes pleasure in heaping upon you His graces, both ordinary and extraordinary, out of the excess of His goodness, He also derives extreme joy from seeing that you fly from all greatness in the eyes of men, out of a true sense of your unworthiness and the desire to resemble Him in His humility. And whoever is not thus disposed will lay himself open to many deceptions and illusions of the spirit of vanity.

Notice, however, that I am here referring to extraordinary things, and not to acts that are common and usual to all true servants of God, such as frequent communion, or kneeling down at least once each night and morning to perform your duties to God, no matter where one may be; or accompanying the Blessed Sacrament when It is being taken to the sick; or mortifying our flesh with fasting, discipline and penance; or reciting the Rosary, or praying in a church, or at home, or serving and visiting the poor, or doing some other good work. Be on your guard lest, wishing to omit the practice of such acts under pretext of false humility, you actually give them up out of real cowardice! If human respect and shame before the world stand in the way of your duty to God, they must be overcome. Remember that you are not to be ashamed, but to take great pride in being a Christian and acting as a Christian, and serving and glorifying God before men, in the face of the whole world.

But if fears, arising from vanity and the vain show of humility that is donned for the benefit of an audience, would seem to prevent you from doing what has been outlined, you must thrust those fears aside, protesting before Our Lord that you want to do nothing except for His glory alone. Realize then, that all these works are so common to God's true servants, and should be so frequently practised by all Christians, that they offer no cause for vanity, being things done by many good persons.

I fully realize that our Lord Jesus Christ teaches you to fast, give alms and pray in secret. But the great St. Gregory asserts that this refers to the intention and not to the act itself. That is, Our Lord does not mean that you should not perform these or similar actions, in public, or before men, for He says, in another place: "Let your light shine before men, that they may see your good works, and glorify your Father who is in heaven" (Matt. 5, 16). But He wants your intention to be secret and hidden: that is, in the public acts that you perform, He desires you to have, in your heart, the intention of doing them not to please men or to win their empty applause, but to please God and gain His glory.

Finally, the true humility of heart that our Lord Jesus Christ wants you to learn from Him, which is perfect Christian humility, consists in being humble as Christ was on earth. That means, to be horrified by any spirit of notoriety or vanity, to love contempt and obscurity, to choose always, in all things, whatever is more cheapening and humiliating, and to be ready to be humbled even to the point to which Jesus Christ was humbled in His Incarnation, His life, His passion and His death.

In His Incarnation, as St. Paul says, "He emptied himself, taking the form of a servant" (Phil. 2, 7). He willed to be born in a stable. He subjected Himself to the weakness and dependence of childhood, and in a thousand other ways He made Himself lowly. In His passion, He Himself says that He is a worm and no man, the opprobrium of men and the outcast of the people. He bore the anger and judgment of His Father, and so severe were they that they made Him sweat blood so plentifully, in the garden of Olives, that the ground was soaked with it. He gave Himself in subjection to the powers of darkness, that is, to the devils, who through the Jews, Pilate, Herod and their instruments, took possession of Him and made Him suffer every indignity in the world. Uncreated Wisdom was treated like a vagabond by Herod and the soldiers. He was whipped and nailed to a Cross like a slave and a thief. God, who should be His infinite refuge, abandoned Him and regarded Him as if He alone had committed all the crimes in the world. And finally, to use the words of His Apostle, "Christ hath redeemed us from the curse of the law, being made a curse for us" (Gal. 3, 13). Indeed, He even became the embodiment of sin through the power and justice of God. For St. Paul says: *Deus eum pro nobis peccatum fecit*—"Him he hath made sin for us" (II Cor. 5, 21). In other words, He bore not only the confusion and abasement deserved by sinners, but also all the ignominy and infamies due to sin itself, and that is the vilest and most ignominious state to which God could ever reduce the greatest of His enemies.

O God, what humiliation for a God, the Only Son of God, Sovereign Lord of the universe, to be brought down to such a level! O Lord Jesus, is it possible that Thou dost love man so much as to annihilate Thyself so completely for his love? O man, how is it possible for you still to retain any vanity, seeing how your God is brought so low for love of you? O my Saviour, let me be humiliated and destroyed with Thee, let me enter into the sentiments of Thy most profound humility, and let me be ready to bear all the shame and humiliation which are deserved by the sinner and even by sin itself!

It is in this, then, that perfect Christian humility consists; in being ready, not only to desire the treatment deserved by a sinner, but to bear all the ignominies and degradations which are the just due of sin itself, since our Head, Jesus, the Saint of saints, and Sanctity Itself, bore them, while you, at the same time, fully deserve them since of yourself you are nothing but sin and accursedness. If these truths were only deeply engraved upon your minds, you would find that you had very good reason to cry out and often say, with St. Gertrude: "Lord, one of the greatest miracles Thou dost accomplish in the world is to allow the earth to bear me."

## XIX Practice of Christian Humility.

Since, as has been said, Christian humility is so important and so necessary, you must seek out every means to give yourself a solid foundation in this virtue.

For this purpose, I repeat my advice that you frequently read and reread, consider and intently ponder the truths I have set forth relating to humility of mind and of heart, as well as those which I am about to set down here. I urge you to pray to Our Lord to impress them upon your mind, and make you ever carry with you, in heart and soul, the sentiments and effects proceeding from them. It is not enough for you to know superficially and vaguely that you are nothing, that you are powerless to do good or avoid evil, that all good is from on high, from the Father of lights, and that every good work comes to you from God through His Son. You must also become firmly rooted in a profound realization of your imprisonment under the law of sin, of your uselessness, incapacity and unworthiness in God's service, of your deficiency in all good things, of your nothingness, your extreme poverty and urgent need of Jesus Christ and of His grace.

This ought to make you cry out unceasingly to your liberator, and at all times fly to His grace, never relying upon anything except His omnipotent and infinite goodness.

God sometimes permits you to work for a long time to conquer a passion and become established in a virtue, and to advance very slowly towards your goal, so that the experience may teach you what you are, and how little you can do of yourself, thus obliging you to seek outside yourself, in Jesus Christ our Lord, the power to serve God. God did not will to give His Son to mankind until the world had longed for Him for four thousand years, and had learned by the experience of two thousand years that it was incapable of keeping the Law, and freeing itself from sin, and that it needed a new spirit and a new power to resist evil and do good. By this He showed you that He wants you to recognize your wretchedness very clearly before He gives you His grace.

This truth should lead you to recognize once every day, before God, your wretchedness as it is in His eyes, and to renounce Adam and yourself, since Adam and you yourself have sinned and surrendered your nature to the devil. Renounce yourself, then, altogether. Renounce your own judgment and every power and ability you may be conscious of in yourself. For all the power left by Adam in human nature is powerless, and any sense of power you may have is mere illusion, presumption and a mistaken estimate. Nor will you ever have any real power or perfect freedom to do good, except by renouncing yourself, and emerging from yourself and all that belongs to you, in order to live in the spirit and virtue of Jesus Christ.

Following this renunciation, adore Christ Jesus; give yourself entirely to Him, and ask Him to take over Adam's rights as well as your own, since by His Precious Blood and death He acquired the rights of all sinners. Beg Him to dwell in you to dispossess your nature, to appropriate and make free use of all that you are in His hands, and protest to Him that you desire to depart from your own way of looking at things, which is a spirit of pride and vanity, and from all your intentions, tendencies and dispositions, so that you may no longer live save in His spirit, His divine and adorable dispositions.

Implore Him by His great mercy to draw you out of yourself as from a hell and to establish you in Himself, in His spirit of humility. Ask this favor not for your benefit or satisfaction, but for His pleasure, and His glory, pure and simple. And again, pray that He may make use of His divine power to destroy your pride, and that He may no longer wait upon your weakness to establish His glory in you by means of perfect humility. Remember that, of yourself as a sinner, you are, as has been said, a potential demon, a Lucifer and an antichrist, because of the sin, the pride and self-love which always remain in each one of us. Frequently, and especially at the beginning of the day, place yourself at the feet of Jesus and of His holy Mother, and say to them:

"O Jesus, O Mother of Jesus, keep this wretched demon well under foot, crush this snake, exterminate this antichrist with Your precious breath; bind this Lucifer, that he may do nothing today against Your holy glory."

Now I do not intend that you should, every day, repeat before God all these prayers in the exact form in which I have set them down, but in whatever way it shall please Our Lord to make them appeal to you.

When you make resolutions to be humble, do so by giving yourself to the Son of God, that He may fulfil your desires, and say to Him:

"I give myself to Thee, my Lord Jesus, that I may enter into Thy spirit of humility. I wish to spend all the days of my life with Thee, in this holy virtue. I call down upon myself the power of Thy spirit of humility in order to annihilate my pride and bind me close to Thee in humility. I offer up to Thee all the opportunities for humility that shall present themselves in my life. Deign, I beseech Thee, to bless them. I renounce myself and all things which may prevent me from sharing in the grace of Thy humility."

But after this do not place your confidence in your own resolutions, nor in this practice, but rely solely upon the bounty of our Lord Jesus Christ.

You can follow a similar course with each of the other virtues or pious intentions you wish to present to God. In this way, they will be based not on you yourself, but on our Lord Jesus Christ and on the grace and mercy of God which are upon you.

When you present to God your desires and intentions to serve Him, it should be with a profound belief that you can neither fulfil these, nor deserve to do so yourself. If God treated you as you deserved, He would not even suffer you to think of such resolves, and it is because of His very goodness and because of the merits of the Precious Blood of His Son that He tolerates you in His presence, and allows you to hope for the grace to serve Him.

You must not be surprised when you fail in your good resolutions. We are all sinners, and God is not obliged to give us His grace. "I know," says St. Paul, "that there dwelleth not in me, that is to say, in my flesh, that which is good. For to will, is present to me; but to accomplish that which is good, I find not" (Rom. 7, 18).

So great is our weakness that it is not sufficient for God to inspire us with a good thought; it is also necessary for Him to grant us the will and resolve to put it into effect. Nothing will come of a good resolution if God does not grant the grace to accomplish and perfect the act. Finally each one of us needs also the special grace to persevere until the end of his life.

You ought, therefore, to submit yourself to God in your search for virtue. You should desire His grace and ask Him for it, but you should be surprised when He grants it. When you fall, you should adore His judgment of you, yet not become discouraged, but rather humble yourself and constantly persevere in giving yourself to Him, that you may enter with more virtue into His grace. You should live constantly in great gratitude and thanksgiving towards Him, because He tolerates you in His presence and inspires you with the desire to serve Him. And even though, after much effort on your part, God should give you no more than one good thought, you should recognize that you do not deserve even this one, and prize it so highly that you should consider it well worth all your trouble. If, after a thousand years of hell, the damned could form even one good thought of God, they would consider it much honor and great gain, and the devil is ever in a rage because he knows that he will never have a holy thought, for he looks upon goodness as a perfection which his pride desires, yet beholds himself deprived of it by the curse that is upon him. We, like the demons, are sinners and the only thing that sets us apart from them is the mercy of God, a mercy which should lead us to value His gifts and be satisfied with them. For, however little they may be, they are always more than we deserve. Enter, then, reflectively and deeply into this spirit of humble admission of your unworthiness, and by so doing you will draw down upon your soul a thousand blessings from God and He will be greatly glorified in you.

When God has granted you some favor, either for yourself or for someone dear to you, do not ascribe this to the power of your prayers but to His mercy alone.

If in the good works God gives you the grace to accomplish, you feel any complacency or spirit of gratification, humble yourself, remember that all good comes to you from God alone, and that from yourself nothing can come but evil. Bear in mind that you have much stronger reasons for being afraid and humbling yourself in view of the many faults and imperfections with which you perform your actions, than for puffing yourself up and feeling pleased when you see the slight good you are doing, a good, moreover, that does not proceed from you.

If men censure and sneer at you, accept it as being fully deserved, in honor of the contempt and calumnies suffered by the Son of God. If you are accorded any honor or receive thanks, refer all such praises to God, and see that you do not appropriate them to yourself, nor rest on your laurels, because these may prove to be the only reward of your good actions. You may thus come to feel the effect of these words of the Son of God: "Woe to you when men shall bless you: for according to these things did their fathers to the false prophets" (Luke 6, 26). These words teach you to consider and fear the praise and applause of the world not only as mere wind and smoke and illusion, but also as a danger and a curse.

Perform with a ready will lowly and menial acts that involve abjection, so as to mortify your pride. But see that you act in a spirit of humility, with inward sentiments and dispositions corresponding to the things done.

At the beginning of everything you do, always humble yourself before God, remembering that you are not worthy to exist or to do anything, and that you have no power to please Him, unless He gives you grace for that purpose.

In a word, engrave deep in your heart these words of the Holy Ghost, and systematically put them into practice: *Humilia te in omnibus, et coram Deo invenies gratiam, quoniam magna potentia Dei solius, et ab humilibus honoratur.* "Humble thyself in all things, and thou shalt find grace before God: for great is the power of God alone, and he is honored by the humble" (Eccli. 3, 20-21).

XX. CONFIDENCE AND SELF-ABANDONMENT IN THE HANDS OF GOD.

Humility is the mother of confidence. When you realize that you are destitute of all good and of every virtue, and of all power and capacity to serve God, and that you are a true hell full of all kinds of evil, you can no longer rely in any way upon yourself, or upon what is yours. You are obliged to emerge from yourself, as you would go out of hell, to enter into Jesus as into Paradise, where you find in great abundance all that is lacking in yourself. You must place your reliance and trust in Him, as in the One given to you by your Eternal Father to be your redemption, your justice, your virtue, your sanctification, your treasure, your strength, your life and your all. It is to this that He would draw you when He lovingly and compellingly urges you to come to Him with confidence, saying: "Come to me, all you

who labor, and are burdened, and I will refresh you" (Matt. 11, 28),
and will relieve you of the weight of your sorrows. Our Lord assures
us that He will reject no one who will come to Him: *Eum qui venit
ad me non ejiciam foras* (John 6, 37).

In order to compel us to become confident, He tells us in various
texts of Holy Scripture [1] that accursed and wretched are they who
place their trust in any other thing but Him; but happy and blessed are
they who entrust themselves to Him (Jer. 17, 5-7); they shall abound
in all kinds of graces and blessings, and shall lack nothing (Ps. 22,
1-2). His eyes are fixed upon those who hope in His mercy (Ps. 32, 18).
He is good to those who hope in Him (Lam. 3, 25). His mercy shall
compass them about (Ps. 31, 10) and He Himself will always be by
their side (Prov. 3, 26). He is the shield of all that trust in Him
(II Kings, 22, 31); He is their protector and helper (Ps. 113, 11). He
will protect them in His tabernacle and He will hide them in the
secret of His face, or, as another version has it, "in the apple of his
eye" (Ps. 30, 21). He will be their defense in the day of trial, and will
help them and deliver them from the hands of sinners because they
have put their trust in Him (Ps. 90, 14-15); He will let them taste in
its perfection the great multitude of His sweetness (Ps. 30, 20); they
will always be full of joy, and He will abide in them (Ps. 5, 12). He
lavishes upon them His graces and the effects of His mercy, in proportion to the hope and confidence they have in Him (Ps. 32, 22);
those who trust in Him will know truth (Wis. 3, 9), that is, He
the Sovereign Truth will manifest Himself to those who trust in
Him; they will not sin, or, according to the Hebrew version, they will
not be condemned and will not perish, that is, He will not allow them
to fall into sins that would separate them from Him and reduce them
to perdition (Ps. 33, 23); those who place their hope in Him will
sanctify themselves as He is sanctified (I John 3, 3). Never has anyone who entrusted himself to Him been disappointed or defrauded
of his expectations (Eccli. 2, 11). God grants to them everything that
they confidently ask of Him (Matt. 21, 22). Finally, nothing is im-

---

[1] St. John Eudes weaves into this passage several scriptural texts on confidence. We
have not attempted to quote the exact words from the Douay version but have merely
inserted the biblical references. (Editors' note—English translation.)

possible to those who have faith and confidence in Him, but they can accomplish all things, relying on His goodness and power (Mark 9, 22).

I could go on for ever, if I began to quote here all the texts from Holy Scripture in which God commends to you the virtue of trust. It seems as if He were not satisfied even with the thousand instances in Holy Scripture by which He proves how dear and delightful this holy virtue is to Him, and how much He loves and favors those who place their trust in His goodness and abandon themselves entirely to the fatherly care of His Divine Providence.

You may read in the third book of *Intimations of Divine Piety*, by St. Gertrude, that Jesus once told her that the filial confidence of a Christian soul is the eye of the holy spouse, of which the Divine Bridegroom says in the Canticle of Canticles: *Vulnerasti cor meum, soror mea, sponsa: vulnerasti cor meum in uno oculorum tuorum.* "Thou hast wounded my heart, my sister, my spouse: thou hast wounded my heart by one of thine eyes" (Cant. 4, 9). In other words, the soul that has firm confidence in Christ, and trusts that He can and desires to help it faithfully in all things, pierces His heart right through with an arrow of love; and such confidence does such violence to the piety of Jesus that He can in no way absent Himself from it.

St. Mechtilde's *Book of Special Grace* tells us that Jesus said to her also: "It is a special delight to Me when men trust in My goodness and rely upon Me. And so, whoever shall have great trust in Me, yet always with humility, shall be favored by Me in this life, and in the next receive more than he deserves. The more anyone trusts in Me and avails himself of My goodness, the greater will be his gain, since it is impossible for a man not to obtain what he believes with holy conviction, and hopes to gain because it has been promised him. And so it is most advantageous to a man to have firm trust in Me, when he hopes for great things from Me." And again, when St. Mechtilde asked God what was the main thing she should believe of His ineffable goodness, He replied: "Firmly believe that after death I will receive you as a father receives a dear son, and that no father ever so faithfully and lovingly gave all his possessions to an only son, as I will make you a sharer in all that is Mine. Whoever shall believe this of My goodness, firmly and with humble charity, will be happy indeed."

## XXI. Additional Points on Confidence.

To strengthen you further in holy confidence, our most gentle and amiable Saviour gives Himself all the most sweet and loving names and qualities imaginable, to describe His relationship with you. He calls Himself your friend, your advocate, your physician, your shepherd, your brother, your father, your soul, your spirit and the bridegroom of your soul. He calls you His sheep, His brethren, His children, His portion, His heritage, His soul, His heart. Your souls he regards as His cherished spouses.

At various places in Sacred Scripture He assures you that He exercises continual care and watchfulness over you (I Peter 5, 7); He carries you, and will always carry you in His heart and in His bosom (Isa. 46, 3-4). Nor is He satisfied with saying once or twice that He bears you so tenderly; He repeats this beautiful thought as many as five times in a single passage. And elsewhere He says that even if a mother were to forget the child she bore in her womb, He would never forget you, and that He has written you in His hands, that He might always have you before His eyes (Isa. 49, 15-17); whoever touches you touches the apple of His eye (Zach. 2, 8); you should have no care for the things that are necessary to you to sustain life and clothe yourself; He well knows that you need such things, and He takes care of them on your behalf (Matt. 6, 31-33); He has numbered every hair of your head (Matt. 10, 30), and of these, not one shall perish (Luke 21, 18): His Father loves you as He loves the Son Himself and the Son loves you as He is loved by His Father (John 15, 9); He wants you to be where He is, that is, to be at rest with Him in the bosom and heart of His Father (John 17, 24), to sit with Him upon His throne (Apoc. 3, 21), and in a word, He wants you to be one with Him, and, indeed, to be consummated in unity with Him and with the Father of Heaven (John 17, 21-23). If you have offended Him, He promises, provided you come back to Him with humility, repentance, confidence in His goodness, and the resolution to make a clean break with sin, that He will receive you, He will embrace you,

He will forget all your sins, and clothe you with the garment of His grace and His love, of which you had been stripped by your sins (Ezech. 18, 21; Luke 15, 22).

Who, after all this, will not have confidence? Who will not become entirely abandoned to the care and guidance of a brother, a father, a bridegroom, endowed with infinite wisdom to know what is most advantageous for you and to foresee everything that could possibly happen to you, and to select the most appropriate means to bring you to the goal of your supreme happiness? Not only this, but He is also filled with extreme goodness with which He wills all kinds of good for you, together with immense power to turn aside any evil which might befall you, and to pour forth upon you the complete wealth of benefits He wills to grant you.

Lest you think His words and promises ineffectual, look for a moment at all He did and suffered for you in His Incarnation, His life, His Passion and His death, as well as the wonderful graces He still brings to us daily in the Blessed Sacrament of the Eucharist. Consider how He came down from heaven to earth, out of love for you, how He humbled Himself to the extent of willing to become a little child, to be born in a stable and embrace all the woes and needs of a human and mortal life. See how He devoted all His hours, all His thoughts, words and actions to you; how He delivered up His holy body to Pilate, to the executioners and to the Cross; how He laid down His life and shed His blood even to the last drop; how He gives you every day, in the Holy Eucharist, His body, His blood, His soul, His divinity, all His riches, all that He is, all that is most dear and most precious to Him.

O Thou who art goodness! O Love! O Most Great and Amiable Jesus! Let them trust in thee, who know Thy Name (Ps. 9, 11), which is none other than love and goodness, for Thou art all love, all goodness and all mercy. Yet I am not surprised that there should be so few who trust in Thee perfectly, since there are so few who study themselves to find out and observe the effects of Thy infinite goodness. O my Saviour, surely I am most worthless if I do not have confidence in Thy goodness, after Thou hast displayed so very many proofs of Thy love for me! If Thou hast done and suffered so much, and if Thou hast given us such great things, what wouldst Thou not do yet again, what wouldst Thou not add now to these gifts, if only I came to Thee with humility and confidence?

Cultivate a great desire to be firmly rooted in the sublime virtue of confidence. Do not fear, but be courageous in serving and loving our Most Adorable and Amiable Jesus, with great perfection and holiness. Undertake courageously great tasks for His glory, in proportion to the power and grace He will give you for this end. Even though you can do nothing of yourself, you can do all things in Him and His help will never fail you, if you have confidence in His goodness.

Place your entire physical and spiritual welfare in His hands. Abandon to the paternal solicitude of His Divine Providence every care for your health, reputation, property and business, for those near to you, for your past sins, for your soul's progress in virtue and love of Him, for your life, death and especially for your salvation and eternity, in a word, all your cares. Rest in the assurance that, in His pure goodness, He will watch with particular tenderness over all your responsibilities and cares and dispose all things for the greatest good.

Do not rely on the power or influence of friends, on your own money, on your intellect, knowledge or strength, on your good desires and resolutions, or on human means, or on any created thing, but on God's mercy alone. You may, of course, use all these things and take advantage of every aid that you can marshal on your side to conquer vice, to practise virtue, to direct and conclude all the business that God has placed in your hands, and acquit yourself of the obligations of your state in life. But you must renounce all dependence or confidence you may have in these things, to rely upon Our Lord's goodness alone. You ought to take as much pains and work as hard for your own part, as if you expected nothing from God: nevertheless, you should no more rely upon your own resources and labor than if you had done nothing at all, but had looked to God's mercy alone for all things.

To this we are exhorted by the Holy Ghost, saying, by the mouth of David, the royal prophet: *Revela Domino viam tuam, et spera in eo, et ipse faciet.* "Commit thy way to the Lord, and trust in him, and he will do it" (Ps. 36, 5). And in another place *Jacta super Dominum curam tuam et ipse te enutriet.* "Cast thy care upon the Lord and he shall sustain thee" (Ps. 54, 23). And, speaking through St. Peter, the Prince of the Apostles, He advises us to cast all our cares and worries upon God, since He watches over us: *Omnem sollicitudinem vestram projicientes in eum, quoniam ipsi cura est de vobis* (I Peter 5, 7). This is what Our Lord said to St. Catherine of Sienna: "Daughter, forget thyself and think of me, and I will ever think of thee."

Accept this teaching as if addressed to you personally and to no one else. Let your chief care be to avoid everything that displeases Our Lord, trying to serve and love Him perfectly, and He will turn everything, even your faults, to your advantage.

Acquire the habit of making frequent acts of trust in God, but especially when you happen to be assailed by thoughts or feelings of fear and mistrust, either with regard to your past sins, or for any other reason. At such times lift up your heart at once to Jesus, and say to Him, with the Royal Prophet: *Ad te, Domine, levavi animam meam: Deus meus in te confido, non erubescam.* "To thee, O Lord, have I lifted up my soul. In thee, O my God, I put my trust; let me not be ashamed" (Ps. 24, 1-2).

*In te, Domine, speravi, non confundar in aeternum.* "In thee, O Lord, have I hoped, let me never me confounded" (Ps. 30, 1). *Deus meus sperabo in eum.* "My God, in him will I trust" (Ps. 90, 2). *Dominus mihi adjutor, non timebo quid faciat mihi homo.* "The Lord is my helper: I will not fear what man can do unto me" (Ps. 117, 6). *Dominus mihi adjutor, et ego despiciam inimicos meos:* "The Lord is my helper and I will look over my enemies" (Ps. 117, 7). *Bonum est confidere in Domino, quam confidere in homine.* "It is good to confide in the Lord, rather than to have confidence in man" (Ps. 117, 8). *Et si ambulavero in medio umbrae mortis, non timebo mala quoniam tu mecum es:* "For though I should walk in the midst of the shadow of death, I will fear no evils, for thou art with me" (Ps. 22, 4).

Or else join the prophet Isaias, saying: *Ecce Deus salvator meus fiducialiter agam et non timebo.* "Behold, God is my saviour, I will deal confidently and will not fear" (Isa. 12, 2). Or say with holy Job: *Etiam si occiderit me, in ipso sperabo.* "Although he should kill me,

I will trust in him" (Job 13, 15). Or, repeat the words of the poor man in the Gospel: *Credo, Domine, adjuva incredulitatem meam.* "I do believe, Lord: help my unbelief" (Mark 9, 23).

At other times, say with the holy apostles: *Domine, adauge nobis fidem:* "Lord, increase our faith" (Luke 17, 5).

Or else speak to Him thus: "O Good Jesus, it is in Thee alone that I have placed all my trust. O Thou my strength and only refuge, I give and abandon myself entirely to Thee; do with me whatever Thou dost please."

"Oh my sweet love, O my dear hope, I place my whole being in Thy hands and sacrifice it to Thee, with my life, my soul and all that belongs to me, that Thou mayest dispose of them in time and in eternity howsoever it pleases Thee, for Thy glory."

In conclusion, confidence is a gift of God that follows in the wake of humility and love. Therefore, ask it of God, and He will give it to you. Strive to perform your every action in a spirit of humility for the pure love of God, and you will soon taste the sweetness and peace that accompany the virtue of confidence.

## XXII. Submission and Christian Obedience.

Continual submission to the holy will of God is the most universal of all virtues and its practice should be most familiar to you, since at every moment there arise opportunities of renouncing your own will and submitting to the will of God. His will is always easy to recognize. God has willed that all things that are extremely necessary should also be very easy to obtain. The sun, for instance, and air and water, and the other elements are most necessary for man's natural life; so, also, these things are common and freely available to everyone.

In the same way, since God has placed you in this world only to do His holy will, and your salvation depends upon this, it is, therefore, extremely necessary that you should easily know God's will in all that must be done. So, He has made it easily recognizable, manifesting His holy will in five chief ways which are very certain and evident: 1. by His commandments; 2. by His counsels; 3. by the laws, rules and obligations of our state in life; 4. by the authority of those placed over you or directing you; 5. by events, since every hap-

pening in an infallible sign that God so wills, either by absolute or by
permissive will. So, if you would but open the eyes of faith even a little,
you could easily, at all times and in every situation, recognize God's
most holy will, and this knowledge would lead you to love Him and
to submit yourself to Him.

But if you are to become really and truly submissive, you must store
away in the deepest recesses of your souls these four truths taught us
by faith:

1. Faith, which tells us there is but one God who created all
things, also obliges us to believe that this great God orders and governs
all things without exception, either by absolute or by permissive will;
and that there is nothing accomplished in the world that does not
come under the ordering of His divine guidance, or pass through the
hands of His absolute will, or His permission, which are like the two
arms of His Providence, by which He controls all things: *Tua, Pater,
Providentia gubernat* (Wis. 14, 3).

2. God neither wills nor permits anything except for His greater
glory, and, in fact, He does draw forth greater glory from all things.
Since God is the Creator and Governor of the world, He has made all
things for Himself and is imbued with infinite zeal for His glory
and is infinitely wise and powerful in knowingly and effectively directing all things to that end. It is, therefore, very certain that He
neither wills nor permits anything whatever to happen, in the world,
that does not contribute to His greater glory and to the good of those
who love God. If, then, we would only desire to love God and adore
His holy will in everything that happens, all things would work out
for our greater profit. And this result depends upon us alone.

3. God's will, whether absolute or permissive, is infinitely holy, just,
adorable and worthy of love, and deserves to be infinitely and equally
adored, loved and glorified in all things just as they are.

4. Our Lord Jesus Christ, from the very first moment of His life,
made it His whole purpose in existing to execute, not His own, but
His Father's will, according to the authentic testimony of St. Paul
writing to the Hebrews: "When he (Jesus) cometh into the world,
he saith (speaking to His Eternal Father): Behold I come; in the head
of the book it is written of me: that I should do thy will, O God"

(Heb. 10, 5-7); and according to what Christ afterwards said Himself: "I came down from heaven, not to do my own will but the will of him that sent me" (John 6, 38). In fact, He never followed His own will, although it was holy, divine and adorable. He renounced and, as it were, annihilated it, in order to follow His Father's will, saying incessantly to Him in all things, the words He uttered on the eve of His death, in the Garden of Olives: "Father, not my will, but thine be done" (Luke 22, 42).

If you ponder these truths, you will acquire considerable facility in submitting yourself in all things to God's most adorable will. If you reflect that God orders and disposes everything for His glory and your greater good, and that His disposition is most just and deserving of love, you will not ascribe things that happen to you to luck or chance, nor to the malice of devils or of men, but to God's ordaining, which you shall then love and tenderly embrace, knowing for certain that it is most holy and worthy to be loved, and that it neither orders nor permits anything except for your greater good and for the greater glory of God. You should love this glory above all things, since you are only in the world to live and procure the glory of God.

If you give attentive consideration to the fact that Jesus Christ, our Head, abandoned so holy and divine a will as His, to follow the most rigorous and strict will of His Father in His regard—a will that demanded that He suffer so many extraordinary things and die so cruel and shameful a death for the salvation of His enemies, will you, after all this, have any trouble in renouncing a will that is so depraved and corrupted by sin as yours, in order to set up in its place the reign of the most holy and sweet and amiable will of God?

Submission and Christian obedience consist then in continuing Christ's most perfect obedience not only to the desires expressed directly by His Father, but also to those communicated to Him through His most holy Mother, through St. Joseph, through the angel who led Him into Eygpt, through the Jews, Herod and Pilate. For He not only submitted to His Father, but became subject to all creatures, for His Father's glory and for love of you.

### XXIII. Practice of Submission and Christian Obedience.

To put into practice the truths that have just been explained, it is necessary to adore in Jesus the divine submission which He exercised so perfectly. Frequently shatter at His feet all your own will, assuring Him that you desire none other but His desires and inclinations, praying Him to make His will reign perfectly in you.

Live in the continual resolution to suffer all kinds of tortures, even to die, rather than transgress the least of God's commandments, and be ever disposed to follow His counsels, according to the light and grace He gives you, in harmony with your state in life and under the guidance of your spiritual director.

Respect those who have authority over you and honor them as representatives of Christ on earth. Obey their will as if it were the will of Jesus Christ, provided their orders are not manifestly contrary to what is commanded or forbidden by God.

St. Peter, the Prince of the Apostles, goes much farther than this. He exhorts us to submit to every human being for the love of God *Subjecti estote omni humanae creaturae, propter Deum* (I Peter 2, 13). And St. Paul would have us regard one another as superiors. *Superiores sibi invicem arbitrantes* (Phil. 2, 3). Following the divine teachings of these two great apostles, you ought to consider and honor persons of every kind as your superiors, and be ready to give up your own judgment and will in deference to others. In your capacity as a Christian bound to live with the same sentiments and dispositions as Jesus Christ, you ought to make it your professed aim in life, with Jesus Christ, never to follow your own will, and thus to obey the will of God in all its manifestations. In doubtful cases, that is, in cases where you cannot tell with certainty what is the will of God, you should obey the will of another person, no matter who he may be, looking upon all men as your superiors, and submitting to their will as far as possible in all that is not contrary to God and to the duties of your state in life. You should, however, always give preference to those who have fuller authority and more right over you.

Consider and observe all the laws, rules and obligations of your state, position or condition as unmistakable indications of what God asks of you. In honor of the most exact obedience and perfect sub-jection rendered by Jesus, not only to the rulings of His Father, and to the hours and minutes prescribed and determined for the per-formance of all His actions, but even to human laws, place yourself in subjection to the rules and obligations of your condition, to the hours and minutes prescribed for the fulfilment of the duties and functions of your occupation, and also to human and civil laws. Do all this for the love of Him who, for love of you, showed you the way by first entering into such subjection Himself.

In every event that happens, whether by God's absolute or His per-missive will, adore and bless and love both these wills, and declare to Him, in union with His Beloved Son and as far as possible, with the same spirit, and with the same love, submission and humility of His Most Obedient Son: *Pater, non quod ego volo, sed quod tu; non mea voluntas, sed tua fiat,* "Father, not what I will, but what thou wilt. Not my will, but thine be done" (Mark 14, 36; Luke 22, 42). *Ita Pater, quia sic fuit placitum ante te,* "Yea, Father; for so hath it seemed good in thy sight" (Matt. 11, 26).

When you become aware of some inclination or desire for any object, instantly cast it down at the feet of Jesus. If the attraction is powerful, continue to renounce it, and to dash it down and implore Jesus Himself to eliminate it, until you feel yourself disposed to want the very contrary to that desire, if He were to have you make the choice.

When some thought or fear enters your mind, concerning the loss of your health, your reputation, your property, your parents or your children or your friends, surrender your will to Jesus, adore and bless and love His will, just as if you had already sustained the loss—or else anticipate, at this time, the moment when it will occur, and say:

"O Jesus, I annihilate all my will and inclinations at Thy feet. With my whole heart, I adore and praise Thy most holy and lovable will. In spite of all my repugnances and contrary feelings, I desire to love, bless and glorify Thee in everything it may please Thee to ordain for me and all that concerns me in time and in eternity. Live Jesus! Live the most holy will of my Jesus! May my own will be annihilated and destroyed forever, and may His reign be accomplished eternally on earth as it is in heaven!"

## XXIV. Perfection of Submission and Christian Obedience.

Not only did our Lord Jesus Christ do everything His Father willed, and submit to Him and to all things for love of Him, but He also found all His contentment, His happiness, His paradise in doing so: *Meus cibus est, ut faciam voluntatem ejus qui misit me:* "My meat," He said, "is to do the will of him that sent me" (John 4, 34). In other words, "I find nothing more desirable, nor more delightful than to do the will of my Father." In the performance of everything that He did, He took infinite satisfaction, because it was His Father's will. He found His joy and happiness according to the spirit in the sufferings He bore, because they were His Father's good pleasure. And so, speaking of the day of His passion and death, the Holy Ghost calls it the "day of the joy of his heart" (Cant. 3, 11). He likewise found peace and satisfaction of soul in all the things He saw happen and destined to happen in the world, since in all things He considered nothing but His Father's most adorable will.

So also, in so far as you are Christians, who ought to be invested with the sentiments and dispositions of your Head, you should not only submit to God and to all things for love of God, but you should also find all your satisfaction and your paradise in so doing. It is in this that the highest perfection of Christian submission consists. This is our prayer each day to God as we say: *Fiat voluntas tua, sicut in coelo, et in terra:* "Thy will be done on earth as it is in heaven" (Matt. 6, 10). For the saints in heaven, the accomplishment of the will of God is so completely adequate to give them felicity and heavenly bliss, that many of them, even beholding their dearest loved one punished in hell, must rejoice in the manifestation of God's eternal justice. This is possible because the saints are completely one with God and have no choice or understanding of things other than His Holy will. God, however, wills that His justice be carried out upon these wretches who have fully deserved it, and He finds infinite satisfaction in the effects of His justice, just as He does in the works of His mercy. Therefore, the saints also find satisfaction in them

*Laetabitur justus cum viderit vindictam; manus suas lavabit in sanguine peccatoris:* "The just shall rejoice when he shall see the revenge; he shall wash his hands in the blood of the sinner" (Ps. 57, 11). Thus you must seek all your joy in the effects of the divine will, since you ought to strive to do that will on earth as it is done in heaven.

There are two reasons why you are bound to do this:

1. Since you are created only to glorify God, and God's glory is your last end, it follows that all your joy should spring from God's glory, and, therefore, from all the effects of His divine will, because they all operate for His greater glory.

2. Since Our Lord has told you that it is His divine wish for you to be one with Him and with His Father, it follows that you should be of but one mind and sentiment with Him, just as are the blessed in heaven. You must, consequently, find all your joy, your blessedness and your heaven in that very same thing which is the heaven and blessedness of the saints, the most Blessed Virgin, the Son of God and the Eternal Father.

Now the saints, the most Blessed Virgin, the Son of God and the Eternal Father take pleasure and find heaven in all things, because they see God's will in all things. God takes infinite satisfaction and joy in all that He wills or permits, and in all His works: *Laetabitur Dominus in operibus suis* (Ps. 103, 31). He would not be God if He were not infinitely satisfied with everything that He does. So true is this, that He is just as much pleased with the enforcement of divine justice He inflicted upon the damned, as with the effects of providential goodness lavished upon the blessed. Holy Scripture says: "As the Lord rejoiced upon you before doing good to you, so he shall rejoice destroying and bringing you to nought" (Deut. 28, 63). Hence also, you must find all your joy and your heaven in all that is willed, or permitted or worked by God, and in all things in general, excepting in sin, which you must detest and abhor; yet you must adore and bless God's permission and the ordering of His justice, which by a just judgment permits that, as punishment for one sin, the sinner may fall into another.

Thus, by Our Lord's grace, you have a means of being always satisfied in life and of possessing heaven on earth. You would indeed be very hard to please, if you were not satisfied with what satisfies God, the angels and the saints, who rejoice, not so much in their own great glory as in the accomplishment of God's will in them—that is, in the fact that God derives pleasure and contentment from glorifying His faithful servants. Nor do you have any cause for complaint if you are in the paradise of the Mother of God, the Son of God and the Eternal Father.

### XXV. Practice of Perfect Christian Submission.

If, then, you desire to possess a real heaven on earth, pray that Jesus may fill you with these holy dispositions of perfect submission to all that He divinely wills. In order to do your own share and co-operate with Him, try not only to submit to God in all things, but also to submit to Him with joy and satisfaction.

When performing any action, try to perform it not only for love of Our Lord, but out of so much love for Him that all your satisfaction, your joy and your heaven consist in performing it, simply because it is an act of love of Him, and because it is His will and His good pleasure that you should do it.

When anything happens to you against your will and contrary to your hopes, take satisfaction in it, because it is God's will. If anything is favorable to your will or your plans, be glad, not because your wish has come true, but God's will has been accomplished.

In all that happens in the world, see only God's will and permission. In view of the fact that He takes pleasure in all that He wills, whether absolutely or permissively, and that all things ever accrue to His gain, and that He ever draws forth greater glory from everything, you must detest the sins committed against Him, in the events of daily life and be pleased with the things in which He takes His good pleasure.

I do not say that you should derive sensible pleasure and joy from all that you do or suffer, or from all that happens in the world, for that is possible only to the blessed. But I am here speaking of joy and satisfaction of the spirit and of the will, which you may easily obtain, with the help of Our Lord's grace, since all you have to do is to say: "My God, if it be pleasing to Thee, I desire for Thy love to take all my pleasure in willing, doing or suffering this or that, because it is Thy will and pleases Thee." Thus you will obtain satisfaction of your mind and will in all things. Furthermore, a frequent repetition of this practice will diminish and destroy whatever pain and natural distaste you may happen to feel, in various situations, and will help you to enjoy sweetness and satisfaction, even of the senses, in cases where you found bitterness and pain before.

To familiarize yourself with this practice, acquire the habit of lifting up your heart to Jesus, on the occasion of everything you see happen in the world and say to Him:

"O Jesus, it is Thee Who dost ordain, or permit these things, and Thou dost will all things with an infinite satisfaction. O my God, I give myself to Thee; may it please Thee to make me one with Thee in spirit, will and disposition. Make me will all that Thou dost will and make me will it as Thou dost, contentedly. May I find all my joy and heavenly bliss in all that Thou dost will or do."

With regard to things that arouse repugnance and distaste in you, say:

"O Jesus, in spite of all my repugnance and the contrariness of my self-will and self-love, I desire to suffer this pain or affliction for love of Thee. I desire to suffer it with so much love for Thee, as to find in it all my joy and heavenly bliss, because it is Thy holy will."

Concerning things which give you consolation and satisfaction, say:

"O Jesus, I am glad this has turned out as it has (or else, I desire to do this act) not merely because it has turned out in a way that is pleasing to me (or because it gives me satisfaction to perform this act), but because it is Thy will and Thy pleasure that it should happen thus (or that I should do what I am about to do)."

In so doing, you will begin to enjoy heaven even in this world. You will taste perpetual peace and contentment. You will perform your actions as God performs His own, even as Jesus Christ our Lord performed His, when He was on earth, in a spirit of joy and contentment. This is the true joy He asked of His Father for you on the eve of His death, in these words: *Ut habeant gaudium meum impletum in semetipsis.* "That they may have my joy filled in themselves" (John 17, 13).

Here, then, is the supreme perfection of Christian submissiveness and of pure love of God, for the highest degree of divine love consists in doing, suffering and accepting all things for the love of God, with joy and contentedness. Anyone who makes a holy use of all the things that occur in the world, who will suffer with these dispositions all the trials that come upon him and perform his actions in this spirit of submission, will give God more glory and satisfaction, will make more progress, in one day, in the paths of His love, than he would do in his whole life by following any other course.

## XXVI. CHRISTIAN CHARITY.

When the Son of God tells you, in His Gospel, that the first and greatest commandment is to love God with your whole heart and your whole soul and with all your strength, it is with good reason that He went on to declare that the second commandment, by which you are obliged to love your neighbor as yourself, is like unto the first. For the love of God and of your neighbor cannot be separated. These are not two different loves, but a single, uniform love. And you are bound to love your neighbor with the same affection and with the same love with which you love God, because you should love your fellow men not in and for themselves, but in and for God. Briefly, it is God Himself that you should love in your neighbor.

Jesus loves you in this way. He loves you in and for His Heavenly Father, or rather He loves His Father in you, and He wants you to love one another as He loves you. "This," He says, "is my commandment, that you love one another as I have loved you" (John 15, 12).

This, then, is what constitutes Christian charity: to love one another as Jesus loves you. So great is His love for you that He gives you all that He has, His riches, His own self; and He devotes all the powers of His wisdom and goodness to doing good to you. So exceedingly great is His charity toward you that, for a great length of time and with very much gentleness and patience, He tolerates your defects. He is the first to seek you out when you have offended Him. He seems almost to prefer your comforts, pleasures and interests to His own, since, during His earthly life, He subjected Himself to every form of trouble, sorrow and suffering to deliver you from affliction and make you happy. He has, in a word, so much love for you that He devotes to you His whole life, His soul, His time, His eternity, His divinity and His humanity—all that He is, all that He has and all that He can do. In His thoughts, His words, and His actions He is all charity and love for you.

This is the standard and model of Christian charity. This is what He asks of you, when He commands you to love one another as He loves you. This is how you ought to love one another, acting towards your neighbor as Jesus did to you, according to the power He gives you.

To excite and urge yourself to love your fellow men with true charity consider your neighbor as existing in God and God in him. I mean, look upon him as a being who has come forth from God's Heart and His goodness; as a being participating in God, created to return to God, to be one day ensconced in the bosom of God to glorify God eternally, and as a creature in which God will, indeed, be eternally glorified, either through mercy or through justice. Consider your neighbor as the object of the love of God, no matter what his condition may be: for God loves everything He has created, even the devils, in so far as they are His creatures and He does not hate anything that He has made. Sin alone He holds in abhorrence and sin was not made by Him. Your neighbor is an individual who has sprung from the same principle as yourself, a child of the same Father, created for the same end, belonging to the same Lord, redeemed at the same price, the infinitely Precious Blood of Jesus Christ. See in him a member of the same Head, Christ, and of the same body, the Church of Christ, nourished by the same food, the precious body and blood of Jesus Christ. Consequently you should be of one mind, one soul, and one heart with him.

You must also regard your neighbor as the temple of the living God, bearing in himself the image of the Blessed Trinity and the character of Jesus Christ. He is part of Jesus Christ, bone of His bone, flesh of His flesh. See him as one for whom Jesus labored and suffered so much, spent so much precious effort and time, and gave His blood and His life. Finally, consider him as one recommended to you, by Jesus, as His own equal: for He said that whatsoever you should do to the least of His little ones, that is, of those who believe in Him, He would consider it as done to Himself (Matt. 25, 40). Oh, if you only pondered and thoroughly thought out the importance of these truths, what charity, what respect, what honor you would entertain for one another! How you would fear to offend against unity and Christian charity, whether in thoughts, words or deeds! What would you not do, what would you not suffer for one another! How charitably and patiently would you bear with the faults of others, and excuse them! With what gentleness, modesty and restraint would you converse one with another! How careful would you be to "please your neighbor unto good, to edification" as St. Paul says (Rom. 15, 2). O Jesus, God of love and charity, impress these truths and these dispositions upon our minds and our hearts.

## XXVII. Practice of Christian Charity.

If you desire to live in the spirit of Christian charity, which is nothing else but a continuation and fulfilment of the charity of Jesus, you must frequently exercise yourself in the following practices.

Adore Jesus, who is all charity. Bless Him for all the glory He gave to His Father by His continual acts of charity. Ask Him to forgive all the failings of which you have ever been guilty, with respect to this virtue, praying Him to offer His charity to His Father for you, as reparation for these failings. Give yourself to Him, begging Him to destroy all that is contrary to charity, in your thoughts, words and actions, and to cause His own most perfect charity to live and reign in you.

Often ponder these beautiful words of St. Paul: "Charity is patient, is kind: charity envieth not, dealeth not perversely; is not puffed up; is not ambitious, seeketh not her own, is not provoked to anger, thinketh no evil; rejoiceth not in iniquity, but rejoiceth with the truth; beareth all things, believeth all things, hopeth all things, endureth all things. Charity never falleth away" (I Cor. 13, 4-8).

Adore Jesus who pronounces these words by the lips of St. Paul. Offer yourself to Him, with the firm purpose of making this living charity a real part of your life. Beg the All-loving Christ to give you grace for that purpose.

Whenever you render a service to another person, and in all the actions you perform for others, whether as a duty or out of charity, lift up your heart to Jesus and say to Him:

"O Jesus, I desire to perform this action, if it please Thee, in honor of and together with Thy charity towards this person, and for love of Thyself, Whom I desire to see and serve in him."

When necessity demands that you give your body some rest, nourishment or refreshments, do so with this same intention, looking upon your health, your life and your body not as belonging to yourself but as one of Christ's members, according to St. Paul, as something pertaining to Jesus, *Corpus autem Domino,* "The body for the Lord" (I Cor. 6, 13), which you must, consequently, protect and nourish not for yourself but for Jesus, in so far as your body is necessary for His service. And imitate St. Gertrude in remembering, in this connection, the fact that Our Lord said whatever was done to the least of His little ones, would be done to Him (Matt. 25, 40).

When you greet someone, or show him respect, greet and respect him as the temple and image of God and as a member of Jesus Christ.

Where an occasion presents itself for polite conversation, or an exchange of compliments, do not allow your lips to utter friendly words that do not come from your heart. There exists the following difference between Christian souls and worldly souls, namely, that, while they both make use of the same compliments and polite phrases that are customary when one meets a friend or goes visiting, the Christian utters them from his heart, while the worldling has them only on his lips, and speaks them in a spirit of falsehood and simulated friendliness.

I do not say that it is necessary for your mind to be always alert and busy at the task of forming these thoughts and intentions every time you meet somebody, or say a word or two in courteous greeting, or lend a helping hand even though that would be a good thing. But at least have the general intention of doing all things, always, in this spirit of Christ's charity; and try to renew the intention before God, when He brings the thought to your mind.

Whenever another person arouses in you any distaste or aversion, or feelings of envy, be sure to renounce them vigorously, at once, and dash them down at the feet of Our Lord, asking Him to eliminate these sensations and fill you with His divine charity. Be sure to make interior acts of charity towards that person, in the following terms:

"O Jesus, I desire to love this person for love of Thee. Yes, my Saviour, I want to love him with my whole heart, together with and in honor of Thy charity towards Him. And I offer myself to Thee to do and suffer whatever Thou dost please, for that person."

Moreover, make the effort to speak to him and to perform some external acts of charity towards him, and do not stop until you have utterly wiped out, within yourself, this feeling of aversion and antipathy.

If you have been offended, or have offended another, do not wait for him to seek you out, but remember that our Lord said: "If therefore thou offer thy gift at the altar, and there thou remember that thy brother hath anything against thee; leave there thy offering before the altar, and go first to be reconciled to thy brother" (Matt. 5, 23-24). So, to do honor to the fact that He was the first to seek you out, He Who is so bountiful and generous in favors to you, Who receives from you nothing but hurts and offenses, and to obey these words of His, go and find the one you have offended or who has offended you, and be reconciled with him, disposing yourself to talk to him in a spirit of forgiveness, gentleness, peace and humility.

If unfavorable remarks about someone else are made in your presence, disregard them; change the subject if possible, in a prudent and tactful way trying to manage it so that nothing further will be said; if the conversation goes on, it would be better to keep quiet and evince no awareness of or interest in the subject.

Pray to Our Lord, especially, to implant in your heart charity and warm affection for the poor, strangers, widows and orphans. Consider such as these to be persons recommended to you by your greatest friend, Jesus Christ, who in Holy Scripture very often and very emphatically recommends them to you as deserving all the attention you would give to Him in person. With this in mind, then, be kind in speaking to them, treat them charitably and give them all the help you can.

## XXVIII. Charity and Zeal for the Salvation of Souls.

Above all, have a particular charity for the souls of all men, especially of those who are related to you or depend upon you, and do everything you possibly can to effect their salvation. For St. Paul tells us that "if any man have not care of his own, and especially, those of his house, he hath denied the faith, and is worse than an infidel" (I Tim. 5, 8). Remember that these souls were bought at the price of the labors of God made Man, of His thirty-three years of suffering, of His blood and His life, and that the greatest and most Godlike work, the task most pleasing to Jesus that you could do on earth, is to labor with Him for the salvation of souls, so dear and precious in His sight.

And so, offer yourself to Him to share the work for souls in every way He asks. Consider yourself most unworthy to be employed in so great a work. Yet, whenever you see a chance to help in the salvation of some poor soul (and if you are alert, such chances will occur most frequently), do not let it slip by, but first ask grace of Our Lord and then apply yourself, according to your condition and to the means He puts at your disposal, with all the care, diligence and love you can muster, just as you would in the case of some business of the highest importance, or if all temporal goods and the lives of all the men in the world were at stake. Do this purely for the love of Jesus, so that God may be eternally loved and glorified in souls, knowing that you should consider it a great favor and blessing to employ all your time, your health, your life and all the money in the world, if they were in your possession, to help in the salvation of a single soul for whom Jesus Christ shed all His Precious Blood, spent all His time, His strength and His life.

O Jesus, zealous lover of souls, and lover of the salvation of men, may it please Thee to implant in the hearts of all Christians the sentiments and dispositions of Thy zeal, and of Thy most ardent charity for souls.

# TRUE CHRISTIAN DEVOTION AND THE FORMING OF JESUS WITHIN YOU

## XXIX. True Christian Devotion.

After what has been said so far about Christian virtues, it is easy to see what true Christian devotion is, and in what it consists. Since all the Christian virtues are nothing else but the virtues which our Lord Jesus Christ practised on earth, which must be continued by us while we are in this world, it necessarily follows that true Christian devotion is simply Jesus Christ's holy and divine devotion, that we are bound to perpetuate and fulfil in ourselves.

Now, for our Lord Jesus Christ devotion was a matter of accomplishing, with the greatest perfection, everything that His Father willed, and of taking all His pleasure in this alone. His devotion consisted in serving His Heavenly Father, and in serving even men for the love of His Father, since He willed to take the form and lowly condition of a servant, in order to pay more honor and homage to the supreme greatness of His Father by His own abasement. His devotion consisted in loving and glorifying His Father and in causing His Father to be loved and glorified in the world; of doing all that He did purely for the glory and love of His Father, with most holy, most pure and most divine dispositions—namely, with the most profound humility, the most burning charity for men, the most perfect detachment from self and from all created things, the closest union with His Heavenly Father, the most rigorous submission to His Father's will and with all joy and satisfaction. Finally, His devotion consisted in being altogether immolated and sacrificed purely for the glory of His Father, since He willed to take upon Himself the role of victim, and in this capacity to undergo every sort of contempt, humiliation, privation, interior and exterior mortification and, finally, a cruel and shameful death, for the everlasting glory of His Divine Father.

These were three solemn professions, three vows, as it were, pronounced by Jesus from the moment of the Incarnation. And these He carried out most perfectly in His life and in His death.

1. At the moment of His Incarnation, He vowed obedience to His Father, that is, He made profession never to do His own will, but to obey most perfectly everything willed by His Father, and to find in so doing all His bliss and joy.

2. He professed servitude to His Father. This is the character given to Him by His Father, speaking through a prophet: *Servus meus es tu, Israel, quia in te gloriabor* (Isa. 49, 3). And this is the character which He Himself adopts: *Formam servi accipiens* (Phil. 2, 7), lowering Himself to the state and condition of a humble and servile life with respect to His creatures, even to the cruel shame and servile death of the Cross, for love of us and for His Father's glory.

3. He professed to become a host and victim entirely consecrated and immolated to His Father's glory from the first moment of His life to the very last.

Such was the devotion of Jesus. Since Christian devotion is simply Jesus Christ's devotion, our own devotion must, therefore, consist of similar vows of submission. In order to make it so, we should enter into the closest and most intimate contact and union with Jesus, and adhere to Him most closely, concentrating upon Him all our attention, throughout our whole life, in all our functions and acts.

This is the solemn vow, the first and most important public profession, which is made at baptism in the presence of the entire Church. At that time, to use the terms of St. Augustine, St. Thomas' *Summa,* and the *Catechism of the Council of Trent,* we made a solemn vow and profession to renounce Satan with all his works and to be united with Jesus Christ as members are one with their head, to deliver and consecrate ourselves entirely to Him and to dwell in Him. A Christian who professes to adhere to Christ and dwell in Him, professes to adhere to His devotion, His dispositions, His intentions, His laws and rules of conduct, His spirit and His behavior, His life, His qualities, and His virtues, and all that He did and suffered.

Thus, when we vow to adhere to Jesus Christ and dwell in Him—and this is "the greatest of all our vows," says St. Augustine, *votum maximum nostrum*—we make three great professions, which are very sacred and sublime, deserving frequent consideration.

1. We profess, with Jesus Christ, never to do our own will but to submit to everything willed by God, to obey persons of all kinds, in whatever is not contrary to God, and to seek all our satisfaction and heavenly bliss in acting so.

2. We profess servitude to God and His Son Jesus Christ, and to all the members of Jesus Christ, according to the words of St. Paul: *Nos servos vestros per Jesum* (II Cor. 4, 5). In consequence of this avowal, no Christian can call anything his own, any more than a slave can. Nor has a Christian the right to make any use of the faculties of his soul, or of his life, or his daily time, or his temporal goods, except for Jesus Christ and the members of Jesus Christ—that is, all who believe in Him.

3. We profess to become victims continually sacrificed to God's glory—*Spirituales hostias* (I Pet. 2, 5), as St. Peter, the Prince of the Apostles, expresses it. *Obsecro vos, fratres, per misericordiam Dei, ut exhibeatis corpora vestra hostiam viventem, sanctam, Deo placentem* says St. Paul: "I beseech you therefore, brethren, by the mercy of God, that you present your bodies a living sacrifice, holy, pleasing to God" (Rom. 12, 1). What is here said of our bodies must also be said of our souls. So we are obliged to glorify and love God, in proportion to all the powers of our body and soul, to do everything possible that He may be glorified and loved, and in all our acts and in all things to seek nothing but His glory alone, His love alone, and to live in such a way that each Christian life may be a ceaseless sacrifice of praise and love. And we should be ready to be completely immolated and consumed for His glory.

In a word: *Christianismus est professio vitae Christi:* "Christianity is the profession of the life of Christ," says St. Gregory of Nyssa. St. Bernard assures us that Our Lord does not admit to the ranks of those professed in his religion, anyone who does not live His life: *Non inter suos deputat professores, quos vitae suae cernit desertores.* That is why we profess Jesus Christ at Holy Baptism. We profess the life of Christ, Christ's devotion, His dispositions and intentions, His virtues and His perfect detachment from all things. We profess to believe firmly everything that He teaches, either by His own words and example or through His Church, and to choose death before swerving, however little, from this belief. We profess to join Him in a fight to the finish with sin; to live, as He lived, in a spirit of uninterrupted prayer; to carry His Cross with Him, as well as to bear His mortification in our bodies and souls; to continue the practice of His humility, His trust in God, His submissiveness and obedience, His charity and zeal for the glory of His Father and the salvation of souls. We profess to live, on earth and in heaven, only in order to belong to Jesus and to love and honor Him in all the states and mysteries of His life, in all that He is, in Himself and in the universe. Finally, we profess to be ever ready to undergo every form of torture and to die a thousand deaths, if it were possible, purely for His love and for His glory.

Such are the vow and profession made by all Christians at their baptism. This is what constitutes true Christian devotion. Any other devotion, if it be possible for any other to exist, is mere deception and perdition.

## XXX. Practice of Christian Devotion.

If you would enter upon the path of this holy devotion, adore Jesus in His most perfect devotedness, and in the profession He made to His Father at the instant of His Incarnation, which He observed most perfectly throughout His whole life. Bless Him for the glory rendered to His Father by consecration. Beg Him to pardon your faults against the vow you made at baptism, and to atone for them in His most great mercy. Consider in the presence of God what great obligations go with this vow and profession. Frequently renew your desire to live up to these obligations, pray that Jesus Christ will give you the grace to do so and implant His devotion within you. Make all your devotions consist in the practices described above, the essentials that comprised the devotion of Jesus Christ. In all that you do or suffer, make a point of uniting yourself with Christ's devotion as follows:

"O Jesus, I give myself to Thee, to do this action, or bear this affliction, in union with the most perfect devotion with which Thou didst perform all actions and suffer all afflictions."

In so doing, you will live in true and perfect devotion, by means of which Christ will be shaped within your own souls, according to the Apostle's wish: *Donec formetur Christus in vobis* (Gal. 4, 19). You will be transformed into Jesus; *in eamdem imaginem transformamur* (II Cor. 3, 18). This means that you will cause Jesus to live and reign in you; you will become one with Him, and He will be all in you, according to Holy Writ: *Consummati in unum, et omnia in omnibus* (John 17, 23). This is the goal toward which all Christian life, piety and devotion must tend. Hence it is necessary to show you how important is this work of forming Jesus in your souls, and what needs to be done in order to form Him there.

## XXXI. FORMATION OF JESUS WITHIN YOU.

The mystery of mysteries, and work of works, is the formation of Jesus, indicated in these words of St. Paul: *Filioli, quos iterum parturio, donec formetur Christus in vobis,* "My little children, of whom I am again in labor until Christ be formed in you" (Gal. 4, 19). It is the greatest mystery and the greatest work that is ever accomplished, either in heaven or on earth by the most excellent Beings in existence, namely, the Father, the Son, and the Holy Ghost, the Blessed Virgin, and Holy Mother Church.

This is the greatest act performed by the Eternal Father, in all that eternity during which He is continually occupied in producing His Son within Himself. Nor did He accomplish anything more astounding outside of Himself, in forming the human nature of His Divine Son, at the moment of the Incarnation. It excels all works effected by the Son of God on earth, forming Himself within His holy Mother, and in His Eucharist. It is the noblest of all the works of the Holy Ghost, Who formed Him in the sacred womb of the Virgin Mary. Neither did she ever, nor will she ever do anything more perfect, than when she cooperated in this divine and wonderful formation of Jesus in herself. It is the greatest and holiest of all the works of Holy Church, who exercises no function more exalted, even when she brings Him forth, in a sure and wondrous way, by the lips of her priests, in the Holy Eucharist, than when she brings Him to life in the hearts of her children. For, in all that she does, she has no other aim than that of forming Jesus in the souls of all Christians.

So it should be your desire, your care and your chief occupation to form Jesus in you, to make Him live and reign in you together with His spirit, His devotion, His virtues, His sentiments, His inclinations and dispositions. This should be the aim of all your good works. God places this task in your hands, for you to work at it without interruption.

Two most compelling reasons should stir you up to work energetically for the completion of this task:

1. You should desire the accomplishment of the Eternal Father's plan and of His great yearning to behold His Son living and reigning in you. Since His Beloved Son destroyed Himself for His glory and your love, He wants to repay Him, for His annihilation, by establishing Him in all things and making Him reign over all creatures. He loves His Most Amiable Son so much that He desires to see nothing but Him in all things, nor does He wish any other object to contemplate, delight in, or love. Thus He wants Him to be in all things *omnia in omnibus* (I Cor. 15, 28), so as to see and love nothing but Him in all things.

2. You should desire that Jesus, once established in your hearts should there give His Eternal Father and Himself the love and glory they deserve, according to the words of St. Peter: *ut in omnibus honorificetur Deus, per Jesum Christum* (I Peter 4, 11), since He alone is capable of glorifying His Eternal Father and Himself worthily or adequately.

These two reasons ought to enkindle in you a most ardent desire to form and establish Jesus within yourself and to seek out every possible means of achieving this end. A few of these methods will now be proposed for your consideration.

XXXII. Manner of Forming Jesus Within You.

There are four things to be done, in order to form Jesus within you.

1. You must make it your practice to see Him in everything, in your devotions and in all your acts, to have no other objective than Him and all His states, mysteries, virtues and actions. He is in all

things. He is the being of things that exist, the life of things that live, the beauty of things beautiful, the power of the strong, the wisdom of the wise, the virtue of the virtuous, and the sanctity of the saints. There is hardly any action of your ordinary lives that does not find some counterpart in the actions He performed during His time on earth, so you must keep your eyes on every similar act of His, and imitate it in performing your own. By this means you shall fill up your understanding with Jesus, and shall form and establish Him in your mind, by thus frequently thinking of Jesus, and seeing Him in all things.

2. You ought to form Jesus, not only in your mind, by thinking of Him, seeing Him in everything, but you must also keep Him alive in your hearts by the frequent practice of His divine love. To do this, you should become accustomed to lifting up your hearts frequently to Him in love, after the manner of the various exercises in this book, and to do everything purely for love of Him and to consecrate every affection of your heart to Him.

3. You ought to form Jesus in yourself by a complete annihilation of yourself and of all things within you. If you want Jesus to live and reign in you perfectly, you must destroy all creatures in your minds and hearts. You must no longer look at them or love them in themselves, but only in Jesus, seeing and loving Jesus in them. You must see to it that the world and all that is in the world, so far as you are concerned, is put to death, and that nothing remains for you but Jesus, and that you no longer seek to please, contemplate or love anyone but Him.

You must also labor to destroy yourself, your own opinion, your own will, self-love, pride and vanity, all your perverse inclinations and habits, all the desires and instincts of a depraved nature, and everything that comes from yourself. Everything in you is depraved and corrupted by sin and, by that fact, is contrary to Jesus Christ and opposed to His glory and love, therefore it is necessary for all to be destroyed and consumed in order that Jesus Christ may live and reign perfectly in you.

Here you have the main foundation, the first principle and the first step in Christian living. It is what is called, in Holy Scripture and in the lives of the saints, being lost to self, dying to self and self-renunciation. It is one of the chief cares incumbent upon you, one of your principal tasks to practise abnegation, humiliation and mortification, both inward and outward: and this development of self-denial is one of the most effective means to form and establish Jesus in you.

4. This great work of forming Jesus in you is incomparably beyond your own achievement, so the fourth and most important means is to have recourse to the power of divine grace, and to the prayers of the most Blessed Virgin and of the saints.

Pray often and fervently to the most Blessed Virgin and all the angels and saints, asking them to help you in this task by their prayers. Surrender yourself to the omnipotent power of the Eternal Father and to His most burning love and zeal for His Divine Son, begging Him to annihilate you altogether, in order to make His Son live and reign in you.

Offer yourself with the same intention, and address the same prayer to the Holy Spirit.

Abandon yourself, and all your possessions at the feet of Jesus, begging Him, by the very great love in which He did annihilate Himself, to come with His divine power to destroy you and establish Himself in you, saying to Him, to this end:

"O Good Jesus, I adore Thee in Thy divine annihilation which the Apostle describes in the words: *Exinanivit semetipsum* (Phil. 2, 7). I adore Thy most great and strong love for Thy Father and Thyself, which did so annihilate Thee. I give and abandon myself altogether to the power of that divine love, that it may destroy me completely. O Most Powerful and Most Good Jesus, do Thou employ Thine own power and infinite goodness to annihilate me and establish Thyself in me, to destroy in me my self-love, my own will, my own mind, my pride, and all my passions, sentiments and inclinations, in order to establish Thy holy love and make it reign in me, together with Thy divine spirit, Thy most deep humility and all Thy blessed virtues.

"And also annihilate in me all attachments to creatures, and erase me from the minds and hearts of all creatures. Establish Thyself in their place and in mine, so that men may no longer see, esteem, desire, seek or love anything else but Thee, and that men may speak of

Thee only, and do nothing except for Thee. Thus mayest Thou be all and do all in all things, to love and glorify Thy Father and Thyself in us and for us, with a love and glory such as He and Thou deserve."

# PROPER USE OF CONSOLATIONS AND AFFLICTIONS

XXXIII. Proper Use of Spiritual Consolations.

The life of the Son of God on earth included two contrasting states: a state of consolation and joy, and a state of affliction and suffering. In the sublime heights of His divine soul He rejoiced in all eternal delight and contentment, but in the depths of His human soul and in His body, He endured all kinds of bitterness and pain. So also the life of His servants and members, being a continuation and imitation of His own, is ever a mixture of joy and sadness, of consolation and affliction. The Son of God imparted divine accomplishment to both these opposing states and glorified His Eternal Father just as much in one as in the other; therefore, you must likewise study how to make a holy use of them, so as to give God all the glory He requires of you, that you may be able to say with David, the holy king: "I will bless the Lord at all times, his praise shall be always in my mouth" (Ps. 32, 2).

It is for this reason that I discuss, at this point, the use you should make of sorrow and consolation, if you are to be faithful to God and glorify Him in times of joy and affliction.

Every saintly writer who has treated of the matter teaches that you should not set much store by consolations, whatever they may be, whether interior or exterior. You should not desire them, nor ask for them when they are wanting in you, nor fear to lose them when they are present, nor consider yourself better than other souls on account of your fine thoughts, your great lights, your various sensible feelings of devotion, your inner sweetness or tears or other such manifestations; for you are not in this world to enjoy yourself but to suffer. The state of bliss is reserved for heaven and the state of suffering is assigned to this earth, out of homage to the sufferings borne here below by the God of earth and heaven.

Nevertheless, when God is pleased to grant you consolations, you must not reject or despise them, lest you become guilty of pride or presumption. Indeed, your sole concern should be to use them profitably and to direct all things to the service of God as follows:

1. You must fully humiliate yourself before God, recognizing that you are most unworthy of any grace or consolation. You must remember that He is treating you as weak and imperfect creatures, as little children not yet able to eat solid food, or to stand on their own feet, but needing to be fed with milk and carried in protecting arms, without which care they would perish.

2. Your self-love must not be allowed to feast on these spiritual tastes and feelings, nor is your mind to relax and rest in them at ease. Rather, you must trace these joys to their source, and give them back to Him who favored you with them; that is, refer them entirely to God, since He is the principle of all consolation, and He alone is worthy to be enjoyed. Protest before Him that you desire no pleasure but His pleasure and that, with the help of His grace, you are ready to serve Him forever for love of Him, without seeking or claiming any consolation or reward.

3. You should place all your good thoughts, sentiments and consolations in the hands of Jesus Christ, and beg Him to turn them to whatever use He designs for His glory. You should direct them to the advantage of God, using them as means to spur you on to a more ardent love, and a more courageous and loyal service of One who treats you with such gentleness and love, after you have so often deserved to be stripped of all His graces and utterly abandoned by Him.

## XXXIV. Holy Use of Spiritual Dryness and Affliction.

Since the whole life of our Father and Head, our Lord Jesus Christ, was filled with labors, bitterness and pain, both inward and outward, it is scarcely reasonable that His children and members should travel by any other road but His. He is giving you a great grace, so you cannot murmur in complaint when He gives you what He took for Himself and makes you worthy to drink with Him from the chalice, that chalice of suffering given Him by the Eternal Father with so much love, which He presents to you with equal love. This is His way of showing you more love and giving you unmistakable indications that your trifling services are pleasing in His sight. Do you not hear His Apostle exclaim that "all that will live godly in Christ Jesus shall suffer persecution" (II Tim. 3, 12); and the Angel Raphael saying to holy Tobias: "Because thou wast acceptable to God, it was necessary (note well this word) that temptation should prove thee" (Tob. 12, 13); and the Holy Ghost speaking to us as follows, in Ecclesiasticus: "Son, when thou comest to the service of God, stand in justice and in fear, and prepare thy soul for temptation. Humble thy heart, and endure: incline thy ear, and receive the words of understanding: and make not haste in the time of clouds. Wait on God with patience: join thyself to God, and endure, that thy life may be increased in the latter end. Take all that shall be brought upon thee: and in thy sorrow endure, and in thy humiliation keep patience. For gold and silver are tried in the fire, but acceptable men in the furnace of humiliation" (Eccli. 2, 1-6). These words are divinely inspired and teach you that real piety and devotion are always accompanied by some trial or afflictions, either from the world, or the devil, or else from God Himself, who sometimes seems to withdraw from souls who love Him, in order to test and prove their fidelity.

Therefore, do not be deceived into imagining that the paths of God are nothing but roses and delights. You will find there many thorns and labors. But whatever happens, always faithfully love Our Lord, and His love will turn the gall into honey and the bitterness into sweetness. Do better still: resolve to seek all your joy and satisfaction, as long as you are in this life, in crosses and sufferings. They are the means by which you may give God more glory and prove that you love Him, and in which your Father and Bridegroom, your Head, Jesus Christ, took all His joy and pleasure while in this world, since the Holy Ghost calls the day of His Passion, "the day of the joy of his heart" (Cant. 3, 11).

Such is the use you should make of every kind of bodily or spiritual affliction. It is not my intention, however, to speak in this place of outward and bodily afflictions, since I am reserving that for the sixth part of this book, where you will find an exercise that will help you to bear those trials with true Christian spirit. For the moment, I should like to set before you the way to make use of inward and spiritual afflictions, such as dryness, sorrows, annoyances, fears and troubles within yourself, feelings of distaste for the things of God, and all the other sufferings of the spirit that come upon souls devoted to the service of God. It is a matter of great importance to know how to use these things well and so remain faithful to God. Here is the way to set about doing so:

1. Adore Jesus in the sufferings, privations, humiliations, anxieties, sorrows and desolations which He bore in His holy soul, according to His own words: "My soul is filled with evils" (Ps. 87, 4); "now is my soul troubled" (John 12, 27); "my soul is sorrowful even unto death" (Matt. 26, 38). Adore the dispositions of His divine soul in this state of trial and the good use He made of it for the glory of His Father. Give yourself to Him to enter into the same dispositions and to employ your sufferings with merit even as He did. Offer them to Him in honor of His sufferings. Beg Him to unite your afflictions with His own, to bless and sanctify them by His own and to supply for your defects, and on your behalf, employ them as He made use of His own sufferings for His Father's glory.

2. Do not waste energy trying to discover, in detail, the reason for the state in which you find yourself, or in scrutinizing your sins. Humble yourself in face of all your faults and infidelities as a whole, and adore God's justice, offering yourself to Him to suffer all the pains ordained by His holy will, in homage to His justice, and considering yourself most unworthy that this divine justice should be exercised upon you. You must admit that the least of your sins deserves that you should be utterly forsaken by God. When you are in the state of dryness and distaste with respect to the things of God, and you can scarcely think of God or pray except with a thousand distractions, you ought to remember that you are most unworthy of any grace or consolation, and that Our Lord is indeed doing you a great favor when He permits you to live. You have most often deserved to share the lot of the damned, who will not be able for all eternity to entertain any thoughts but those of blasphemy and horror for God. So you must deeply humble yourself before God.

As a matter of fact, that is the intention God has in mind for you at such moments, and that is what He expects. He wants you to recognize what you are of yourself and to develop a vivid, immediate and profound knowledge and consciousness of your own nothingness, so that, when He gives you some helpful thought or pious inspiration or some other grace, your pride and self-love may not claim it as your own, ascribed to your own effort, vigilance and cooperation but rather refer it to Him, recognizing that the inspiration comes, not from yourself, but from His mercy alone. Thus you may place all your trust in His goodness alone.

3. Above all, never let yourself be carried away by sorrow and discouragement. Instead rejoice in three special considerations:

(1) That Jesus is always Jesus, always God, always great and worthy of love, always in the same unchanging state of glory, joy and contentment, and there is nothing capable of lessening His joy and bliss. *"Scitote quoniam Dominus ipse est Deus"* (Ps. 99, 3). Say to Him: "O Jesus, it is enough for me, merely to know that Thou art ever Jesus! O Jesus, be Jesus forever, and I will always be happy, no matter what happens to me!"

(2) Be glad that Jesus is your God, that He is all yours and that you belong to so good and so lovable a Lord, remembering what the prophet David says: *Beatus populus cujus Dominus ejus,* "Happy is that people whose God is the Lord" (Ps. 143, 15).

(3) Be glad in the knowledge that now you can serve Our Lord with more purity of intention and show Him that you love Him in truth, for love of Himself alone and not for the consolations He has given already. As an effective demonstration of the fidelity and purity of your love for Him, take care to perform your every activity with all possible purity and perfection. The more coldness, tepidity and weakness you feel in yourself, the more should you have recourse to Him Who is your strength and your all, giving yourself to Him yet more earnestly and lifting up your mind to Him more frequently. Continue to make constant acts of love for Him, paying no attention to the fact that you may be making them with less than your usual consolation and fervor. After all, what difference does it make whether you are satisfied or not, provided your Jesus is satisfied? As a matter of fact, it often happens that the acts we make while in a state of dryness and spiritual desolation are more pleasing and agreeable to Him,

provided we strive to make them with a pure intention of honoring Him, than the things we do with much fervor and sensible devotion. For the latter are generally accompanied by self-love, while the former are more purified. Finally, do not become discouraged over the failings and weaknesses of which you may be guilty in this state; humble yourself before Our Lord, begging Him to repair your faults in His great mercy, and have great confidence that He will do so in His goodness. Above all, keep constantly alive in yourself an intent purpose and powerful resolution to serve and love Him perfectly and to be faithful to Him, no matter what happens, until your life's last breath, ever trusting in Him to give you that grace in His great kindness, regardless of all your infidelities.

# SPIRIT OF MARTYRDOM

XXXV. Martyrdom, the Perfection and Fulfilment of Christian Life and Sanctity.

The culmination and perfection of Christian life is holy martyrdom. The grace of martyrdom is the most powerful miracle that God can possibly work in Christian souls, and to suffer martyrdom for His sake is the greatest and most magnificent thing a Christian can achieve for God.

This immeasurable favor, conferred by Jesus Christ on chosen souls by perfecting their resemblance to Him not only in life but in their very death, and making them worthy to die for Him even as He died for His Father and for them, is the most excellent favor He can grant to those whom He loves with the most special love. Nowhere is the astounding power of His divine love more evident than in the lives of the holy martyrs. Among all the saints, the blessed martyrs command the greatest admiration in the presence of God. So you see that all the greatest saints of Paradise, such as St. John the Baptist and the Apostles, are martyrs. They are Christ's own saints. He Himself calls them that, speaking through the oracle of His Church, *Sancti mei,* "My saints" (*Brev. Rom.* Com, mart. 8 resp.). Although each and everyone of the saints belongs to Jesus, the holy martyrs belong to Him in an entirely unique and special manner, because they lived and died for Him. For that reason, He shows them extraordinary love and promises them the greatest and most beneficent rewards.

1. Speaking by the voice of Holy Church, He promises that He will give them a special, prominent place in His Father's Kingdom: *Dabo Sanctis meis locum nominatum in regno Patris mei* (*Brev. Rom.,* Com. mart. 2 noct., 1 ant.).

2. He says that He will give them to eat of the tree of life which is in the Paradise of His God, namely, Himself, as the learned doctors explain. This is equivalent to saying: You have lost a human and

temporal life for Me, I will give you being that is eternal and divine. For I will make you live by my life, and I myself will be your life in eternity.

3. He declares that He will give them hidden manna: *Vincenti dabo manna absconditum* (Apoc. 2, 17). What else is this hidden manna but the divine love which reigns perfectly in the hearts of the holy martyrs? What is it but the surpassing love that, even on earth, transforms the bitterness of tortures and the hell of torments into a paradise of incredible sweetness and delight, and in heaven heaps upon them eternal and unspeakable joys, in exchange for the brief sufferings they have withstood on this earth?

4. He assures them that He will give them power over all nations, just as He received it from His Father, and such great power that they will be able to shatter the nations as the potter breaks the vessel he has made (Apoc. 2, 26-28). In other words, He will make them reign and dominate over the whole universe; He will set them up at His right hand as judges of the whole world: *Judicabunt nationes et dominabuntur populis* (Wis. 3, 8). With Him, they shall judge and condemn the wicked on the day of reckoning.

5. He promises to invest them with His colors, namely, white and red, the colors of the King of martyrs, according to the words of the divine spouse: "My beloved is both white and ruddy" (Cant. 5, 10). These are also the colors of the martyrs, for they wear their Master's livery, and are garbed in white. "They have washed their robes and have made them white in the blood of the lamb," says Holy Scripture (Apoc. 7, 14). "They shall walk with Me in white," says the Son of God, and "he that shall overcome, shall thus be clothed in white garments" (Apoc. 3, 4-5), because martyrdom is a fiery baptism that purges every kind of sin and clothes the souls of the martyrs in undying light and glory. They are also clad in red (*rubri sanguine fluido,* sings Holy Church), which signifies their flowing blood as well as the burning love with which they shed it.

6. Christ tells the martyrs that He will write upon them the name of His God, and of His Father, and the name of the city of His God (Apoc. 3, 12), which means, as the pious and learned Rupert explains, that they shall be Christ's father and mother; He shall look upon

them and treat them as such. For he said: "Whosoever shall do the will of my Father, he is . . . my mother" (Matt. 12, 50). Martyrdom represents the most perfect operation and fulfilment of the will of God. Therefore, the Son of God, speaking of His Father and the holy martyrs, says that He has marvelously wrought all that He willed in them: *Sanctis qui sunt in terra ejus, mirificavit omnes voluntates meas in eis.* (Ps. 15, 3). He says, moreover, that "He will write also upon them a new name" (Apoc. 3, 12), which is Jesus. The holy martyrs imitated Jesus most perfectly in His life and in His death, while they were on earth, therefore they shall so admirably resemble Him in heaven as to be called Jesus, and even actually to be Jesus, in a certain and wonderful manner, through a perfect resemblance and a wondrous transformation.

7. He gives them His word: "I will give to sit with me in my throne, as I . . . am set down with my Father in His throne" (Apoc. 3, 21). And Holy Church, on the feast of every martyr, shows Him to us speaking thus to His Father: *Volo, Pater, ut ubi ego sum, illic sit et minister meus.* "I will, O My Father, that where I am My servant should also be" (*Brev. Rom.,* Com. mart., 5 ant. ad Laudes), that is, he should dwell and rest with Me in Thy bosom and Thy fatherly heart.

I am well aware that most of these promises made to the martyrs are also addressed to the other saints. But they are nevertheless addressed to the martyrs in token of a most special recompense, because these are Christ's own saints, who bear His stamp and Godly character, saints whom He loves with a particular love, and to whom He gives extraordinary privileges.

O bounty! O love! O excessive love and goodness of Jesus for His holy martyrs! O Bountiful Jesus, how blessed are they whom Thou dost love and who love Thee in return! O how blessed are they who bear, in themselves, a perfect image of Thy holy life and of Thy most loving death! How blessed are they who are called to the wedding feast of the Lamb: *Beati qui ad coenam nuptiarum Agni vocati sunt* (Apoc. 19, 9). How blessed are they who wash their robes in the blood of the Lamb: *Beati qui lavant stolas suas in sanguine agni* (Apoc. 22, 14). How blessed are they who want no life on earth, except to spend it all for the glory, and sacrifice it for the love of this most sweet Lamb, so worthy to be loved! And all the more so, because, to borrow the words of the Holy Ghost, this is the end of all fulfilment and perfection, the final and perfect consummation of all sanctity (John 15, 13); because man can do nothing greater for His God than to sacrifice to Him what he holds most dear, that is, his blood and his life, and to die for Him (St. Thomas, *Summa,* 2ᵃ 2ᵃᵉ, Q. 124, a. 3).

There are, however, various kinds of martyrs and martyrdoms. Those who are truly disposed and willing to die for our Saviour are martyrs before God in a certain sense, even though they may not actually die for Him. St. Cyprian affirms that those who are ready to die rather than offend Almighty God are also martyrs in a certain sense. St. Isidore says, furthermore, that to mortify the flesh and the passions, to resist unruly appetites and to persevere to the end in self-abandonment for love of Our Lord is likewise a kind of martyrdom. And, according to St. Gregory the Great, if, for pure and sacrificing love of Christ, one patiently suffers the privations and miseries of poverty, starvation, deformity or any other sore affliction; or else meekly endures insults, calumny and persecution, not returning evil for evil, but blessing those who harm him by hurtful words, and loving those who hate him, this also is a species of martyrdom.

But true martyrdom consists not only in suffering, but in loss of life. Consequently, death belongs to the essence and nature of full and perfect martyrdom. This means that it is necessary to die, and to die for Jesus Christ, if one is to be a real martyr, in the sense in which the word *martyr* is taken by Holy Church.

It is true that one may perform some action for love of Our Lord, or suffer for Him some pain which should in the ordinary course of events, cause death; yet he is miraculously preserved by the power of God. In this case, God, who delivered Him from the death he was ready to suffer, will not deprive him of a martyr's crown, even though he may live long and die a natural death, provided he persevere until the end in the grace and love of the God of martyrs. Witness St. John the Evangelist, St. Thecla, the first of her sex to suffer martyrdom for Christ, St. Felix of Nola, and others honored by the

Church as true martyrs, although they did not die in the clutches of the tyrants, or in the torments they underwent for Our Lord. In fact, they lived for many years afterwards and died ordinary deaths, having been preserved by a divine and extraordinary power from the death they were ready to endure for Jesus Christ.

But apart from such miraculous intervention preventing the occurrence of death, if one is to be a true martyr, he must die, and die for Our Lord Himself, or for the honor of His mysteries and sacraments, in defense of the Church, or in support of an article of Faith or a point of morals, or to avoid yielding to sin because it offends Him, or by the fact of loving Him so ardently that the sacred violence of His divine love actually causes death.

St. Thomas Aquinas, the angelic doctor, assures us that any act whatsoever, even if it be merely human and natural, can make us martyrs if referred to the glory of God and done for His love, and actually does so, if it happens to bring about our death (*Summa, $2^a 2^{ae}$, Q. 124, a. 5, ad 3*).

For this reason, I advise and urge you to make a point of lifting up your heart to Jesus at the commencement of your actions, offering them to Him and affirming that you desire to do these things for His love and His glory. If the spiritual or bodily help you give to the sick, for instance, causes you to contract a mortal illness, and if you really gave your services or performed your duty to the sick out of love for Our Lord, you will share in the glory of the holy martyrs who are in heaven. And much more will this be true if you love Him with such strong and burning love that the intensity and power of holy love end by consuming your bodily life. This kind of death is a super-martyrdom, the noblest and holiest of all martyrdom. This is the martyrdom of the Mother of Fair Love, the most holy Virgin, Mother of God. This is the martyrdom of great St. Joseph, St. Mary Magdalen, St. Theresa, St. Catherine of Genoa, and many other saints. It is even the martyrdom of Jesus, for He died not only in love and for love, but also from the excess and power of His love.

## XXXVI. Spirit of Martyrdom.

All Christians, irrespective of their state in life, ought always to be prepared to suffer martyrdom for our Lord Jesus Christ. Several reasons oblige them to live in the dispositions and spirit of martyrdom.

1. They belong to Jesus Christ by an infinite number of bonds. They are bound to live for Him alone; therefore, they are bound also to die for Him, according to the words of St. Paul: "None of us liveth to himself; and no man dieth to himself. For whether we live, we live unto the Lord; and whether we die, we die unto the Lord. Therefore, whether we live, or whether we die, we are the Lord's. For to this end Christ died and rose again; that he might be Lord of the dead and of the living" (Rom. 14, 7-10).

2. Since God gave us life and being for His glory only, we are bound to glorify Him as perfectly as possible, by sacrificing to Him our being and our life in homage to His life and His supreme being, and by proclaiming thus that He alone is worthy to be and to live, and that every other life should be immolated at the feet of His sovereign and undying life.

3. God commands us to love Him with our whole heart, our whole soul and our whole strength, that is, with the most perfect love possible to us. Now if we are to love Him so, we must love Him to the extent of shedding our blood and laying down our life for Him. This is the highest degree of love, as the Son of God tells us: "Greater love than this no man hath, that a man lay down his life for his friends" (John 15, 13).

4. From the very moment of His Incarnation, Our Lord had a most intense desire to shed His blood and to die for His Father's glory and our love; yet He was unable, at that time, to fulfil His desire by Himself, because the time appointed by His Father's ordinance had not yet come. So He chose the Holy Innocents as martyrs, and accomplished, through them, His own desire, and, in a certain manner, died in them. So also ever since He rose from the dead and ascended into Heaven, He has always kept the infinite desire to suffer and die for His Father's glory and our love. He can no longer suffer nor can He die a second death; nevertheless, He still desires to suffer and die

in His members, and seeks everywhere for souls in whom He can accomplish this desire. Hence, if we have any zeal at all for the accomplishment of His divine plans, we ought to offer ourselves to Him as candidates for His renewed martyrdom that He may find in us a means to quench that burning thirst in the fulfilment once more of His yearning to shed His blood and die for love of His Father.

5. As I have said, every Christian made a solemn promise at baptism to adhere to Jesus Christ, to follow and imitate Him and consequently to be victims consecrated and sacrificed to His glory. This pledge obliges us to follow and imitate Him in His death as well as in His life, and to be ever prepared to sacrifice our lives and all that we have, according to these holy words: "Because for thy sake we are killed all the day long: we are counted as sheep for the slaughter" (Ps. 43, 22).

6. Jesus Christ is our Head and we are His members. We must live by His life, so, too, we are also obliged to die His death, since it is evident that the members must necessarily live and die by the life and death of their head, as St. Paul says: "Always bearing about in our body the mortification of Jesus, that the life also of Jesus may be made manifest in our bodies,—that the life also of Jesus may be made manifest in our mortal flesh" (II Cor. 4, 10-11).

7. But, above all, the most valid and compelling reason that imposes upon us the obligation to become martyrs is the most agonizing martyrdom suffered by our Lord Jesus Christ on the Cross, for love of us.

Our most lovable Saviour was not content merely to spend His whole life for our sake, but also willed to die for our love the cruellest and most ignominious death in the history of the world. He laid down an infinitely precious life, one moment of which was worth more than all the lives of angels and men. He would be ready, if necessary, to die over again a thousand times. He remains continually present upon our altars both as host and victim, and there He is and will be immolated every day and every hour, until the Day of Judgment, as often as the divine sacrifice of the altar, bloodless and without pain, shall be celebrated until the end of time.

O what goodness, what love! I am not surprised that three hundred thousand martyrs shed their blood and gave up their life for Jesus Christ. Christ Himself died for all men; surely, therefore, all men should die for Him. No wonder the holy martyrs, and all those to whom Christ has given to know and feel the holy fire of that divine love, which nailed Him to the Cross, possessed so burning a thirst and so flaming a desire to suffer and to die for love of Him. No wonder that so many glorious saints have actually suffered such frightful torments, with so much happiness and joy that the executioners grew weary of inflicting tortures before they wearied of enduring them, while their cruellest torments were nothing to them in the face of their insatiable desire to suffer for Jesus Christ. What does make me wonder is the coldness of our love for so lovable a Saviour, and what cowards we are in the presence of the least of sufferings! How strong is our attachment to so wretched and trivial a thing as earthly life, and how far we are from desiring to sacrifice it for Him Who sacrificed so noble and precious a life for us!

What truth can there be in the claim that we are Christians and adore a crucified God, a God agonizing and dying upon a Cross, a God who for love of us gives up so noble and excellent a life, a God who sacrifices Himself every day, before our eyes upon our altars for our salvation, if we are not ready to sacrifice to Him all that we hold dearest in the world, and even life itself, which in any case belongs to Him by all rights? Surely we are not Christians if we are not in these dispositions. Therefore I say, and this will immediately be clear to anyone who gives a little thought to the truths I have outlined, that all Christians ought to be martyrs, if not in actual fact, at least in intention and in will. So true is this, that if they are not martyrs of Jesus Christ, they will be martyrs of Satan.

Choose whichever of the two you love more. If you live under the tyranny of sin, you will be a martyr to your self-love and your passions, and consequently a martyr of the devil. But if you desire to be a martyr of Jesus Christ, you must strive to live in the spirit of martyrdom.

What is the spirit of martyrdom? It is a spirit that has five excellent attributes:

1. It is the spirit of strength and constancy which fears only God and sin, and cannot be shaken or overthrown, either by promises or threats, by persuasion or violence.

2. It is the spirit of deepest humility, which feels only horror for the vainglory and publicity of the world, and loves contempt and humiliations.

3. It is the spirit of self-mistrust and of most firm confidence in Jesus Christ our Lord, our Strength, in whom all things can be done.

4. It is the spirit of perfect detachment from the world and everything that is in the world. Those who are to sacrifice their lives to God must also sacrifice to Him all else besides.

5. It is the spirit of most burning love for our Lord Jesus Christ, who leads those animated by this spirit to do all and suffer all for love of Him, who did and suffered all for them. It so inflames them that, for love of Him, they consider mortification and suffering to be a paradise of joys, to be sought and desired while they avoid and detest the pleasures of this world as much as they would hell itself.

That is the spirit of martyrdom. Implore Our Lord, who is the King of Martyrs, to fill you with this spirit. Pray to the Queen of Martyrs, and all the martyrs, too, that they may obtain this spirit for you from the Son of God, by their holy prayers. Cultivate a particular devotion to the saintly martyrs. Make a point, also, of praying for all those who will have to suffer martyrdom, in order that God may grant them the spirit and grace of martyrdom. Pray especially for those who will have to suffer the persecution of antichrist at the end of the world, for it will be the most cruel and horrible of all persecutions.

Finally, strive to develop within yourself, by imitation, a perfect image of the lives of the holy martyrs and, what is more, the life of the King and the Queen of martyrs, Jesus and Mary, so that they may make you worthy to resemble them in death.

## XXXVII. Prayer to Jesus, King of Martyrs.

O Jesus, most worthy to be loved, prostrate at Thy feet in the very depth of my nothingness and in union with all the humility, devotion and love in heaven and on earth, I adore, glorify and bless Thee as the first and sovereign martyr of Thy Eternal Father, and King of all the martyrs. I adore and bless Thee in the consummate martyrdom Thou didst suffer in Thy Passion on the Cross. I honor and reverence Thee in the most dolorous martyrdom Thy most holy Mother sustained at the foot of Thy Cross, where her pure soul was pierced with the sword of anguish, where she suffered, in her mother's heart, the same martyrdom Thou didst endure in Thy sacred body. So, also, do I praise and magnify Thee in the various forms of martyrdom suffered by Thy saints, who endured so many and so great torments for love of Thee.

I give Thee a thousand thanks for the great glory which Thou didst give to the Heavenly Father and to Thyself by these martyrdoms which Thou didst undergo in Thyself, in Thy most Blessed Mother and in Thy saints. I offer Thee all the love, glory and praises which were rendered unto Thee by Thy most holy Mother and Thy saints in their martyrdom. What joy for our hearts to contemplate the infinite glory accorded to the Omnipotent Father by Thy sufferings and death, and the glory Thy Heavenly Father didst give to Thee because of the death and torments Thou didst suffer for Him and for us! What consolation to behold Thee so loved and glorified by Thy holy martyrs, and to see them so glorified and so loved by Thee and in Thee!

O Jesus, object of all desires, Thou art no longer able to suffer or to die in Thyself; yet Thou dost still possess a most great desire to suffer until the end of the world in Thy members, to glorify Thy Father by the way of suffering and death, even until the end of time. Thou dost everywhere seek for souls in whom Thou mayest accomplish Thy designs. Behold us, O good Jesus, who now offer ourselves to Thee with all our heart, indeed, with a thousand hearts and a thousand wills, that Thou mayest design to make use of us for that end. Behold my body is ready, with Thy grace, to suffer all kinds of tortures for the accomplishment of Thy desire, so that Thy most burning thirst to suffer and to die in Thy members, for love of Thy Father, may be somewhat slaked in us.

O Most Adorable Jesus, since Thou hast created us for Thy glory alone, grant that we may glorify Thee in the most perfect manner possible to us, by dying for Thy honor.

O sole object of all our love, Thou dost command us to love Thee with our whole heart, our whole soul and our whole strength. This is what we desire, O Lord, and to that end, we long to shed our blood and sacrifice our life for Thy love. But this will never be more than a wish, unless Thou, in Thy great mercy, dost fulfil the desire Thou hast been pleased to impart to us.

O Most Benign Jesus, since in an excess of admirable goodness Thou art pleased to be our Head, and to let us be Thy members, grant by that same goodness that we may live by the life of our Head and die by His death.

Such is our obligation, since Thou hast made us one body with Thyself by holy Baptism, in which Thou didst make us solemnly promise to adhere unto Thee and to follow Thee everywhere, and consequently, to imitate Thee by being victims destined to sacrifice for Thy glory. Give us, then, the grace to fulfil perfectly this holy, sacred promise and profession. Grant that we may follow Thee in Thy life and in Thy death, and that we may be immolated, like Thee, for Thy love and for Thy Father's glory.

O Thou, the well-beloved of our souls, when we contemplate Thee on the Cross, we see Thy most holy body all torn with wounds and anguish and drenched with blood from head to foot. Alas, O my Saviour, behold how Thou art in the utmost extremity of pain, anguish and agony. Behold Thee dying the most cruel and shameful of all deaths. Not satisfied with that, behold Thee again, as victim upon our altars, where Thou art sacrificed every day and every hour, to prove that Thou art yet ready to suffer and die a thousand times for love of us, most wretched and unworthy creatures.

Good Jesus, what return shall we make to Thee, what shall we suffer for love of Thee? It is not enough, no, not enough to have but one body to immolate for One who immolated so holy and noble a body for us. It is not enough to have but one life to lose for One who surrendered, on our behalf, a life of which one single moment was worth more than all the lives of men and angels. It is not enough to die but once for Him who died a death of infinite merit for love of us. Surely, dear Jesus, if we had all the human bodies that ever were or shall be, we would most willingly, with Thy grace, deliver them up and abandon them to every kind of torment for Thy sake. And if we had all the lives of men and angels, with how glad a heart would we not offer them to be sacrificed to Thy glory? Would it were possible to die as often, for Thy love, as there are moments of time in all past, present and future centuries! How happy would we then esteem ourselves!

Thou one and only love of our hearts, who will grant us to behold ourselves redeemed with our own blood and filled with wounds and suffering for love of Thee, as Thou wast once for love of us? If only we might one day see ourselves in this enviable state, how we would then praise and bless Thee! Oh blessed be that day, yes, a thousand times blessed, in which Thou shalt accomplish the extreme desire to be sacrificed for Thy pure love! Come fires, flames, swords, guns, gibbets, gehennas! Come all things that confound us, come all contempt and shame! Come all you torments, all rage and cruelty of men and devils, earth and hell, come upon us! We defy you, if only we may ever love our most lovable Jesus; if only we may love Him by our death, and die for His love, in order to love and bless Him forever in eternity!

Well we know, O Good Jesus, that of ourselves we do not have the power to endure the least suffering in the world. Yet we have the greatest confidence that in Thy infinite goodness Thou wilt be our strength and enable us to accomplish all things. We know that we are most unworthy of such great things. Since Thou hast died for us, Thou art most worthy that we should die for Thee, and Thou hast infinite goodness and power to make us worthy of this high achievement.

This, then, is what we beg of Thee most humbly and most urgently, O Most Kind Jesus, by the burning love that compelled Thee to die for us on the Cross, by that Precious Blood which Thou didst shed, by that most painful death which Thou didst suffer, by the very great love which Thou hast for all Thy holy martyrs, and by their abounding love for Thee, in a word, by everything that Thou dost treasure in heaven and on earth.

Make us worthy of this mercy, by Thy great goodness, for love of Thyself and for the glory of Thy Holy Name. To that end grant us now, we beseech Thee, the spirit of martyrdom with the grace and dispositions required for it. Make us strong and firm to do and suffer all things with courage for Thy love, fearless of all the world except Thee and Thy displeasure. Let us have no reliance on our strength, nor on anything that is of ourselves; but let all our trust be in Thy goodness only. Make us abhor worldly glory, ambitions and delights, as we abhor hell; and let us seek all our happiness in contempt, abjection, labors and persecutions. Make us live in complete unawareness and oblivion of the world and in detachment from ourselves and all worldly things. Above all, may we be so consumed by the fire of Thy holy love that it may be our very life's breath, and that we may continually burn with a flaming desire to love Thee ever more and more, and to do and suffer yet greater things, for Thy pure love. May our life be consumed at last in the flames of that divine love!

O Good Jesus, deeply implant in us these divine characteristics of the spirit of martyrdom, and imprint them also upon all whom Thou hast chosen from all eternity to be numbered among the ranks of the holy martyrs, especially those who will have to suffer and die for Thee in the last, terrible persecution of antichrist.

O Mother of Jesus, Queen of martyrs, and O you holy martyrs of Jesus, we implore you to pray that, in His infinite goodness, He may fulfil these things in us; for His glory alone and for purest love of Him.

Finally, O Jesus Christ, most worthy of all love, grant, we beseech Thee, that we may live a life of perfect imitation of Thy most holy life, of Thy Blessed Mother and of the glorious martyrs, so that we may deserve to resemble Thee and them in death as well as in life, and to sing forever in their company with Thee the most sweet canticle of Thy holy praise and Thy divine love.

## XXXVIII. Prayer in Honor of all the Martyrs.

*Ant.* Mirabilis es, Domine Jesu, magnus et laudabilis nimis in sanctis Martyribus tuis. Mirificasti omnes voluntates tuas in ipsis, et desiderium animae eorum tribuisti eis. Omnis spiritus laudet te, et omnes virtutes tuae benedicant tibi.

V. Orate pro nobis, omnes sancti Martyres.
R. Ut digni efficiamur amore Jesu, et societate passionum ejus.

### Oremus.

Domine Jesu, qui maxima potentiae et amoris tui miracula in passione ac morte tua, et in sanctis Martyribus demonstrasti: da nobis quaesumus, intercedentibus sanctis martyribus tuis, Stephano, Laurentio, Eustachio, Blasio, Clemente et Agathangelo, Thecla, Catharina, Felicitate, Caecilia, Agnete, et omnibus aliis, pro amore tuo prospera mundi despicere; nulla ejus adversa formidare; in omnibus nos humiliare; te semper magis atque magis toto corde, ore et opera diligere; passionibus tuis sociari; morti tuae configurari; ac denique tibi viventes et morientes, velut hostias sanctas atque placentes, in sacrificium laudis, gloriae, et amoris immolare. Qui vivis et regnas cum Deo Patre, in unitate Spiritus Sancti Deus, per omnia saecula saeculorum. Amen.

## PART TWO

*Some Devotional Exercises Necessary to*
*Live a Christian and Saintly Life and*
*to Make Jesus Reign in Your Soul*

Illustration in the 1648 French Edition of
*The Life and the Kingdom of Jesus*

## Part Two

*SOME DEVOTIONAL EXERCISES NECESSARY TO
LIVE A CHRISTIAN AND SAINTLY LIFE AND
TO MAKE JESUS REIGN IN YOUR SOUL*

### MORNING EXERCISE

#### I. Everything That You Do Should Begin and End With Jesus.

Jesus, the Only Son of God and the Only Son of Mary, is, to use the words of St. Paul, "the author and finisher of faith" (Heb. 12, 2), and of Christian piety. He is, to quote His own words, "Alpha and Omega, the first and the last, the beginning and the end" (Apoc. 22, 13) of all things. It is, therefore, most just that He should be the beginning and the end of your whole life, of every year, of every month, of every week, and of every day of your life and of every one of your devotional exercises. For this reason you ought to have consecrated the beginning of your life to Him, if you had been gifted with the use of reason at that time; and you earnestly seek to end it in His grace and in the exercise of His love. So, if you wish to obtain this favor from His goodness, you should take care to consecrate to Him by some special exercise of piety and love the beginning and end of each year, of each month, of each week, and especially of each day.

Consequently, it is a matter of great importance to begin and to end each day well; but especially to begin it well by fitting your mind first thing in the morning with good thoughts and by offering up your first actions to Our Lord, because on this depends the blessing of the rest of the day.

#### II. What You Should Do Upon Waking up in the Morning.

As soon as you awake in the morning, raise your eyes to heaven and your heart to Jesus, thus consecrating to Him the first use that you make of your sense and the first thoughts and affections of your mind and your heart.

Let your first words be the Holy Names of Jesus and Mary: *Jesus, Maria.* "O Jesus! O Mary, Mother of Jesus! O Good Jesus, I give Thee my heart forever. O Mary, Mother of Jesus, I give thee my heart; give it, I beseech thee, to thy Son."—*Veni, Domine Jesu.* "Come, Lord Jesus, come into my mind and my heart to possess and fill me entirely. O Jesus, be Jesus to me!"

Let your first exterior action be the Sign of the Cross: "In the Name of the Father, and of the Son, and of the Holy Ghost," at the same time giving yourself with your whole heart to the Father, the Son, and the Holy Ghost in order that they may possess you entirely.

When the time to rise has come, recall to mind the very great love with which at the moment of His Incarnation the Son of God came forth from the bosom of His Father—a place (if one may use the word) full of delights, of repose and of glory. He came down to earth to become subject to our miseries and to take upon Himself our sorrows and afflictions. In honor of this same love and in union with it, get up promptly and courageously saying: *Surgam et quaerum quem diligit anima mea.* "I will arise and seek him whom my soul loveth" (Cant. 3, 2). As you pronounce these words: *quem diligit anima mea,* "whom my soul loveth," have the desire of pronouncing them, as far as possible, with all the love that is offered to Jesus both in heaven and on earth.

Then kneel down and adore our Lord Jesus Christ, saying: *Adoramus te, Domine Jesu, et benedicimus tibi, et diligimus te ex toto corde nostro, ex tota anima nostra, ex totis viribus nostris.* "We adore Thee, Lord Jesus; we bless Thee and we love Thee with our whole heart, with our whole soul, and with all our strength." And in saying these words, desire to say them with all the humility, devotion, and love in heaven and on earth, and on behalf of all the creatures in the universe.

III. What You Should Do While Dressing.

While you are putting on your clothes, to prevent the devil from filling your mind with useless or bad thoughts, fill it with good ones. Remember that by His Incarnation our Lord Jesus Christ put on, like garments, our humanity, our mortality, and all the human miseries and needs to which we are subject; and that He lowered Himself to a condition in which, like you, He had need of clothing; and that He did this all for love of you. Then lift up your heart and speak to Him as follows:

"O Lord Jesus, mayest Thou be blessed and exalted forever, because Thou didst so humble Thyself for love of me. O my Jesus, I offer Thee the action I am now performing, in honor of the action Thou didst perform when Thou didst clothe Thy Divinity in our humanity, and also when Thou didst clothe Thy humanity in garments like these which we put on. I desire to dress myself in the same dispositions and with the same intentions with which Thou didst perform this human act."

Think also of the many poor people who have only rags to cover themselves. They have offended God less than you have. Yet Our Lord, by an excess of His goodness, has given clothing to you rather than to them. With this thought in mind raise your heart and speak to Him thus:

"O my God, I bless Thee a thousand times for all the mercies Thou hast shown in my regard. I beg Thee to provide for all the needs of the poor. And I also beg that, just as Thou hast given me clothing for my body, Thou mayest also clothe my soul with Thy own self, that is, with Thy spirit and Thy love, Thy charity, humility, meekness, patience, obedience, and all Thy other virtues."

IV. Your Whole Life Belongs to Jesus and Ought to be Consecrated to His Glory and Employed for it Alone.

Your whole life, with everything that pertains to it and depends upon it, belongs to Jesus by reason of five general claims which include a countless number of special ones.

1. Jesus is your Creator, who gives you life, who impresses His image and likeness upon your soul. Because of this, your life belongs to Him absolutely and universally no matter what you do, and must be continually referred to Him as the image of its prototype.

2. He is your Preserver, who sustains you each moment in your

being, and carries you incessantly in His arms with more care and love than a mother carrying her tiny child.

3. He is the Son of the Heavenly Father, who has given Him from all eternity, and still gives Him all things as a whole, and likewise each person individually.

4. He is your Redeemer, who has delivered you from the slavery of Satan and sin and bought you at the price of His Precious Blood. He has, therefore, purchased everything that is in you, your entire life, your time, your thoughts, words, and deeds, all the powers of your body and soul, as well as all external things that surround you in the world. By His death on the Cross He has acquired for you not only the graces necessary for the sanctification of your souls but also the things needed for the conservation of your bodies. Because of your sins you should have no right to walk upon the earth, to breathe the air, to eat a morsel of bread, to drink a drop of water, nor to use anything in this world, unless Jesus had acquired that right for you by His blood and His death. All that is in you, therefore, and all your use of things outside of you, belong to Jesus and must be employed only for Him, as beings which He has acquired at the price of His blood and His life.

5. Jesus Christ has given you all that He has and all that He is. He has given you His Father as your Father, by making you sons of His own Father. He has given you His Holy Spirit to teach you, to direct you and to lead you in all things. He has given you His holy Mother to be your Mother. He has given you His angels and saints to be your protectors and intercessors. He has given you all the other countless beings that exist in heaven and on earth for your use and to fill your needs. He has given you His own Person in the Incarnation. He has given you His whole life, of which He spent not a single moment that was not for your benefit. Nor did He have a single thought, utter a single word, perform one action or even take a single step that was not devoted to your salvation. Finally, He gives you His body and blood in the Blessed Eucharist, as well as His soul and His divinity and all the infinite treasures that are enclosed in His divinity and humanity. He does this every day for all men; and for you as often as you dispose yourself to receive Him.

Considering all these countless gifts, you must realize how important it is to give yourself entirely to Him, and to offer and consecrate to Him all the functions and exercises of your life. Indeed, if you had the lives of all the angels and of all the men who have ever existed, now exist and will exist, you would be obliged to spend them in His service, even if He had devoted but one moment of His life to you, since a single moment of His life is worth more than a thousand eternities, if I may use such words, of lives of angels and of men. How great, then, is your obligation to consecrate and expend in His service and for His glory, the short life and the brief time you have on earth!

The first and most important thing to do is to keep yourself with all care in His grace and friendship, fearing and flying from all that might make you lose Him, that is, from every kind of sin. Fly from sin more than the most terrifying things in the world, even death itself. But if by some unhappy chance you fall into sin, rise immediately by means of confession and contrition, of which I shall speak later on. For just as the branches, leaves, flowers, and fruit of a tree belong to the one who owns the trunk of the tree, so also, as long as you belong to Jesus Christ and are united to Him by His grace, all your life, with all that comes from it, and all the acts you may perform that are not evil in themselves, will belong to Him. But in addition, I am going to set before you three other methods, which are very satisfying and very easy to use, by which your whole life may be employed in a far more perfect and holy manner for the love and glory of Jesus.

## V. THREE METHODS BY WHICH YOUR WHOLE LIFE CAN BECOME A CONTINUAL EXERCISE OF PRAISE AND LOVE.

Over and above what has been said, there are three others things to be done, if you are to spend your whole life for the glory of Jesus. These things are contained in the morning prayer that follows.

1. Once you are dressed, before you go out of the house or do any other action, go down on your knees and take at least five minutes to adore Jesus, to thank Him and to offer yourself to Him, together with all the acts that you will do during the day, having the intention of

performing them all for His glory. The writings of St. Gertrude tell us that Our Lord assured her that he took considerable pleasure in her offering up to Him all her very smallest acts, even every breath she took and every beat of her heart. By virtue of this oblation, every step that you take, every breath that you draw, every beat of your heart, every use that you make of your interior or exterior senses and in general all the actions that you may perform, which are not in themselves evil, will belong to Jesus Christ, and will all be so many acts redounding to His greater glory.

Note that, when I urge you to kneel down each morning in your home to adore our Lord Jesus Christ, to thank Him and offer yourself to Him, I do not mean that these acts are to be made only in the sight of the Son of God and no other, but also in the sight of the Most Holy Trinity, the Father, the Son and the Holy Ghost. This infallibly happens even when you do not expressly intend it. Since Jesus Christ is one with the Father and the Holy Ghost and since the entire Holy Trinity, or, as St. Paul says, the plenitude of the divinity dwells in Christ (Col. 2, 9), it must necessarily follow that to adore and glorify the Father and the Holy Ghost and to offer Jesus all the glory that is given Him in heaven and on earth is to offer that same glory to Father and the Holy Spirit. And when you beg the Father and the Holy Spirit to glorify Jesus, you are supplicating Them to glorify Themselves. This brings me to the second thing that you should do in the morning, if you want your whole life to be an exercise of glorification and love of Jesus, and consequently of the Father, the Son and the Holy Ghost.

2. Offer up to Our Lord all the love and glory that will be given Him this day in heaven and on earth and unite yourself with all the praises that will be given to Him by His Eternal Father, by Himself, by His Holy Spirit, by His Blessed Mother, by all His angels and saints and by all His creatures. Thus you will be associated with the love and the praise that will continually ascend to Him during that particular day.

3. Pray to the Eternal Father, the Holy Spirit, the Blessed Virgin Mary, all the angels and saints to glorify and love Jesus for you during this day. They will surely do so, because this is the most agreeable

petition you could possibly make to them and the one which they most willingly hear and grant. Thus you will have a special share in the love and glory that Jesus continually receives from those Holy and Divine Persons. And He will receive this glory and love as being rendered, in a certain manner, by you, since it is rendered at your request and insistence.

If you make faithful use of these three practices every morning, then every day of your life and your life as a whole will be a perpetual act of love and glorification of Jesus Christ. If it were possible to find in the world a man so detestable, that he would want all his actions and his every breath to be so many blasphemies against God, and if he also had the intention of uniting himself with all the blasphemies committed on earth and in hell: and if, not satisfied with that, he were to excite and urge all the demons and wicked men to blaspheme for him, is it not true that by reason of his abominable intention, all his acts and his every breath would be blasphemies and all the blasphemies on earth and in hell could be imputed to him? So then, on the other hand, if you use the three practices I have proposed above, it is most certain that by virtue of your holy intention all the acts of your life will be as many acts of praise to God and you will be associated in a special manner in all the honor that is incessantly given to Him on earth and in heaven.

It would also be a good thing, over and above all this, if you were to make, every morning, out of love for Our Lord, an act of acceptance of all the afflictions you may have to bear during the day and also an act of renunciation of all the temptations of the devil and all the feelings of self-love and other passions which may come upon you during the day. These two acts have considerable importance, because a thousand little annoyances occur in the course of the day, and they pass on and you often do not take thought and offer them to God. In the same way many temptations and impulses of self-love creep into your acts without your taking notice of them. By virtue of the first act, however, God will be glorified by all the pains, both of body and soul, which will make themselves felt during the day, if you accept them first thing in the morning out of love for Him. Then, by virtue of the second act, He will give you strength to resist more easily all evil temptations and to destroy more easily all effects of self-love and other vices.

These two acts, together with the three practices that precede them, are all embodied in the following prayer.

## VI. Morning Prayer to Jesus.

O Most Lovable Jesus, I fall at Thy feet in the utmost depths of my nothingness. I adore and glorify Thee in the immense extent of Thy spirit, the infinite greatness of Thy love and all the virtues and powers of Thy divinity and humanity. I bless Thee and love Thee in all that Thou art universally, both in Thyself and in all things. I give Thee infinite thanks for Thy care and watchfulness over me during this night. I offer Thee all the honor that has been given Thee during this night in heaven and on earth.

O my Saviour, I offer and consecrate myself entirely and forever to Thee and through Thee to Thy Eternal Father. I offer Thee my body, my soul, my mind, my heart, my life, all the parts of my body, all the powers of my soul, every breath I draw, every throb of my heart and veins, every step I take, every look, every use I make of my senses and in general everything that has been, is and shall be in me. It is my desire that all these things may be consecrated to Thy glory and become so many acts of praise, adoration and love of Thee. Then may it please Thee, O my God, in Thy great power and mercy, to make this be so, in order that everything in me may render to Thee continual honor and homage.

I likewise offer up to Thee, O Most Lovable Jesus, and through Thee to the Blessed Trinity, all the love and glory that will be given Thee today and for all eternity in heaven and on earth. I unite myself to all the praise that ever has been, is now, and ever shall be given to the Father by the Son and the Holy Ghost, to the Son and the Holy Ghost by the Father, and to the Father, the Son and the Holy Ghost by the Blessed Virgin, by all the angels, all the saints and by all creatures.

O Jesus, adore and love the Father and the Holy Spirit for me.

O Father of Jesus, love and glorify Thy Son Jesus for me.

O Holy Spirit of Jesus, love and glorify Jesus for me.

O Mother of Jesus, bless and love thy Son Jesus for me.

O blessed St. Joseph, O angels of Christ and His saints, adore and love my Saviour for me.

And besides this, I now accept for the love of Thee, O my Lord Jesus, all the annoyances, contradictions, and afflictions, whether of body or of spirit, which may befall me today and during my whole life, offering myself to Thee to suffer everything Thou art pleased that I should suffer for Thy pure glory and good pleasure.

Furthermore, I declare that from now on I shall renounce all the suggestions and temptations of the devil and I disavow and detest all the motions, feelings and effects of pride, of self-love and of all other passions and evil inclinations that are in me.

And I beg Thee, O my Saviour, to imprint in my heart the hatred and horror and fear of sin, which is greater than all the evils in the world. Grant that I may die rather than offend Thee wilfully. Give me the grace to serve Thee today and all the rest of my life, with fidelity and love, meekness, patience, obedience and humility.

## VII. Another Morning Prayer to Sanctify all Your Actions and to Make Them Pleasing to God.

O my God, my Creator and Sovereign Lord, since I belong entirely to Thee, so also everything that proceeds from me should belong to Thee. Thou hast created me for Thyself; therefore, it is fitting that I should offer Thee myself and all my acts, which can have no value unless they be referred to Thee. And so do I, Thy truly insignificant creature, now and for all the moments of my life offer Thee myself and all my works, especially those that I am to do today, the good as well as the indifferent, the free as well as the natural acts. In order that they may be more pleasing to Thee, my God, I unite them to all the works of Our Lord and of His most holy Mother, as well as to those of all the souls of the blessed and of just men in heaven and on earth. I consecrate to Thee every step I take, every word, every breath, in short, all my actions, with the intention and the desire of giving Thee infinite glory and of losing Thee with an infinite love.

I offer Thee my heart, my will, my understanding and myself not only in the manner most agreeable to Thee (for this is my intention in each one of my acts), but also with these acts, I refer to Thee the actions of all other creatures, especially those actions that are not offered to Thee. I offer Thee the perfection of all the angels, the virtue of the patriarchs, of the prophets and of all the apostles, the sufferings of the martyrs, the penance of the confessors, the purity of the virgins, the sanctity of all the blessed and finally Thy very Self. All this I do, not to obtain favors from Thee, not even paradise, but only to please Thee more and give Thee greater glory.

Moreover, I mean to offer Thee from this moment on in my present state of freedom, all the acts of love by which I shall love Thee necessarily in the blissfulness of eternity, as I hope to do by Thy bounty. In like manner, I offer Thee all the virtuous acts that I shall ever perform and all the perfect acts to be done by the blessed in the homeland of glory. Since all things are excellent in proportion as they are pleasing to Thee and in conformity with Thy divine will, I desire not only to conform my will to Thine in everything, but I also long to accomplish nothing but what is pleasing to Thee, desiring that Thy holy will and not my own may be done in all things. And I would do this, saying always with my lips and with my heart and by all the actions of my life: *Fiat, Domine, voluntas tua sicut in caelo et in terra.* "Lord, may Thy will be done on earth as it is in heaven."

May it please Thee, O my God, to grant me this grace, in order that I may always love Thee more ardently, serve Thee more perfectly and act more purely for Thy glory, that I may become so transformed into Thee as to live in Thee alone, for Thee alone, and to find my paradise both in time and eternity in giving pleasure to Thee.

### Prayer to the Most Blessed Virgin Mary

O Mother of Jesus, Queen of heaven and earth, I hail thee and honor thee as my sovereign Lady, to whom I belong by right and upon whom I depend after God. I pay thee all the honor that I can and must, according to God's will and thy own greatness. I give myself all to thee; may it please thee to give me thy Son. Grant that by thy prayers all that is in me may be consecrated to His glory and to thine and that I may die rather than lose His grace.

### Prayer to St. Joseph

O blessed St. Joseph, foster father of Jesus and worthy spouse of Mary, be my father, my protector and my guide today and all my life.

### Prayer to Your Guardian Angel

O my holy guardian Angel, I give myself to thee: offer me to Jesus and His most holy Mother and ask them to give me the grace to honor and love them with all the perfection they demand of me.

### Prayer to all the Angels and Saints

O holy angels, O blessed saints, I offer myself to you; offer me to Jesus and beg Him to give me His holy blessing, that I may faithfully employ this day in His service and that I may die rather than offend Him.

### Prayer to beg a blessing from Jesus and Mary

O Jesus, O Mary, Mother of Jesus, I beseech you to give me to your holy blessing. *Nos cum prole pia, benedicat Virgo Maria.* "May the Virgin Mary with her Divine Child bless us. Amen."

# EXERCISE DURING THE DAY

VIII. Jesus is the Center of Your Being and Should be the Sole Object of Your Life.

The first, most important, and, indeed, the only object of the contemplation, love, and delight of the Eternal Father is His Son, Jesus. I repeat: the *only* object. The Divine Father has willed that His Son Jesus should be "all in all things" (Eph. 1, 23), and that "He is before all, and by Him all things consist (Col. 1, 17), according to the words of St. Paul. This is why God the Father beholds and loves all things in His Son and sees nothing but Him in all things. The same Apostle also teaches that God made all things in Jesus and by Jesus (Col. 1, 16), and that likewise He made all things for Jesus (Heb. 2, 10). He has embodied in His Son "all the treasures of wisdom and knowledge" (Col. 2, 3), of His goodness and beauty, of His glory and joy, and of all His other divine perfections. He tells us most clearly, and on several occasions, that He has placed all His complacency and delight in this Only and Well-beloved Son. This does not, of course, exclude the Holy Spirit, since He is the Spirit of Jesus and is one with Jesus.

After the example of the Heavenly Father, whom you are obliged to follow and imitate as your own Father, you must make Jesus Christ the sole object of your mind and heart. You must see and love all things in Him; you must not see nor love anything except Him in all things. You must perform all your actions in Him and for Him. You must seek all your happiness and your paradise in Him; as He is the paradise of the Eternal Father, and as the Father takes all His pleasure in Him, so also this Holy Father has given Him to you to be your paradise. Therefore, He commands you to dwell in Him: *Manete in me,* "Abide in me" (John 15, 4). And His beloved disciple twice repeats this commandment to us. "Abide in him" he says, "And now little children, abide in him" (I John 2, 27-28). And St. Paul would lead you to do this by assuring you that "there is . . . no condemnation to them that are in Christ Jesus" (Rom. 8, 1). You may truly say even further that outside of Him there is nothing but perdition, malediction and hell.

Yet notice once more at this point, that when I say that Jesus Christ must be the only object of your life I do not exclude the Father and the Holy Ghost. As Jesus Himself assures you that "he that seeth me seeth the Father also" (John 14, 9), it follows that whoever speaks of Him also speaks of His Father and of His Holy Spirit; whoever honors and loves Him likewise honors and loves His Father and His Holy Spirit; and whoever makes Him the only object of his life, includes the Father and the Holy Ghost.

Make our most amiable Saviour the sole object of your thoughts, desires and affections, the single end of all your actions, the centre of your being, your paradise, and your all. Wherever you may be, have recourse to Him, as to a place of refuge, by lifting up your mind and heart to Him. Remain always in Him, that is, let your mind and your heart, all your thoughts, desires and affections be His. Let all your actions be done in Him and for Him, in the manner that will be explained in greater detail in "Part Three" of this book.

Meditate often His own words: *Unum est necessarium,* "but one thing is necessary" (Luke 10, 42), namely to serve, love and glorify Jesus.

Consider that apart from Him all is but madness, deceit, illusion, loss of time, affliction of body and spirit, nothingness, vanity of vanities; that you are on earth for this one thing alone, the principal, the most necessary, the most urgent, in fact, the only business you have in this world. It must be your chief and only care. All your thoughts, words, and actions must be directed to this one end. So you must be most careful, at the beginning of all your actions, especially the most important ones, to offer them to Our Lord, protesting that you wish to do them for His glory.

If you should fall into some sin, do not be discouraged—not even if you fall many times—but profoundly humble yourself before God in spirit and retire sometimes, if circumstances permit, into some secluded place where you may kneel down and ask His pardon, making an act of contrition and begging our Lord Jesus Christ to repair your fault and to give you fresh grace and strength to keep you from falling again. Ask Him to implant within you, once again, your resolution to die rather than to offend Him.

Remember from time to time that you are before God, in fact, in God Himself (Act. 17, 28); that our Lord Jesus Christ, in His divinity, surrounds you on all sides, and so completely penetrates and fills you that He is more intimately in you than you are in yourself; and that He is constantly thinking of you and keeps His eyes and heart ever turned toward you. May this arouse you in turn if not to think always of Him, at least never to allow a full hour to go by without lifting up your mind and heart to Him by one or another of the following aspirations or other prayers, it may please His divine spirit to inspire in you.

## IX. Aspirations to be Said During the Course of the Day.

O Jesus! O Good Jesus! O Possessor of my heart! O Beloved of my soul!

O Object of all my love, when shall I love Thee perfectly?

O Divine Son, fill with light the shadows of my mind, set fire to the coldness of my heart!

O Light of my eyes, let me know Thee and know myself, that I may love Thee and hate myself!

O my sweet light, make me clearly see that all that is not Thee is nothingness, deceit and vanity!

O my God and my All, take away all that is not Thee, to unite me all with Thee!

O my beloved All, be all to me, and may all else be nothing to me!

O my Jesus, be Jesus to me!

O Life of my soul, O King of my love, live and reign in me perfectly!

Live, Jesus, live, King of my heart, live, Life of my life. Glory and love to Thee forever, in all and from all things!

O divine Fire, immense Fire, who art everywhere, consuming and devouring Fire, why dost Thou not consume me altogether in Thy sacred flames?

O Fire, O celestial Flame, come, transform me into a pure flame of love for my Jesus!

O Jesus, Thou art all fire and all flame of love for me! Oh, why am I not all flame and fire of love for Thee?

O Jesus, Thou art all mine; may I be all Thine forever!

Ah, God of my heart! Ah, my soul's only heritage! What is there for me to desire on earth or in heaven save Thee?

*O Unum Necessarium! Unum quaero, unum desidero, unum volo, unum mihi est necessarium, Jesus meus et omnia!* O Thou only Necessary One! It is Thou whom I seek, it is Thou whom I desire, it is Thou whom I long for, it is Thou whom I need, my Jesus, who art in all things and beyond whom all is nothing!

*Veni Domine Jesu!* Come, Lord Jesus, come into my heart, into my soul, there to love Thyself in all perfection!

Alas, Jesus, when will there be nothing left in me to oppose Thy love?

O Mother of Jesus, show me that thou art the Mother of Jesus by forming Him and making Him live in my soul!

O Mother of Love, love thy Son for me!

O Good Jesus, give back to Thyself a hundredfold all the love I ought to have given Thee in all my life, and the love of all creatures ought to have given Thee!

O Jesus, I offer Thee all the love in heaven and earth!

O Jesus, I give Thee my heart; fill it with holy love!

O Jesus, may all my steps pay homage to the steps that Thou didst take on earth!

O Jesus, may all my thoughts be consecrated to the honor of Thy holy thoughts!

O Jesus, may all my words give homage to Thy holy words!

O Jesus, may all my acts give glory to Thy divine actions!

O my Glory, may I be wholly sacrificed to Thy glory forever!

O my All, I give up all that is not Thee and give myself to Thee forever!

> Jesus, without whom all is nothing, is my all.
> Thus I want all things, though I want not one!
> For, having nothing, then will I have all,
> If you take all, and leave me Him alone!

# EVENING EXERCISE

IT IS JUST as important to end as it is to begin the day well and to make a special consecration to God of the last actions of each day as well as the first. To this end, before taking your rest in the evening, make a point of going on your knees for a quarter of an hour to thank God for the graces He has given you during the day, to examine your conscience and to renew the offering of yourself to Him by the following exercises and practices.

## X. ACT OF THANKSGIVING.

O Jesus, my Lord, I adore Thee as the One who, together with Thy Father and Thy Holy Spirit, art the source of all that is good and holy and perfect in heaven and on earth, in the orders of nature, of grace, and of glory. To Thee do I refer all the gifts and benefits, both earthly and heavenly, temporal and eternal, which ever came forth from Thee, but especially this day, both on earth and in heaven.

I give Thee infinite praise and thanks for all that Thou art in Thyself, and for all the effects of Thy goodness that Thou hast ever brought about, especially during this day, for the benefit of all Thy creatures. But I thank Thee more especially for those Thou hast accomplished for me, the most insignificant of Thy creatures, as well as for all the benefits Thou hast designed on my behalf from all eternity.

I offer Thee all the love and all the praises that have ever been given Thee, especially all those that have been given Thee today in heaven and on earth. May all the angels, all the saints, all creatures and all powers of Thy divinity and Thy humanity bless Thee forever.

## XI. EXAMINATION OF CONSCIENCE.

O Lord Jesus, I adore Thee as my sovereign Judge. Most willingly do I submit to Thy power of judging me and I rejoice that Thou hast this power over me. May it please Thee to let me share a little of that light by which Thou wilt show me my sins, when I shall appear before Thy judgment seat at the hour of death, so that, in the brightness of that light, I may know the sins I have committed against Thy divine majesty. Let me share in the zeal of Thy divine justice and in Thy hatred for sin, so that I may hate my sins as Thou dost hate them.

Having said this prayer, make a brief examination of the whole day to see whether you have offended God. When you have recalled your sins, accuse yourself before Him and ask pardon of Him, making use of the following acts of contrition.

## XII. Act of Contrition Before Retiring.

O my Saviour, I accuse myself before Thee and before all Thy angels and saints, of all the sins that I have committed in my whole life, especially today, against Thy divine majesty. I implore Thee, my Lord, by Thy great mercy, by the Precious Blood which Thou didst shed for me and by the prayers and merits of Thy most holy Mother and of all Thy angels and saints, to give me grace, at this time, to conceive true contrition and repentance for my sins.

O my God, I detest my sins with my whole heart and with all the power of my will. I detest them because of the offense, injury and dishonor which I have given Thee by means of them. I hate them because Thou dost hate them and because they are infinitely displeasing to Thee. O Good Jesus, these sins of mine have been the reason for which Thou didst suffer the most frightful tortures that have ever been suffered, and Thou didst die the most cruel of all deaths. That is why I hold them in abhorrence, O my good Saviour, and renounce them forever. Oh, who will give me all the anguish of St. Peter or St. Mary Magdalen and all the penitent saints, that I may weep for the offenses I have committed against my God with all the feeling and all the regret with which they wept for theirs! Oh, who will bring me to hate all my iniquities as much as the angels and saints hate them!

Oh, my God, if it were only possible for me to have as great a horror for my sins as Thou hast Thyself! Lord, let me detest them, let me hold them in abhorrence even as Thou dost and let me abominate all that is not pleasing to Thee!

O my sweet Lord, let me die a thousand times rather than offend Thee mortally again, or, indeed, rather than offend Thee in any way at all, by a deliberate act of will. I promise, with the help of Thy grace, that I will accuse myself of all my sins at my next confession and I assure Thee of my firm resolution to avoid them in the future for love of Thee. Yes, my God, with my whole heart, I renounce every sort of sin forever and I offer myself to Thee to do and to suffer all Thou dost please, in satisfaction for my sins. In homage to Thy divine justice, I now willingly accept all the sufferings and penances it shall please Thee to inflict upon me, whether in this world or in the next, in expiation of my faults, to satisfy for the dishonor I have given Thee today by Thyself, Thy holy Mother, by Thy angels and saints and by all the holy souls there are on earth.

O Good Jesus, I give myself all to Thee. Destroy in me all that does not please Thee. Make reparation, on my behalf, for all the offenses I have committed before Thy Eternal Father, Thyself, Thy Holy Spirit, Thy Blessed Mother, Thy angels, Thy saints and all Thy creatures. Give me the strength and grace to offend Thee no more.

O angels of Jesus, saints of Jesus, Mother of Jesus, make up for my defects, I beg you; atone on my behalf for the dishonor I have given God by my sins, and return to Him a hundredfold all the honor and glory I should have given Him today and in my whole life.

O Mother of Jesus, Mother of Mercy, ask thy Beloved Son to show me His mercy. Mother of Grace, implore thy Son to give me grace never to offend Him again and to serve and love Him faithfully.

O blessed St. Joseph, O my Guardian Angel, O blessed St. John and blessed St. Mary Magdalen, intercede for me that I may obtain mercy and grace to be more faithful to God.

## XIII. Act of Oblation.

O Jesus, I offer Thee the rest I am about to take, in honor of the eternal rest Thou dost enjoy in the bosom of Thy Father, and in honor of the sleep and temporal rest Thou didst take in the bosom of Thy Mother, as well as during Thy whole life on earth.

I offer Thee every breath I shall draw during this night, every pulse of my heart and my veins, desiring that they may be so many acts of praise and adoration of Thee. I unite myself with all the praises which will be offered up to Thee, this night and forever, in heaven and on earth. I beg all Thy angels and saints, Thy Blessed Mother and Thy very Self to love and glorify Thee for me this night and for all eternity.

When you have said this and are lying down, you should make the sign of the Cross. Then say the last prayer that Jesus said to His Father at the last moment of His life: *Pater, in manus tuas commendo spiritum meum.* "Father, into thy hands I commend my spirit" (Luke 23, 46). You should say this prayer with your life's last hour in view, and try to say it with just as much devotion as you would wish if you were indeed in that last hour. To do this, you must desire to make the offering, as far as possible, with the love, the humility, the confidence and all the divine and holy dispositions with which Jesus said these words Himself. At the same time unite yourself, as of that moment, with the final disposition in which Jesus ended His life, saying this prayer and imploring Him to impress those dispositions deeply within you and to keep them there for you in your last hour, so that, by this means, you may die in Christ, that is, in the holy and divine dispositions in which He died, and thus you may be one of those of whom it is written: *Beati mortui qui in Domino moriuntur.* "Blessed are the dead who die in the Lord" (Apoc. 14, 13).

Finally, take care that your last action before falling asleep is the sign of the Cross; and that your last thought is of Jesus, that your last inward act is an act of love for Jesus and Mary. Thus you may merit the grace that the last words you say in your life will be these: *Jesus! Maria!* Live Jesus and Mary! O Good Jesus, be Jesus to me! O Mary, Mother of Jesus, be the Mother of my soul!

# CONFESSION

## XIV. Preparation for Confession.

The frequent use of the Sacrament of Penance is a very useful, holy and necessary means for the glory of God and the sanctification of souls.

But it is a deplorable thing to see what a strange abuse many souls make of this Sacrament in our own day, when they come to the feet of the priest to receive absolution for their sins, but get up and bear away their own condemnation because they have come without the dispositions necessary for true and solid repentance. This is a matter to be feared extremely, even by those who confess frequently, because there is a real danger of their going to confession more as a matter of routine than in a real spirit of penance, especially when they can detect no change in their life and no progress in Christian virtues. Therefore, the more you frequent this Sacrament, the more you should see that you make the proper preparation for receiving it. There are three things that will enable you to do so.

1. You must fall on your knees before Our Lord, in some quiet place, if possible, to consider Him and adore Him in the rigorous penances, in the contrition and humiliation which He had to bear for your sins all through His life, especially in the Garden of Olives. And you should beg Him with great insistence to let you share in His spirit of penance, and to give you the grace to know your sins, to hate and detest them as much as He would wish, to confess them clearly, and to give them up absolutely and to be converted perfectly to Him, flying from all occasions of sin, while making use of the remedies necessary for the healing of the wounds of your soul.

To do this, you may use the following prayer:

O my dear Jesus, as I contemplate Thee in the Garden of Olives when Thou didst enter upon Thy Sacred Passion, I behold Thee prostrate upon the ground before Thy Father's face in the name of all sinners, since Thou hast taken upon Thyself all the sins of the world and, especially, my own. I see that by Thy divine light Thou dost place all those sins before Thy own gaze, to confess them to Thy Father in the name of all sinners, taking upon Thyself all the humiliation and contrition for them in His sight, and offering Thyself to Him to make whatever satisfaction and perform whatever penance is pleasing to Him.

O my Good Jesus, I behold Thee, as a result of this spectacle of the horror of my crimes and of the dishonor they give to Thy Father, reduced to an astounding agony, a frightful sorrow and to such an extremity of anguish and contrition, that the violence of the suffering makes Thy soul sorrowful unto death and causes Thee even to sweat blood, so terribly as to stain the ground about Thee.

O my Saviour, I adore, love and glorify Thee in Thy holy agony and in this spirit of penance to which Thou hast been reduced by Thy love and my offenses. I give myself to Thee now, that I may enter with Thee into this spirit. May it please Thee to give me some little share of the light that gave Thee cognizance of my faults, that I may know them and confess them humbly. Give me some small share of the humiliation and contrition Thou didst bear before the Eternal Father, as well as some measure of the love with which Thou didst offer Thyself to Him in atonement and some fraction of Thy hatred and horror for sin. Give me the grace, I beseech Thee, to make this confession with perfect humility, sincerity and repentance and with a firm and strong resolution never to offend Thee again.

O Mother of Jesus, I implore thee to obtain for me those graces from thy Son.

O my holy guardian Angel, pray to Our Lord for me, to give me the grace to know my sins and confess them well, and to have true contrition for them and to be perfectly converted from them.

2. When you have said this prayer, you should examine your conscience with care and try to remember the sins you have committed since your last confession. Once you have recognized them, try to form in your heart real regret, perfect repentance and contrition for having offended so good a God, asking Him pardon for your faults, detesting them and renouncing them because they displease Him, making a firm resolution to avoid them in the future, with the

help of His grace, flying from all occasions of sin, and making use of the proper and efficacious means to bring about a genuine conversion: for contrition is composed of all these elements.

Since, however, contrition is extremely necessary and important, not only in confession but in several other matters as well, I should like to show you in more detail the nature of contrition, and when and how you ought to make acts of contrition. This will be done after I have told you the third thing necessary for a perfect confession and what to do after you have confessed.

3. The third thing you must do, if you want to make a perfect confession, is to kneel before the priest as before one who represents the Person of Jesus Christ and takes His place. Present yourself to him as a criminal who has outraged the majesty of God, with the full intention of humiliating and confounding yourself, taking God's side against yourself, as against His enemy which you are in so far as you are a sinner, and being ready to arm yourself with His zeal for justice against sin and His infinite hatred for it. Do not fail to bring with you the firm resolve to confess your sins humbly, completely and clearly, without disguises, without excuses, and without trying to shift the blame on to somebody else. But rather accuse yourself as though you were on the point of death. For it would be well to reflect that it is far better to state your sins in the ear of the priest than to bear the shame of them on the day of judgment, before the entire world, and then be damned forever.

Remember that you ought to be willing to accept with cheerfulness and courage the pain and confusion that go with the confession of sins, out of homage for the confusion and torments suffered by our Lord Jesus Christ upon the Cross for those very same sins, as well as to glorify Our Lord by your humiliations, remembering that the more you abase yourself, the more He is exalted in you.

## XV. THANKSGIVING AFTER CONFESSION.

After you have confessed your sins and received pardon for them through the Sacrament of Penance, do not forget to thank Our Lord for having given you so great a grace. When He delivers you from some great sin, either by preventing you from falling into it, or by pardoning you after your fall, even if it is only the smallest venial sin in the world, He is giving you a greater grace, for which you owe Him more thanks, than if He had preserved you from all the plagues, diseases and other afflictions of the body that might beset you. Therefore, thank Him in such words as these, praying Him to preserve you from sin in the future.

Be Thou blessed, O Good Jesus, be Thou blessed a thousand times! May all Thy angels and Thy saints and Thy holy Mother bless Thee now and forever, for having established in Thy Church the holy Sacrament of Penance and for having given us so accessible, so easy and so efficacious a means of wiping out our sins and becoming reconciled with Thee! Be Thou blessed for all the glory that has been and will be given Thee by this sacrament until the end of the world! Blessed be Thou, also, for all the glory Thou hast Thyself rendered to Thy Father by the confession, if one may say such a thing, which Thou didst make to Him of our sins, in the Garden of Olives and by the humiliation, contrition and penance Thou didst bear for them! O my Saviour, engrave deep within me a great hatred, abhorrence and fear of sin, greater than all the other evils on earth and in hell and let me die a thousand deaths rather than offend Thee again.

## XVI. Nature of Contrition.

Contrition is so powerful, so holy and so desirable that a single act of true contrition is capable of wiping out a thousand mortal sins, if they were to be found in the soul.

Contrition is an act of hatred and abhorrence, of sorrow and repentance at the sight of a sin you have committed, because this sin offends God. It is an act of the will, by which you tell God that you desire to hate and detest your sins, that you are filled with shame for having committed them, and that you renounce them earnestly, not for your own interests but because of His. By this I mean, not so much because of the evil, injury and harm you have done to yourself, as because of the dishonor, great sufferings and most cruel death you have caused Our Lord to suffer by your sins.

It is true that the very slightest offense against the infinite good-

ness of God is so detestable that even if you were to weep until the
day of judgment, or even if you were to die of grief over the smallest
of your faults, it would not be enough. Nevertheless, in order to have
contrition it is not absolutely necessary to shed tears, nor to conceive
a pain that can be felt, nor a sensible feeling of anguish over our
sins. Contrition is an interior and spiritual act of the will which is
a spiritual power and not a faculty of sense; therefore, you may make
an act of contrition without any sensible pain. It is enough to assure
Our Lord, with the real will to carry out what you promise, that you
want to hate and detest your sins and to avoid them in future, because they displease Him, and that you shall confess them at your
next confession.

It should also be remembered that contrition is a gift of God and
an effect of grace. Even if you had perfect knowledge of its essence
and applied all the strength of your mind and will to make an act of
contrition, you would never be able to do so if the Holy Spirit did
not give you grace. But you may console yourself with the thought
that this grace will never be refused if you ask for it with humility,
confidence and perseverance, and if you do not wait until the hour
of your death to ask for it. For grace is ordinarily refused, in that
last hour, to those who have neglected it during their lifetime.

Notice, also, that four things are necessary for true contrition. The
first of these is to make restitution, at the earliest possible opportunity
of things belonging to others, if you have anything that it is possible
to return; also to restore the good name of another when you have
robbed him of it by calumny or backbiting.

The second thing is to do everything in your power to bring about
reconciliation with those with whom you are at odds.

The third is to have a firm and constant will, not only to confess
your sins and renounce them, but also to use the necessary remedies
and means to overcome evil habits, and to begin to live a truly Christian life.

The fourth thing is effectively to give up all active and passive
occasions of sin—that is, the occasions you give others to offend God,
as well as those by which you yourself are led into sin.

Such occasions are, for instance: for the promiscuously impure and the adulterous, their partners in evil; for drunkards, their taverns; for gamblers and blasphemers, their games, when they have the habit of swearing and blaspheming or losing very much time and money at these pastimes; women and girls should avoid the least thing that tends to immodesty in dress, as well as excessive novelty and vanity in the matter of fashions; others should give up bad books, improper pictures, the wrong kind of parties and shows, and avoid certain groups, or certain individuals, as well as certain occupations which lead them into sin.

The Son of God Himself says: "If thy hand, or thy foot scandalize thee, cut it off, and cast it from thee. It is better for thee to go into life maimed or lame, than having two hands or two feet, to be cast into hell fire. And if thy eye scandalize thee, pluck it out, and cast it from thee. It is better for thee having one eye to enter into life, than having two eyes to be cast into hell fire" (Matt. 18, 8-9). He is giving you here an absolute commandment under pain of eternal damnation (as the holy Fathers explain these words of Sacred Scripture), to cut off from yourself and entirely renounce all things that are occasions of ruin for yourself and others, even those which are not in themselves evil, even occupations and professions, if you cannot follow them without sinning, as well as things that are most close and dear and precious to you, if these things might occasion the loss of your soul.

Acts of contrition may be made at all times and in every situation, but they should be made particularly at such times as:

1. When you go to confession, for perfect contrition or at the very least attrition, which is imperfect contrition, is a necessary part of Penance. That is why I said above and here repeat, that, before you go to confession and after your examination of conscience, you should ask God for contrition and then try to make genuine acts of sorrow for sin.

2. When you have fallen into sin, so that you may instantly rise again by means of contrition.

3. In the morning and evening, so that if you have committed any sins during the night or in the day, they may be wiped out by contrition, and so you may always keep in God's grace. For this cause I

# HOLY COMMUNION

## XIX. Preparation for Holy Communion.

Our Lord Jesus Christ comes to you in the Blessed Eucharist, with the greatest humility, abasing Himself so far as to take the form and appearance of bread, to give Himself to you, and with the most ardent love that impels Him to give you, in this Sacrament, all the greatest, most dear, and most precious things He has. You also should receive Him in this same Sacrament with the deepest humility and the greatest love. These are the two principal dispositions you should have when you go to Holy Communion.

## XX. Prayer Before Holy Communion.

O Jesus, my light and my sanctification, open the eyes of my spirit and fill my soul with Thy grace, so that I may realize the importance of the action I am about to perform, and do it in a holy and worthy manner for Thy glory.

O my soul, I pray thee, consider attentively how great and marvelous is the action thou art about to perform and how great is the holiness and dignity of Him whom thou art about to receive. Thou art about to partake of the greatest, most important, holiest and most divine action thou couldst ever perform. Thou art about to receive on thy tongue, in thy breast and in the most intimate recesses of thyself, thy God, thy Sovereign Lord and thy Saviour. Yes, thou art about to receive, really and actually, Jesus Himself in His own Person, who lives for all eternity in the bosom of His Father; Jesus Himself, who is the Life, the glory, the riches, the love and the delight of the Eternal Father; the very same Jesus whom so many patriarchs, prophets and just men of the Old Testament desired to see; the same Jesus who dwelt nine months in the womb of the Blessed Virgin, whom she nursed and carried so often in her arms; the same Jesus who was seen walking and living on the earth, eating and drinking with sinners; the same Jesus who was nailed to the Cross.

Thou art about to receive the same body that was bruised and torn and shattered for love of thee; the same blood that was shed upon the ground. Thou art about to receive next to thy own heart the very Heart which was pierced by a lance. Thou art about to receive in thy soul the soul of Jesus, which, when dying on the Cross, He commended into the hands of His Father. What a miracle of wonder! To think that I should receive into myself the very same Saviour who ascended in glory and triumph into heaven, who sits at God's right hand, and will come in power and majesty at the end of time to judge the universe.

O Most Great, Most Admirable Jesus, the angels purer than the sun do not esteem themselves worthy to look upon Thee, to praise Thee and to adore Thee; and today Thou dost not only allow me to contemplate Thee, Thou dost even desire me to take Thee into my heart and soul so that I may then have within myself all divinity, all of the most Holy Trinity and all Paradise. Ah, my Lord, what goodness is this! Whence comes this happiness to me, that the Sovereign King of heaven and earth should desire to take up his abode in me, who am a hell of wretchedness and sin, in order to change me into a paradise of graces and blessings? O my God, how unworthy I am of such a favor! For I do indeed avow, in the presence of heaven and earth, that I far rather deserve to be cast into the bottommost depths of hell, than to receive Thee into my soul, so full of vices and imperfections.

Yet since it pleases Thee, O my Saviour, thus to give Thyself to me, I desire to receive Thee with all possible purity and love and devotion. With this intention, O Good Jesus, I give Thee my soul. Do Thou Thyself prepare me as Thou Thyself dost desire. Destroy in me everything that is contrary to Thee, fill me with Thy divine love and with all the other graces and dispositions with which Thou dost will me to receive Thee.

O Father of Jesus, annihilate in me everything that is displeasing to Thy Son and impart to me a share of Thy love for Him, with which Thou didst receive Him into Thy paternal bosom on the Day of the Ascension.

O Holy Spirit of Jesus, I offer Thee my soul; adorn it with all the graces and virtues necessary to receive our Saviour.

O Mother of my God, may it please thee to let me share the faith and devotion, love and humility, the purity and sanctity with which thou didst so often receive Communion after thy Son's Ascension.

O holy angels and blessed saints, to you also do I offer my soul. Offer it to my Jesus and pray Him to make it ready Himself, and that He may allow me to share in your purity and holiness, and in the very great love you bear for Him.

O my Dear Jesus, I offer Thee all the humility and devotion, all the purity and sanctity, all the love and all the preparation with which Thou hast ever been received by the holy souls that are, and ever have been, on the earth. Would that I had in myself the holy fervor, the divine love of all the angels, of all the seraphim, of all the saints on earth and in heaven, in order the more worthily to receive Thee. O my sweet Love, Thou art all love for me in the Sacrament of love and Thou dost come to me with an infinite love. Alas, why am I not also all love for Thee, that I might receive Thee into a soul entirely transformed into love for Thee.

And yet, O my Lord, nothing is worthy of Thee but Thine own Self, and there is no love by which Thou couldst be worthily received, except thine own divine love. Therefore, in order to receive Thee, not into myself, as being too unworthy of such a thing, but into Thy own Self, with the love which Thou hast for Thyself, I reduce to nothingness before Thee both myself and all that is mine. I give myself to Thee; I beg Thee to take up Thy abode in me, and to establish in me Thy divine love, so that when Thou dost come to me in Holy Communion, Thou mayest be received not into me, but into Thyself, with all the love with which Thou lovest Thyself.

Take special note of the last part of this prayer, for in it is to be found the true disposition with which we are to receive the Son of God in Holy Communion. I have placed it here at the end for the benefit of more spiritual and more advanced souls.

Notice also that it is by no means useless to desire to have in you all the devotion and love of all holy souls, because Our Lord revealed to St. Mechtilde, a nun of the holy Order of St. Benedict, that if,

when she went to Communion, she did not feel any devotion in herself, she should desire to have the devotion and the love of all the
holy souls who had ever received Communion and He would consider her as if she did indeed possess it.

We also read of St. Gertrude, a contemporary of St. Mechtilde, a
member of the same order and of the same monastery, that one day,
when she was about to receive Communion, and did not feel herself
to be as well prepared or as full of devotion as she desired, she turned
to Our Lord and offered Him all the preparation and devotion of all
the saints and of the Blessed Virgin. The result of this was that He
appeared to her and spoke to her the following words: "Now indeed
thou dost appear in my sight, and in the sight of my saints, clad in
just those garments and ornaments that thou hast desired!"

Ah, Lord, how good Thou art thus to accept our good desires as
real effects!

## XXI. Thanksgiving after Holy Communion.

There are three things you should do after Holy Communion:

1. You should prostrate yourself in spirit at the feet of the Son of
God abiding within you, to adore Him and ask His pardon for all
your sins and ingratitude and for having received Him into so unworthy a place, with so little love and so poorly disposed.

2. You must thank Him for having given Himself to you, and invite all things in heaven and on the earth to bless Him with you.

3. Since He has given Himself all to you, you should give yourself
all to Him, and beg Him to destroy in you everything that is contrary to Him and to establish in you forever the empire of His love
and glory.

## XXII. Prayer after Holy Communion.

O Jesus, O my God and my Creator, my Sovereign Lord, what
marvel is this? That I should truly, at this very moment, possess in
my heart the One who resides eternally in the bosom of the Father!
That I should indeed bear within me the same Jesus whom the most
holy Virgin bore within her pure womb! That the most amiable
Heart of Jesus, upon which the well-beloved disciple rested, which

was pierced by the lance upon the Cross, should truly rest in me, so close to my heart! That His most holy soul should be living in my own soul! That the divinity, the Most Holy Trinity, all that is most admirable in God and in heaven should have become merged in me, a most insignificant and most unworthy creature! O God, what mercies, what favors are these! What can I say, what can I do when I behold such great and astonishing marvels?

Ah, my Lord Jesus, let all the powers of my soul and body prostrate themselves before Thy divine majesty to adore Thee and render Thee fitting homage! May heaven and earth, and all the creatures that are in heaven and on earth come now and cast themselves at Thy feet that, with me, they may render to Thee a thousand acts of homage and adoration! But, O my God, how great is my boldness, that I should receive Thee, the Saint of saints, into so vile an abode, with so little love, so little preparation! Forgive me, my Saviour; with all my heart I beg forgiveness for this as well as for all the other sins and acts of ingratitude during my past life.

O Most Gentle and Amiable Jesus, O Thou the only One of my heart, O well-beloved of my soul, O object of all my affections, O my sweet life, my dear soul, my one and only love, my treasure and my glory, my joy and my only hope! My Jesus, what am I to think of Thy bounties, so exceeding great to me? What am I to do for Thy love, when Thou hast wrought so many wonders for me? What thanks can I give Thee? My Saviour, I offer Thee all the blessings that ever have been and ever will be given Thee for all eternity by Thy Father, Thy Holy Spirit, Thy holy Mother, by all Thy angels and by all the holy souls who have ever received Thee in Holy Communion.

My God, may all that is in me be transformed into love and praise of Thee! May Thy Father, Thy Holy Spirit, all Thy angels, Thy saints, and all Thy creatures bless Thee eternally for me! Father of Jesus, Holy Spirit of Jesus, Mother of Jesus, angels of Jesus, saints of Jesus, bless Jesus for me!

O Good Jesus, Thou hast given Thyself to me with a love most great. In this same love I give myself to Thee. I give Thee my body, my soul, my life, my thoughts, my words and my deeds, and all that depends upon me. I give myself all to Thee, that Thou mayest dispose of me and of all that belongs to me, in time and in eternity, according to Thy most adorable will. O my Lord and my God, do Thou Thyself make use of the power of Thy own hand to ravish me from myself, from the world and from all that is not Thyself, that Thou mayest entirely possess me. Destroy all my self-love, my own will and all my vices and unruly desires. Establish in my soul the kingdom of Thy pure love, of Thy holy glory and of Thy divine will, so that I may henceforth love Thee perfectly. And let me love nothing, except in Thee and for Thee.

May all my pleasure be in pleasing Thee, all my glory in glorifying Thee and in leading others to give Thee glory. May my most perfect happiness consist in carrying out Thy holy desires. O Good Jesus, establish in me the reign of Thy humility, Thy charity, Thy gentleness and patience, Thy obedience, Thy modesty, Thy chastity and all Thy other virtues. Clothe me in Thy spirit, Thy thoughts and inclinations, so that I may no longer have any thoughts, desires, or inclinations except Thy own. Finally, annihilate everything in me that is opposed to Thee, and so in me love and glorify Thyself in all the ways Thou dost desire.

O my Saviour, I offer Thee all the persons for whom I am bound to pray, and especially N.N. . . . Destroy in them all that is displeasing to Thee. Fill them with Thy divine love. Accomplish all the plans of Thy divine goodness for their souls, and give to them everything that I have asked for myself.

## XXIII. THREE OTHER ACTS OF ADORATION, OF OBLATION AND OF LOVE.

Since you are on earth only for the purpose of honoring and loving Jesus, and you belong to Him by an infinite number of ties, your chief preoccupation and business in life should be to adore and love Him, and to give and unite yourself without ceasing to Him. Thus, it would be a good thing to add to the preceding morning and evening exercises another quarter of an hour, either before or after noon, to make the three following acts. They are easy to make and take but little time; nevertheless they are most useful, for they gradually and imperceptibly establish those who persevere in their practice, in a very close union and submission, and in a spirit of love and trust for Jesus. They should be made, not with haste or excitement, but in repose and tranquillity of mind. You should dwell upon the one you find most attractive or appropriate. Here is the way to make these acts.

### 1. *Act of Adoration:*

O Great and Admirable Jesus, I adore and honor Thee as my God and Sovereign Lord, upon whom I depend and to whom I belong. I adore and honor Thee with all my power, and in every way possible to me. I offer up to Thee all the adoration and all the honor that ever has been, is now, or ever shall be offered to Thee in heaven or on earth.

Oh, would that I were entirely transformed into adoration and praise of Thee! May heaven and earth adore Thee now with me, and may all that is in heaven and on earth be transformed into adoration and glorification of Thee.

### 2. *Act of Oblation:*

O Jesus, my Lord, I belong of necessity to Thee by a thousand ties, but I also desire to belong to Thee of my own free will. I, therefore, entirely offer, give and consecrate to Thee my body, my soul, my life, my heart and my mind, all my thoughts and my acts, everything that goes with or belongs to my being and my life. I desire that all that ever has been, is now, or ever shall be in me may belong totally, absolutely, exclusively and eternally to Thee. And I make to Thee this oblation and gift of myself, not only with all my strength and power, but also I give myself to Thee in all the virtue of Thy grace, in all the power of Thy spirit, and in all the strength of Thy divine love, which is mine since all that is in Thee is mine. I beg Thee, O my Saviour, do Thou in Thy great mercy Thyself make use of the strength of Thine arm and the power of Thy spirit and love to tear me away from myself and from all that is not of Thee and to possess me perfectly and forever for the glory of Thy Holy Name.

### 3. *Act of Love:*

O Most Amiable Jesus, Thou art all goodness and all love, and all infinitely worthy of love. Thou hast created me to love Thee, and dost ask no other thing of me except that I should love Thee. I desire to love Thee, O my Dearest Jesus, I desire to love Thee with my whole heart, my whole soul and all my strength. I desire, besides, to love Thee to the full extent of Thy divine will, with all the strength of Thy heart, and in all the virtues and all the powers of Thy love. For all these things are mine, and I can make use of them as of things belonging to me, since in giving Thyself to me Thou hast given me all that is Thine. O my Saviour, I desire to annihilate, at any cost, whatever in me is opposed to Thy love. O Good Jesus, I give myself to Thee to love Thee in all the perfection Thou dost ask of me.

Do Thou Thyself remove in me every obstacle in the path of Thy love, and do Thou love Thyself in me in all the ways Thou dost desire, since I give myself to Thee to do and suffer all it may please Thee, purely for Thy love.

O Jesus, I offer Thee all the love that ever has been, is now, and ever shall be borne for Thee in heaven and on earth. Oh, may the whole earth love Thee now with me, and may everything that is in the world be transformed into a pure flame of love for Thee! O Father of Jesus, Holy Spirit of Jesus, Mother of Jesus, Blessed St. Joseph, Blessed St. Gabriel, angels and saints of Jesus, love Jesus for me and repay Him a hundred times over, all the love I should have given Him in my whole life, as well as the debt of love owed to Him by all the wicked angels and all ungrateful men.

## XXIV. Prayer to the Blessed Virgin Mary, Mother of God.

O Blessed Virgin, Mother of God, Queen of Men and Angels, Wonder of Heaven and Earth, I pay thee all possible reverence, according to God's word, according to the desires of thy Only Son, our Lord Jesus Christ. I offer thee my soul and my life, and desire to belong to thee forever and to render thee particular homage and service, in time and in eternity. Mother of Grace and Mercy, I choose thee as Mother of my soul because it pleased God Himself to choose thee for His Mother. Queen of Men and Angels, I accept and recognize thee as my sovereign, in honor of the dependence upon thee, as His Mother, that the Son of my God, my Saviour and my God, willed to have. I give thee, as my sovereign, all possible power, in accordance with God's holy will, over my soul and my life. O Holy Virgin, look upon me as thy very own, and in thy goodness treat me as the subject of thy power, and as the object of thy mercies.

O Fount of Life and Grace, Refuge of Sinners, I have recourse to thee to be delivered from sin and saved from everlasting death. Let me remain under thy patronage and share in thy privileges. May I obtain through Thy powers and privileges, and through my right as thy bondsman, the graces I do not merit to obtain, because of my sins. Let my life's last hour, that hour which will determine my eternity, be in thy hands, in honor of that happy moment of the Incarnation in which God became man and thou didst become the Mother of God.

Virgin and Mother, Holy Temple of the Godhead, Marvel of Heaven and Earth, all thy glories entitle thee to make me thine own. But I desire to belong to thee by my own choice and free will. Therefore, I give myself to thee and to thy Only Son, Jesus Christ, our Lord, and I wish to let no day go by without rendering to Him and to thee some particular homage and some token of my dependence and servitude, in which I desire to die and to live forever. Amen.

# PROFESSIONS OF CHRISTIAN VIRTUES

CHRISTIAN LIFE and sanctity are founded upon eight principal bases, which have been explained in "Part One" of this book. The eight foundations of Christian holiness are faith, hatred of sin, humility, self-denial, renunciation of the world and of all things, the abandonment and submission of oneself to the divine will, the love of Jesus and His most holy Mother, the love of the Cross, and charity to our neighbor. These are the principles of heavenly theology, of Christian philosophy, of the science of the saints, which our Lord Jesus Christ taught by His words and still more by His example. You are obliged to follow these teachings if you wish to be true Christians. You are bound by the solemn profession you made at Baptism.

It is, therefore, very important to renew each day this profession, which is included in the eight following prayers. But be especially careful not to make them in haste, cursorily; take plenty of time, weighing what you say and letting it make a deep impression on your mind. If time does not permit, select one profession, or two, each day, and leave the others until a later hour or even another day. If you have few leisure moments, it would be better to employ only one prayer each day, with firm attention, rather than to use them all in a rush, without the application of mind demanded by the importance of these matters.

## XXV. PROFESSION OF FAITH.

O Jesus, I adore Thee as the author and consummation of faith, as eternal light and the source of all light. I give Thee infinite thanks that it hath pleased Thee, in Thy very great mercy, to call me forth from the shadows of sin and of hell into Thy admirable light, the light of faith. I beg pardon a thousand times over, because in the past I have not acted in accordance with this divine light, and I realize that I have often deserved to be deprived of that light. I protest that I wish to live in future only in accordance with the word of Thy holy Apostle, St. Paul, who tells us that "the just man liveth by faith" (Rom. 1, 17).

To this end I give myself to the spirit of Thy holy faith and, in the power of that spirit as well as in union with the most lively and perfect faith of Thy Blessed Mother, the holy apostles and of all Thy holy Church, I make my profession before heaven and earth. And I am prepared, with the help of Thy grace, to make it also before all the enemies of that same faith. I profess entire and firm belief in all that Thou dost teach us both by Thyself and by Thy holy Church; I desire to give my blood and my life and to suffer all kinds of tortures, rather than to abandon one single item of that faith and adhere in the smallest degree to the errors opposed to it: I desire to live and conduct myself no longer according to the senses, as do the animals, or merely according to human reason like the scientists, but according to the light of faith like true Christians, and according to the maxims of faith, which Thou hast left us in Thy holy Gospel. Preserve these holy resolutions in me, O my Saviour; make them grow and give me the grace to carry them out perfectly for the glory of Thy Holy Name.

## XXVI. Profession of Hatred and Detestation of Sin.

O Jesus, I adore Thee in Thy incomprehensible sanctity and in Thy infinite hatred for sin. From the bottom of my heart I beg Thee to forgive all the sins I have committed in my whole life. I give myself to Thy spirit of sanctity and to Thy spirit of hatred for sin. In this spirit, I make profession of a hatred and detestation of sin more than of death, or of the devil, or hell, and more than of all the most detestable things imaginable; of hatred for sin alone: I profess that I will never grieve over anything but the offenses committed against Thy divine majesty, since there is nothing in the world which deserves to be the object of our enmity and the subject of our sorrows, save only this hellish monster. I profess to hate it so much that, with the help of Thy grace, if I were to behold on one hand all the tortures of earth and of hell, and on the other sin, I would choose the former sooner than the latter. O my God, preserve and increase more and more this hatred in my heart.

## XXVII. PROFESSION OF HUMILITY.

O Most Adorable and Most Humble Jesus, I adore and bless Thee in Thy profound humility. I reduce myself to nothingness and confusion before Thee, when I consider my pride and vanity, and I most humbly beg Thee to forgive me. I give myself with all my heart to Thy spirit of humility. In this spirit, as well as in all the humility in heaven and on earth, plunging down into the depths of my own nothingness, I recognize before the whole world that I am nothing, have nothing, can do nothing, know nothing, and have no value whatsoever, and, therefore, of myself I have no power to resist even the slightest evil, or to do even the smallest good act; that, left to myself, I am capable of all the crimes of Judas, Pilate, Herod, Lucifer, and antichrist, and, in general, of all the sins of earth and of hell, and that, if thou didst not uphold me with Thy very great goodness, I should fall into a hell of all kinds of abominations; that I have deserved the wrath of God, and of all God's creatures, and merit only everlasting punishment. Such is my heritage. This is all I have to boast about—this, and not one thing more.

Therefore, I make profession of the desire to abase myself below all other creatures, considering and esteeming myself, and desiring to be considered and esteemed in all things and in every place, as the least of all men. I profess horror for all praise, honor, and glory, as of a curse and a poison, according to Thy words, O my Saviour, "Woe to you when men shall bless you" (Luke 6, 26). I profess the desire to embrace and love all scorn and humiliation as something that is due to a wretched reprobate such as I am, because I am a sinner and a child of Adam, which makes me, as I learn from Thy Apostle, *natura filii irae* (Eph. 2, 3), a child of wrath and malediction by my own natural condition. I profess the desire to be totally reduced to nothing in my own estimation and in that of others, so that I may no longer have any regard for esteem of, or preoccupation with myself; and also so that no one may see me or esteem me any more than they would something that does not exist, but rather that all may see and esteem Thee only. O Good Jesus, eternal Truth, deeply impress upon me these truths and sentiments, and grant that they may manifest their effects in me by Thy great mercy, for Thy holy glory.

## XXVIII. Profession of Abnegation.

O Jesus my Lord and my God, I adore Thee uttering these words: "If any man will come after me, let him deny himself, and take up his cross, and follow me," and also, "Every one of you that doth not renounce all that he possesseth, cannot be my disciple" (Matt. 16, 24; Luke 14, 33). I give myself to the spirit of light and grace with which Thou didst speak these words, so that I may recognize their importance and show their effects. In this spirit, I recognize three great truths, which exercise upon me a powerful compulsion to renounce myself and all things.

I see that Thou alone art worthy to be, to live, to act, and, therefore, that every other being must be reduced to nothing before Thee. If I am to exist and live in Thee, as it is Thy very great desire that I should do, it is necessary that I emerge from myself and all things, by reason of the corruption which sin has put into me and into all things. And I see that, by my sins, I have deserved to be stripped of all things, even of my own being and of my own life.

Therefore, I make the following profession, in the power of Thy grace, and in union with that same love by which Thou didst desire to live stripped of all worldly things, as well as in the power of the divine spirit by which Thou didst utter these terrible words: "I pray not for the world" (John 17, 9), and these also, in speaking of Thy followers: "They are not of the world, as I also am not of the world" (John 17, 16). In public, and most solemnly do I now profess that I desire henceforth to view the world and abhor it as being excommunicated, damned and another hell, and to renounce entirely and forever all the fame, money and enjoyment the world can offer; that I desire to take no voluntary satisfaction, pleasure or repose of spirit in any of these things, but to employ them as if I used them not, making no account of them, and not attaching myself to them in the least, but only using them through necessity, to obey Thy holy will in all things, and only for Thy pure glory.

I will try to live in this world of the old Adam as though I were not in it, and as one belonging to the other world, that of the new Adam, which is heaven. I resolve to live in this world as if it were a hell, that is, not only with detachment from it, but hatred, opposition and horror towards all that is in it. And I will live in love, desire and longing for the world to come, with patience towards this world, suffering it as Thou dost suffer it, my Saviour, in spite of Thy great hatred of it, and Thy infinite desire to destroy it and reduce it to ashes, as Thou wilt do in the day of Thy wrath.

May I live in the same manner, in the midst of this world, as a truly Christian soul would live if such a soul had been placed in the midst of hell by Thy command. May I remain on earth as one who is not on earth; and let my mind and heart and my conversation be in heaven, that is, in Thyself, for Thou art my heaven, my paradise, my world and my all.

And yet, my Lord, I do desire to progress further, even beyond this. I want to follow Thy word in which Thou dost declare to me that if I wish to come after Thee I must not only renounce all things, but my own self as well. To this end, I give myself to the power of the divine love by which Thou didst reduce Thyself to nothingness, and in union with that same love I profess to renounce entirely and forever everything belonging to myself and to the old Adam; to annihilate at Thy feet, as far as possible, my mind, my self-love, my own will, my life and my being. I most humbly beg Thee to exert Thy divine power to annihilate me, in order to establish Thy kingdom in my heart, that Thou mayest live and reign and work in me in accordance with Thy designs.

I desire no longer to exist, or live, or act, or speak in and by myself, but in Thee and by Thee. I make this profession not only for now, but for all the moments, all the actions of my life, and I beg Thee with my whole heart to look upon my resolution and accept it as if I were making it every minute, and in every one of my acts, and to bring about that I may put this profession into practice for Thy glory, through Thy great goodness and power, so that I may say, together with Thy holy Apostle: "I live, now not I; but Christ liveth in me" (Gal. 2, 20).

## XXIX. Profession of Submission and Abandonment of Self to the Divine Will.

O my Saviour, I adore Thee speaking these divine words: "I came down from heaven, not to do my own will, but the will of him that sent me" (John 6, 38). I adore Thee in the most perfect submission rendered by Thee to all the desires of Thy Father. I implore pardon for all the obstacles I have placed in the way of Thy holy desires. I yield myself to Thy spirit in order to follow Thee, from now on, in the practice of this virtue of submission. In the light of this divine spirit, I recognize that Thy holy will governs and disposes all things, whether by absolute command, or by permission. I also recognize that Thou hast placed me upon the earth only that I may here do Thy divine will. Consequently, this is my end, my centre, my element and my sovereign good.

And so, in union with the most perfect submission which Thou and Thy most holy Mother and all Thy saints render to the divine will, I profess to renounce entirely and forever all my wishes and inclinations. I desire never to have any other will but Thine, and to fix my eyes always upon it, and follow it wheresoever it leads, as perfectly as possible, in time and in eternity. I prefer to die, and to suffer a thousand hells, rather than to do anything against Thy most lovable will; and I wish in life and in death, in this world or the next, no other treasure, no other glory of joy or satisfaction, no other paradise but Thy most adorable will. O most dear will of my God, Thou art henceforth my heart, my soul, my life, my strength, my riches, my delight, my honor, my crown, my empire and my sovereign good. Live and reign in me perfectly and forever.

## XXX. Profession of Love for Jesus and Mary.

O Most Amiable Jesus, and dearest Mary, Mother of Jesus, I honor you in all your perfections and in the intensity of your great mutual love. I beg a thousand pardons for having loved you so little up to now, and for having so often offended you. I surrender myself totally to your divine love. And in this same love, as well as in all the love in heaven and earth, recognizing that I am on earth only that

I may love and glorify you, that I am obliged to do so for an infinite number of reasons. I profess my constant desire to employ myself with all my strength in loving and serving you; to desire to do all that I shall ever do, as perfectly as I can, for love of you; to desire rather to be annihilated than to give away, to anything whatever, the slightest spark of the love I owe to you; to place all my happiness and delight in honoring, serving and loving you; to desire to cause you to be loved and glorified by as many souls as I can and in all the different ways that lie in my power.

## XXXI. Profession of Love for the Cross.

O Jesus, my dear crucified Love, I adore Thee in all Thy sufferings. I beg Thy forgiveness for all the failings of which I have been guilty in the afflictions it has pleased Thee to send me. I give myself to the spirit of Thy holy Cross, and in this spirit, as well as in all the love in heaven and on earth, I embrace, with my whole heart and for love of Thee, all the crosses of body and of spirit that shall come to me. I profess to seek all my glory, my riches and my satisfaction in the Cross, that is, in humiliations, privations and sufferings, saying with St. Paul: *Mihi autem absit gloriari nisi in cruce Domini nostri Jesu Christi* (Gal. 6, 14). "God forbid that I should glory, save in the Cross of our Lord Jesus Christ." "For my part, I solemnly profess that I desire no other paradise in this world but the Cross of my Lord Jesus Christ."

## XXXII. Profession of Charity Towards Your Neighbor.

O Jesus, God of love and of charity, I adore Thee in all the excesses of Thy divine charity. I beg Thy forgiveness for my failings in this virtue, which is the queen of all virtues. I surrender myself to Thy spirit of charity. And in this spirit, as well in all the charity of Thy holy Mother and of all the saints, I profess never to hate anything, except sin; to desire to love all men, for love of Thee; never to think or do any evil to anybody, but always to think and judge and say and do what is good, in regard to everybody; to excuse and bear the faults of others; to put a favorable interpretation upon things; to have compassion for the spiritual and bodily woes of my neighbor and to conduct myself towards each and every one with all gentleness, benignity and charity. O Eternal Charity, I give myself to Thee. Annihilate everything in me that is opposed to Thee, and establish Thy kingdom in my heart and in the hearts of all Christians.

# PART THREE

*Devotional Exercises to Be Done Each Day*
*to Live a Christian and Saintly Life and*
*to Make Jesus Reign in Your Soul*

# Part Three

## DEVOTIONAL EXERCISES TO BE DONE EACH DAY TO LIVE A CHRISTIAN AND SAINTLY LIFE AND TO MAKE JESUS REIGN IN YOUR SOUL

### SANCTIFICATION OF YOUR DAILY ACTIONS

I. OBLIGATION AND METHOD TO PERFORM YOUR ACTIONS DEVOUTLY.

I have already explained to you, in "Part Two" of this book, the way to begin and end each day well. My present purpose is to offer you a few practices by which it will be very easy, with the grace of Our Lord, to sanctify every one of the actions which you are obliged to do not only as a religious but also as a Christian. For I cannot repeat too often that it is most important for everyone to understand that not only religious but all Christians no matter what their state in life, are obliged, as members of Jesus Christ, to live the life of their Head, that is, a thoroughly holy life, and to perform all their actions, whether great or small, in a Christian manner. What do I mean when I say in a Christian manner? I mean in a divine and holy manner, in the manner which characterized Jesus Christ in everything that He did. I mean with the spirit of Jesus Christ, with His holy and divine dispositions.

You are obliged by countless reasons to act in this way, and in the first part of this book I presented some of the most compelling of these reasons. But in addition, I beg you to return often to the consideration of the fact that Jesus Christ is our Head and all of us are His members, and that our union with Him is much more perfect and intimate than that of the members of a natural body with their head, because the principle of this union is His grace. Hence you are obliged to do everything in Him and for Him; for Him because the members belong to Him, because everything in the members belongs to the

151

Head; in Him, that is, in His spirit, dispositions and intentions, because the members must follow and imitate their Head, and must be animated only by His spirit, with no other dispositions and intentions but His.

This is a matter of the highest importance, because the greater part of your life is taken up with a succession of repeated little acts such as drinking, eating, sleeping, reading, writing, conversing with one another and so on. Now by all these little actions, if you would only set your mind on doing them well, you might give great glory to God and make rapid progress along the road of His love. By your neglect of these little things God is deprived of the glory you owe Him, and you lose the graces He would otherwise give you.

For this reason St. Paul exhorts you to do everything, whether you eat or drink or do any other thing, no matter how insignificant or trifling, for the glory of God in the name of our Lord Jesus Christ (Col. 3, 17). What does it mean, to do what you do in the name of Jesus Christ? It means to do it in the spirit of Jesus Christ, with the dispositions and intentions with which Jesus Christ performed the same actions that you perform, while He was on earth, with which He would yet again perform them, were He in your place now. Whoever acts in the name of another has to act, as far as possible, in the spirit of the person represented, that is, with his dispositions and intentions, just as he himself would act, if he were present.

You may object: Who is able to know the dispositions and intentions with which Jesus Christ performed His actions? By way of answer, let me tell you two things:

1. The light of faith reveals to us that His dispositions were humility, meekness, patience, charity towards others, recollection of God and all kinds of virtue: His intentions were to love His Eternal Father, to glorify Him, to give Him pleasure and to carry out His divine will.

2. It is not even necessary to know them; it is sufficient to have the desire and intention of performing your actions in the spirit of Jesus Christ, with His dispositions and intentions. And so it is really easy, with the help of God's grace, to do all that you do in a Christian and holy manner.

Make a point, then, of lifting up your heart to Jesus when you begin any action or at least any of your most important acts, and of assuring Him: (1) that you renounce yourself, your self-love and your own mind, that is, all your own personal dispositions and intentions; (2) that you surrender yourself to Him, to His holy love and to His holy spirit, in your desire to perform your various acts with the dispositions and intentions with which He performed His. By this means, you will give Him very much glory in everything that you do, and you will make great progress, in a short time, along the road of His grace.

Now turn to the practice of this holy exercise, as set forth in divers ways in the following prayers. These may be uttered with the lips or with the heart alone, now in one way, now in another. You do not have to follow the exact words given here, but need only to keep to the meaning and substance of the words.

## II. Prayers to Sanctify the Performance of All Your Actions.

1. O Jesus, I renounce myself, my own mind, my self-love and all that pertains to me. I give myself to Thee, to Thy holy spirit and Thy divine love, in order to carry out what I am about to do through Thee, under the guidance of Thy spirit and Thy pure love.

2. O Jesus, as far as it is possible to me, I cast at Thy feet my own mind, my own self-love, my own dispositions and intentions, everything that is mine. I give myself entirely to Thee; destroy me Thyself and take up Thy abode in me, so that it may be Thou that speakest and workest in me, according to Thy spirit and Thy dispositions and intentions.

3. O Good Jesus, I surrender myself totally to Thy divine power and Thy holy love. Draw me out entirely, if it please Thee, from myself, hide me in Thyself and absorb me into Thyself that I may no longer live or speak or act save in Thee and by Thee and for Thee.

4. O Good Jesus, I offer Thee this action in honor of the action Thou didst perform in the world. I desire, if it be pleasing to Thee, to do this in union with the same dispositions and intentions as those with which Thou didst perform all Thy holy actions.

5. O my God, since it is true that Thou art always with us, and

that Thou dost operate in all our works, grant, I beseech thee, that I may also be always with Thee, and perform each action with the same intentions as Thou, in union with the same love, perfections, and sanctity with which Thou dost now perform it with me.

6. O Good Jesus, let there be nothing for me, nothing for self-love, nothing for the world; but all for Thee, O my Saviour, all for Thy glory, and all for Thy pure love.

### III. How to Sanctify a Prolonged Activity, or One Requiring the Full Attention of the Mind.

When you have to perform some action which by its long duration or its demands upon your concentration threatens to distract you from God's presence, make a point of turning to your good angel, to the other angels and saints, and to the most Holy Virgin, before you begin and say to them: "Angels of Jesus and His saints, Mother of Jesus;" and say this with the intention of asking them to love and glorify Jesus on your behalf as long as you are engaged in the performance of this action.

### IV. Prayer Before Conversation.

O Jesus, I give myself to Thee. Inspire my lips with things Thou dost wish me to speak and grant that all my words pay homage to Thy holy words.

O Jesus, may all my conversations be consecrated to the honor of Thy divine converse with men on earth. Grant me, if it please Thee, a share in the humility, meekness, modesty, and charity which marked Thy friendly discourse with persons of every type.

### V. Prayer Before Meals.

O my God, there are many people who have nothing to eat, and yet they have not offended Thee as much as I. But by an excess of charity, Thou dost give this meal to me rather than to them. My dearest Lord, I desire to eat it for love of Thee, because it is Thy holy will. I wish to partake of this food in union with the same love with which Thou dost give it to me; and I desire, if it please Thee, that all the motions

I shall make, taking each bite, may be so many acts of praise and love for Thee.

O Jesus, I offer Thee this repast in honor of the meals Thou didst take on earth. I renounce all self-love, and I desire to eat now in union with the love which subjected Thee to the need of eating and drinking, and in union with all the holy dispositions and intentions with which Thou didst partake of earthly nourishment.

### VI. Prayer Before Recreation.

O Jesus, I offer Thee this recreation in honor of and in union with the holy recreation and divine rejoicings of Thy mortal life in company with the Eternal Father, the Holy Spirit, Thy Blessed Mother and the angels and saints. Referring to Thyself, Thou didst say: *Delectabar per singulos dies, ludens coram eo omni tempore, ludens in orbe terrarum; et deliciae meae esse cum filiis hominum.* "I was delighted every day, playing before him at all times; playing in the world. And my delights were to be with the children of men" (Prov. 8, 30-31). The holy Gospel tells us that Thou didst rejoice in the Holy Spirit, and didst command the apostles to rest after work.

### VII. Prayer for a Journey.

O Jesus, may all my journeys, my travels, my goings and comings, and my every step, give glory to the various journeys, the travels up and down, the goings and comings and every step of Thy blessed feet on earth.

O Jesus, may every movement of my eyes, lips, feet and of all my exterior and interior senses pay homage to the divine use of Thy deific eyes, Thy sacred lips, Thy blessed hands, Thy holy feet, and all Thy outward and inward senses.

### VIII. Prayer to Be Said While at Work.

O Jesus, may this work I am doing give honor to Thy holy labors in the world. Please impart Thy blessing to my activity.

## IX. Prayer Before Hearing a Sermon.

O Jesus, I offer this sermon in honor of Thy sublime preaching upon earth. I desire to take part in this function in honor of and in union with the profound devotion of Thy holy Mother as she listened to Thy divine teachings.

O Good Jesus, grant that I may share in the love, attention and devotion with which Thou dost hear the pronouncements of the Father. He is ever speaking to Thee, and Thou dost listen most attentively to Him, and dost most faithfully carry out all His counsels and instructions.

## X. Prayer Before Spiritual Reading.

There are many holy activities which can help souls to maintain their position and to make progress in divine love, but one of the most excellent is spiritual reading, of which I have already spoken in "Part One." Hence, with all the earnestness I can muster, I renew my advice and exhortation to you never to let a day go by without reading, for at least half an hour, from some good book. Now in order to do this reading in the right way, in addition to following suggestions already made, you should also call to mind what is related of the Son of God in the fourth chapter of St. Luke's Gospel, namely that having entered into the synagogue upon the Sabbath day, He took up a book and read (Luke 4, 16). Offer Him your reading in honor of His, as follows:

O Jesus, I offer Thee this reading in honor of Thy holy reading; I wish to read in union with the same love, and the same dispositions and intentions with which Thou didst read. I give myself to Thee. By means of this reading, work in me all that Thou desirest to operate for Thy glory.

## XI. Prayer Before Writing.

You should recall that several Doctors of the Church tell us that Our Lord wrote letters to Abagar, King of Edessa. You should offer Him your action in writing, in honor of His, thus:

O good Jesus, I offer Thee this action in honor of Thy holy

writing. I desire to do this in union with the charity and other dispositions and intentions with which Thou didst write. May all the words and letters that I write be so many praises and blessings of Thee.

O my Dear Jesus, guide my spirit and my pen, that I may write nothing except what is of Thee, by Thee and for Thee. During the time I am writing upon this paper, do Thou please write upon my heart the law of Thy divine love and the virtues of Thy holy life.

## XII. Prayer Before Giving Alms.

O Jesus, it is for Thy pure love, in honor of and in union with Thy charity towards the poor, that I desire to make this donation.

## XIII. Prayer to Be Said When Visiting the Poor, the Sick or the Afflicted.

O Jesus, I offer Thee this action in honor of and in union with Thy great love as Thou didst come from heaven to earth, to visit the poor and to console the sorrowful. I give myself to Thee to console and assist the afflicted and the poor as much as Thou dost will me to do. Grant that I may share Thy exceeding great charity towards afflicted mankind.

## XIV. Prayer When Fasting, or Doing Penance or Mortification.

O Good Jesus, I offer Thee this act in honor of Thy divine justice and Thy holy Passion. I desire to suffer this privation, this penance and mortification purely for Thy love in union with that same love with which Thou didst bear so many and such extraordinary privations and mortifications on earth, as well as in satisfaction for my sins, and to accomplish Thy divine design for my soul.

## XV. Prayer When Performing Some Act of Humility.

O Most Humble Jesus, I offer Thee this act with all similar acts that ever were or ever shall be performed in honor of Thy holy humiliations and those of Thy Blessed Mother. O Good Jesus, destroy all pride and vanity in me, and cause Thy divine humility to reign in their stead.

### XVI. Prayer Before Doing a Charitable Act.

O Most Charitable Jesus, I offer Thee this action, with all the others like it that ever were, are now, or ever shall be performed, in honor of and in union with Thy infinite charity. Destroy all self-love and self-interest in me, and establish in me the kingdom of Thy divine charity.

### XVII. Prayer Before Doing an Act of Obedience.

O Most Obedient Jesus, I offer Thee this act of obedience to my superior, to my father or mother, or this act of submission to the rules and obligations of my state in life, in honor of Thy most perfect obedience, and in honor of the subjection which Thou didst will to undergo not only to the rules and laws of Thy Father, but also of men, and even of Thy enemies. Eliminate my own judgment and my own will, and cause me to have no longer any other will but thine and the will of those who represent Thee in my regard.

### XVIII. Prayer for all Other Actions.

In all other actions, of every sort, you may follow the method indicated in the foregoing prayers, for there is hardly any act or virtuous practice possible in human and Christian daily life that does not find its counterpart among the actions of our Lord Jesus Christ on earth. And if you wish to sanctify your actions, you should offer them to Him in honor of and in union with His own.

I have suggested these little practices to point out the way you must follow in order to walk ever before God and live in the spirit of Jesus. This spirit will inspire many other methods in your heart if you make a point of giving yourself to our Blessed Lord at the beginning of everything you do. For I beg you to note carefully that the one essential practice, the secret of secrets, the devotion of devotions, is to be attached to no one practice or exercise of devotion in particular, but to take care, in all your exercises and activities, to surrender yourself to the holy spirit of Jesus, with humility, confidence and detachment from all things.

When you are thus free from attachment to your own way of looking at things, or to your own devotions and tastes, He will have complete power and freedom to act in you according to His holy will and to arouse in your soul whatever dispositions and devout sentiments He desires, and to lead you by whatever paths He may choose. After you have given yourself to Him, you should progress and be faithful in cultivating the good sentiments and dispositions He will arouse in you, and in following His impulsions, inspirations, and guidance. If He inspires you to make use of the above and the following exercises, and if they prove to be a source of grace and blessings to you, well and good! If He attracts you to other more perfect ways, or methods in which you find more grace and devotion, follow His attractions with simplicity and humility.

XIX. The Practice of Offering all Actions to Jesus is the Real Way to Remain Constantly in God's Presence.

By means of the practice I have explained, and by frequent lifting of your mind and heart to God, your whole life will belong to Jesus; all your acts will give Him glory, you will walk ever before Him and will be always in His presence. For this is the true secret and the easiest way of keeping always in the presence of God and of living a life that is a single uninterrupted act of love for Him.

Of course I know that if a person is in God's grace, and offers Him in the morning everything that he may do in the course of the day, all his actions (so long as they are not evil in themselves), will give glory to God even if he should not think of God at all for the rest of that day. But Our Lord offered up for you to His Father all the acts He performed on earth, and never allowed a moment to go by in which He did not think of you and love you; consequently it would show very little gratitude and love for Him if you were to think of Him only once or twice a day. Indeed, if you really loved our most amiable Saviour, you should find all your happiness in thinking of Him, and in frequently lifting up your mind and heart to Him. This may be done without the least trouble or mental strain, with great ease and most pleasantly. With His precious grace, which He will never fail to give you, together with the exercise of a little care and fidelity on your part, you can soon develop this holy practice into a habit so strong that it becomes almost second nature to you.

I can prove it by telling you in all truth that I know a certain ecclesiastic (May his name be written in the Book of Life!) who by frequent use of this exercise has reached the point where it is easy for him, even when at table, actually to make nearly as many acts of love for Jesus as he takes mouthfuls of food. He accomplishes this not only without mental strain or any injury or inconvenience to his health, but even with so much ease and so readily that it does not prevent him from conversing, enjoying fitting recreation, and being specially charitable towards other persons. I am not telling you this in order to make you do as much yourself, for some would meet this suggestion with loud complaints that I was asking them something far too difficult. I only mention it to show you how strong a holy habit can become, and how wrong the world is in imagining a thousand difficulties and repellent obstacles where there is really nothing but pleasantness and delight.

## XX. Employing the Actions and Sufferings of Others for the Glory of God.

Not only is it possible, but it is necessary to make a holy use of every personal occurrence for the glory of Our Lord, but also of everything that ever has happened, is happening now, or ever shall happen in the world. You can do this because it is within your power to make use of what is your own. Now, as has been said, St. Paul assures you that *all things* without a single exception, past, present or to come, *belong to you* (1 Cor. 3, 22). You must make use of them because you are bound to utilize and employ everything that is yours for the glory of Him Who gave you everything.

Hence, when you perform some act, the love and zeal you are bound to have for the glory of Our Lord ought to incite you not only to offer Him this action, but also to unite it with all other actions, past, present and future, similar to the one being performed, to offer and consecrate them to His glory together with your own act.

For instance, when you are at work, consider how many people there have been, are now, and shall be in the world who did, are doing, and will do the same work as you, only they neglect to offer it to God. Unite all that work with your own and offer it up to Jesus as belonging to you, in honor of His labors. Do the same thing whenever a trial or affliction, whether of body or mind, comes upon you, as well as whenever you engage in any mental or physical activity.

This is the way you ought to take holy advantage of all things for God's glory. This is the way you ought to carry on and express in yourself Christ's exceeding great zeal for the glory of His Father, making use of all things to glorify Him. His zeal for His Father's glory was infinitely great, and every action that ever was, or is, or shall be done on earth was just as present to Him as what He was doing then, and He looked upon them all as His own, given to Him by the Omnipotent Father. Therefore, you can not doubt that He consecrated all the acts of mankind together with His own, to the glory of His Father. He compensated for the deficiencies of men and made use of every gift to glorify His Father. What I have said of actions may also be applied to sorrow and suffering, since the Son of God left nothing on earth unemployed for the glory of His Father. Let us enter into His sentiments and dispositions, and unite ourselves with Him in His sacred employment of all things to honor His Father; allow nothing to slip by, whether good or evil, in yourself or in others, but take advantage of everything to lift up your heart to Jesus, and to make everything that occurs a means of glorifying Him, just as He Himself makes all things cooperate for your good and utilizes everything for the advantage of your soul.

## XXI. In Time of Affliction.

As soon as any affliction of body or spirit visits you, go at once and cast yourself down at the feet of our Blessed Lord Who said: "Him that cometh to me I will not cast out" (John 6, 37), and "Come to me, all you that labor and are burdened: and I will refresh you" (Matt. 11, 28). Adore His divine will. Humble yourself before Him at the sight of your sins, which are the cause of all your trials; offer Him your affliction; ask Him for the grace to bear it in a holy manner, and reconcile yourself with Him by means of Confession and Holy Communion. For if you are not in His grace and love, even though you were to suffer martyrdom, it would be useless both for God's glory and your own sanctification. You are robbing God of the very great honor you might give Him in time of tribulation, if you were only in fit condition, and you yourself suffer the loss of incalculable riches of grace and glory.

## XXII. PRAYER TO JESUS IN TIME OF AFFLICTION.

O Jesus, my Lord, I cast myself down at Thy feet, adoring, blessing and loving Thy Divine Providence with my whole heart, in all that it ordains and permits now and ever in regard to me and my affairs. For what Thou dost ordain and dost permit, O great God, are to be equally adored and loved. Yes, my Saviour, may Thy holy will be done in all things, everywhere, in spite of the weakness of my own will. May Thy divine ordinances and permissions be forever adored and glorified.

I admit, O my God, and I confess before heaven and earth, that Thou art just and that I fully deserve this suffering a hundredfold for the least of my sins. And so, in spite of the reluctance of my own mind, I desire to embrace this affliction to the full extent of my will, in homage to Thy divine justice, in submission to Thy holy will, in honor of Thy extreme sufferings on earth, in satisfaction for my sins, to accomplish Thy designs for me, and as something which comes from Thy beloved hand and from Thy Heart overflowing with love for me.

Blessed be Thou, Good Jesus, because Thou art pleased to give me the opportunity to suffer something for love of Thee. Grant that I may share in the love, humility, patience, meekness and charity of Thy Passion; and give me grace to endure all things for Thy glory and for Thy pure love.

## XXIII. PRAYER AGAINST TEMPTATIONS.

When some bad thought or other kind of temptation comes to you, do not become upset, but turn with confidence of mind and heart to Jesus. Humble yourself deeply before Him and ask for strength.

"O my Saviour, I confess that my sins fully deserve that Thou shouldst permit me to be harassed by all sorts of temptations, nay even vanquished and overwhelmed by them. I admit that, of myself,

I have no strength to resist the slightest temptation, and that if Thou didst not sustain me now and always, I should fall into a terrifying hell of sin. Alas, my Jesus, what frightful danger confronts me now! I behold myself on the edge of the abyss and the jaws of the lion of hell open wide to devour me. I am on the point of losing Thy grace, of being cut off from Thee, of being led away by Satan as a slave and, most terrible of all, of crucifying Thee with the utmost cruelty and infinite dishonor, if I allow myself to be overcome by this temptation. O dearest Lord, prevent this. Free me from this danger, give me the grace and strength to turn this temptation to good use and to make it an occasion for glorifying Thee. My God, with all my might I renounce the evil spirit, sin, and everything that displeases Thee. I surrender my will to Thee; take it into Thy safe-keeping and do not allow me to take sides, in any way, with the will of Thine enemies. My Saviour, I conjure Thee by Thy holy Passion, by Thy boundless goodness and mercy to grant me the favor of suffering all the ignominies and torments in the world, and indeed, of dying a thousand deaths rather than ever offend Thee."

# THE HOLY SACRIFICE OF THE MASS

XXIV. Manner of Assisting Worthily at the Holy Sacrifice of the Mass.

To assist worthily at the Holy Sacrifice of the Mass and to give God the glory He deserves, there are four things you must do.

1. As soon as you leave the house to go to Mass, you should realize that you are going not merely to attend or watch, but actually to perform an action more holy and divine, greater and more sublime, more noble and admirable than any other in heaven or on earth. Consequently, you must perform it in a holy and divine manner, that is, with thoroughly holy and divine dispositions, with great care and attention of mind and heart, and with the realization that what you are going to do is more vitally important to you than anything else in the world. I stress the words "you are going to perform" because all Christians are one with Jesus Christ, the Sovereign Priest, and, therefore, they share in His divine Priesthood. Hence, they are called priests in Holy Scripture (I Peter 2, 9). The faithful are consequently entitled not only to assist at the Holy Sacrifice of the Mass, but also to participate in the action of the priest, that is, to offer with him and with Jesus Christ Himself the Sacrifice that is offered to God on the altar.

2. Upon entering the Church, you should profoundly humble yourself in spirit, considering yourself most unworthy to enter the house of God, to appear before His face, and to take part in so great a mystery, —a mystery which contains in itself all the mysteries and all the wonders of heaven and earth. Remember your nothingness and your sins, for which you ought to enter into a spirit of penance, humiliation and contrition at the beginning of the Mass, accusing yourself of your sins with the priest at the *Confiteor,* asking God's forgiveness, and begging Him to give you the grace and strength to keep yourself free from sins in future. To make reparation, offer your Heavenly Father the Holy Sacrifice of the Precious Body and Blood of His Son,

once offered to Him on the Cross, and now about to be offered to Him on the altar.

3. Having adored our Lord Jesus Christ, Who becomes present on the altar to receive the homage and adoration we owe Him, pray that He, who changes the base and earthly nature of bread and wine into His body and blood, may also change and transform the heaviness, frigidity and dryness of our earthly and arid hearts into the ardor, tenderness and vitality of the holy dispositions of His divine Heart. Then remember that all Christians are one with Jesus Christ, as members with their Head, and, therefore, share all His qualities. Recollect that Jesus Christ consummates this sacrifice as both Priest and Victim at the same time, so all present must likewise attend Mass both as priests and sacrificers, to offer up one and the same Sacrifice with Jesus Christ, the Sovereign Priest, and as hosts and victims, forming one Host with Jesus Christ just as they form one Priest with Him, one Host to be immolated with Jesus Christ, to the glory of God.

Thus you participate in the divine priesthood of Jesus Christ. As a Christian and member of Jesus Christ you bear the name and character of priest; therefore you ought to act in that capacity and exercise the rights it confers upon you, the right of offering up to God, together with the priest and with Jesus Christ Himself, the Sacrifice of the divine body and blood of God the Son in Holy Mass, and to offer it as far as possible, with the very dispositions with which it is offered by Jesus Christ, His Son, with holy and divine dispositions. What holy and filial dispositions! What humility, what purity and sanctity, what detachment from self and from all things, what attentiveness to God, what charity towards man and what love towards His Father! Unite yourself in desire and intention with these sublime dispositions. Pray to Jesus to implant them in you, enabling you to offer up this divine Sacrifice with Him in union with the dispositions of His adorable Heart.

Unite yourself also to the intentions for which Christ offers His endless Sacrifice. There are five principal intentions. The first is to honor God the Father in all that He is in Himself and in all things, and to pay Him fitting honor, glory, and love. The second is to render the All-bountiful Father a tribute of thanksgiving that measures up to His goodness and all the benefits He has ever bestowed on all His creatures. The third is to make complete satisfaction for all the sins of the world. The fourth is to perfect the fulfilment of all His designs and His holy will. The fifth intention is to beseech Divine Providence to grant you the things necessary to all men, both for their bodies and their souls. So, in conformity with these intentions of Jesus Christ, you ought to offer the Holy Sacrifice of the Mass as follows:

(1) In honor of the Most Holy Trinity, in honor of all that Jesus Christ is in Himself, in all His states, mysteries, qualities, virtues, actions and sufferings, and in honor of all that He is and achieves whether through mercy or justice, in His Blessed Mother, in all the angels and saints, in His whole Church Militant, Suffering and Triumphant, and in all creatures of heaven, earth and hell.

(2) In thanksgiving to God for all the benefits and graces whether temporal or eternal, imparted to the sacred humanity of His Son, to the most Blessed Virgin, to all angels and men, to all creatures and especially to yourself.

(3) In satisfaction to His divine justice for all your sins and for all the sins of the world, especially for those of the poor souls in Purgatory.

(4) For the fulfilment of all His designs and desires, especially those He entertains on your behalf.

(5) To obtain from His goodness all the graces necessary to you and to all mankind, so that He may be served and honored by all creatures with the perfection He demands of each one.

All this you should perform in the Christian role of priest. But over and above that, in the role of host, when you offer Jesus Christ to God in Holy Mass as a victim you are obliged to offer yourself also, like Him, as a victim. Better still, pray that Jesus Christ will enter into you and draw you into Himself to unite and incorporate you with Himself as host, to sacrifice you with Him for the glory of His Father.

The Host to be sacrificed must be slain and consumed by fire; so you must implore Our Lord to make you die to yourself, to your passions, to your self-love and to all that displeases Him, that He may consume you in the sacred fire of His divine love, and cause your whole life to be henceforth a perpetual sacrifice of praise, glory and love for His Eternal Father and for Him.

4. You should prepare yourself for communion—if not sacramental, at least spiritual communion. Consider that our Lord Jesus Christ, Who loves you beyond measure, becomes present in the Sacrifice not only to be with you, but to be with you in intimate friendship and to impart to you His gifts and graces. And what is far more, He wills to be actually within you. He has a most ardent desire to dwell in your very heart, and give Himself to you in sacramental or spiritual communion. Therefore, you ought to prepare yourself to receive Him by fostering dispositions necessary to communicate sacramentally, namely, sentiments of humility and love. Humble yourself before Him, considering yourself most unworthy to receive Him; nevertheless, since He so earnestly desires to have communion with you, you must also long to receive Him and invite Him, by countless acts of love, to enter your heart and to live and reign in you perfectly.

5. Finally, after having thanked Our Lord for the graces He has given you in Holy Mass, leave the church with a firm resolution to spend the day well in His service, with the thought that you must henceforth be a host at the same time living and dead: dead to all that is not God, living in God and for God, totally consecrated and sacrificed purely to the glory and love of God. Declare to Our Lord that you will be a victim of His love, and that you offer yourself to Him to do and suffer, for that end, whatever may please Him. Pray that He may accomplish this in you by His very great mercy; ask Him to give you the grace to lift up your heart to Him frequently during the day, to do everything for His glory, and choose to die rather than offend Him. For all these intentions, ask Him to give you His holy blessing.

Such is the way you should make use of so divine an event as the Most Holy Sacrifice of the Mass. If you do not feel the need of so many intentions to keep your mind devoutly occupied during Mass, select the most helpful and inspirational. To assist you to acquire greater facility in the use of these exercises, I now present them in the form of prayers, which you are to use not in haste and confusion, but in a leisurely and recollected state of mind and heart, if you want to reap fruits for God's glory.

## XXV. Prayer at the Beginning of Holy Mass.

O my God and Sovereign Lord, behold me prostrate at the feet of Thy mercy. Deign to look with kindness upon so insignificant a creature, who recognizes and confesses before heaven and earth, that he is the most unworthy and ungrateful of all creatures.

O Father of mercies, I accuse myself before Thee, before the angels and saints, of all the lapses of my past life, all the offenses I have committed against Thy divine majesty, my great coldness in Thy ardent love, my neglect in Thy holy service and in following Thy inspirations, and countless other faults of which Thou well knowest me to be guilty. O my God, when I consider that Thy well-beloved Son, whom I am here to adore, gave me even the first moment of His life, I account myself exceedingly guilty for not having consecrated to Thee the very first use of reason given me by Thy divine majesty.

O my Lord Jesus, Thou didst spend all Thy days in poverty and suffering and didst end them on the Cross for love of me. Thou didst spend Thy whole life in uninterrupted works of ardent and exceeding great charity towards my soul. Yet I, treating my days and my life as something all my own, spend them ordinarily in useless or indifferent neglect, and often in offending Thy divine majesty. O my Saviour, grant that I may detest all my faults, since the very least of them was a reason why Thou didst will to be born in a stable and die on the Cross to expiate even that fault before the justice of Thy Father.

O my Jesus, the very least of Thy humanly divine and divinely human actions, repeated so often for my benefit during the thirty-four years of Thy life on earth, possesses such value and merit, that even if it had taken place no more than once, it could rightfully claim that my whole life should be devoted to doing Thy will, as a mark of gratitude and thanksgiving and by way of repayment to Thy divine majesty. Yet I do not do this. On the contrary, it would seem that I was born for the sole purpose of offending and insulting Thee. O what ingratitude! What infidelity! How I detest my treachery! How

sorry and ashamed I am, Most Lovable Jesus, of having been so unfaithful and ungrateful, and of having corresponded so miserably with
so great and strong a love as Thine for me! My God, I cast all my
sins into the stream of Thy Precious Blood, into the abyss of Thy
mercies, into the fire of Thy divine love. Cleanse me and utterly consume my sins. Atone for all my failings, O Good Jesus, and accept in
satisfaction this most holy Sacrifice of the Precious Body and Blood,
which Thou didst offer on the Cross, and I now offer Thee in
reparation.

O my sweet Saviour, the disordinate love of myself and of the
world is the source of all my offenses. Forever and with all my might
I renounce that love. O Most Amiable Jesus, annihilate in me all
earthly affections and establish in me the kingdom of Thy divine
love.

## XXVI. Prayer During Holy Mass.

O Jesus, my Lord and my God, Thou dost descend upon this altar
that I may contemplate and adore Thee, love and glorify Thee, to
recall to my memory the great love that caused Thee to suffer and
die for me on the Cross. O great God, I adore Thee and glorify Thee
to the full extent of my limited powers. O abyss of love, O infinite
goodness, O immense charity, would that I were all love for Thee!
O Most Beloved, Most Loving and Most Lovable Jesus, when will the
time come when I shall love Thee perfectly? O ye Seraphim, angels
and saints of paradise, give me your love, that I may employ its
ardor to love my Jesus. O ye men, O creatures capable of love, give
me all your hearts that I may sacrifice them to my Saviour. O loving
Redeemer, would that I possessed all the love of heaven and earth!
With what willingness would I direct it all to Thee! O Thou Well-
beloved Son of the Eternal Father, O Thou treasure and delight of
heaven and earth, how art Thou now adored, loved and glorified on
this altar by the thousands of angels who there surround Thee! How
much shouldst Thou be venerated, praised and loved by men, since it
is not for the angels but for love of men that Thou art present! Let all
angels and men, all creatures on earth and in heaven be transformed
into adoration, glorification and love of Thee! May all the powers of

Thy divinity and humanity be employed in magnifying and loving Thee forever!

O Most Mighty Jesus, I adore the power of Thy sacred words by which Thou dost change the earthly nature of bread and wine into the substance of Thy most Precious Body and Blood. I surrender myself absolutely to Thy might, so that it may transform my sluggishness, apathy and aridity into the warmth, tenderness and vitality of Thy celestial and divine Heart. Grant that I may be so transformed into Thee as to be of one heart, one mind, one will, one soul and one life with Thee.

O my most gentle Redeemer, Thou art present on this altar to recall and re-enact before us Thy bitter Passion and cruel death. Grant that I may possess a continual remembrance and vivid realization of all Thou didst do and suffer for me. Grant that I may bear with humility, submission and love all the contradictions that may befall me to-day and during my whole lifetime. O Good Jesus, Thou dost so abhor sin that Thou didst die to put it to death; and Thou dost so cherish and prize my soul as to give Thy life to make it live. Grant, O my Saviour, that I may henceforth fear and abhor nothing save sin alone, that I may prize and seek only Thy glory, and that I may hold everything else as unworthy of my love or hatred.

## XXVII. PRAYER TO JESUS CHRIST, HIGH PRIEST.

O Jesus, I adore Thee as High Priest, Thou who dost ceaselessly exercise this function in heaven as well as on earth, sacrificing Thyself for Thy Father's glory and our love. Blessed be Thou a thousand times, O Good Jesus, for the infinite honor Thou dost give the Heavenly Father, and for the exceeding great love Thou dost manifest for us in this divine Sacrifice. Thou art not satisfied with sacrificing Thyself for us so many times, but Thou dost further desire to associate us with Thee in this great work, causing us all to participate in the character of high-priest, giving us the power to participate with Thee in this supreme and wonderful act, that is, to offer Thee in sacrifice when Thou dost offer Thyself, at the hands of Thy holy priests, for the glory of the Almighty Father and for our salvation. Unite me with Thee, O Divine Jesus, since it is Thy will that I should now offer with Thee this most Holy Sacrifice. Grant that I, too, may offer it with holy and divine dispositions like Thine. Oh, with what devotion, what purity and sanctity, what charity for us, what recollection and love for Thy Father dost Thou perform this holy action! Implant these dispositions in me, that I may accomplish with Thee and like Thee this act which Thou dost perform in a manner so holy and divine.

O Father of Jesus, Thou hast given us Thy Son and Thou hast, as it were, placed Him in our hands, in our power and possession. Hence I offer Thy Divine Son to Thee as though He were truly mine to give, and I desire to offer Him in union with the humility, purity, charity, love and all the other holy dispositions with which He offers Himself to Thee.

So also I desire to offer Thy Beloved Son for the same intention, with which He sacrificed Himself. Hence I offer Him to Thee:

1. In honor of all that Thou art, O my God, in Thy divine essence, in all Thy divine perfections, in Thy Three Eternal Persons, and in all the great external works Thou dost effect. I offer this sacrifice in honor of all that Thy Son Jesus is in Himself and in all His states, mysteries, qualities, virtues, acts and sufferings, and all that His external dispensations, either of mercy or of justice, in heaven, on earth and in hell.

2. I offer this sacrifice to Thee in thanksgiving for all the benefits and graces, both temporal and eternal Thou didst ever impart to the sacred humanity of Thy Son, to His most Blessed Mother, to all angels and men, and above all to me, the most unworthy of all creatures.

3. I offer this sacrifice to Thee in satisfaction for all the dishonor given Thee by all the sins of the world, past, present and future, and above all by my own, and those of the people for whom I am especially bound to pray, both living and dead.

4. I offer this sacrifice to Thee for the fulfilment of all Thy designs, especially Thy providential designs for me and all my associates, begging Thee never to permit us to impede Thy holy will.

5. I implore Thee, O my God, that in virtue of this holy oblation and precious gift that I render unto Thee, Thou mayest grant us all

the spiritual and bodily graces we need, to serve and love Thee perfectly and to be Thine entirely and forever.

## XXVIII. Prayer to Jesus Christ, Sacrificial Victim.

O Jesus, I contemplate and adore Thee in this mystery as the sacred Host laden with the sins of the world which Thou dost expiate, and as the Victim immolated by Thine own self for the glory of God and the salvation of men. I learn from St. Paul that Thou dost desire us all to be living and holy hosts, worthy of being sacrificed with Thee to the glory of God the Father (Rom. 12, 1). O my Saviour, in honor of and in union with Thy supreme oblation and sacrifice, I offer myself to Thee to be for ever a victim of Thy will, a victim immolated to Thy glory and to the glory of Thy Eternal Father. Unite me to Thee, O Good Jesus. Absorb me into Thy sacrifice so that I may be sacrificed with Thee and by Thee and, since it is necessary that the host of a sacrifice should be slain and consumed by fire, make me die to myself, that is, to my vices and passions and to all that displeases Thee. Consume me utterly in the sacred fire of Thy divine love, and grant that henceforth my whole life may be a continual sacrifice of praise, glory and love of Thy Father and Thyself.

## XXIX. Prayer for Spiritual Communion.

O Most Good and Lovable Jesus, I am not worthy to think of Thee, nor that Thou shouldst think of me; still less am I worthy to appear before Thee, or that Thou shouldst deign to become present to me. Yet Thou dost not only think of me and become present to me in the Holy Eucharist, but Thou dost even long to give Thyself to me, with an infinite desire of abiding in my heart and in my soul. O dearest Lord, how wondrous are Thy mercies and how great is Thy kindness! Alas, what is there in me, wretched creature full of filth and sin, what is there capable of attracting Thee to me? Surely it is nothing but the excess of pure charity that urges Thee to come into my soul. Come, come then, O Dearest Jesus, for I love and desire Thee beyond measure! Would that I were utterly transformed into aspirations, desire, longing and love for Thee! Come, my sweet light, come, my dearest love, hasten and delay not to come into my heart which renounces all else and desires nothing save Thee alone. O Thou king of my heart, O Thou life of my soul, O my treasure beyond all price, my only joy, my most dear, most desired and most beloved Jesus! O my all, come into my mind, come into my heart and into my soul! Annihilate my pride, my self-love, my self-will and all my other vices and imperfections. Come and establish Thy humility, charity, sweetness, patience, obedience, zeal and all Thy other virtues. Come to me, there to love and glorify Thyself and perfectly unite my spirit with Thy divine spirit, my heart and Thy Sacred Heart, my soul with Thy holy soul. Grant that this heart, this soul and this body, which are often so closely and so intimately united with Thy Heart, Thy soul and Thy body by the Blessed Eucharist, may never have any other ideas, affections, desires or emotions save those of Thy holy Heart, Thy sacred body and divine soul. Come, my Jesus, enter into me there to live and reign absolutely and forever. *Veni, Domine Jesu.*

## XXX. Prayer at the End of Holy Mass.

O Jesus, most worthy of love, I praise and thank Thee countless times. I summon all the angels, all the saints and creatures to bless and glorify Thee with me, for all the graces Thou hast given me by this divine sacrifice. May it please Thee to preserve and multiply in my soul all the holy desires, thoughts, affections and sentiments which Thou hast implanted in my soul during this Holy Mass, and to give me the grace to bring forth the fruit Thou dost expect of me. Thou hast lowered Thyself to become present to me by this holy mystery. Grant, I beseech Thee, that during this day I may not let one hour go by without lifting up my heart and becoming present to Thee in spirit. Thou didst descend to this altar to take possession of our hearts and receive from us the homage we owe Thee as our Sovereign Lord. Then take possession of my heart, Good Jesus; consecrate it to Thee forever. I recognize and adore Thee as my King and Sovereign Lord. I render homage with my being, my life and all my acts, especially those I shall perform today. Take them and do with them whatever pleases Thee. Give me the grace to die rather than offend Thee, and to be a host at the same time living and dead

—dead to all that is not Thee, living in Thee and for Thee. May my whole life be a perpetual sacrifice of praise and love for Thee, and may I be utterly immolated and consumed for Thy pure glory and for Thy holy love. To this end I implore Thee with my whole heart, O Good Jesus, to give me Thy most holy blessing.

# THE DIVINE OFFICE

## XXXI. PREPARATION FOR THE DIVINE OFFICE.

The chief reason why you are often harassed by distractions and useless and wandering thoughts during vocal prayer is because your mind needs to be occupied with some thought, whether good or bad. So, if you prevent evil and useless thoughts, you have to take great care, from the very beginning of your prayer, to give your heart and your mind quite definitely to Jesus, that He may take full possession of them. You must develop the habit of filling your mind at the outset with good thoughts and holy dispositions, taking care not to slip into performing so holy an action in a careless and perfunctory fashion, more as a matter of habit than out of true devotion.

So, therefore, at the beginning of the Divine Office, remember that you are about to perform one of the greatest and most important functions possible to you, or, for that matter, to anyone in heaven or on earth. So great and exalted an act is this, that it not only is ever the ceaseless occupation of so many millions of angels and saints, with the Queen of Angels and Saints, but it always is the eternal concern of the Three Divine Persons of the Blessed Trinity, who are continually rapt in mutual praising, blessing and glorification. An action so thoroughly holy and divine—it is called the Divine Office—must necessarily be performed with holy and divine dispositions.

Consider, then, the greatness and sanctity of this act and realize that of yourself you do not possess the least qualification to recite it worthily, but rather that your whole nature hinders you. Realize that you are completely unworthy to stand before the face of God and enter into the presence of such exalted majesty. Annihilate yourself, therefore, at the feet of your Heavenly Father. Offer yourself to Jesus, and implore Him to annihilate you and to establish Himself in you, so that He Himself may perform this function on your behalf, that He Himself may glorify His Father and Himself in you, since He alone is worthy to do so. Surrender yourself to the zeal and exceeding great love with which He praises His Father, without ceasing, in heaven, on earth and in hell. For, strictly speaking, it is Jesus alone, in the whole universe, who praises and glorifies God in heaven forever by Himself and through His Blessed Mother, His angels and His saints. He praises and glorifies Him in heaven by Himself and through His Blessed Mother, His angels and His saints. He praises and blesses Him on earth ceaselessly in the Blessed Sacrament of the Altar, where He remains in a continual state of praise and adoration, and in all holy souls who praise God on earth, whether in public or privately. He praises and magnifies His Eternal Father in hell where He ceaselessly operates before the eyes of His Father as He does in heaven. Finally, He praises and exalts Him without interruption throughout the whole universe, which is entirely filled with His divine presence and majesty and with the unending praises and blessings He everywhere renders to His Father.

Unite yourself with all these everlasting praises which Jesus gives to His Father and to the Holy Trinity in every time and place and unite yourself also with the humility, recollection, love, purity, sanctity and all the other divine dispositions of Jesus Christ as He constantly renders fitting praise to His Father and the most Holy Trinity.

## XXXII. Manner of Reciting the Divine Office Devoutly and of Honoring the Whole Life of Jesus in Each Day's Office.

Having thus devoutly prepared yourself for the sublime action of the private or public recitation of the divine office, you may honor the whole life of Jesus in the course of each day as follows:

When you recite the first nocturn of *Matins,* offer it to Jesus in honor of His divine and eternal life in the bosom of the Father from all eternity, before the creation of the world.

The second nocturn is offered in honor of Christ's life in the world from the creation to the Incarnation.

The third nocturn is offered in honor of His life in the sacred womb of His most holy Mother.

Offer *Lauds* in honor of His Holy Childhood, from His infancy until He reached the age of twelve.

Offer *Prime* in honor of His hidden life of labor, which lasted until He was thirty.

Offer *Tierce* in honor of His public life and ministry, lasting from the time He was thirty until His death.

Offer *Sext* in honor of His passion, death and burial.

Offer *None* in honor of His Resurrection and Ascension, and His glorious life in heaven, not only in Himself, but in His Blessed Mother, His angels and His Saints.

Offer *Vespers* in honor of His life on earth since the Ascension, in the Holy Eucharist and in His Church.

Offer *Compline* in honor of His universal kingship over the world of nature, grace and glory, over men, angels and all creatures; also in honor of all that He ever did or shall accomplish for His Father, Himself, His Holy Spirit, His Blessed Mother, His angels, saints and all creatures.

So, when you recite each part of your office, you should reflect attentively on the mystery designated for each particular hour. You should consider the details of each mystery of His life, for instance, His thoughts and designs, His affections and dispositions, the things He did, the virtues He practised, His inward activity in relation to the Father, His own self, the Holy Spirit, the Blessed Mother, the angels and saints, and especially the thoughts, designs and love He cherished for you in particular. Consider also the glory and praises rendered to Him in that part of His life by the Omnipotent Father, the Holy Spirit, the Blessed Mother, the angels and saints.

After these considerations you should reflect upon yourself. When you see how far removed your life is from the perfection and sanctity of the life of your Head, whom you are obliged to imitate, you should profoundly humble yourself and ask His forgiveness. Then give yourself to Him to honor and imitate that aspect of His life in all the perfection He requires of you. Pray that He will implant it within you and there glorify it Himself, destroying everything in you that might place an obstacle in its way. And finally, unite yourself with all the praises that ever were, are, or shall be given Him, in this phase of His life, by His Father, His Holy Spirit, His Blessed Mother, His angels and saints.

If in reciting the office you are honoring a mystery of the temporal life of Jesus, you ought to offer and consecrate to Him the phase of your life which corresponds to the part of His life you are honoring. Implore Him to destroy all the evil in that part of your life and to cause all its happenings to render honor and glory to what took place in the corresponding phase of His own life.

For instance, when saying *Lauds,* after you have considered the Holy Childhood of Jesus Christ and reflected upon your own childhood, considering how different it was from the perfect holiness of the Sacred Childhood of Jesus, and having profoundly humbled yourself for all this, you should then offer yourself to Him to honor His divine childhood in whatsoever manner He pleases. You should consecrate your childhood in honor of His own, imploring Him to destroy all that was evil in your youth, and to cause all that took place in it to give undying honor and glory to His most adorable Childhood.

Similar reflections should be employed in the recitation of other parts of the Divine Office.

You should realize, however, that there is no necessity to stop or to interrupt the recitation of office to engage in these exercises. All this may be done by concentration on these subjects while you are chanting or reciting the office. If you have any familiarity at all with the interior life, you will not need to take extra time to perform these acts. On the contrary, the time spent thus will seem very short, so great will be the sweetness and devotion derived from the inward application of your mind and heart to Jesus, the source of all unction and consolation.

XXXIII. Another Method of Saying the Divine Office
With Devotion.

Here is another exercise which may be of great help to you in chanting or reciting the Divine Office with devotion.

1. Prepare yourself in the manner suggested above. Then lift up your mind to heaven, and consider with what love, attentiveness, purity and sanctity the Son of God is there ceaselessly praised, blessed and glorified by His Father, Himself, His Holy Spirit, His Blessed

Mother and all His angels and saints. Unite yourself with these loving praises and blessings, as follows:

During the first psalm, unite yourself with all the praises that the Eternal Father gives to His Divine Son and with all the love with which He glorifies Him forever, offering all these praises to Jesus Christ in satisfaction, or reparation for all your failures to praise and glorify Him during your life.

During the second psalm, unite yourself with all the glory Jesus gives to Himself by His Divine Person and by His sacred humanity, offering Him all this glory in reparation for your deficiency in praising Him.

During the third psalm, unite yourself with all the blessings which the Holy Spirit renders to Jesus Christ offering Him all these blessings in reparation for the maledictions which your sins caused Him to suffer on earth.

During the fourth psalm, unite yourself with the praises given by the Most Blessed Virgin to her Son, for of herself alone she praises Him more worthily than all the angels and saints together. Unite yourself with all her attention, her very great love and all her other holy dispositions as she sings His praises without ceasing, offering her praise to Jesus in satisfaction for all your negligence.

During the fifth psalm, unite yourself with all the praises of the seraphim, eternally offered before the throne of Jesus Christ, and with all the fervor and love of their endless chant of adoration, offering Him these praises in reparation for your coldness, distractions and lack of devotion.

And so, as you recite each psalm, unite yourself successively with each choir of angels and order of saints, one after another, in their perpetual chorus of praise to the Son of God. Here is a list of them, which it would be well to memorize for your use in the present exercise.

*The nine choirs of angels:* Seraphim, Cherubim, Thrones, Dominations, Virtues, Powers, Principalities, Archangels and Angels.

*The orders of saints:* Patriarchs, Prophets, Apostles, Martyrs, Priests, Confessors, Virgins, Widows, Innocents.

2. Next, descending from heaven to earth, unite yourself with all the

praises of Christ proclaimed by the various orders of Holy Mother Church, that is: by the order of pontiffs and bishops, the order of pastors and priests, the Orders of St. Benedict, St. Bernard, St. Norbert, St. Francis, St. Dominic, St. Theresa, St. Ignatius of Loyola, by all religious orders and the many good souls who are in the world and there greatly glorify Our Lord.

Consider how many people there are in the world who have no knowledge of the Son of God, who do not love Him and, instead of blessing Him, do nothing but dishonor Him. Then stir yourself up to bless and glorify the divine Redeemer on their behalf.

You should likewise rejoice in the thought that all the irrational creatures and inanimate objects in the universe are engaged in blessing and magnifying their Creator without interruption, with their entire being. The beloved disciple St. John assures us that he heard all the creatures in heaven, on earth, in the sea and under the earth, that is, in hell, giving blessing, honor and glory to God and to the Lamb of God, Jesus Christ, each according to his state. Some praised God out of love and of their own will, others by a happy necessity, others again by compulsion and by force. Unite yourself with all these blessings given to Jesus by all creatures.

3. Leaving the earth, descend in spirit to purgatory, to unite yourself with all the praises that are given to the Son of God by the holy souls in that blessed place of purification. Go down also in spirit to hell, there to adore and praise Jesus in the midst of His enemies and to glorify Him with a fervor and attention at least equal to the intentness of those unhappy souls in blaspheming Him. Unite yourself with all the glory and praises given in hell to the infinite justice of Jesus Christ by His Eternal Father, the Divine Judge, and His Holy Spirit. In conclusion, you should desire that everything in heaven, earth and hell, and especially everything that is in yourself, in your body or your soul, may be transformed into praise, benediction and glory for Him who can never be blessed or glorified enough. The words of David, the holy psalmist, should be your inspiration: *Benedic anima mea Domino, et omnia quae intra me sunt, nomini sancto ejus,* "Bless the Lord, O my soul: and let all that is within me bless his holy name" (Ps. 102, 1).

## XXXIV. DEVOUT RECITATION OF THE OFFICE OF OUR LADY.

The preparation suggested for the Canonical Office may also serve to stimulate the right dispositions for saying the Little Office of Our Lady. There you may use the following method, assisted by Our Lord's grace. In saying the Canonical Office, it is possible in the course of the day to honor the whole life of Jesus; so too, in reciting the Little Office of the Blessed Virgin, you may honor in each day her whole beautiful life, or, to express it more aptly, the whole life of Jesus in Mary and of Mary in Jesus. Thus you may never separate the Son from the Mother, nor the Mother from the Son, and you may behold nothing but Jesus in Mary and Mary in Jesus. Here is the way to do this:

Offer *Matins* to Jesus in honor of His life in the Blessed Virgin, and her life in Him, from her Immaculate Conception to her Nativity. For, from the very first, the Son of God was abiding in the mind and soul of the Blessed Virgin. He dwelt in her, sanctifying and illuminating her from the moment of her conception, beautifying her soul with glowing virtues, utterly filling her with grace, sanctity and love. And she in turn was living a most holy and admirable life in Him; and her mind, her soul and her heart indeed dwelt more in the divine object of her sacred love than in her own self.

Offer *Lauds* to Jesus in honor of His life in the most holy Virgin and hers in Him from her birth to the time of His Incarnation by the wonderful works of grace, virtue, light and love which the Son of God effected during this time, without interruption, in the holy soul of this blessed child, as well as by the faith, hope, desire, contemplation, love and praise of Him which were the constant occupation of the divine soul of the most holy Virgin.

Offer *Prime* in honor of the wondrous and most delectable life of Jesus in Mary and Mary in Jesus during the nine months in which He dwelt in her sacred womb.

Offer *Tierce* in honor of the life of Jesus in Mary and Mary in Jesus from the birth of Jesus until the end of His Childhood, that is, until He was twelve years of age.

Offer *Sext* in honor of the life of Jesus in Mary and of Mary in Jesus until the end of His hidden life—that is, until He was thirty.

Offer *None* in honor of the life of Jesus in Mary and of Mary in Jesus from the beginning of His public life and ministry until the beginning of His life of glory, that is, from the time He was thirty until His Resurrection.

Offer *Vespers* in honor of the life of Jesus in Mary and of Mary in Jesus from His Resurrection and Ascension until the Assumption of the Blessed Mother. For even though Jesus had ascended to His Father in heaven, He nevertheless remained with His Blessed Mother and in her until her Assumption. And in a certain sense He lived more fully in her than in heaven during this time, because He was ever producing in her greater graces and more love than in all the citizens of heaven. So, too, she was more truly in heaven with her Son than on earth, and lived more fully in the life of her glorious Son than in her own.

Offer *Compline* in honor of the glorious and immortal life of Jesus in Mary and of Mary in Jesus amid the joys of paradise.

As you recite each part of this office, you should consider quietly, without too much mental exertion, the particular part of the life of Jesus in Mary and of Mary in Jesus honored by each hour of the office. You should meditate on the intercourse of Jesus and Mary in that part of their life: their sentiments, dispositions and relationship toward each other, their holy discourses and conversations, their divine actions, their most eminent virtues, as well as how the Mother uninterruptedly contemplated, glorified and loved the Son, and how the Son filled the soul of His Mother with light, grace and divine love.

Then you should reflect upon yourself, and when you see how remote is your life, full of sin and imperfection, from that most holy and most perfect life of Jesus and Mary, whom you should regard and imitate as your father and mother, you ought to humble yourself profoundly and beg Jesus for forgiveness. You should offer Him all the honor which His most Blessed Mother gave Him, or, rather, which He gave to Himself through her by His most perfect life in her, and hers in Him, to atone for the dishonor you have given Him by your sinful and imperfect life. And finally implore him to cause your whole life, past, present and future to render eternal homage and glory to His most adorable life and the most lovable life of His Blessed Mother, destroying all in you that goes against this glory.

## XXXV. ANOTHER METHOD OF SAYING THE OFFICE OF THE MOST BLESSED VIRGIN WITH DEVOTION.

The second method suggested for the recitation of the canonical Office may also be applied to the Office of the Most Blessed Virgin, uniting the Mother and the Son in the following manner:

When you say the first psalm, unite yourself with all the praises which the Eternal Father ever gave and shall give forever to His Son Jesus and to the most Blessed Virgin, offering to the Son and the Mother all these praises to satisfy for your many failures to praise and glorify them.

When you say the second psalm, unite yourself with all the glory Jesus ever gave and shall give forever to Himself and to His Mother most worthy of honor, offering to the Son and to the Mother all this glory in satisfaction for your faults.

At the third psalm, unite yourself with the Holy Spirit in all the praises He ever gave or ever shall give to Jesus and Mary, offering them these praises in reparation for your negligences.

At the fourth, unite yourself with the seraphim, with all the other choirs of angels, with the glorious company of saints and with the orders of creation, as outlined in the second method of reciting the Divine Office.

offer ourselves to Him to die and shed our blood a thousand times, were it possible, for His pure love, for the glory of His mysteries, and in preference to the slightest deviation from the faith of His Church. So also, we must surrender ourselves to Him to be filled with a great love and devotion for all the mysteries of His life and of His Church, that He may implant and glorify them in us according to His holy will.

With the recitation of the Our Father and the three Hail Marys introducing the first decade, we should annihilate ourselves at the feet of the Son of God and His holy Mother, considering ourselves most unworthy to appear before them or to think of them, or to have them think of us. And we should give ourselves to Jesus, imploring Him to annihilate us Himself, and to take up His abode in us, that He Himself may honor His most blessed Mother on our behalf, for He alone can give her fitting honor. Each one of us must also unite himself to His zeal, love and devotion for her. Then we should offer our prayer to the Blessed Virgin, in union with the devotion, love, humility and purity of her Dear Son and in union with all the devout prayers and all the glory and praise, past, present and future, ever addressed to her Son and herself.

This should be offered for the accomplishment of their heavenly design, especially on behalf of ourselves.

After that, as each decade of the Rosary is said, we should offer it to the Son and the Mother, in honor of one or another of their most eminent virtues, never separating Jesus from Mary or Mary from Jesus. The offering of the decades proceeds as follows:

The first decade should be offered to Jesus and Mary in honor of the deep humility that characterized all their thoughts, words and actions.

The second decade should be said in honor of the perfect purity of the Heart of Jesus and Mary. This virtue consists chiefly of two elements, namely: first, a very great hatred, horror and flight from sin, together with perfect detachment from all that is not God; and second, a most holy union with God and the pure glory of God, which existed most eminently in the holy soul of the Son of God and that of His most holy Mother.

The third decade should be recited in honor of the divine meekness and charity which Jesus and Mary practised towards others in their thoughts, words, actions and sufferings.

The fourth decade should be said in honor of the most holy obedience of Jesus and Mary to every operation of God's holy will. They never sought to do their own will, but rather chose the will of God in all and by all things, and the will of others for the love of God. What is more, they sought their entire satisfaction and joy in submitting to all that was willed by God and in fulfilling His every command or wish.

The fifth decade should be offered in honor of the boundless and ardent pure love of Jesus Christ for His Heavenly Father and of Mary for Jesus: for they both lived in an uninterrupted act of this pure love, and never had a thought or uttered a word or performed any action save in this pure love. It should also be said in honor of the last day, the last hour, the moment, and the death of Jesus and Mary—a death all divine and all for love.

Now, as you say each decade:

1. You should meditate on each of these virtues of Jesus and Mary, considering their eminent sanctity and with what perfection they practised each virtue throughout their lifetime in thought, word and action.

2. You should consider yourself and see how far removed you are from this virtue, and how little you resemble your Father and Mother (that is, Jesus and Mary) in this. Then, you should profoundly humble yourself on this account and beg them to forgive you, to make reparation for your failures and to offer to the Eternal Father all the honor accorded Him by their practice of this virtue, in satisfaction for the faults you have committed against it.

3. Offer yourself to Jesus and to His holy Mother with an earnest resolution to attend with more care to the practice of this virtue in future, imploring the Divine Son, by His absolute power and the inviolate Mother by her prayers and merits, to destroy in your soul all that can possibly prevent you from making this progress, and to establish the reign of this virtue for His pure glory.

But please remember well what I have said elsewhere, that in all

these devotions, even though I may suggest various ideas and practices to you, there is no need for you to make use of them all every
time, but only of those from which you happen to derive the most
spiritual benefit. Or else, use now one, now another, according to
the inspiration of Our Lord's grace. For instance, if your mind finds
enough to occupy it in contemplation of one or two of the virtues
that have been mentioned, or in some other virtues of Jesus and
Mary, there is no need to go on to the consideration of the others,
which may be considered at another time.

It remains to be said that, when you recite the last decade in honor
of the last hour and most holy death of Jesus and Mary, you should
offer them the last moment of your life and the instant of your death,
in honor of the last day, the last hour, and the last moment of their
life, and their most holy death, imploring them to grant that all
that shall occur in your last day and moment may be consecrated to
the homage and the glory of what took place on their last day and
at the moment of their death and that you may die in the state and
practice of divine love, and that your last breath may be an act of
most pure love for Jesus.

## XXXVIII. ROSARY OF JESUS, MARIA.

You should earnestly desire that the last words you utter in life
should be: *Jesus, Maria.* And in order to dispose yourself to obtain
this grace from divine mercy, it would be a good thing to end each
day with the recitation of this very brief rosary, which I call the rosary
of *Jesus, Maria,* because it is composed of these two words alone:
*Jesus, Maria,* "Jesus, Mary." These Holy Names contain all that is
greatest and most admirable in heaven and on earth, together with
the entire virtue and sanctity of the most excellent prayers and devotions that could possibly be practised.

This rosary is made up of thirty-four small beads in honor of
Christ's thirty-four years on earth, in honor of Mary's participation
in them and the honor she gave Him always.

To begin with, you should say three times *Veni Domine Jesu:*
"Come Lord Jesus," with the intentions suggested for the Rosary of
the Glory of Jesus, which may be found in "Part Six" of this book.

On each small bead pronounce the words *Jesus, Maria,* "Jesus,
Mary," trying to say each with all the love and devotion you would
want to have if you were at the hour of death, and as if it were
the last word you should ever utter. Your intention should be to
pronounce each name with all the love, or in union with all the love
(for these two terms mean but one thing), which ever was offered
or shall be offered forever in heaven and on earth, to Jesus and Mary.
You should give them this totality of love as something of your
own, since, as has been said, everything belongs to you, making the
offering in satisfaction for all your failures to love and serve them
during your life.

On the large beads say the words: *Benedicta tu in mulieribus et
benedictus fructus ventris tui, Jesus,* "Blessed art thou amongst
women and blessed is fruit of thy womb, Jesus"; and as you
say them, offer to Jesus and Mary all the praises and blessings
that ever were, are, or shall be given to Him forever on earth and
in heaven, in reparation for your failures to bless and glorify them.

# PART FOUR

*Devotional Exercises to Be Done Each Week*
*to Live a Christian and Saintly Life and*
*to Make Jesus Reign in Your Soul*

## DEVOTIONAL EXERCISES TO BE DONE EACH WEEK TO LIVE A CHRISTIAN AND SAINTLY LIFE AND TO MAKE JESUS REIGN IN YOUR SOUL

### I. THE THREE SPECIAL DAYS OF THE WEEK.

There are three week-days that should stand out above the others, and be spent with more devotion and attention to God.

Monday should be consecrated to the honor of the first day of Christ's life in the world. On this day you should renew your desire to begin a new life for Our Lord, and resolve to spend the week devotedly in His service.

Friday is dedicated to the last day of Our Lord's life on earth. You ought to regard every Friday as though it were the last day of your life, and spend it accordingly.

Saturday is consecrated to the honor of the life of Jesus in Mary and of Mary in Jesus, a life to which all Christians are bound to have special devotion. On Saturday you should render love and praise to the most Blessed Virgin with more than usual zeal and affection, and try to make reparation for having fallen away during the week from your duties to her and her Son. So, too, at the close of this day, it is well to honor the Blessed Virgin in the last day and the last hour of her life as I shall set forth in "Part Six."

### II. MANNER OF HONORING THE WHOLE LIFE OF JESUS IN THE COURSE OF EACH WEEK.

In order to spend the remaining days of the week devoutly, it is a good thing to dedicate each day to some mystery of the life of Christ, in order to give particular honor to His life on that day and to try to implant its special virtues in your soul by consideration and imitation. According to St. Paul, we are all dead in Adam and living in Jesus Christ (I Cor. 15, 22), and since Jesus Christ is our life (Col.

3, 4), none of us have any right to live on earth except by the life of Jesus Christ. Remember that God lets you remain here only that you may work to destroy in you the wicked and sinful life of the old Adam and to establish there the holy and divine life of Jesus.

Hence, your chief care and occupation should be to consider, adore, and imitate the life of Jesus, in order that, by this means, you may form and establish within yourself a perfect image of that life.

Here are a few meditations for each day of the week, which sum up the whole life of Jesus, and which I present in the form of prayers, so that every type of person may use them to honor the various phases of the life of Christ.

# MEDITATIONS FOR EACH DAY OF THE WEEK

III. First Meditation—Sunday.

## *The Divine Life of Jesus in the Bosom of His Father*
## *from all Eternity*

1. O Jesus, my Lord and my God, I contemplate, adore and glorify Thee in Thy divine life from all eternity in the bosom of the Eternal Father, before Thy Incarnation in the virginal womb of Thy Mother. Oh, how holy a life this is, how pure, divine, wonderful and filled with glory, greatness and delights! What joy to see Thee living, from all eternity, a life so filled with perfection, contentment and wonders! Blessed be Thou, O Father of Jesus, for having imparted such a life to Thy Well-beloved Son! O Jesus, I offer Thee all the glory, love and praise Thou dost derive from the Father and the Holy Spirit throughout the eternity of Thy divine life.

2. O Jesus, when I consider Thy divine and eternal life, I see that Thy chief function for all eternity is to contemplate, glorify and love Thy Father, to refer Thyself to Him as to Thy principle, to give Him Thy being, Thy life, Thy perfections and all that Thou shalt be forever, as gifts received from Him, to be employed in glorifying and loving Him, and to offer Him infinitely worthy praise and love. Blessed be Thou, O Jesus, for all these things. O Most Amiable Father, how I rejoice to behold Thee so loved and glorified by Thy Son! I offer Thee all love and glory that Thou dost receive from Him during all eternity, by His divine life in Thy fatherly bosom before His Incarnation.

3. O good Jesus, Thou hast expended all Thy divine life for my benefit. From all eternity Thou dost think of me, love me and offer me to the Father, and Thou dost offer Thyself also to Him, to come one day upon earth to be made flesh, to suffer and die on earth for love of me. O Dearest Jesus, Thou hast loved me from all eternity, and I hardly know if I have yet begun to love Thee as I ought.

Forgive me, my Saviour. From now on, and for all eternity, let me live but to love Thee!

## IV. SECOND MEDITATION—MONDAY.

### The First Moment of the Temporal Life of Jesus

1. O Jesus, I adore Thee at the moment of Thy Incarnation, which is the first instant of Thy mortal life. I adore all the marvelous things that took place in Thee at that moment. What great accomplishments were effected in Thee and by Thee, in that blessed instant, in the eyes of the Father, the Holy Spirit, Thy sacred humanity, and Thy Blessed Mother! What thoughts, what affections, what love! How Thy holy soul in that instant devoted itself, before Thy Father's face, to adore and glorify Him and sacrifice Thee entirely to His glory, and to accomplish all that He willed! O Good Jesus, I adore Thy first thoughts and Thy first acts of adoration, oblation, love and praise, which Thou didst offer to Thy Father at that time. How exalted and divine were the love and glory Thou gavest Him then! Truly Thou didst give Him infinitely more honor and love in that moment alone than all the angels and all men accorded Him in the five thousand years that preceded Thy Incarnation, or ever shall give Him for all eternity. O Father of Jesus, what satisfaction for my soul to behold Thee so loved and glorified by Thy Son! O Jesus, be Thou blessed, adored and glorified forever for the honor and love Thou didst give to Thy Father at the blessed moment of Thy Incarnation!

2. O Jesus, when I consider Thee in this mystery, I see by the light of faith that Thou dost entertain most exalted thoughts and great designs upon her in whom the Incarnation was accomplished, and that Thou dost indeed effect great and marvelous things in her. O Jesus, I adore Thy first thoughts, Thy first acts of love and movements of grace, of light and of eminent sanctity which Thou didst produce in Thy Blessed Mother at the moment of Thy Incarnation. So, too, do I adore the first acts of adoration, praise and love of the most admirable Mother for the Most Adorable Son. Blessed be Thou, O Jesus, Son of Mary, for all the wonders Thou didst work in Thy divine Mother by this stupendous mystery. Blessed be Thou, O Mother

of Jesus, for all the glory thou hast given thy Son in this same mystery. Unite me, I implore Thee, to all the love and honor thou didst give thy Dear Son in the first instant of His life, and grant that I may share in thy peerless love for Him and in thy zeal for His glory.

3. O Most Amiable Jesus, at the same instant that Thou didst look up to the Father, after the Incarnation, Thou didst also look upon me. Thou didst begin to think of Him, refer Thyself to Him and love Him and Thou didst likewise begin to think of me, to give Thyself to me and love me. At the very instant Thou didst begin to live, it was to live for me, to prepare and acquire for me most extraordinary graces, and to form plans for my salvation. From that very moment Thou didst plan and desire to create in me an image of the mystery of Thy Incarnation and to become incarnate in me, that is, to unite me to Thyself, and Thyself most intimately to me, both physically and spiritually by Thy holy grace and Thy divine sacraments, and then to fill me with Thyself, and establish Thyself in me to live and reign perfectly in me.

O what goodness! What boundless love! Infinitely blessed be Thou, O Good Jesus! May all Thy mercies and all Thy wonders for the children of men bless Thee forever! I most humbly beg Thy forgiveness for the obstacles which I have put in the way of the accomplishment of the great designs Thou hast deigned to have in my regard. Never allow me to impede Thy grace again. From now on I desire to annihilate, at all costs, everything in me that opposes Thy holy will. My Jesus, may it please Thee to grant me the grace and strength to do this.

## V. Third Meditation—Tuesday.

### The Holy Childhood of Jesus

1. O Great and Admirable Jesus, Thou wast not satisfied to become man for love of men, but Thou didst also will to become a child, subject to all the lowliness and weakness of infancy, in order to honor the Eternal Father in every condition of human life, and to sanctify all the states of our life. Blessed be Thou, Good Jesus, for

these favors. May all Thy angels and saints bless Thee eternally. O most amiable Child, I offer Thee my own childhood, although it is past, imploring Thee most humbly that, by virtue of Thy divine Childhood, Thou mayest wipe out all that was bad or imperfect and cause my whole life as a child to render homage to Thy most adorable Childhood.

2. O Divine Jesus, when I contemplate Thee in Thy holy Childhood, I see that Thou art never idle, but dost effect great things for Thy Eternal Father, contemplating, adoring and loving Him, and also for Thy Blessed Mother, heaping upon her a world of graces and blessings, also for St. Joseph, and little St. John the Baptist and the other saints with whom Thou didst associate as a Child, accomplishing in them most wonderful works of illumination and sanctity. I adore Thee, love Thee and bless Thee in all Thy divine occupations and in the marvelous effects of Thy divine Childhood. I offer Thee all the honor and love Thou didst receive in Thy holy Childhood from Thy Father, Thy Blessed Mother, St. Joseph, St. John the Baptist, St. Gabriel, and from the other angels and saints who are in any special way associated with Thy divine Childhood.

3. O most amiable Child, I adore all Thy thoughts and designs and Thy most burning love for me. Thou wast thinking of me, and didst love me without interruption in Thy Childhood. Thou didst cherish the plan and the strong desire to imprint upon my heart an image of Thy divine Childhood, that is, to make me enter upon a state of holy and sacred childhood, which should imitate and honor the meekness, simplicity, humility, purity of body and spirit, the obedience and innocence of Thy holy Childhood. O my Jesus, I give myself to Thee to accomplish Thy plan and desire and to enter into this state. I shall henceforth strive, with the help of Thy holy grace, which I invoke with my whole heart, to become meek, humble, simple, pure, obedient, free of all arrogance, bitterness and malice, like a child, so that I may render some small honor to Thy Childhood which so deserves to be honored.

VI. Fourth Meditation—Wednesday.

## The Hidden Life of Jesus

1. O Jesus, although Thou didst have so many and such great things to do on earth, converting so many souls, working so many miracles, doing so much good by Thy blessed example and holy preaching, if Thou hadst gone out among men, yet Thou didst not will to do this. Instead, Thy choice on earth was a life hidden and unknown until the age of thirty, performing in that time no outward act that might make Thee known to men. Thou didst remain hidden and withdrawn into the Father, in whom Thy mind, heart, thoughts, desires and affections were uninterruptedly enclosed. And Thou didst choose this hidden life to honor Thy hidden life from all eternity in the bosom of Thy Father, and to teach us that solitude and retirement are pleasing to Thee. Of the thirty-four years of Thy life upon earth, no more than four were spent in active intercourse among men, while thirty were spent in retirement and solitude. Blessed be Thou, O Good Jesus, for all the glory Thou didst give Thy Father during these thirty years of Thy hidden life! Grant that I in their honor may henceforth love retirement and solitude, both interior and exterior. Draw me apart and hide me in Thee. Absorb my mind into Thine, my heart into Thy Heart and my life into Thy life. I desire henceforth, with the help of Thy grace, to make every effort to withdraw my thoughts and affections from all things into Thee, O my Jesus, as into my place of refuge, my center, my element and my paradise, outside of which all else is hell and perdition. I wish to dwell ever in Thee, following thy commandment: *Manete in me;* "Abide in me" (John 15, 4), that is, in Thy spirit, Thy love, Thy sentiments and inclinations, never to leave Thee again.

2. O Most Great and Most Adorable Jesus, Thou didst will to lead an unknown and despised life, a life base and abject in the eyes of men, a life of poverty, labor and suffering, bearing the name and following the trade of carpenter, to teach us first by example what Thou didst later teach us by words, namely, that "what is high to men is an abomination before God"; *quod hominibus altum est,*

*abominatio est ante Deum* (Luke 16, 15). O Jesus, imprint this truth deeply in my mind and firmly implant in my heart a great hatred and horror of all fame, praise, greatness and vanity, and for all that catches and dazzles the eyes of men, giving me a very strong love for all that involves lowliness, abjection and humiliation.

3. O Jesus, Thou art God like Thy Heavenly Father and Thou art but One God with Him; Thou hast but one power and operation, and with Him Thou art the Creator, Preserver and Governor of our vast universe. From all eternity Thou dost send forth with Him a God and a Divine Person, that is, the Holy Ghost, who is God even as the Father and Thou. This and other exalted things worthy of Thy supreme greatness, Thou dost accomplish. Yet in Thy hidden and laborious life on earth, I see that Thou dost lower Thyself to the commonest and most lowly actions of human life, such as eating, drinking, sleeping, working, earning Thy living with the toil of Thy hands and in the sweat of Thy brow. I am filled with wonder and consolation because Thou art no less great and admirable in small things than in great. In these lowly commonplace activities Thou didst render infinitely great glory to the Omnipotent Father because, O Jesus, Thou didst perform all actions, even the smallest and most ordinary, not with common or ordinary dispositions, but with an infinite love for the Father and for us. Thou didst merit and acquire, by the power of Thy holy actions, a special grace for all our acts, to enable us to perform them meritoriously. Hence we can and must do everything, in a devout manner. Otherwise we nullify and waste the graces Thou hast acquired for us in the performance of like things. Do not allow this to happen, O Good Jesus! Give me the grace Thou hast acquired for me by Thy holy actions, so that I may perform all my own acts with holiness. This is my desire and my resolve. Grant me grace to carry it out purely for Thy glory, that in future I may offer up all my acts, even the smallest, in honor of Thine and that I may, as far as possible, perform my tasks with the dispositions and intentions that exalted the lowliness of all Thy most humble, human deeds.

## VII. Fifth Meditation—Thursday.

### The Public Life of Christ on Earth and in the Most Blessed Sacrament

1. O Most Amiable Jesus, Thou dost live, reign and commune for all eternity with the Eternal Father and the Holy Spirit. How rich is this association and how delightful to Thee! What glory and praise Thou dost receive from the Father and Holy Spirit! Yet Thou didst will to come forth from the bosom of the Father to appear on earth, to associate, eat and drink in familiar visible companionship, not only with Thy Blessed Mother, St. Joseph and the holy apostles and disciples, but even with sinners, from whom Thou didst receive all kinds of outrages and indignities. Thou didst will to do this: (1) By association with Thy Blessed Mother, St. Joseph, the holy apostles and the disciples, to give homage to Thy divine and holy association with the Father and Holy Spirit from all eternity. (2) By the pain Thou didst suffer from associating with sinners, to deliver us from the punishment, so rightly deserved by our sins, of being reduced for ever to the wretched company of demons, and to make us worthy to live eternally in the company of the angels and saints, Thy Blessed Mother, and the Three Divine Persons. (3) In order to show us how true are thy words: Thy delights are to be with the children of men (Prov. 8, 31). (4) To acquire for us, by the merit of Thy active life, the grace we need to behave virtuously in our relations with one another. (5) In order that the perfection of Thy holy and divine conduct in Thy relations with other men might serve as a model and example of the way we should act towards our neighbor.

2. I adore Thee, O Jesus, I bless Thee and love Thee for all these things. I adore Thee in Thy public life and active ministry, which lasted from Thy thirtieth year to the day of Thy death. I adore and give Thee glory for everything in this period of Thy life, inward and outward, that is, all the actions, words, teachings, miracles, journeys, labors and weariness, and for all Thy thoughts, feelings, intentions, affections and inner dispositions. I bless Thee for all the glory Thou didst render to the Eternal Father. I offer Thee all the love and

honor accorded during the time of Thy active life by all the holy souls who came in contact with Thee. I also offer Thee all my own associations and contacts, whether past or future, in homage to Thine own, and I implore Thee to cause all my actions relating to my neighbor to be consecrated to the glory of Thy public life.

3. O Jesus, I adore the thoroughly holy and divine dispositions which characterized Thy activity among men. With what dignity, charity, meekness, patience, modesty, detachment from creatures and attention to God didst Thou move and act in the world of men! O my Saviour, I desire that such dispositions may henceforth characterize all my relations with my neighbor. Alas! How far I am from such perfection and how many faults I have committed in the days gone by! For all these I beg Thy forgiveness, imploring Thee to implant in me all the dispositions I have set down above.

4. O Lord, Thou wert not satisfied with having lived and associated with mankind during Thy mortal life. When Thou wast on the point of returning to heaven, Thy most insatiable love and Thy exceeding great desire to prove the tremendous truth that Thy delight is to be with the children of men inspired Thee to devise a most admirable invention that would keep Thee ever with us, and give Thyself to us with all the essence of Thy riches and wonders. All this was accomplished by means of the Holy Eucharist, which is a compendium of all Thy wonders and the greatest of all the effects produced by Thy love for us. O love, O goodness, how is it that I am not utterly transformed into love and praise for Thee? O Jesus, forgive me my past abuse of so great a grace, grant that in the future I may make a better use of this Divine Sacrament and that, as Thou dost find Thy delight in being with me, I may also find all my delight in Thy company, in thinking of Thee, and in loving and glorifying Thee.

## VIII. Sixth Meditation—Friday.

### The Sufferings and Death of Jesus

1. O Jesus, Thou art the love and the delight of God and the angels, of heaven and earth. Thou art the God of consolation, the

source of all joy and bliss, joy and blessedness itself. And yet, when I behold Thee on the final day of Thy mortal life, I see that Thou art the object of the wrath and persecution of heaven, earth, hell, of God, men and all creatures. I see the universe and the powers of evil leagued against Thee, expending all their energies in making Thee suffer. Thou art, as it were, a target exposed to every volley of contradiction and outrage. I behold Thee so filled with sorrow, anguish and torments in every part of Thy body and soul, that Thou dost seem to be transformed into pain and sufferings. Hence the Prophet Isaias calls Thee the Man of Sorrows, *Virum dolorum* (Isa. 53, 3). O my Dearest Jesus, what has reduced Thee to so pitiable a state? It is Thy goodness, my Saviour, and the excess of Thy love. O my sweet love, let me adore and love and bless Thee in all Thy sufferings, both interior and exterior; let me adore in Thee the holy and divine dispositions of Thy suffering. With what submission to Thy Father's will, with what deep humiliation under the burden of all the sins of the world, with what charity for us, with what meekness and patience towards Thine enemies Thou didst endure the magnitudes of all sufferings. How ashamed I am to behold my Jesus suffering so extremely, with such dispositions, while I see how sensitive I am to the slightest pain, and so far from sharing His dispositions! O Good Jesus, I give myself to Thee to suffer all Thou dost will and I offer Thee all that I have suffered and am yet to suffer in my whole life. May it please Thee to unite my works and trials with Thine; bless them through Thine; use them as Thine own, to glorify the Father and to honor Thy holy Passion. Grant that I may share in the love, humility and other dispositions with which Thou didst suffer!

2. O Most Amiable Jesus, the torments of the Cross and of death were borne with so much love for the Father and for us that the Holy Spirit speaks of the day of Thy Passion as the day of Thy Heart's joy (Cant. 3, 11) to show that Thou didst find joy and satisfaction in suffering. O my Saviour, let me also find my joy and all my happiness in this world in trials and labors, in contempt and sufferings, if by them I can give Thee greater glory and love! Implant these dispositions in my soul, and imprint upon my heart in-

tense hatred for the delights and pleasures of this earth, and a particular affection for hard work and suffering.

3. O Jesus, I contemplate and adore Thee agonizing and dying on the Cross. I adore Thy last thoughts, words, actions and sufferings, the last use of Thy bodily senses and of the faculties of Thy soul, the last graces Thou didst infuse into the soul of Thy Blessed Mother and the other persons who remained at the foot of the Cross; Thy last acts of adoration and love for the Heavenly Father; the last sentiments and dispositions of Thy Heart and soul and the last breath that yielded up Thy life. I offer Thee the last moment of my life and my death in honor of Thy holy death and the consummation of Thy life. Bless my death, O Jesus, my Saviour, and sanctify it by Thine own; unite it to Thine; grant that I may share the holy and divine dispositions with which Thou didst die. Grant, if it please Thee, that the last things of my life, that my last breath may be consecrated to the honor of Thy last breath, and that it may be an act of most pure and perfect love for Thee.

IX. SEVENTH MEDITATION—SATURDAY.

## The Life of Jesus in Mary and that of Mary in Jesus

1. O Jesus, Thou only Son of God, only Son of Mary, I contemplate and adore Thee living and reigning in Thy most holy Mother, the divine Author of her existence. St. Paul says: Thou art all and dost all in all things (Eph. 1, 23; I Cor. 12, 6), so surely Thou art and dost all in Thy most holy Mother. Thou art her life, her soul, her heart, her spirit, her riches. Thou art in her, sanctifying her on earth and glorifying her in heaven. Thou art in her, accomplishing greater works and giving to Thyself, in and by her, greater glory than in all the other creatures of heaven and earth. Thou art in her, clothing her with Thy qualities and perfections, inclinations and dispositions, imprinting in her a most perfect image of Thyself, of all Thy states, mysteries, and virtues, and making her so like Thee, that whoever sees Jesus sees Mary, and he who sees Mary beholds Jesus. Blessed be Thou, O Jesus, for all that Thou art and all that Thou dost accomplish in Thy most holy Mother! I offer Thee all the delights,

all the love and all the glory Thou didst ever have or ever shalt have in her.

2. O Mother of Jesus, I honor and venerate thy most holy and admirable life in Thy Son Jesus: a life resplendent with every kind of virtue and perfection; a life of which one single moment is more dear to God than all the lives of angels and men; a life that gives more honor and love to God than all other lives combined in heaven and on earth. This life is none other than the life of thy Son Jesus, which He communicates to thee from moment to moment by a most particular and ineffable favor. Blessed be thou, O holy Virgin, for all the honor thou hast given to thy Well-beloved Son in thy whole life. I offer thee all my life, O Mother of life and grace, and I consecrate it all to the honor of thy life, and with my whole heart I beg thy Son Jesus, the God of life and love, to grant by His great goodness that my whole life may pay continual and eternal homage to His most holy life and to thine.

3. O Jesus, God of my life and of my heart, Thou hast a very great desire to dwell in me, and to make me live in Thee an entirely holy and heavenly life. Forgive me for all the ways I have obstructed the fulfilment of Thy desire by my sins and infidelities. Eradicate the corrupt and depraved life of the old Adam in me, and in its place establish Thy holy and perfect life. Dwell in all Thy fulness in my spirit, heart and soul, and therein accomplish all the works Thou dost desire for Thy glory. Love Thyself in me, and in me glorify Thyself in every way that Thou mayest desire. O Mother of Jesus, if it please thee, obtain from Thy Son the accomplishment of these things in me.

## X. Eighth Meditation—Second Meditation for Sunday.

### Christ's Life of Glory in Heaven, after His Resurrection and Ascension

1. O Jesus, having considered and adored Thee in Thy mortal life, in the agony of the Cross, in the shadow of death and in the chill of the Sepulchre, let me now adore and contemplate Thee in the exaltation, brightness and delights of the life of glory and blessedness Thou

didst enter by Thy Resurrection, which Thou hast enjoyed in heaven in the bosom of the Father since Thy Ascension. O immortal and glorious life of my Jesus! O life entirely free from the sorrow and suffering of this earth! O life completely hidden and absorbed in God! O life of nothing but love, and of love most pure, since, in His heavenly life, Jesus has no other thought than to love His Father, and to love us for His Father, to love, bless and glorify His Father for us, to offer us to His Father and to intercede for us with Him! O most holy life, most pure and most divine! O life replete with unutterable joy and exultation! O life that enjoys the fulness of glory, greatness and bliss which is God! O my Dear Jesus, what joy for my heart to behold Thee living such a life! May Thy most amiable Father be blessed forever for having brought Thee into heaven.

2. O Jesus, most worthy of love, not only art Thou in Thyself living a life of glory and blessedness, but so also are all the angels and saints who are with Thee in heaven. Thou livest in them, Thou dost communicate to them Thy glorious and immortal life, Thou art glorious and blessed in them, as St. Paul testifies in the words: *omnia in omnibus* (I Cor. 12, 6). It is Thou who dost adore, praise, and love Thy Eternal Father in them and by them. Blessed be Thou for all these things, O Good Jesus. I refer and offer to Thee the glorified and blessed life of all the citizens of heaven, together with all the love and praise they give Thee now and shall give Thee forever, in homage to the life of bliss and glory which Thou hast in Thyself. I beg all Thy angels and saints to love and glorify Thee for me, and to associate me with all the love and glory they give Thee and shall give Thee forever.

3. O Jesus, Thou object of all desire, I know that Thou dost bear me an infinite love, and by Thy extreme zeal for Thy glory, dost most ardently desire to be perfectly loved and glorified in me, and also that Thou hast an infinite desire to draw me to Thee in heaven, that Thou mayest live perfectly in me and fully establish in me the kingdom of Thy glory and Thy love. Thou wilt not live and reign perfectly in me so long as I am on earth. Therefore, O my Saviour, I no longer desire to live on earth except to long without ceasing after heaven. Heaven! O heaven! How desirable art thou; how thou dost

call to our love! O God of heaven, when will the time come for me
to see Thy holy face? When wilt Thou live fully in me and when
will I love Thee perfectly? O earthly life, how hard, how unbearable
art thou! O God of my life and of my heart, how long and cruel is
this life in which Thou art so little loved and so much offended! But
what consoles me, Lord, is that the great apostle, St. Paul, tells me
that Thy Father has given us life and raised us from the dead, and
caused us to sit down with Thee and in Thee in heaven: *Convivifi-
cavit nos in Christo, et conresuscitavit; et consedere fecit in coelestibus
in Christo Jesu* (Eph. 2, 5). Hence I live with Thee in heaven, O
Jesus, and there I share in all the love, glory and praises Thou dost
give to the All-glorious Father, whether by Thyself or through the
angels and saints. Indeed, if I am united to Thee by grace, I can
say that I am uninterruptedly loving and praising and glorifying the
Eternal Father most perfectly, in Thee and with Thee, with the same
love, praise and glory with which Thou dost glorify and love Him.
Because I am one with Thee, as the member is one with the head, I
can say with St. Augustine: wherever my head is, I am, and I live by
His life, and all that is His is mine, and I share in all that He does,
all His acts and activities belong to me, and in Him and with Him
I do everything that He does.

Consequently, O my dear Jesus, I am even now in heaven with
Thy Blessed Mother, with all Thy angels and saints, and especially
in company with those to whom I am particularly united. I participate in all their praise and love of Thee, and indeed I can say with
truth that I ceaselessly love and glorify Thy Father and Thee in them
and with them; for both they and I are members of one identical
Head and one identical body and are, therefore, all one: consequently,
all that is theirs is mine. I share, therefore, all they do; indeed I do
in them and with them all that they do. What a consolation it is for
me to know that I am already in heaven, and that I there love and
glorify God without ceasing! Lord Jesus, how can I possibly love
Thee or thank Thee enough for having united me in so close and
so holy a union with Thee and with all Thy saints, and for having
given me, by this union, such great and profitable means of praising
and loving Thee perpetually in heaven and on earth? O my Saviour,

let me praise Thee and love Thee on earth as in heaven! May I live on earth a life in conformity with the life I lead in Thee and in Thy saints in heaven! May I do on earth what I do with Thee and with Thy saints in heaven, that is, may I be ever engaged, without interruption, in loving and praising Thee! May I begin my heaven in this world, seeking all my joy and satisfaction in blessing and loving Thee and in doing all Thy holy will, in striving courageously and faithfully to complete the work of grace Thou dost desire to accomplish in me, so that once this work is finished and perfected, Thou mayest come and take me with Thee into the kingdom of Thy eternal love, that I may there love and magnify Thee perfectly, without ceasing, and forever!

XI. Prayer to Jesus on All the Phases and Mysteries of His Life, and a Consecration of Every Phase and Detail of Your Life to Him.

O Jesus my Lord, I cast myself down and annihilate myself at Thy feet; I surrender myself to the might of Thy divine spirit and Thy holy love, in their immense power and greatness; I adore, glorify and love Thee in Thyself and in all the mysteries and phases of Thy life. I adore Thee in Thy temporal life on earth for thirty-four years. I adore Thee in the first moment of that life, in Thy holy Childhood, in Thy hidden life of labor, in Thy public ministry among men, both when Thou wast living and walking on earth for all to see, and now that Thou art still among us in the Blessed Eucharist. I adore Thee in all Thy sufferings, whether interior or exterior, and in the last moment of Thy passable life. I adore Thee in Thy life of glory and bliss in heaven ever since the Ascension. I adore Thee in Thy life in the most Blessed Virgin and in all the angels and saints, whether in heaven or on earth. And, in general, I adore, love and glorify Thee in all the other mysteries and wonders that are embraced in the measureless expanse of Thy life, divine, temporal, and glorified. I bless Thee and give Thee infinite thanks for all the glory Thou didst ever and ever shalt give to the Father in all the phases of Thy life.

I offer Thee all the love and honor Thou ever didst or shalt receive forever, in all Thy mysteries and states, from all the angels and all the saints, begging them most humbly to love and glorify Thee, for me, in every way possible and proper to Thy glory.

O Jesus, I give myself to Thee and beg Thee with my whole heart to enter into me, there to destroy all that is not Thee, and to imprint a perfect image of Thyself, the states and mysteries of Thy life, Thy qualities and Thy virtues. Come, Lord Jesus, enter into me to destroy all that is not Thee and establish Thyself perfectly, there to be all and do all, that thus my being and my life, in all its aspects and ramifications, may be totally dedicated to the honor of Thy life and Thy sovereign being. May my birth in nature and in grace, my childhood, adolescence and my years of activity as a mature man, my agony, death and burial, together with all the other phases of my temporal and eternal life, be consecrated to the honor of each successive part of Thy life, Thy birth, childhood, adolescence, Thy maturity, Thy Passion, death and burial, and all the other states of Thy temporal and eternal life. May all my thoughts, words and actions give honor to Thine. May every step I take, all my works and sufferings give honor to every step Thou didst take on earth and all Thy works and sufferings. May all the powers of my soul and all the senses of my body be dedicated to the honor of Thy holy soul and senses of Thy deified body. Finally, may everything that ever was, is, and shall be in me be transformed into ceaseless and eternal adoration, praise and love for Thee. Come Lord Jesus, enter into me; live and reign over me perfectly, and there love and glorify Thyself as befits Thee, to carry out the designs of Thy goodness in my being, to accomplish the work of Thy grace and to establish forever in my heart the kingdom of Thy glory and Thy pure love. *Veni, Domine Jesu, veni in plenitudine virtutis tuae, in sanctitate Spiritus tui, in perfectione mysteriorum tuorum, et in puritate viarum tuarum. Veni, Domine Jesu.*

Come, Lord Jesus, enter into me in the fulness of Thy virtue, to destroy all that displeases Thee and execute all that Thou dost desire for Thy glory. Come in the sanctity of Thy spirit to detach me entirely from all that is not Thyself, to unite me perfectly with Thee and to lead me in the path of sanctity in all my actions. Come in the perfection of Thy mysteries, that is, to perfect in me what Thou dost deign to operate by Thy mysteries. Come in the purity of Thy ways, to accomplish in me, no matter at what price, and without sparing me in any way, all the designs of Thy pure love, and lead me in the straight path of that same pure love without permitting me to turn aside, without yielding anything to the inclinations and feelings of corrupt nature and self-love. Come, Lord Jesus!

## PART FIVE

*Devotional Exercises to Be Done Each Month to Live a Christian and Saintly Life and to Make Jesus Reign in Your Soul*

## DEVOTIONAL EXERCISES TO BE DONE EACH MONTH TO LIVE A CHRISTIAN AND SAINTLY LIFE AND TO MAKE JESUS REIGN IN YOUR SOUL

### I. EXERCISE FOR THE FIRST AND LAST DAYS OF THE MONTH.

The first and last day of each month ought to assume great importance for you. You should treat the first day as a new beginning of your life, and excite a fresh desire and resolution to serve and love God perfectly, and to spend that month well in His love and glory, looking upon it as though it were to be the last month of your life. But especially should you consider and make use of the last day of the month as you would wish to spend the last day of your life. The first and last day of each month should be dedicated in honor of the first and last day of the life of Our Lord, just as you consecrated the first and last day of each year. Thus you will begin and end each month as well as each year in union with Our Lord. The spiritual exercises to be proposed in "Part Six" for the beginning and ending of the year may be adapted for each month.

### II. THE MONTHLY RETREAT.

In addition to your annual retreat, it is beneficial to set aside one day in each month, for example, the first Thursday or any other special day, to renew and stimulate the good desires and resolutions adopted in the yearly retreat; to make reparation for your failures in God's service and love during the month. You should apply yourself particularly to God on that day, performing all your ordinary actions with more than ordinary attention and perfection, giving yourself with special care and fervor to exercises of praise and love of Jesus. That is why I insert here various exercises and rosaries of praise, glory, and love for Jesus, which you may use on this day of retreat, selecting now one, now another, according to the graces God may give you.

But, first, I must tell you that, in order to stir you up and enkindle you with a greater desire to praise and love Jesus, it would be a good thing for you to set apart some time that same day for the attentive consideration of the thoughts I shall set forth in the following meditation.

### III. Meditation to Stir You up to Praise and Glorify Jesus.

1. Consider that Jesus is infinitely worthy of all praise, glory and blessing, for every reason in the universe. He deserves infinite praise for all that He is and all that He does for His Eternal Father, glorifying and loving Him infinitely and continually from all eternity and to all eternity; likewise for all that He is in Himself, in His divinity, in all His divine perfections, in His Divine Person, in His sacred humanity, in His body, in His soul, the very least elements of which deserve infinite praise; in all His states and mysteries; in all His qualities and offices; in all His words, thoughts, deeds, and sufferings; in all His virtues, and in everything that subsists in Him, the very least of which is so deserving of praise that, even if all the angels and saints were to be occupied for all eternity in glorifying and praising it with all their might, they would never be able to render it the glory deserved.

Furthermore, He deserves undying praise for everything that He is and everything that He has accomplished with respect to His holy spirit, His Blessed Mother, all His angels, all His saints, all men, all Christians, and all creatures on earth and even in hell. He deserves no less praise for the effects of His justice than for those of His mercy, since all His divine attributes are equally holy and worthy of adoration. Many are the reasons to bless and glorify Jesus, who so commands your adoration and love! But always remember that you should be much more ready to praise and love Him for what He is and what He does with respect to His Father, Himself, and His Holy Spirit, than for what He is and does for you and for other creatures, because the interests of God ought to be infinitely more dear to you than your own.

2. Consider that the only reason for your existence on earth is to love Jesus and give Him glory. To this you are bound by an infinite number of special reasons, because of the countless graces He has given you. Hence, it should be your chief, nay, your only care and business to make your active life a ceaseless offering of love and glory to Jesus. All your thoughts, words, deeds, and affections should have only this one object in view, to which should be directed the employment of all your time and all the powers of your body and soul. And you see how, instead of loving and glorifying Him, you have done practically nothing else, in your whole life, but offend Him in your thoughts, words, and actions, and in all the functions of your body and soul. Humble yourself profoundly before Him; ask His forgiveness, and cultivate a fervent desire to make up for all these faults, and to exert yourself from now on to love and glorify Him perfectly.

3. Look back on your whole life and examine it, together with your actions and your behavior, and consider what it is in you that most obstructs the love and glory of Jesus. Then firmly resolve to fight, overcome and destroy this defect at all costs, giving yourself withal to your Loving Jesus and imploring Him to eradicate your predominant fault by the power of His grace and His divine love.

After that, exert all the powers of your soul to praise and glorify your divine Saviour in the following manner, or in any other way He may inspire you, whether it be vocal, or only in your heart in the form of a meditation.

## IV. Exercise to Praise and Glorify Jesus.

O Jesus, most worthy of honor and glory, since Thou art so full of grandeur and perfections that command praises without end, and since I am in this world only to give Thee glory, I now desire to exert all the powers of my soul and body in blessing and magnifying Thee. I implore Thy Eternal Father, Thy Holy Spirit, Thy Blessed Mother, Thy angels, and saints, and all the creatures in heaven and on earth, to join with me in blessing Thee, for all that Thou art to Thy Eternal Father, to Thyself, to Thy Holy Spirit, to Thy Blessed Mother, to all Thy angels, all Thy saints, to all men, to all Christians, to myself in particular, and to all created things.

O Kind Jesus, with all my heart I beg Thee to forgive me for having hitherto, instead of praising and glorifying Thee, done hardly anything but dishonor and offend Thee. To satisfy for this, I offer Thee all the praises that ever have been, and ever shall be rendered to Thee in heaven and on earth.

O my Dear Jesus, I give myself all to Thee. Destroy all in me that militates against Thy glory; transform every thought and function of my body and soul into praises and blessings of Thee. O Jesus, Thou art worthy of praise without end; may I be all praise for Thee! If I possessed all the strength of all the creatures in heaven and on earth, I should be obliged to exert all of it in praising Thee. How great, then, is my obligation to exert what small powers I have. So then, let everything in me be employed and consumed in blessing and magnifying Thee. *Benedic, anima mea, Domino et omnia quae intra me sunt, nomini sancto ejus* (Ps. 102, 1).

O Jesus, so worthy to be admired, I hear Thy holy word commanding me to bless Thee from all eternity to all eternity: *Benedicite Domino Deo vestro ab aeterno usque in aeternum* (II Esd. 9, 5). For this purpose I offer Thee all the blessings that have ever been or ever shall be accorded Thee, from all eternity, by Thy Eternal Father, by Thyself and Thy Holy Spirit, uniting myself with all these blessings, and imploring Thee, in Thy great bounty, to unite my humble praise to the endless voice of all who bless Thee forever.

O Great Jesus, Thou art omnipresent. By Thy divinity, Thou dost fill up heaven, earth, and even hell with the immense greatness of Thy divine majesty; Thou art most worthy to be loved and glorified in every place. So, too, art Thou loved and glorified beyond all measure in heaven, on earth and even in hell, by Thy Father and Thy Holy Spirit, who are everywhere with Thee, and everywhere love and glorify Thee without ceasing.

Thus heaven, earth, and even hell are filled with Thy love, Thy glory and praise: *Pleni sunt coeli et terra gloria tua* (Isa. 6, 3). I say even hell, because it is filled with the love, glory, and praise there given Thee by the infinite justice of The Father and The Holy Spirit. O Dearest Jesus, what pleasure and joy for me to behold how the whole world is filled with Thy glory!

Indeed, my Saviour, since Thou art thus in every place, and dost everywhere deserve to be praised, I also desire to praise Thee wherever Thou art. To that end I unite myself with all the glory that is given Thee now in heaven, on earth and in hell, and shall be given Thee forever.

Furthermore, I desire now to descend in spirit into hell and there, in the midst of Thine enemies, in spite of all their hatred and fury against Thee, to unite myself with the exceeding great love borne for Thee by Thy Father and Holy Spirit in that place. I adore and love and bless Thee with my whole heart, O Jesus, my Lord, for all that Thou art in Thyself and in all things, and even for all the effects of justice which Thou dost visit upon the demons and the damned.

O Jesus, exceedingly to be adored, would that I had in myself all the powers and all the capacity to praise and glorify Thee that were once in the possession of these miserable souls which, by their malice, they have lost, so that I might now exert them in praising and loving Thee! These traitors now surrender themselves with all their might, with never a pause. Would that I could show at least as much fervor and concentration in praising Thee as they show fury and concentration in blaspheming Thee! Would that I could make some slight reparation for the insults and curses they heap upon my Saviour!

O Good Jesus, these unhappy souls received from Thee the priceless gifts of being, life and natural perfections, and should use them all for Thy glory; yet they are doing just the contrary. But I must, and I will, give what they fail to give, and in their stead to the things they ought to be doing. For the being, the life and natural perfections of demons and of all reprobates belong to Thee, O my God, because they emanate from Thee. Consequently they belong to me, since all things are mine, according to the Holy Apostle: *Omnia vestra sunt* (I Cor. 3, 22), because, in giving Thyself to me, Thou didst give me all that was Thine. Thus, it necessarily follows that I can, and must exercise on behalf of Thy glory the being, life and natural perfections of the demons and the damned, because I am bound to exert all the power that belongs to me to give Thee glory and praise. Hence, I offer and refer these things to Thee, O my Jesus, as my own possessions and I render Thee homage for them; I cast them at Thy feet and sacrifice them entirely and forever to Thy praise and Thy glory. Such is the use and employment to which I desire to put the faculties of the damned so that in spite of themselves they may give glory to Thy Holy Name.

O my God, I desire to descend again in spirit into hell, and put myself in the place that Thou knowest I have deserved by sins, where I should indeed be, if Thou hadst not delivered me by Thy mercy. There I desire to adore and love Thee, O my sovereign Judge, and to glorify Thee in all the effects of the terrible justice Thou wouldst have inflicted upon me for all eternity, if Thy mercy had not taken pity on my wretchedness.

O Most Kind Jesus, I have exceeding great confidence that, in Thy infinite goodness, Thou wilt give me grace to become one of the elect who shall bless Thee forever. But none the less, supposing I were to be so unhappy as to resist the designs of Thy goodness, and by my sins cause myself to become a victim of Thy justice, I should desire at this present moment, O great God, voluntarily and through love to do what I should do then, through necessity and compulsion. I mean that I should desire to adore, love and bless, with my whole heart and all my strength, Thy most equitable judgment against me, and all its effects as Thy prophet has said: *Justus es, Domine, et rectum judicium tuum:* "Thou art just, O Lord: and thy judgment is right" (Ps. 118, 137). And yet, O Dearest Jesus, whom I so desire, I recover again my unshakable confidence that in Thy immense mercy Thou wilt deliver me from so great a disaster. For, alas! *Non mortui laudabunt te, Domine, neque omnes qui descendunt in infernum.* The dead, that is, those who have died the eternal death, shall not praise Thee, O Lord, nor shall all those who go down into hell (Ps. 113, 17). *Hic ure, hic seca, modo in aeternum parcas.* "Burn, tear, and cut me to pieces, provided only Thou dost pardon me in eternity" (St. Augustine), and provided that I may be numbered among those who shall praise and love Thee forever.

## V. CONTINUATION OF THE FOREGOING EXERCISE.

Once I have thus adored and blessed Thee in hell, O Jesus exceedingly worthy of love, I desire to proceed in spirit to purgatory, there to adore, love and glorify Thee similarly, in all the works wrought by Thy justice there, and even in the punishment Thou wilt one day visit upon me, when I shall be in purgatory. So, too, I desire to go there to unite myself with all the love and glory that ever was, is and ever shall be given Thee in that blessed place of purification.

From purgatory I come to the visible world of creation, where I behold three different orders of being, in which I desire to bless and magnify Thee, O Jesus, Sovereign Lord of the World.

The first is the order of irrational and inanimate creatures, concerning which Sacred Scripture teaches me that they praise and magnify Thee without ceasing, to the full extent of their being and natural power, and their existence is entirely one of confession, that is, praise and magnificence of Thee. *Confessio et magnificentia opus ejus* (Ps. 110, 3). O my divine Creator, how I rejoice to behold Thee incessantly glorified by all Thy creatures, and to see that all Thy works are filled with Thy glory, according to the divine testimony: *Gloria Domini plenum est opus ejus* (Eccli. 42, 16), and to hear that the whole universe resounds with Thy praise! How guilty I am, and what a source of confusion it is to me to understand that I have to learn, from insensible creatures, the lesson of the glory I must render to Thy divine majesty. O Lord, permit me to unite myself with all the blessings accorded Thee without ceasing by all creatures. O you beloved creatures of my God, bless Him, praise Him, exalt Him for me through all the ages: *Benedicite omnia opera Domini Domina, laudate et superexaltate eum in saecula* (Dan. 3, 57). Divine Creator, do not allow me to live on earth except to join all Thy creatures in ceaselessly blessing Thee.

The second order in the world is the state of the wicked, that is, those who are devoid of all knowledge or love of Thee, O most kind Jesus, and who begin to do on earth what the damned do in hell— that is, to dishonor and offend Thee continually. Let me, O my Jesus, with the help of Thy grace, make up for all they fail to give Thee. Let me love and bless Thee for them, and for all the favors Thou hast given them, of which they make not the slightest acknowledgment to Thy bounty. Let me refer and sacrifice to Thy glory the being, life and natural perfections Thou hast given them, just as I have referred and sacrificed to Thy glory the being, life and natural perfections of those who are in hell.

The third order which I behold in the world, O Jesus, is the good, which embraces the vast number of holy souls living in the world and in many religious communities, who are employed without ceasing in Thy praise, with such affection and discipline that not a single hour or minute of the day or night goes by without Thy receiving great glory and praise from them. For this do I rejoice beyond measure, O my God, and I desire to unite myself, if it please Thee, with all the benedictions that ever have been, or are now, or ever shall be given Thee on earth by all the precious souls that belong to Thee.

From earth my thoughts ascend to heaven, where I behold the Eternal Father, the Holy Spirit, Thy Blessed Mother, together with so many millions of Seraphim, Cherubim, Thrones, Dominations, Virtues, Powers, Principalities, Archangels, Angels, Patriarchs, Prophets, Apostles, Martyrs, Priests, Confessors, Virgins, Widows, Innocents and other saints, who are forever engaged in loving and glorifying Thee with all their might, with radiant love and concentration. My Dear Jesus, how glad I am to behold Thee so loved and magnified! I offer up to Thee all this glory and all this praise. O Father of Jesus, Holy Spirit of Jesus, Mother of Jesus, and His angels and saints, with all the blessings that you give to Jesus my Lord, include, I pray you, my own also, and allow me to share in the love, attention, purity and sanctity with which you incessantly praise Him, so that I may praise Him with you forever and thus commence here below what I hope and desire to do eternally with you in heaven.

O Most Divine Jesus, I rejoice beyond all measure that Thou art so full of greatness and perfection, and consequently so deserving of glory and praise that all the creatures on earth and in heaven together are unable to praise Thee according to Thy worth. Thy dignity and worthiness of praise infinitely surpass the whole capacity of heaven and earth to praise Thee, as the Prophet David said: *Confessio ejus super coelum et terram* (Ps. 148, 14). Only the Father and Holy Spirit give Thee praise worthy of Thy infinite greatness. All the other praises rendered on earth or in heaven are unworthy of Thee, for they are finite, while Thou art deserving of praise that is infinite.

O Father of Jesus, Holy Spirit of Jesus, what shall I do for You? How shall I repay You for the glory You give to Jesus Christ my Lord? Yes, even though (to imagine the impossible) I had never received nor ever should receive any favor from You, I should none the less desire to love and serve You eternally for the love and the glory that You give to Him who is my all, whom I love more than myself.

O Father of Jesus, O Holy Spirit of Jesus, I implore You with my whole heart, by Your very great love for my Lord, and by Your most ardent zeal for His glory, to atone for all my neglect in pleasing Him, and to make Him a hundredfold return for all the glory I ought to have rendered Him all my life. O Good Jesus, I give myself to Thee, to praise and glorify Thee in every way that shall please Thee. Grant that my life may henceforth be a continual sacrifice of praise and benediction for Thee, but do Thou render infinite blessing to Thyself on my behalf: *Benedicite omnes virtutes Domini Domino.* Let all the virtues, that is, all the might and powers of Thy divinity and humanity, Lord Jesus, be employed in blessing Thee for me, and in exalting and magnifying Thee incessantly and forever (Dan. 3, 61).

## VI. Rosary of the Eternal Father.

On this monthly day of recollection devoted to a more particular love and praise of Jesus, you may, if you like, say a rosary which I call the Rosary of the Father of Jesus, because it is addressed to the Eternal Father, and beg Him to praise and glorify His Son Jesus in you and for you.

This rosary is made up of thirty-four small beads, in honor of the thirty-four years of Our Lord's life on earth.

First, repeat three times *Veni Pater Jesu,* "Come, Father of Jesus," to invoke and draw down to you the Father of Jesus, and to give yourself to Him that He may destroy all in you that is contrary to the glory of His Son, and glorify Him in you according to His holy will.

Then on each small bead say: *Pater clarifica Filium Tuum, ut*

*Filius Tuus clarificet Te:* "Father, glorify thy Son, that thy Son may glorify thee" (John 17, 1).

This is the prayer which the Son of God addressed to His Eternal Father on the eve of His death. Therefore, no prayer can be said by you that is more pleasing to Him than this invocation, nor can you ask Him anything that would please Him more than what you request of Him in this perfect prayer.

But when you recite this invocation, remember that it came forth from the heart and lips of Jesus. Unite yourself with the humility, the purity, the love, and all the holy dispositions and intentions with which Jesus Christ uttered it, begging the Eternal Father to glorify His Divine Son throughout the whole world, and to destroy in you and in all mankind everything that is contrary to His glory. Implore Him to implant in your soul all the graces and virtues required for His perfect glorification, and to exert the power of His own zeal and love for His Son to glorify Him there, according to His holy will.

On the large beads say: *Gloria tibi, Domine Jesu, qui natus es de Virgine,* "Glory to Thee, Lord Jesus, who wast born of the Virgin Mary." When you say this, offer to Jesus Christ all the glory that ever has been, is now and ever shall be rendered to Him forever in heaven and on earth.

## VII. EXERCISE OF LOVE FOR JESUS.

Of all the duties and functions of a truly Christian soul, the most noble, most holy, most elevated that God asks of you before all others is to exercise yourself in divine love. For this reason you must make a point of affirming to Jesus Christ our Lord, in all your pious practices and other actions, that you desire to perform them, not for fear of hell, nor for the reward of heaven, nor for the merit attached, nor for your own satisfaction and consolation, but only for the love of God Himself, for His satisfaction, His glory and His pure love.

So, too, you ought frequently to exercise yourself by contemplation and acts of this divine love.

I have already indicated many such acts in the preceding exercises. But in addition, here are thirty-four more, in honor of the thirty

four years of Our Lord's life on earth, a life that was all love. Added
to these are one or two others which may be used at any time, but
chiefly for the monthly day of recollection or any other day in the
month set aside expressly for your conscientious application to this
divine contemplation, which is the greatest, the holiest, and most
noble occupation of the angels and saints, and of God Himself, in
which He always has been, is now, and ever shall be engaged throughout all the infinite extent of eternity.

VIII. Thirty-four Acts of Love of Jesus Christ in Honor of the
     Thirty-four Years of His Life on Earth.

1. O Jesus, my Saviour, Thou art all lovable, infinitely lovable and
infinitely worthy of love. O my God, I need no other knowledge but
this. What concern have I with so many studies and ideas and considerations? It suffices me to know that my Jesus is all lovable, and
that there is nothing in Him that is not worthy of being loved beyond
measure. Let my mind then be satisfied with this knowledge; but
may the hunger of my heart to love Him Who can never be loved
enough, never be sated.

2. Alas! My Saviour, I know that this poor, insignificant, imperfect
heart of mine is not worthy to love Thee. But Thou art exceeding
worthy to be loved, and Thou didst create this poor heart only that
it might love Thee. Thou dost command it to love Thee under pain
of death, eternal death. God of my heart, Thou hast no need to command. To love Thee is what I want, what I desire, what my heart
sighs after. Yes, my Jesus, I no longer want any other desire. Farewell all other thoughts, all other inclinations, all other wishes. I wish
to have but one increasing purpose here on earth; I desire nothing,
only to love Jesus, who is the love and delight of heaven and earth.
Ah, Jesus! Ah, My Dear Jesus! What do I desire on earth? Nothing,
O my all, but only to love Thee.

3. O Jesus, worthy of all desire, indeed I long to love Thee, not
only with all the power of my too feeble will, but to the full extent
and with all the might of Thy divine will, which is mine since Thou
hast given me all. Add to that the will of all men and angels. They
also are mine, since in giving Thyself to me Thou hast given me

everything. O sweetest Lord, would that I were entirely transformed into desires, aching, yearning, and longing to love Thee ever more and more!

4. O Thou desire of my soul, grant me the favor I implore; hearken to the cry of my heart. Thou knowest, Lord, what I ask of Thee; my heart has so often told Thee. I ask nothing but the perfection of Thy holy love. I desire only to love Thee and ever to grow progressively in that desire. O Thou object of all my desires, increase in me the desire to love Thee, which Thou hast given me. Increase it so much and make it so burning and strong that I may henceforth glow incessantly with the desire of Thy love.

5. O Jesus, worthy of all love, crown of all desire, enkindle in my soul so burning a thirst and so extreme a hunger for Thy holy love that it may be to me a ceaseless martyrdom not to love Thee enough, and let nothing more in this world be able to cause me sorrow, except that I love Thee too little.

6. O Good Jesus! Who is there who would not wish to love Thee? Who would not desire to love ever more and more such lovable goodness? My God, my life and my all, I cannot be content to tell Thee that I desire to love Thee as perfectly as possible, and that I desire it so much that, if it were possible, I should will my whole spirit to be transformed into wishing, my whole soul into desire, my heart into yearning, my life into longing.

7. O King of my heart, take pity on my misery. Thou knowest that I want to love Thee. But alas! Thou seest how much there is in me that goes against Thy love. Thou seest the innumerable multitude of my sins, my self-will, my self-love, my pride and all the other vices and imperfections which keep me from loving Thee perfectly. I detest and abhor all these defects which so obstruct my desire to love Thee! What must I do to destroy them? I stand ready to do and suffer all that pleases Thee for that end. Exert the strength of Thy powerful arm to exterminate in my soul all the enemies of Thy love.

8. O Jesus, everything in Thee is love, and all love for me. And although I ought to be all love for Thee, there is in me nothing of myself, whether in body or in soul, that is not opposed to Thy love. Oh, what pain! Oh, what anguish! How can I tolerate my own self? Where art Thou, divine love? Where is Thy power? Where the

force of Thy mighty arm? O consuming and devouring fire, where are Thy heavenly flames? Why dost Thou not totally annihilate this wicked and sinful life of mine, and establish Thy life, divine and holy?

9. O all-powerful love, I surrender myself entirely to Thy holy might. Come, I beseech Thee, into my soul, there to destroy all that displeases Thee, and to establish Thy heavenly kingdom. If suffering is all that is required to effect this change, I offer myself with my whole heart to Thee, that I may suffer all the martyrdom and torments that ever have been and ever shall be suffered in the world. Spare me not, love! Nothing matters except that I be set free from all that displeases my Saviour and of all attachments that keep me from loving Him. I long to love my Jesus and I will to love Him perfectly, no matter what the cost, no matter what the sacrifice.

10. O God of love, Thou art all lovable, all loving, all love and all love for me. Why am I not also all love for Thee? Why are not heaven and earth transformed into a pure flame of love for Thee?

11. My sweet love, who shall henceforth prevent me from loving Thee, now that I realize Thy immense goodness? Shall my body? I will grind it to dust first! Shall my past sins? O Jesus, I plunge them deep into the sea of Thy Precious Blood. Take my body and my soul and make me suffer all that pleases Thee, to purge them utterly, so that they may no longer prevent me from loving Thee. Shall the world, or creatures stop me? No. With all my might I renounce all affections of sense and all created things. I consecrate my whole heart and all my affections to Jesus, my Creator and my God. And as for you, O world, excommunicated from Jesus, since He and His disciples are not of this world, and since He said that He prayed not for the world, know once and for all that I give you up forever. I fly from you as from an excommunicate; it is my will to consider you as an antichrist, the enemy of my Lord Jesus Christ. I will set no more store by your praises and censures, your pleasures and ambitions, or by all that you most highly value and cherish than I would by a dream or a puff of smoke that vanishes away. I will hold in abhorrence your spirit, your code of behavior, your opinions and your accursed maxims. Finally, I will hate and persecute your malice just as

much as you hate and persecute the goodness of my Lord Jesus Christ.

Farewell then, world, and once again farewell to all that is not God. Jesus shall henceforth be my world, my fame, my fortune, my delight and my all. I no longer desire to see anything but Jesus Christ. Eyes, close yourselves up against all else, for He alone is a worthy object of vision. I no longer want to please anyone but Jesus. I no longer want to have any love or affection save for Him. I no longer want to rejoice except in His love and in performing His most amiable will. Nor do I any longer wish to grieve except for what offends Him and is contrary to His divine love. O love! O love! Let me love or let me die: nay, rather let me both die and love! Die to all that is not Jesus, and then love Him alone to perfection.

12. O King of my love, Thou hast placed me on earth only that I may love Thee. Oh, how noble, how holy and how lofty is the end for which Thou hast created me! O what a favor, O my heart! What an honor was given Thee, when Thou wast created for the same purpose as the God who made Thee, and to employ thyself in the same divine activity which is His ceaseless concern! This great God exists only to contemplate and love Himself eternally and continually. My soul is created only to love the God who made it, and to be forever employed in loving and blessing Him. May He be forever loved and blessed, the King of all hearts, who has given to me a heart capable of loving Him!

God of my heart, since Thou hast created me only to love Thee, do not allow me to live except in love of Thee, ever growing in Thy love. Death or love! Give me more life, my God, only that I may love Thee more. Better a thousand deaths than the loss of Thy love.

13. O divine love, be the life of my life, soul of my soul, heart of my heart. Let me live no more save in Thee and by Thee. Let me no more subsist save by Thee and for Thee.

14. Thou sole object of my heart, Thou alone art worthy to be loved. All that is not Thee is mere nothingness and deserves not even one passing glance. It is Thee alone that I desire, Thee alone that I seek, Thee alone I long to love. Thou art my all; the rest is nothing

to me now and I no longer want to regard anything or love anything, save Thee in all things.

O Dearest Jesus, Thou art my greatest friend; indeed Thou art my one and only friend. To me Thou art Father, Brother, Spouse and Head. Thou art all mine. I desire to be all Thine forever.

15. O Jesus, who alone art worthy to be loved, who alone dost love and alone art loved by the Eternal Father and by all the elect who love in heaven, grant that I may love Thee above all things, alone in all things, and that if I love any created thing, I may love it only in Thee and for Thee.

16. O Thou only love of my heart! O Thou sole object of my love! Nothing in heaven or on earth is worthy of love save Thee. When, therefore, shall it be ordained that men will see nothing and love nothing in heaven and on earth save Thee?

17. O Jesus, O my one and only love, detach me altogether from myself and from all things. Draw me inescapably close to Thee. Possess me so fully and so absolutely that nothing but Thee may ever retain any part of my mind or my heart.

18. O Dearest Jesus! How lovable Thou art, and yet how little loved! The world thinks not of Thee, nor of loving Thee. It thinks only of offending Thee and of persecuting those who desire to love Thee. Let me then think of Thy love instead of the world and concentrate all my thoughts on loving Thee! Grant that I may love Thee as much as the world ought to love Thee.

19. O Eternal Son of the Eternal Father, Thou art all lovable, all loving, and all love. From all eternity Thou didst begin, without beginning, to love me forever. If I had existed from all eternity, I should have been bound to love Thee always. As I have only existed in time I should at least have loved Thee from the first moment I obtained the use of reason. Alas! I have begun to love Thee late indeed, nor do I even dare to say that I have even now begun to love Thee as I should. O Eternal God, Thou hast never passed a moment without loving me, through all the extent of Thy eternity, and yet I hardly know if I have ever spent a single moment of my life in loving Thee as I ought. On the contrary, I know only too well that I have never spent a day without offending Thee. What pain, what heart-

break for my soul, O Lord; I can not tolerate myself when I think of this. Break with grief, O my heart. Dissolve into tears, O eyes! Why am I not dissolved into a sea of tears of penance and of blood, to lament and wipe out my prodigious ingratitude towards such great kindness! O love, no more offenses, no more sin, no more infidelity, no longer anything but love!

20. O eternal love, Thou art loved from all eternity by the Eternal Father and by the Holy Spirit. Boundless is my joy at this; I unite myself with this love, and I lose myself in the ceaseless love of the Father and the Holy Spirit for Thee from all eternity.

21. O everlasting beauty! O eternal goodness! If I had an eternity on earth, I should be bound to employ it all in Thy love. How great, then, is my obligation to use what little life and time remain for me to love Thee! O dearest Lord, I consecrate it all to Thy holy love. Grant that I may no longer live save to love Thee, and that no moment of my life may pass without being employed in Thy divine love! But above all, grant me to love Thee for all eternity. Whatever happens, I unite myself now with all the love that shall be Thine throughout eternity.

O eternity of love! My Dearest Jesus, consume me with thy divine Fire; dismember me, reduce me to dust and make me suffer every thing Thou dost please in this world, provided only that I may love Thee eternally.

22. O King of Ages, Thou hast bought, at the price of Thy blood, every minute of my time and of my life so that I might use them in loving Thee. Too much, too much, alas, have I wasted on self-love, on love of the world and on attachment to created things. Too much time have I lost, time that has cost Thee so dearly, which ought to be so precious to me, since it could be employed in such great and important work as the infinite concerns of Thy divine love. It is indeed time, O Jesus, high time, that I begin seriously to practise the holy exercises of Thy sacred love. Let me have no more days and hours, except to love Thee. Let me so dispose my life that there may remain for me in all the world only myself and Thee. May I have nothing to do but think of Thee and converse with Thee, heart to heart, spirit to spirit. And may nothing, of all the things that happen in the world,

touch me or pertain to me, save only the one care and the one desire to love Thee. O Jesus, increase in me this desire, and make it become so burning and so urgent that it may grow from a simple desire, into continual longing. May I aspire to Thee incessantly; may I tend towards Thee perpetually; may I yearn for Thee night and day without ceasing. O Sweetest Jesus, Thou only love of my desires, when will the time come when I shall be utterly transformed into a pure flame of love for Thee?

23. O immense love, God of the Universe, Thou dost fill heaven and earth; Thou art everywhere and in all things. Everywhere dost Thou infinitely love the Father and the Holy Spirit, and art infinitely loved by Them. So, too, Thou dost love me infinitely in all places and in all things. Let me love Thee also in all places and all things, and let me love all things in Thee and for Thee. To that end, I unite myself to Thy divine immensity, and in its fathomless power, I direct my mind and my will everywhere and into all places in the world. There, in all the power and immensity of Thy spirit and Thy love, I love Thee, glorify Thee and adore Thee infinitely. I also unite myself to the all-embracing love of Thy Father and Thy Holy Spirit for Thee, manifested everywhere and in all things that are in heaven, on earth and even in hell.

24. O infinite goodness, an infinite love would be necessary to love Thee as Thou dost deserve. What joy for my soul, what satisfaction for my heart, to know Thou art so good, so perfect, and so lovable that even if all creatures on earth and in heaven were to exert all their strength, throughout eternity, they would never be able to love Thee enough. There is none but Thyself, together with the Father and the Holy Spirit, capable of loving Thee worthily.

25. O infinite goodness, if I had every single heart and the total capacity for love possessed by all men and angels, I should be bound to exert them all in the love of Him who is infinitely lovable, and directs all the sources of His wisdom, power and goodness to loving me and working so many wonders for my love. How great, then, is my obligation to exert my little strength in loving His goodness! Henceforth, O my Dear Jesus, I desire to pour forth all the powers of my body and soul in loving Thee. But that is not enough. I desire

also to gather unto myself all the might of heaven and earth, which belong to me by Thy gift of Thyself, and exert them all in loving Thee. I desire to employ likewise all the powers of Thy divinity and humanity, which are also mine, since Thou hast Thyself given Thyself to me.

I love Thee, then, O Jesus, I love Thee with all my might, with all the strength of my body and my soul, all the capacity of every creature in heaven and on earth, and all the powers of Thy divinity and humanity.

26. But what am I saying, O my God? I am not worthy to love Thee. To Thee alone belongs so holy and divine a function. Therefore I annihilate myself at Thy feet, plunging into the deepest abyss of my nothingness. I give myself all to Thee. Do Thou Thyself destroy me by the power of that most mighty love, which reduced Thee even to our nothingness, and establish Thyself in me in order to love Thyself there with a love worthy of Thee. Let me love Thee, henceforth, no longer by myself nor by the powers of my own mind and my own love, but by Thee and by Thy mighty spirit and Thy flaming love.

27. O Most Lovable Jesus, Thou dost assure us in Holy Writ that the Father loves us even as He loves Thee, that is, with the same affection and the same love with which He loves Thee. Thou dost command us to love Thee as Thou dost love the Heavenly Father and to remain ever in Thy love, even as Thou dost ever dwell in the love of the Father. But, Lord, Thou knowest my powerlessness to love Thee by myself. Grant me the grace to perform what Thou dost command of me; then command me as Thou wilt. Destroy my own heart and my self-love. Implant within me Thy Heart and Thy love, so that I may henceforth love Thee as Thou lovest the Father and as the Father loves Thee. May I always remain in Thy love, as Thou dost remain always in the love of Thy Father; and may I do everything by the power and under the guidance of that love. Yes, my Jesus, it is in that eternal, infinite and immense love of the Father for Thee, and of Thee for the Father for all eternity, that I desire to love Thee from now on, consecrating to that love my every thought, word and deed for Thee. It is Thy infinite love, Thy immense Heart all filled with

treasures of sublime love, that I offer to Thee as my own heart and love, since Thou gavest it to me in giving me Thyself, together with the beloved heart of Thy peerless Mother, the most lovable, the most loved, and the most loving of all human hearts. To these I add the hearts of all the saints and holy persons in heaven and on earth, and I offer them as my own, since Thy holy apostle, St. Paul, teaches us that the Almighty Father, in giving Thee to us, gave us all things together with Thee (Rom. 8, 32).

28. O Jesus, Thou art purity itself and Thou dost love me with an exceedingly pure love. I desire also to love Thee with the purest love possible. Hence, I wish to love Thee in Thyself, in Thy own love; I desire to love nothing but Thee for Thyself alone, and solely for Thy good pleasure. I love Thee, O my Dearest Jesus, I love Thee with that exceeding pure love Thou hast for Thyself. I love thee also in the most pure love of the Eternal Father, the Holy Spirit, Thy most pure Mother, Thy angels and Thy saints. O Father of Jesus, angels of Jesus and His saints, O all creatures, come to my aid. Help me to love your Creator and mine. Come, let us love Him, our most lovable Lord, let us employ and expend all our being and all our powers in loving Him who created us only that we might love Him.

29. O Thou my heart's dear Friend and Thou dear Heart of my love! How desolate it is, and how much to be lamented with tears of blood, to see Thee loved so little even by those who claim to love Thee.

And this is strange because there is no one so worthy of love as Thou; yet it seems there is nothing in the world less loved than Thou art. There are many souls who love the thought of heaven and the sweetness of Thy grace and the consolations of Thy love, but out of a thousand good men scarcely one will be found to love Thee purely for love of Thyself alone. O most pure love, my dearest Saviour, Thee alone do I seek, Thee alone do I desire, Thee alone do I love. I desire to love Thee not for my own interest and satisfaction, not because it is sweet full of consolation, but because Thou art most worthy to be loved for Thyself alone.

30. When shall I love Thee so purely that I shall be able to say with truth: My Jesus is my all and everything else to me is nothing. He

alone sufficeth me, and I desire no other. I desire Him not for myself
but for His own goodness. The joys of Paradise, the consolidation
of heavenly love, are not my aim. I seek the Lord of Paradise and the
divine Author of all consolations. And even if He were never to
favor me with any consolations or reward (which would not be possible to His goodness), yet should I wish to love Him always, because
He is most worthy of love, for love of Himself. I desire no other reward than to have the power to love Him for His own sake alone.

O Good Jesus, implant these loving dispositions in my heart and in
the hearts of all mankind especially those to whom Thou knowest I
am indebted and eager to remember in my prayers. O King of all
hearts, behold I offer to Thee each poor human heart Thou hast
created to love Thee, desiring now only to breathe Thy love. Destroy
in those chosen hearts all that is contrary to Thy sacred affection; fill
them with Thy divine love. O dearest Saviour, draw them to Thyself;
unite them to Thy Sacred Heart; engulf them in Thy love and
number them among the blessed of whom it is said: *vivent corda
eorum in saeculum saeculi:* "Their hearts shall live for ever and ever"
(Ps. 21, 27), that is, they shall live with the life of divine love, in
order to love forever the God of love and of life! How blessed are the
hearts consecrated for all eternity to adore, praise and love the most
adorable and exceedingly lovable Heart of Jesus! Blessed be He who
has created these cherished hearts that He might be glorified and
loved by them forever!

31. O God of my life and of my heart, Thou dost ever love me.
Thou dost employ all Thy powers and all creation in heaven and on
earth, to testify to me of Thy love. I learn from one of Thy dearest
saints: "Heaven and earth and all creation never cease to tell me that
I should love the Lord my God" (St. Augustine., *Manuale,* c.24).
Everything that I hear, everything I see, taste, touch and smell, everything that can be known or desired by my memory, understanding
and will, all things visible and invisible that are contained in the order
of nature, grace and glory, all the temporal and eternal graces I have
received from Thee, all the angels and saints, all the encouraging ex-
amples they have given me by their virtues and their holy lives, all
the wonders Thou hast worked on behalf of Thy most holy Mother,

all the perfections inherent in the essence of Thy Divine Person, all the mysteries of Thy divinity and humanity, all Thy divine attributes and virtues, all Thy thoughts, words, deeds and sufferings, every step Thou didst take on earth, every drop of Thy Precious Blood, all the wounds of Thy sacred body, in a word, all things that are or ever were, in created or uncreated being, in time and in eternity, constitute so many tongues, by which Thou dost continually proclaim to me Thy goodness and Thy love. All these things incessantly testify that Thou dost love me and dost urge me to love Thee in return. All are so many voices by which Thou dost say constantly to me: *Amo te, amo te: dilige me quia ipse prior dilexi te. Dilige Dominum Deum tuum ex toto corde tuo, ex tota anima tua, et ex totis viribus tuis.* "I love thee, I love thee; love Me for I have loved thee first. Love the Lord thy God with thy whole heart and thy whole soul and thy whole strength." Finally, all these things are so many preachers, so many voices crying out to me without ceasing: Love, love for Jesus, who is all love for you, who employs all that He is, all that He has, all that He knows, all that He does and all that depends on Him, in heaven and on earth, to make you realize the love He bears you, and to win your heart and compel you to love Him.

My Lord and my God, how surpassingly great is Thy bounty and how wonderful Thy love for me! Thou dost love, desire and seek me with intensity and fervor, as if I were of great concern to Thee, as if I were indeed truly necessary to Thee. Thou dost desire to possess me and dost fear to lose me as if I were a precious treasure. Thou dost pursue my friendship with as much insistence as if Thy happiness depended upon it. Would there be anything more Thou couldst do for me, O Lord, even if Thy whole happiness and glory did depend upon my love? O profound kindness, I lose myself in Thy fathomless depths. O priceless kindness, how can it be Thou art so little valued, so little loved, and so much offended and persecuted by those whom Thou lovest so? O hearts of men, how hardened you must be not to be softened by so many persuasive and loving voices! How frozen, not to be melted by so many sacred fires and flames! How can I resist so many powerful attractions of Thy infinite kindness? What dost Thou desire or expect of me, O my Saviour, except that I reply to Thee with St. Peter, the prince of the apostles: *Amo te, amo te,* "I love Thee, I love Thee" (John 21, 15-17).

But instead of replying to Thee thus, I have cried out against Thee with the cruel Jews, by the voice of my sins: *Tolle, tolle; crucifige eum* (John 19, 15). O what anguish and heart rending sorrow! All my sins, my ingratitude, my perverse inclinations, my self-love, my self-will, my pride, all my other vices, all my evil thoughts, words and actions, all the misuse of my bodily senses, of spiritual faculties, all are so many voices worthy of hell that clamor against Thee unceasingly with the Jews: *Tolle, tolle; crucifige eum.* O detestable traitor! Is this how you love Him who is all love for you? Is this your answer to Him who calls you with such sweet persuasion to His love? Is this how you repay His unbounded kindness for all the blessings you have received from Him? Forgive me, O most generous Lord, I beseech Thee, forgive me. May all Thy kindness and mercies (if I be permitted to say it thus) ask forgiveness for me. May Thy holy Mother, with all the angels and saints, cast themselves down at Thy feet to win this pardon from Thy clemency. May all the creatures by which Thou dost cry out to me, "I love you," be so many suppliants on my behalf before the throne of Thy benignity, crying with all the humility, repentance and contrition that ever was or ever shall be: "Forgive, forgive, have mercy on this poor sinner!"

O most merciful Saviour, may it please Thee to accept and approve by Thy great mercy the promises I am about to make for the future. O my Most Lovable Jesus, since Thou dost constantly love me, and since Thou dost employ all that is within and without Thyself in loving me, I, too, desire to be ever concerned in loving Thee, employing all that is within and without me in Thy holy love. And even if, to imagine the impossible, I were to be in no way under obligation to love Thee, I should, nevertheless, desire to love Thee with my whole heart and all my strength.

To that end, if it please Thee, I desire to dedicate all my thoughts, words and deeds, all the functions and senses of my body and faculties of my soul, my every breath and heartbeat, every pulse of my veins, every instant of my life, all things that have been, are, and shall be in me, even my sins, so far as it is possible, to Thy wisdom, which well knows how to make all things cooperate for the good of those who love Thee. I desire that all these things may turn into so many voices, by which I may continue ceaselessly and eternally telling Thee, with all the love in heaven and on earth: *Amo te, amo te, etiam Domine Jesu, amo te.* "I love Thee, I love Thee, yes, my Lord Jesus, I love Thee." And if any element of my soul or part of my body says the contrary, I desire that it may be ground into powder and cast to the winds.

32. I also desire that all things that ever were, are and shall be in the orders of nature, grace and glory, in heaven or on earth and even in hell, may be as many voices proclaiming without ceasing forever, on my behalf: *Amo te, amo te, Domine Jesu,* "I love Thee, I love Thee, Lord Jesus." This is the spiritual use I am bound and freely desire to make of all things, in so far as they belong to me and have been given to me by Thee to employ in Thy love.

33. I also desire further, O my Jesus, that all the powers and perfections of Thy divinity and humanity, all Thy states, mysteries, attributes, virtues, thoughts, words, acts and sufferings, all Thy sacred wounds, every drop of Thy Precious Blood, every moment of Thy eternity, if such an expression be permissible, all things that are or ever existed in Thy body, soul and divinity, may be so many voices proclaiming to Thee forever for me: *Amo te, amantissime Jesu, amo te bonitas infinita; amo te ex tote corde meo, ex tota anima mea, et ex totis viribus meis, et magis atque magis amare volo.* "I love Thee, O Most Loving Jesus; I love Thee, O infinite goodness; I love Thee, with my whole heart, with my whole soul, and all my might, and I desire to love Thee ever more and more."

Finally, my Saviour, I desire, if it please Thee, that there may no longer be anything in existence, in my body or in my soul, in my life and my eternity, which is not transformed into love for Thee.

In order to implement my desires and wishes effectively, I desire and will all this, not with my human and natural will, which is too weak and unworthy to be employed in willing such great and holy things, but with Thy divine will, O Jesus, which is all powerful and belongs to me, since Thou art all mine.

O my Lord, if my powers were as great as my desires, I should in-

deed make everything achieve its perfect fulfilment for Thy glory and
love. But it is for me to desire and for Thee to effect—Thou canst do
all things and dost the will of them that fear Thee. Grant, then, these
my cherished and deepest desires, O Most Beloved Jesus. I beg this of
Thee by all that Thou art, by Thy infinite goodness and mercy, by
everything Thou dost love, and by all who love Thee in heaven and on
earth for Thy most pure love and satisfaction. Thy love is mine and
since I will what I have said in the power of Thy divine will, my confidence is firm that, in Thy infinite goodness, all these things shall be
effected as Thy eternal wisdom deems most fitting to the glory of Thy
divine greatness.

34. Good Jesus, when will the time come when there will no longer
remain anything in me to prevent me from loving Thee? Too well I
know that this shall never be on earth, but only in heaven. O beautiful heaven! How you appeal to my desires! O blessed city where
Jesus is perfectly loved and His glorious love fully reigns, where no
hearts dwell that are not completely transformed in this divine love!
O earth, O world, O body, dark prison of my soul, how unbearable
you are! Wretch that I am, who shall deliver me from the body of
this death? Do I still have long to remain in this miserable exile, in
this strange land, in this place of sin and accursedness? Will not that
day soon come, that desirable hour for which I have so often longed, in
which I shall begin to love most perfectly my most lovable Lord?

My Dearest Jesus, shall I then never love Thee as I desire? God of
mercy, wilt Thou not take pity upon my sorrow? Wilt Thou refuse
to hear my supplication? Wilt Thou not grant what I implore with
such pitiful cries? O my Lord, to Thee do I cry, Thee do I desire,
for Thee do I long. Well Thou knowest that I desire nothing on
heaven or earth, in life or in death, except Thy pure love.

Mother of Christ, angels and saints of Christ and all His creatures,
take pity on my sorrow; speak on my behalf to the Beloved of my
soul; tell Him that I pine away with love of Him. Tell Him that I
desire nothing in time or eternity but His pure love; I desire neither
heaven, nor the glory of heaven, nor the great joys of paradise, nor
the delights of His grace, but only His most pure love. Tell Him
that I can no longer live without that pure love. I implore Him to

make haste, to fulfil in me the designs and work of His grace and to consume me utterly in His divine love, in order to take me soon into His eternal kingdom. *Amen. Veni, Domine Jesu!* "Amen. Come, Lord Jesus" (Apoc. 22, 20). Come, my life and my light, come, my love, my all, come unto me and eradicate everything that works against Thy love. Come to me to transform me wholly into love for Thee. Come to draw me to Thee, and to establish me soon in that abode of love where true and perfect love reigns, where all is love, pure and continual, changeless and everlasting. Come, O Dearest Jesus, Thou sole love of my heart.

## IX. Acts of Love for Jesus, Prisoner in the Sacred Womb of His Most Blessed Mother.

O Jesus, my love, I behold Thee a prisoner in the most pure womb of Thy Blessed Mother, but more imprisoned in the sacred bonds of Thy divine love. Let me love Thee, O Good Jesus, in the infinite love that binds Thee and make me with Thee a prisoner of divine love.

O love that holds Jesus captive in Mary and Mary in Jesus, take my heart, my mind, my thoughts, desires and affections prisoner and establish Jesus in me, in order that I may be completely filled with Him, and that He may live and reign perfectly in me.

O Jesus, my sweet love, I love Thee with all the love with which Thou wast loved, during Thy nine months' imprisonment, by Thy Eternal Father, Thy Holy Spirit, Thy Blessed Mother, St. Joseph, St. Gabriel, and all the angels and saints who took some special part in this mystery of love.

O abyss of love, when I behold Thee in the sacred womb of Thy most holy Mother, I see Thee as it were divinely lost and annihilated in the ocean of Thy divine love. Let me lose myself, and be destroyed with Thee in this same love!

## X. Acts of Love in Honor of the Birth and Holy Childhood of Jesus.

O Jesus, Thou art infinite love in all the moments, states and mysteries of Thy life, but, above all, Thou art pure love and sweetness at the moment of Thy birth and during Thy most Holy Childhood.

Let me love Thee at this precious moment, in this hidden state. May heaven and earth join with me and may the whole world be transformed into love for its Creator and God, Who is completely transformed into gentleness and love for the world.

O most amiable Child, Thou art born by love, in love and for love. At the moment of Thy birth, Thou dost love Thy Eternal Father more than all angels and men together could do in all eternity. So, too, the Heavenly Father loves Thee more at this moment than He ever did or will love all men and angels together. O Jesus, I offer Thee all the love concentrated on Thee at birth by Thy Eternal Father, by Thy Holy Spirit, Thy Blessed Mother, St. Joseph, St. Gabriel and all the angels and saints who participated so intimately in this most lovable mystery.

O love of Jesus, that dost triumph over Him in all His mysteries, but particularly in His subline Childhood and the consummation of His Cross, O love that in these two mysteries, dost transform His omnipotence into helplessness, His plenitude into poverty, His sovereignty into dependence, His eternal wisdom into infancy, His joy and bliss into sufferings, and His life into death, conquer my self-love, my own will and my passions, and put me in a state of powerlessness, indigence, dependence, holy and divine childhood, and death to the world and to myself, which state may adore and glorify the powerlessness, the dependence, Childhood and death to which Thou didst reduce my Jesus in the mysteries of His Nativity and of His Cross.

These acts of love upon the Nativity and Childhood of Jesus will suffice to show how to make similar acts in honor of the other mysteries of the life of our Most Lovable Jesus.

## XI. Acts of Love for Jesus Crucified.

Here are ten acts of love for Jesus Crucified, which may be made when you kiss the crucifix, which it would be well to do each day, in the evening, after your examination of conscience, so that you may end your day in the love of your divine Redeemer and obtain from Him the grace to end your life in acts of love of Him. This is how you proceed:

1. Kiss the foot of the cross, saying:

"O Jesus, in honor of and in union with the love with which Thou didst kiss, embrace and love the Cross presented to Thee on the day of Thy holy Passion, but actually embraced from the moment of Thy Incarnation, with all my heart I love and embrace all the crosses, bodily or spiritual, it may please Thee to send me in my whole life, uniting them to Thine, and begging Thee to grant me a share of that great love with which Thou didst bear them."

2. Kiss the wounds in the holy feet of Jesus with the following desire:

"O Jesus, if it please Thee, I desire to kiss Thy holy feet with love like that of St. Mary Magdalen when she kissed those blessed feet in the pharisee's house, when she won the reward of hearing these sweet words from Thy holy lips, "Thy sins are forgiven thee.""

3. Again kiss the feet of Jesus with this desire:

"O Jesus, I desire to kiss Thy holy feet with all the love of all the just souls on earth, offering Thee all their love in satisfaction for all the times in my life when I have let myself fall away from Thy love."

4. Kiss the wound in the left hand with this intention:

"O Jesus, I desire, if it please Thee, to kiss this sacred wound in union with the love of Thy archangel Gabriel, all the Seraphim and all the angels, especially my guardian angel, offering Thee all this love in satisfaction for the many times I have been guilty of falling away from Thy holy love."

5. Kiss the wound in the right hand with this elevation of the soul to Jesus:

"O Jesus, I desire to kiss this holy wound in union with all the love which all the saints in heaven have for Thee, offering Thee their immense love in satisfaction for all the sins I have committed against Thy divine love."

6. Kiss the sacred wound in the side of Jesus, in union with the love of the Blessed Virgin; or rather, consider yourself unworthy to kiss this holy wound, and ask the most Blessed Virgin to kiss it for you:

"O Mother of Jesus, I implore thee to kiss the holy wound in the side of Thy Son for me, and by this holy kiss make Him a hundredfold return for all the love I should have given Him in my whole life."

And instead of kissing the wound in His side, kiss the wound in the feet, with the following desire:

"O Jesus, if it please Thee, I desire to kiss Thy holy feet in union with all Thy holy Mother's love for Thee, offering Thee all this love in reparation for the faults I have committed against Thy love."

7. Kiss the holy wounds of the sacred head crowned with thorns; or rather, considering yourself too unworthy for this, address yourself to the Eternal Father, and say to Him:

"O Father of Jesus, if it please Thee, imprint a most holy kiss on the sacred brow of Thy Well-Beloved Son, and by this kiss render to Him a thousand times the love I should have given Him in my whole life."

And instead of kissing the wounds of the sacred head, once more kiss the feet of the Crucified Saviour saying:

"O Jesus, let me kiss Thy holy feet with all the love Thy Eternal Father bears Thee, and let me offer Thee this infinite love in reparation for my failures to love Thee."

8. Also kiss the holy feet of Jesus in union with the love of the Holy Spirit:

"O Jesus, let me kiss Thy holy feet in union with all the love of Thy Holy Spirit for Thee, offering Thee that burning love in satisfaction for the faults I have committed against Thy divine love."

9. Once again kiss the sacred feet in union with the divine love of Christ for His own person, saying to Him in your heart and with your lips also, if you wish:

"O Jesus, once again I kiss Thy sacred feet, with all the love Thou hast for Thyself. I offer Thee all this love to satisfy for my failings, imploring Thee to recompense Thyself a hundred thousand times for all the love I ought to have given Thee since I came into the world."

10. Finally, kiss these divine feet once more with all the holy love in earth and heaven together, saying:

"O Jesus, let me once more kiss Thy divine feet with all the love that ever was, is now and ever shall be accorded Thee from all eternity to all eternity, in heaven and on earth, by all the divine and holy persons who love Thee. Let me offer Thee this matchless love in satisfaction for all my sins and infidelities, for all the failures to love Thee of which I have ever been guilty in my whole life."

Note that, when you make these acts of love, there is no necessity to pronounce the words with your lips, nor even to have actually present in your mind the thoughts I have set down. It is quite enough to kiss the crucifix ten times, with the above intentions. Each of these acts may be performed in an instant. It is nevertheless a good thing, at the beginning, to apply your mind to these thoughts and intentions. Later on, when you have been following this exercise for some time, the whole veneration of the cross may be performed with great facility in a very short time.

These ten acts may also be made without a crucifix, if you say ten times the holy words: *O Jesus!* and each time will to say them with the above intentions.

## XII. Rosary of the Holy Love of Jesus.

This rosary consists of three decades and four beads, a total of thirty-four small beads, in honor of the thirty-four years of the life of Our Lord on earth, a life all of love.

To start with, you say: *Veni sancte Spiritus, reple tuorum corda fidelium, et tui amoris in eis ignem accende:* "Come, Holy Ghost, fill the hearts of Thy faithful and enkindle in them the fire of Thy love." This invocation draws down upon you the holy love of Jesus, which is His holy spirit, and gives you to Him, that He may destroy everything in you that opposes Him, and perfect the love of the Holy Ghost for the Son of God.

On each small bead, you say the following words, taken partly from the Gospel and partly from St. Augustine, who repeats St. Peter's triple repetition of *Amo te* to Our Lord after His resurrection, when asked whether he loved Him. *Amo te, amantissime Jesu; amo te bonitas infinita, amo te ex toto corde meo, ex tota anima mea, et ex totis viribus meis, et magis atque magis amare volo.* "I love Thee, Most Amiable Jesus, I love Thee, O infinite goodness, I love Thee with my whole heart and with all my might, and I desire ever to love Thee more and more."

The first *Amo te,* "I love thee," should be said in union with all the love of the Eternal Father for His Son, the second should be said with the intention of sharing all the love of the Son of God for Himself. The third should be recited with all the love of the Holy Spirit for Jesus, bearing in mind that, in giving you His Son, the Eternal Father gave you everything with Him, as St. Paul says (Rom. 8, 32), and it follows that the love of the Father, the Son and the Holy Ghost belongs to you, and that you are entitled to employ it in order to love Jesus.

As you say *ex toto corde meo,* "with all my heart," you must understand by this the Heart of Jesus, the Heart of Mary, the heart of each of the angels and saints in heaven, all comprising a tremendous Heart one with the most Sacred Heart of Jesus and of Mary, by virtue of the union existing between all hearts. And this is likewise your heart, for St. Paul assures you that all things, without exception, belong to you: *omnia vestra sunt* (I Cor. 3, 22), and consequently in loving Jesus you can and must use this universal Heart as if it were your own.

The words *ex tota anima mea,* "with my whole soul," denote the holy soul of Jesus, that of the Blessed Virgin, and all the holy souls in heaven which together form one single soul by virtue of the union wrought by charity. This soul is yours, and you must make use of it to love Him who gave it to you.

When you say, *ex totis viribus meis,* "with all my might," you ought to have the intention of employing all the powers of the divinity and humanity of Jesus and all the strength of all the creatures in heaven, on earth and even in hell, as your own power to love Jesus.

When you say the last words: *Et magis atque magis amare volo* "and I desire to love Thee ever more and more," you should have the intention of employing all your will in desiring to love Jesus, and also of exerting the full extent and infinite capacity of the divine will in order to desire to love Jesus with a will that is infinite and worthy of Him, since your own natural will is not capable of loving Him as He deserves.

On the large beads of the rosary say these words of St. Augustine

*O ignis, qui semper ardes et numquam extingueris, O amor, qui semper ferves et numquam tepescis, accende me, accende me totus, ut totus diligam te.* "O fire, who art ever burning and never extinguished, O love, who art ever fervent and never growest cold, enkindle me, set me on fire, that I may be all aflame with love for Thee."

Or else, instead of this, you may say: *Veni Sancte Spiritus* . . . etc.

I might also add at this point that it is sometimes very beneficial to recite the above words: *Amo te, amantissime Jesu,* etc., after Holy Communion, for at that moment you possess within yourself most intimately the love of the Father and of the Son and of the Holy Ghost, with the divine Heart and holy soul of Jesus, and all the powers of His divinity and humanity, and you are then more than ever entitled to direct all these infinite powers as your own in loving Jesus. Then you can indeed say to Him truly *amo te amantissime Jesu, amo te,* etc., with the intentions you have given above.

It is also a good thing to repeat, after Communion, this verse of the Psalmist: *Benedic anima mea Domino, et omnia quae intra me sunt, nomini sancto ejus:* "Bless the Lord, O my soul: and let all that is within me bless his holy name" (Ps. 102, 1). By this you refer to Jesus, Who is at that time within your heart as the soul of your soul, to the Most Holy Trinity, and all the wonders of heaven and earth. For they are within you in the Holy Eucharist, which is a compendium of God's wonders. And you should desire that everything within you may be employed in blessing, glorifying and loving Jesus and the Most Holy Trinity, and all the plenitude of the divinity that dwells in Jesus Christ.

## XIII. Patron Saint for Each Month.

The angels and saints are most pleased, most willingly hear and answer most gladly the prayer that they may love Jesus for you and help you to love Him. It is in this that they place all their happiness and so it should be your chief prayer to them. In addition to the saints to whom you should have special devotion all your life, it is a most holy practice to choose one particular saint every month, and ask him each day to love Our Lord for you and help you to love Him, to make use of you to love and glorify Him, to atone for the faults you commit during the month against His love. You should love and glorify Our Lord in the saint of your choice, uniting yourself to the praises given Our Lord by him, and striving to imitate the works and virtues he practised for Christ's glory.

## XIV. The Month of March.

Of all the months of the year, the month of March deserves your particular consideration. It was in this month that the greatest works and the holiest mysteries of God were accomplished. The world was created in the time corresponding to March. Many learned doctors are of the opinion that during this month the waters of the deluge receded, the People of God were delivered from the captivity of Egypt, and passed dry-shod through the Red Sea. It was in this month that the Son of God was made flesh, suffered, was crucified, died, delivered the souls of the saints from Limbo and rose again from the dead. It was also in this month that the Most Holy Sacrament of the Altar was instituted, that the Blessed Virgin entered upon her dignity of Mother of God, and that the holy apostles were consecrated priests by the Son of God. Thus the month of March is, in a proper and particular way, Christ's own month, because it was in this month that Jesus began and ended His life on earth, and accomplished His greatest works. It is a special month in the life of the Blessed Virgin Mary, because during March she became Mother of God. It is the month of divine love, wherein the Son of God brought about the greatest mysteries of His love namely, the Incarnation, the Passion, and the divine Sacrament of His Body and Blood. It is also specially dedicated to St. Joseph, foster father of Jesus and Spouse of the Most Blessed Virgin, and includes his feast as well as that of St. Gabriel, the angel who ever waited upon Jesus, the guardian angel of the Mother of Jesus and the herald of the Annunciation.

Hence you should make this month the occasion of most special zeal, devotion, and renewal of fervor.

## PART SIX

*Devotional Exercises for the Beginning and
End, and During the Course of the Year, to
Live a Christian and Saintly Life and
to Make Jesus Reign in Your Soul*

*DEVOTIONAL EXERCISES FOR THE BEGINNING AND
END, AND DURING THE COURSE OF THE YEAR,
TO LIVE A CHRISTIAN AND SAINTLY LIFE
AND TO MAKE JESUS REIGN IN YOUR SOUL*

## SPIRITUAL EXERCISE FOR THE NEW YEAR

### I. BEGINNING THE NEW YEAR WITH JESUS.

The great Apostle St. Paul tells us that, "Christ died for all, that they also who live, may not now live to themselves, but unto him Who died for them" (II Cor. 5, 15), and that he "died for us; that, whether we watch or sleep, we may live together with him" (I Thes. 5, 10). Jesus Himself assures us that His "delights were to be always with the children of men" (Prov. 8, 31). Therefore, if you are not to deprive Him of His delight, nor of the efficacy of His most holy death, you must seek all your delight in His society, and exercise your ingenuity in piously contriving to be ever with Him, never losing sight of Him, and having Him as your object in all things; you must wake and sleep, live and die with Him, begin and end all your years, months, and days with Him. I shall now set before you the way to begin and end each year well and how to spend it with Jesus. You shall see in "Part Seven" how to begin and end your lives with Jesus.

To begin each year of your life in union with Jesus, you should begin it as He began His earthly life. For that purpose, at the beginning of every year, you should take a little time to cast yourself at the feet of Jesus, in order to pay Him your tribute and homage by means of the practices which I am about to set before you.

### II. TRIBUTE TO JESUS CHRIST FOR THE NEW YEAR.

O Jesus, my Lord, I adore, bless and love Thee with all the powers of my soul, in the first moment of Thy life of suffering on earth.

I adore all the holy thoughts, sentiments and dispositions of Thy divine soul, and all that took place within Thee in that first moment.

O Admirable Jesus, from the very first moment of Thy mortal life, Thou didst turn towards the Eternal Father to adore, love and glorify Him, to refer to Him Thy being, Thy life and all its consequences. Thou didst give Thyself to Him to do and suffer everything He pleased, for His glory and for love of us. I behold that, at the same instant, Thou didst turn Thy spirit and heart towards me, to think of me, to love me, to make great plans for my soul and to prepare very special graces for me.

Blessed be Thou, O Good Jesus, and may all the creatures of heaven and earth, and all the powers of Thy divinity and Thy humanity eternally bless Thee for all these things.

O Jesus, I give myself to Thee, to commence this year as Thou didst begin Thy life on earth, and to enter with Thee into Thy holy dispositions. I beg Thee, by Thy great mercy, to implant these dispositions in my heart.

O Most Adorable Jesus, in honor of and in union with the humility, love and other holy dispositions with which Thou didst adore and love Thy Eternal Father, giving Thyself to Him at the first moment of Thy life, I adore, love and glorify Thee, as my God and my Saviour, as the Creator of time, the King of years and of centuries, and as the divine Redeemer who purchased for me, at the cost of Thy own blood, all the time which is given to me on earth.

O Jesus, I consecrate to Thee all my minutes, hours, days and years, my being and my life, and all that goes with it. I desire to employ everything for Thy pure glory alone. I desire all my thoughts and acts, every beat of my heart, every breath I draw, and all else that shall take place in me this year, and in my whole life, to become so many acts of praise and love for Thee. May it please Thee, my dear Jesus, to grant that this may be so, through Thy most great power and goodness.

I also offer Thee, O Jesus, all the love and glory that shall be given to Thy majesty. I unite myself with all the honor and praises that shall be given Thee this year and forever, by Thy Eternal Father,

Thy Holy Spirit, Thy holy Mother, Thy angels, saints and all Thy creatures.

O Most Amiable Jesus, I adore all the designs Thou dost deign to shape for me during this year. Do not permit me to put obstacles in their way. I give myself to Thee to do and suffer everything Thou dost please, for the accomplishment of these eternal designs. In honor of, and in union with the same love with which Thou didst accept, at the first moment of Thy Incarnation, all the sufferings Thou hadst to bear in life, I now accept and embrace, for Thy love, all the sufferings of body and spirit I shall have to undergo this year and during my whole life.

O my Saviour, a year will come that will be the last in my life. Perhaps this very year now unfolding is to be my last. If I knew with certainty that this was to be so, with what care and fervor would I spend it in Thy service! However that may be, I wish to spend this year as if I had no more time to love and glorify Thee in this world, and to make up for the occasions in the past, when I have fallen away from my love of Thee. Please grant me, O Good Jesus, all the graces that I need for this.

### III. Prayer to the Blessed Virgin for the Beginning of the Year.

O Blessed Virgin, Mother of my God and Saviour, I honor and reverence thee in the first moment of thy life. I honor and reverence all the dispositions of thy holy soul, and all that took place in thee at that time.

Thou didst begin immediately, O holy Virgin, to love and glorify God most perfectly, and from that first moment to the last of thy life, thou didst ever love and glorify Him more and more. And as for me, in spite of all the years I have been in this world, I have not yet begun to love and serve Him as I should.

O Mother of mercy, beg thy Divine Son to have mercy on me. Atone for my failings, offering Him on my behalf all the love and glory thou didst ever give Him, to satisfy for my neglect in loving and glorifying Him. Grant that I may share in thy surpassing love for Him, and in the fidelity of that great maternal love. Pray for me, that He may give me the grace to begin, at least now, to love Him perfectly, and that all that shall take place during this year, and all my life, may be consecrated to His glory and thy honor.

Ye angels of Jesus and His saints, pray for me, that our loving Saviour may give me new grace and new love for Him, to devote this year and my whole life, purely and solely, to the service of His glory and love.

# DEVOTION TO THE MYSTERIES OF THE LIFE OF
## OUR LORD JESUS CHRIST

IV. Each Year You Must Honor with Special Devotion All the States and Mysteries of Our Lord's Life.

So many and so binding are your obligations to honor and love Jesus Christ in Himself and in all the circumstances and mysteries of His life, that anyone who might wish to undertake the enumeration of them would be attempting the impossible. I shall, however, call attention here to one or two. To begin with, I shall show that, since your duty is to continue and fulfil in yourselves the life, virtues and actions of Jesus Christ on earth, so must you also prolong and fulfil, in yourself, the states and mysteries of Jesus, and frequently implore Jesus Himself to consummate and accomplish them in you and in His whole Church.

You cannot too often realize and reflect on the truth that the mysteries of the life of Christ have not yet reached their full perfection and completeness. Although they are perfect and complete in Christ's own Person, they are not yet completed in you who are His members, nor in Holy Mother Church, which is His Mystical Body. It is the plan of the Son of God that His whole Church should participate in and actually be, as it were, the continuation and extension of the mystery of His Incarnation, birth, Childhood, hidden life, public life of teaching and of labor, His Passion and His death, by the graces He desires to impart to you, and by the effects He wishes to accomplish in you through these same mysteries. By this means, He desires to fulfil His mysteries in you.

Therefore, St. Paul says that Jesus Christ is fulfilled in His Church (Eph. 1, 22-23) and that we all come together in His perfection and His maturity (Eph. 4, 13), which means, as I have said, His mystical Body, which is the Church—a maturity which will not be complete until the Day of Judgment. And St. Paul again speaks elsewhere of the same fulness of God which is accomplished in you, and of the growth and increase of God in you (Eph. 3, 19). And in another place he says that He fills up in His body the Passion of Jesus Christ (Col. 1, 24). Now what he says of the fulfilment of the mystery of the Passion may also be said of the other mysteries of the life of Jesus Christ.

So the Son of God plans to perfect and complete in you all His states and mysteries. He intends to fulfil in you the divine life which has been His for all eternity in the bosom of His Father, imparting a participation in that life, and making you live, with Him, a life entirely pure and holy.

It is His design to complete in you the mystery of His Incarnation, birth and hidden life, by taking flesh in you and being born in your souls, as it were, through the Sacraments of Holy Baptism and the Blessed Eucharist, causing you to live by a spiritual and inward life, a life hidden with Him in God.

It is His design to perfect in you the mystery of His Passion, death and Resurrection, by causing you to suffer, to die and to rise again with Him and in Him. It is His design to fulfil His glorious immortal life in heaven, by causing you to live, in Him and with Him, a glorious and immortal life after death. He likewise intends to perfect and accomplish in you and in His Church all the other mysteries of His life by the communication and participation granted to you by His holy will, through the continuation and extension of these mysteries operating in you.

This universal plan of the Son of God will not be completed until the Day of Judgment. The ranks of the saints will not be filled up until the consummation of the time God has allotted to men for their sanctification. Therefore, the mysteries of Jesus will not be complete until the end of the time determined by Jesus Christ Himself for their consummation in you and in His Church, that is, until the end of the world.

Now the life you have here on earth was given to you only for the accomplishment of the infinite designs of Jesus Christ for mankind. Hence, you should employ all your time, your days, your years, in cooperating with Jesus Christ in the divine task of consummating His mysteries in yourself. You must cooperate in this by good works and prayer, by frequent application of mind and heart to the contemplation, adoration and veneration of the sacred mysteries of His life according to the different seasons of the year, so that, by these very mysteries, He may work in you all He desires to accomplish for His pure glory. This is the first reason why you must have a special devotion to all the infinitely precious details and aspects of the life of Jesus.

## V. Additional Reasons for Honoring the Mysteries of the Life of Christ.

Although you have every reason to cultivate particular devotion to the mysteries of His life, I shall present four special obligations.

1. You are obliged to imitate the Heavenly Father, according to the teaching of St. Paul: *Estote imitatores Dei sicut filii charissimi* (Eph. 5, 1). Now the Divine Father is continually absorbed in contemplating, glorifying and loving His Son, Jesus Christ, and in causing Him to be loved and glorified in Himself, and in all His states and mysteries.

2. You must love and honor especially all things through which God is given love and glory. Everything that exists in Jesus Christ gives infinite glory to God. So you should give particular and, were it possible, infinite honor to all the vast mysteries and the very smallest details that are found in the life of Christ. You are infinitely more obliged to honor them and to thank the Son of God for the glory He rendered to His Father by His mysteries, than you are to pay homage and thanks for the graces and salvation He has acquired for you, inasmuch as God's interests ought to be infinitely more dear to you than your own.

3. The Holy Ghost, speaking through Holy Mother Church, continually invites and urges you to adore and glorify the mysteries of Jesus. At the beginning, middle and end and in all the principal parts of Holy Mass, in the hymn *Gloria in Excelsis,* in the *Credo,* at the last Gospel, *In principio erat Verbum,* and at several other places in the Holy Sacrifice, as well as in the daily recitation of the Creed, in daily prayers, and throughout the Divine Office, the Holy Ghost unceasingly recalls to your thoughts the blessed mysteries of the life of

Jesus. Why is this so, if not in order that they may be the object of your contemplation and adoration and the subject of all your pious exercises, and that thus they may be the daily bread and nourishment of your souls? For your souls should live by faith alone and by the attention and love which they must entertain for the mysteries of God and of Jesus Christ, according to St. Paul's statement: "But my just man liveth by faith" (Heb. 10, 38).

4. All greatness deserves honor and homage, but an infinite greatness deserves infinite honor and homage. This constitutes yet another special obligation. Jesus Christ is the greatest of the great. He is greatness itself, and is an infinite and incomprehensible greatness. Everything that is bound up in His divinity and humanity, all the mysteries of His existence and even the slightest things that took place in Him, all sustain an infinite greatness and dignity and embody an infinity of wonders. Therefore, they deserve infinite honor and glory.

And yet, great and noble and holy as these things are, how little known, how seldom considered, how poorly honored they are, even by the very ones who style themselves the children of Christ, who bear His Name and dwell on earth only to know and love Jesus, His life and His mysteries. They are so meagerly honored even by these who cannot possess any real life except in His love and knowledge, according to these great words of Truth Himself: "This is eternal life: That they may know thee, the only true God, and Jesus Christ, whom thou hast sent" (John 17, 3).

The happiness of heaven consists in this alone, and in this alone consists true life on earth: to know, love and honor the life and mysteries of Christ. This will be the basis of the account you shall be required to give of yourself at the hour of death. One of the greatest reproaches that will be made against you in that hour, will be the scanty and poor attention and honor you have given to the life and mysteries of Jesus. This will be the purpose of the Son of God in holding His universal judgment at the consummation of time, namely, to exact, by the power of His justice, the honor and homage due to His mysteries by all creatures, and even by His own enemies, before the eyes of heaven and earth. This also is the reason for the existence of hell, that those who shall have failed to honor

Christ's mysteries on earth by love and free will, will render this necessary tribute in hell through constraint and force, by the operation of God's justice in them.

That is why, if you are to avoid being among the number of these miserable creatures, you must make it your chief care and devotion to consider and honor the mysteries of the Son of God. Preference should always be given to the feasts of Our Lord, as well as to those of His holy Mother, over all other feasts. And you should dispose your time and your devotional exercises in such manner as to honor the entire life of Jesus, and the orderly sequence of its mysteries during the course of each year.

## VI. SEQUENCE TO BE OBSERVED THAT YOU MAY EACH YEAR HONOR ALL THE STATES AND MYSTERIES OF JESUS.

Beginning with the first of all the states of Jesus, the divine life enjoyed by Him in the bosom of His Father for all eternity, it is recommended to honor it in the time immediately preceding Advent, so that you may adore Jesus in His life in the bosom of His Father for all eternity, before adoring Him in His life in the bosom of the Virgin, in the fulness of time. When I speak of the time before Advent, I mean the months of October and November.

I set aside, however, the last two weeks of November, as being appropriate for honoring the life led by Christ in the world before His Incarnation, for the space of five thousand years, from the creation of the world up to the Incarnation of the Creator of the World. For during this time Christ was living, in a certain manner, in the minds and hearts of the angels of heaven, of the patriarchs, prophets, and just men on earth, who knew that He was to come and loved Him, desired Him, awaited Him and continually asked God for His coming. In the same way He lived in the souls of the patriarchs who were in Limbo. So also did He live in the Mosaic Law, which was promulgated only to prefigure and foretell Him, and to dispose the world to believe in Him and receive Him when He should come.

During Advent you should honor the mystery of the Incarnation, and the dwelling of Jesus within Mary for the space of nine months.

From Christmas to the Purification, honor the Holy Childhood of Jesus, and all the mysteries included in it, as the Church presents them for veneration, such as the mystery of His birth, of His dwelling in the cave at Bethlehem, of the Circumcision, the Epiphany, the Presentation, the Flight into Egypt, His life there up to the age of seven years, of the journeys to the Temple in Jerusalem in company with His holy Mother and St. Joseph, their loss of Him in the Temple, and His session in the midst of the Doctors at the age of twelve years.

From the Purification to Ash Wednesday, honor the infinitely precious and unknown hidden life which He spent working with His Mother and St. Joseph, up to the age of thirty years.

From Ash Wednesday to the First Sunday of Lent, you should honor the Baptism of Jesus in the Jordan and His manifestation by the voice of the Father, saying: "This is my beloved Son, in whom I am well pleased" (Matt. 3, 17), by the descent of the Holy Ghost upon Him in the form of a dove, and by the testimony of St. John the Baptist.

During the first week of Lent, honor the solitary life of Jesus in the desert.

During the second week of Lent you should honor His public and active life among men, from the age of thirty to that of thirty-three years and three months, following closely the daily gospel of the liturgy of the Church for the holy season of Lent. One week is, however, too short to honor Christ's public life, and as you cannot devote any more time to it in Lent, you shall honor it again after the Feast of Corpus Christi.

The other four weeks of Lent will be dedicated to the honor of the penitential life of Christ, which is divided into four parts, namely, humiliations, privations, exterior and interior sufferings. In the first of these four weeks, honor all the humiliations which Jesus bore in His life, both interior and exterior. In the second, His interior and exterior privations. In the third, the exterior sufferings endured in His body. The fourth, the interior sufferings which He bore in His soul.

Holy Thursday, honor the institution of the most Holy Sacrament of the Eucharist at the Last Supper, and the washing of the feet of the Apostles.

From Good Friday to Easter Sunday, adore Jesus in His agony, His suffering, His Cross, His death, the descent of His soul into Limbo, and the burial of His body.

Easter Sunday, Christ's Resurrection and His entry into the life of glory. This, too, you should venerate on all the Sundays of the year, which are especially consecrated to the honor of Christ's Resurrection.

From Easter to the Ascension, honor Christ's life in glory, and His stay upon earth after the Resurrection.

From the Ascension to Pentecost, you shall again honor Christ's glorified life, this time in Heaven after His Ascension. This glorified life should likewise be adored every Sunday of the year.

From Pentecost to the Feast of the Holy Trinity, you are to honor the mission of the holy spirit of Christ, and all the greatness, attributes and mysteries of that divine spirit.

On the Feast of the Holy Trinity, you shall adore the life of the Blessed Trinity in Jesus, and the life of Jesus in the Trinity, which you should also honor every Sunday of the year. The first day of each week is always dedicated to the mystery of the Holy Trinity, the honor of the life of the Holy Trinity in Jesus, and of the life of Jesus in the Holy Trinity, and to the honor of the mystery of the Resurrection and the state of the glorified life of Christ.

The three days following the Feast of the Holy Trinity are dedicated to the Three Divine Persons: Monday, to the honor of the Father; Tuesday, to the honor of the Son; and Wednesday, to the honor of the Holy Spirit.

During the octave of Corpus Christi, as well as on the Thursdays of each week, you shall honor the perpetuation of the life of Our Lord in the Holy Eucharist.

The time remaining between the octave of Corpus Christi and the month of August shall be divided into two equal parts. The first is dedicated to the honor of the public life of Jesus, for which there was not sufficient time during Lent.

The second part shall be devoted to the honor of the mystery of the second coming of Jesus, and of the general and public judgment to take place at the consummation of time, which is one of the mysteries of the glorious life of Christ, and the first mystery which Holy Church proposes to our adoration in the Creed after the mystery of the ascension and .the enthronement of Christ at the right hand of the Father.

During the month of August, honor the four principal attributes of Jesus Christ, as follows:

1. His divinity, or divine essence. This He possesses in common with the Father and Holy Ghost, making Him co-equal with the Father and the Holy Ghost, God infinite, incomprehensible, eternal, immortal, all-powerful, all-wise, all-good, resplendent with all the perfections that inhere in the divine essence.

2. His Divine Person. This is proper and peculiar to Him, in virtue of which He is the Son of God, the image and splendor of the Father, and the divine exemplar according to which the Father formed all things.

3. His holy soul, with all its faculties, memory, understanding, and will.

4. His holy body, with all the members, sensations, and feelings, especially His Precious Blood and His divine Heart.

During the month of September, honor the seven kingdoms of Jesus Christ, which are:

1. Christ's kingdom in the natural world, made up of the four elements of earth, water, air and fire, and all natural things that exist in the world.

2. The kingdom of Christ in the spiritual and mystical world on earth, that is, the Church Militant.

3. The kingdom of Christ in death, in which are honored His sovereignty, His justice, His eternity, His death and His immortal life.

4. The kingdom of Christ in the particular judgment, which He daily and hourly exercises upon souls as they depart from this life, in which His justice, His equity, His truth, His power and divine majesty are greatly honored.

5. The kingdom of Christ in the Church Suffering, Purgatory,

where continual glory is given to His divine will, His justice, His goodness and His sufferings.

6. The kingdom of Christ in hell, where all His divine perfections and all His mysteries are honored in a way that is superlatively terrifying and astounding.

7. The kingdom of Christ in the Church Triumphant, in heaven.

These are the seven kingdoms of Christ to be honored during the month of September. I call them kingdoms because Christ reigns and triumphs in all these states, and in all these things, and because these seven kingdoms are filled with the glory, the honor, the power, the presence and the majesty of Jesus Christ, as I shall show more fully in the proper place, if it may please God to give me the time and the grace to continue this book.

On the feasts of the Blessed Virgin, and on Saturdays, you shall honor the life of Jesus in His Virgin Mother and all the wonders and mysteries He worked in her.

On the feasts of angels and saints celebrated during the course of the year, you shall honor the life of Jesus as manifested in the angels and saints.

So, you must leave no mystery in Jesus Christ without special honor. You should see Him and honor Him in all places, all times and all things. During the course of the year, you must venerate each of His manifestations and all His mysteries. But to make it easier for you, while waiting for God in His good pleasure to give me time and grace to finish another book I have begun,[1] to give a more extensive treatment to all the kingdoms and mysteries of Christ, I shall here set down the chief aspects you must consider and honor in each mystery of the life of Jesus, and outline a method for their veneration.

First, I should like to point out that you are obliged to have particular devotion to certain angels and saints, to whom you should pay special honor during your lifetime. It is also a good thing to single out some order of saints and angels for special veneration during the

---

[1] St. John Eudes probably refers to *All Jesus,* or *Exercises on the Mysteries of Jesus,* a work which was never published. The manuscript is not extant. Cf. P. Costil, *Fleurs de la Congregation de Jesus et Marie,* 1, 644, and R. P. de Montigny, *Vie du P. Jean Eudes* (Paris, 1827), p. 438.

course of each year. But it is much more important for you to select some attribute or mystery of Jesus to honor throughout your lifetime, having first recommended your intention to God, invoked the Holy Ghost and consulted your spiritual directors. It is likewise an excellent practice to choose a special mystery each year, on the Feast of the Ascension of the Son of God, to be the object of particular veneration in the course of that year. This should be done in the manner I shall propose below.

## VII. EACH MYSTERY OF THE LIFE OF CHRIST TO BE VENERATED UNDER SEVEN ASPECTS.

Among the infinite wonders contained in each mystery of the life of Jesus, there are seven main aspects which you should consider and honor in them, for knowledge of them will give you much light and scope, as well as facility in concentrating on His Mysteries.

The *first* is the external aspect of the mystery, that is, all its outward manifestations. For instance, the visible exterior elements in the mystery of the birth of Jesus are the nakedness, poverty, cold and weakness of the newborn Infant, the little swaddling bands in which He was wrapped, His cradle in the crib and on the straw between the ox and the ass, His tears and baby cries, the tiny movements of His sacred feet and hands, the first gaze of His baby eyes, His slumber in the arms of His Blessed Mother, the nourishment He took from her most holy breasts, the sweet kisses He received from her and from St. Joseph, the visit of the shepherds, and all the other touching incidents that took place outwardly in the stable of Bethlehem, on the night of the birth of the Son of God.

This is what I call the body and the exterior of the mystery of the birth of Jesus. Likewise, all that took place outwardly in the mystery of the Incarnation, of the Circumcision, the Presentation in the Temple, the flight into Egypt, the Passion and all the other mysteries. All that was said or done or suffered outwardly, either by the Son of God, or by the other human beings and the angels who were present at the unfolding of the mystery, comprises its body. Every detail deserves your consideration and honor, because there is nothing unimportant in the mysteries of Jesus, but, rather, each aspect is great, divine and worthy of adoration.

If the Son of God, therefore, takes the trouble to concentrate His divine spirit and Heart (which ought not, it seems, to be concerned about anything other than divinity itself), on the consideration of every step you take, even numbering the hairs of your head, as He Himself asserts, and writing and treasuring in His Heart the slightest actions you perform for Him, so that He may do honor and glorify them for all eternity in heaven, how much more should you centre your mind and heart on the consideration, adoration and glorification of the smallest details of the infinite mysteries of His life, seeing that there is not one thing about them which is not infinitely great and admirable, and deserving of infinite honor and adoration!

The *second* aspect to be considered and honored in each mystery of the Son of God is the interior spirit of the mystery, that is, the particular virtue, power and grace which inhere in the mystery and are peculiar to it, since each mystery has its own proper virtue and spirit of grace. This includes the thoughts and intentions, the affections, sentiments, dispositions and interior activity accomplishing the mystery. In a word, it includes all that took place inwardly in the mind, Heart and holy soul of Christ, and in the minds and hearts of all those who participated directly in the mystery.

Take, for example, all the interior content of the Incarnation, the birth, Passion and other mysteries of the Son of God, such as the thoughts in His mind, the affections and sentiments of His Heart, His inward dispositions of humility, charity, love, submission, meekness, patience. Likewise the inward activity of all His mysteries and acts, with respect to His Eternal Father, Himself, His Holy Spirit, His Blessed Mother, His angels and His saints, mankind in general, and each one of us in particular. Add to this the power and virtue and spirit of grace which He exercised in His Incarnation, His birth, Passion and other mysteries. I call at this the spirit, the core and, as it were, the soul of the mystery.

This spiritual aspect ought to engage your principal attention and honor in the mysteries of the life of Our Lord; yet it actually receives the least attention and honor. Many Christians are satisfied to contemplate the body and the externals, without passing on to the inward features of these tremendous mysteries. Yet it is the spirit and the core that are most important, constituting the foundation, the substance, life and truth of the mystery, whereas the exterior is no more than a covering, an accessory, and the accidental being of the mystery. The exterior and body is passing and temporal, but the interior virtue and spirit of grace which dwell in each mystery are permanent and eternal.

Thus you may truly say that Christ's mysteries are not in the past, but are always present, according to the spirit, the interior, the truth and substance of the mysteries, not according to the body and exterior. It is true, however, that one may also say that even according to the body and externals, the mysteries remain ever present in a certain sense, before God, just as all things are always present to Him by virtue of His eternity, because there is nothing past or future in the sight of God.

The *third* aspect to be honored is the effect accomplished and continually renewed in each one of the mysteries of Jesus. In Sacred Scripture, the Son of God is called the "Lamb, which was slain from the beginning of the world" (Apoc. 13, 8), since from the beginning of the world He has by His death, Incarnation and all His other mysteries, brought about many wonderful effects in glory, felicity, light, grace, mercy, justice and terror, in heaven, on earth, in hell, upon men, angels, and all other creatures. This I shall show, God willing, more extensively further on.

The *fourth* aspect to be adored in all Christ's mysteries is the special intention present, for in each mystery Our Lord sought to carry out some particular intention, for instance, the intention to glorify His Father and Himself, to glorify the mystery itself and, in certain special ways that are unknown to us, to sanctify souls and to accomplish all the untold effects of grace bound up in each inscrutable mystery.

The *fifth* aspect to be venerated is the association of the Blessed Virgin with each mystery of Christ. She has a special and extraordinary part in all the mysteries of the life of her Son. She has more share than all the angels and saints and the whole world put together because in her the Son of God wrought greater wonders by each of His mysteries than He operated in all His angels and saints or in the entire universe. So also, the Blessed Virgin gave more honor by herself to all her Son's mysteries than all the angels and saints, and the whole world put together.

The *sixth* aspect is the participation of the angels and saints, who belong specially to each of the mysteries of Christ. Every mystery has its own angels and saints who are dedicated to it by special participation, concern and association.

For example, the angels and saints of the mystery of the Incarnation are St. Joseph, St. Gabriel, all the saints who have ever cultivated special devotion to this mystery and one particular order of angels—we know not which, although it seems likely that it is the Seraphim—who are dedicated to honor this mystery in a special way because it is a mystery of love.

The angels and saints of the mystery of the Nativity are St. Joseph, St. Gabriel, the watchful shepherds, the saints who have cultivated special devotion to this mystery, like St. Bernard, and many others.

The angels and saints of the mystery of the Childhood of Christ are once again St. Joseph and St. Gabriel: for these, together with the most Blessed Virgin, have a part in all the mysteries of the Son of God. There is also St. John the Baptist, who was sanctified by the Child Jesus; then St. Zachary and St. Elizabeth; St. Simeon, the just man who received and held the child Jesus in his arms on the day of His Presentation; St. Anna, the prophetess, who was also in the Temple that day and likewise, as we may readily believe, received Him into her arms. Then the Three Wise Men, the Holy Innocents, and all the guardian angels of these saints, as well as many other saints and angels, unknown to us but dear to Our Lord.

The angels and saints of the hidden life of Our Lord are St. Joseph, St. Gabriel, St. John the Baptist, and all the saints with whom He was associated during His hidden life and all the saints who ever led a hidden and solitary life, and another order of angels, we know not which. For just as the order of Thrones is especially dedicated to honoring Jesus in the Blessed Sacrament of the Altar, as He Himself revealed to Blessed Angela of Foligno, so it is also very probable that each of the other mysteries has some particular order of angels assigned to its special honor.

The angels and saints of Christ's public life and ministry include all the holy apostles and disciples, all the saints who were His companions in the course of His public life and ministry, and the guardian angels of all these saints.

The angels and saints of the mystery of His Passion, Cross and death are especially St. Gabriel, St. John the Evangelist, St. Mary Magdalen, St. Martha, Salome, the other holy women gathered at the foot of His Cross, all the holy martyrs, all the saints who have had remarkable devotion to this mystery and another order of angels unknown to us.

The *seventh aspect* to be considered and revered is your own singular and special share in the mysteries of Jesus Christ. You have a very particular part in each mystery of the Son of God, inasmuch as He had some thought, some plan, some special love for each one of you, and the design to impart to you special graces and special favors, both on earth and in heaven by every mystery of His perfect life. This obliges you also to pay a particular honor to each of His mysteries.

VIII. SEVEN METHODS OF VENERATING THE MYSTERIES OF OUR LORD.

The mysteries of Jesus are so admirable and worthy of honor that we are bound by many obligations to honor them; therefore we should omit nothing that may be done or suffered in their honor, but must glorify them in every possible way. Now here are seven methods by which you can and must honor them.

1. By thoughts, considerations, affections, dispositions and inward acts, applying your hearts and your minds to contemplate and reflect upon these mysteries to adore them and give them glory.

2. By your words, your speech and your conversations with your friends. All the conversation and communication which Christians hold one with another on earth should have no other subject but Jesus Christ and the virtues and mysteries of His life, just as they shall have no other topic in heaven.

3. By all your outward acts of devotion such as the celebration for hearing of Holy Mass, receiving Holy Communion, going to Confes-

sion, or hearing Confessions, reciting the divine office and all the other customary exercises. You should also honor them by the external acts performed each day, referring and offering all these things to Jesus in veneration of the mystery you propose to honor. For example, if you intend to honor the mystery of the Incarnation, you should offer Our Lord the above acts in words like these:

"O Jesus, I offer Thee this Holy Sacrifice of the Mass, this Holy Communion, and all the other acts that I shall perform today, in honor of the most adorable mystery of the Incarnation."

4. By the practice of humiliation, mortification and penance, offering them to Jesus for this same end.

5. By imitation, when you strive to reproduce within yourself the mystery you would honor, in so far as it can be imitated. For instance, if you are to honor the mystery of the Childhood of Jesus, you should try to imitate Him in the simplicity, humility, meekness, obedience, purity and innocence of His holy Childhood, and thus to imprint upon yourself an image of the divine Childhood. This is one of the most perfect ways of honoring the mysteries of Jesus.

6. By your mental attitude, when you honor the mysteries of Jesus not only by a few passing exterior or interior acts, but when you are in a stable and permanent state of mind which of itself pays uninterrupted honor to some mystery of Jesus. For instance, if you live in interior or exterior poverty, and this state is borne with patience and submission to God, you honor by your very state the poverty of Christ, and thus your condition is the means of paying continuous honor to the state of poverty to which Jesus was voluntarily reduced while He was on earth.

If by some infirmity or illness you are reduced to a state of weakness so that you can scarcely move and take care of yourself, and you bear this condition with submission to the will of God, in honor of the helplessness to which Jesus was reduced in His Childhood, your state gives honor to the state of helplessness and feebleness of the Child Jesus.

If yours is a retired and solitary state of life, and you love your solitude for the love of God, you honor, by your state, the hidden and solitary life of Jesus.

If your condition is a cross to you, full of interior and exterior pain and suffering, which you bear with humility and love, in honor of the cross and afflictions of Jesus, you honor by your state the mystery of the Passion and sufferings of Jesus.

7. This method of honoring the mysteries and states of the Son of God is most excellent. They should be honored by a most humble and searching recognition of your unworthiness, incapacity and impotence to accord them the veneration they deserve, recognizing that there is nothing in you worthy to be employed in their honor, but rather that all in you of yourself is an obstacle to the glory you should give them, because Jesus is the only one worthy to honor Himself and His mysteries as they deserve. For this reason you should supplicate Him to glorify them Himself in you, in every way He desires.

## IX. Seven Other Methods of Honoring the Mysteries of Jesus.

I have said above that one of the methods to honor Jesus is by your dispositions and interior acts. Now here are seven of these, which you may use in order to converse inwardly with Jesus on the subject of His mysteries.

1. You must contemplate, adore, glorify and love Jesus in all that is contained, in general, by the complete mystery, in all its circumstances and all that goes with it. Then, if you wish to study the details of the mystery, you may contemplate, adore, love and glorify Him in all that He is (1) in the body and exterior of the mystery; (2) in the spirit and interior of the mystery; (3) in the effects He brought about by the mystery; (4) in His intentions in each mystery; (5) in the participation of the Blessed Virgin; (6) in the part taken by the angels and saints belonging to the mystery; (7) in your own part in it.

2. You should rejoice and behold Jesus so great, so admirable, so full of love, charity, sanctity and every sort of virtue and perfection, in each mystery. So, too, you ought to rejoice to see Him love and glorify His Father so highly and so fittingly in this mystery, and to contemplate Him so perfectly and so magnificently loved and glorified by His Father, by His Holy Spirit, by His Blessed Mother, by His angels and by His saints.

3. You must bless and thank Jesus for all the love and glory He has given and will give forever to His Father and Himself, as well as for all the graces and favors He has imparted to you and to the whole world by each mystery. But you must thank Him far more for the glory rendered to His Father and Himself, than for the graces imparted to you by His mysteries, because God's interest ought to be dearer to you than your own. Indeed, it is quite enough for you to thank Him for the glory given by His mysteries to His Father and Himself, without particularly thanking Him for the graces acquired for you. If He has obtained and imparted to you any graces, by His mysteries, it was in order to glorify His Father and Himself in you. Thus, when you thank Him for the glory He has given His Father and Himself by His mysteries, you are also thanking Him for the graces He has given you in each mystery. You then express your profound thanks to Him in a most holy, most disinterested and single-minded manner, which makes you forget yourself and see only God in your inward acts.

4. You should humble yourself at the feet of Jesus and beg His forgiveness for your failure to honor Him, for dishonoring Him by your sins, for the obstacles, both in yourself and in others, which you have put in the way of the glory of this mystery and the accomplishment of its designs. You should beg Him to atone for your fault and to make to Himself a hundredfold return for all the honor you ought to have given Him in this mystery, and also implore the Eternal Father, the Holy Ghost, the Holy Virgin, and all the angels and saints to make reparation for your failings, and to make on your behalf a hundredfold recompense to your loving Saviour.

5. You should refer to Jesus all the effects of grace, glory and holiness He ever brought about, in heaven and on earth, by each mystery. You should offer Him all the glory, love and praise which ever were or ever shall be rendered to Him in each of His mysteries, by the Eternal Father, the Holy Spirit, the Blessed Mother, the angels and saints, particularly by those who belong more intimately to each mystery, and by all the creatures that exist in heaven, on earth and in hell. I have already said that all the divine mysteries are honored even in hell by the power of His divine justice. You ought to unite yourself

to all the honor which has been, is, and ever shall be given to the mysteries of Jesus in the whole universe and by all things. You should invoke the Eternal Father, the Holy Ghost, the Blessed Virgin, the angels and saints, especially those that have a particular association with the mystery, to join your homage to the honor they give and ever shall give to the mysteries of Jesus.

6. You should surrender yourself to Jesus to honor this mystery, in every way He desires. After you have exerted all the strength and capacity it shall please Him to give you, you should then beseech Him to honor the mystery Himself, in you, with all the power and holy resourcefulness of His mind and love. You should beg Him to annihilate in you all that is contrary to the glory of this mystery, and to produce in you, by this mystery, all the graces and effects He wills, so that He may rule you according to the spirit and the grace of the mystery, and consummate it in you, and, finally, accomplish in us all the designs He has, in this mystery, in your regard. Then you should give yourself to Him to do and suffer all that He wills, with that end in view.

7. You should ask Jesus to imprint on your heart and on the hearts of all Christians a very great zeal for the glory of His mysteries and to destroy everything that presents an obstacle to their glorification. You should implore Him to cause them to be known and glorified by all men as much as He desires and to consummate them in His Church, fulfilling all the designs which He cherishes in His mysteries. You should offer yourself yet again to Him to do and suffer, for this intention, anything He may will.

These are a few ways of honoring the mysteries of Jesus, and you may choose those which best suit your individuality, making your choice according to the grace Our Lord shall give you, and according to the guidance of the Holy Spirit.

But, in order to facilitate the practice, I shall now condense these seven last ways into a prayer which I dedicate to the holy Childhood of Jesus, which you may apply in turn to each of His other mysteries individually.

## X. Prayer to Honor the Holy Childhood of Jesus.

1. O Good Jesus, I adore, love and glorify Thee in all the thoughts, designs, sentiments, dispositions and interior occupations of Thy holy soul as a child, with regard to Thy Father, Thyself, Thy Holy Spirit, Thy Holy Mother, Thy angels and saints and in particular to me.

2. I rejoice, O Good Jesus, to contemplate Thee in the state of Thy Childhood, and to behold Thee love and glorify the Eternal Father so ardently, and so filled with virtues, excellences, and greatness even as a child.

3. I give Thee infinite thanks for all the love and glory Thou hast rendered to the Father and Thyself in the divine mystery whereby Thou didst grow from infancy to manhood.

4. I beg Thee to forgive me, O my Saviour, for my failure to venerate Thy blessed Childhood, and for all the obstacles I have put in the way of the graces Thou didst plan to effect in me by this mystery. Atone, I beg Thee, for my defects and give Thyself for me a hundredfold return to pay my debt. O Father of Jesus, Holy Spirit of Jesus, angels of Jesus and His saints, glorify my Saviour for me in this mystery.

5. O Jesus, I refer to Thee all the effects of grace and glory Thou didst accomplish in heaven and on earth through Thy holy Childhood. I offer all the love and glory that ever has been or shall be given to Thee in this mystery forever, on earth or in heaven, by the Eternal Father, the Holy Spirit, Thy Holy Mother, and all the angels and saints, begging Thee to unite me with their continual praises given forever to Thee in this mystery.

6. O divine Child Jesus, I give myself to Thee to honor the mystery of Thy Childhood in all the ways Thou dost please. Destroy in me everything that opposes the glory of this mystery. Grant me a share in the simplicity, humility, sweetness, purity, innocense, obedience and other virtues of Thy holy Childhood. Place me, by this means, in a state of holy and sacred Childhood and filial devotion which shall be a constant imitation and praise of Thy divine Childhood.

7. O most lovable Jesus, implant in the hearts of all Christians a most ardent zeal for the glory of this divine mystery. Destroy in them

all that stands in the way of that glory. Cause it to be glorified by all men in the manner Thou dost desire, and accomplish all Thy cherished designs in this mystery. I give myself to Thee to do and suffer all Thou dost please, for this intention.

# DEVOTION TO THE MOST BLESSED VIRGIN MARY

## XI. Manner of Honoring Jesus in Mary, and Mary in Jesus.

Devotion to the most Blessed Virgin, Mother of God is so pleasing to her Son, and is so dear and commendable to all true Christians, that it is not necessary to recommend it to those who desire to lead a Christian life.

I shall only tell you that you must never separate what God has so perfectly united. So closely are Jesus and Mary bound up with each other that whoever beholds Jesus sees Mary; whoever loves Jesus, loves Mary; whoever has devotion to Jesus, has devotion to Mary. Jesus and Mary are the two first foundations of the Christian religion, the two living springs of all our blessings, the two centres of all our devotion, and the two objectives you should keep in view in all your acts and works. A man is no true Christian if he has no devotion to the Mother of Jesus Christ and of all Christians. St. Anselm and St. Bonaventure assure us that it is impossible for persons who are not loved by the Mother of Christ to have any part with Him. Conversely, it is impossible for anyone to perish upon whom she looks with favor.

As you must continue the virtues of Jesus and keep with you His sentiments, so you must also continue and maintain in your hearts the love, tenderness and devotion that Jesus cherished for His Blessed Mother. He loved her most perfectly and accorded her the very highest honor in choosing her to be His Mother, giving Himself to her as Her Most Beloved Son, taking from her a new being and life, becoming subject to her, following her guidance in outward things during His Childhood and hidden life, afterwards crowning her Queen of heaven and earth, glorifying her and causing her to be glorified by the whole world.

To continue on earth this love and devotion of Jesus towards His most Blessed Mother, you should have a most especial devotion and veneration for her. Now, to honor her as God requires of you, and as she desires, there are three things for you to do:

1. You must see and adore her Son in her, and see and adore Him alone. It is thus that she wishes to be honored, because of herself and by herself she is nothing, but her Son Jesus is everything in her, her being, her life, her sanctity, her glory, her power and her greatness. You should thank Our Lord for the glory He has given to Himself through His admirable Mother. You must offer yourself to Him and ask Him to give you to her, causing all your life and all your acts to be consecrated to the honor of her life and her actions. You must pray that He will make you participate in her admirable love for Him and in her other virtues. You must ask Him to employ your life in her honor, or rather to honor Himself in her, in whatever way He pleases.

2. You must recognize and honor her first as the Mother of God, then as your own Mother and Queen. You must thank her for all the love, glory and perfect service she rendered to Her Son Jesus Christ our Lord. You must refer to her, after God, your being and your life, subjecting yourself entirely to her as her slave, imploring her to direct you in all your affairs and to assume full power over you, as over something belonging entirely to her, and to dispose of you as she pleases, for the greater glory of her Divine Son. You must beg her to employ all your actions to honor the infinite works of her Son, and to associate you with all the love and praises which she ever gave Him and ever shall give Him throughout eternity.

It is a good thing to make these acts of devotion every day, every week or at least every month.

To that end, you might use a prayer to the Blessed Virgin contained in "Part Two" and another prayer that follows presently.

3. You can and should honor the most holy Virgin Mary by thoughts, meditating on the holiness of her life and the perfection of her virtues; by words, taking pleasure in speaking of her perfections and in hearing them discussed; by actions, offering them to her in honor of and in union with her own; by imitation, striving to imitate our admirable Mother, especially in her charity, her pure love, her detachment from all things and her most divine purity, the thought of which ought to arouse in you a powerful desire to shun and fear more than death the least fault against purity, whether in thought, word or act.

Finally, you may honor the Blessed Virgin by special prayers or works of devotion, such as the Rosary, which ought to be in common use among all Christians, and the Office of Our Lady, which you should recite in union with the love and devotion of her Son Jesus for her, in honor of both their perfect lives and of their sublime virtues.

Let me also add one word more. Each year, you should honor a special mystery of Jesus, as has been said above. It is also good each year, on the day of the Blessed Virgin's Assumption, to choose one of the mysteries of her life for particular veneration during the year. For that reason I have set down the chief of these mysteries.

## XII. Mysteries of the Life of the Blessed Virgin.

The chief states and mysteries of the life of the Most Blessed Virgin are: her Conception; her abiding in the blessed bosom of her mother, St. Anne; her Nativity; the day on which she received the holy name of Mary, eight days after her birth; her Presentation in the Temple; her childhood up to the age of twelve years; her life and service in the Temple until the age of fifteen years; her holy marriage to St. Joseph, the feast of which is kept in some churches on the fifteenth of January; the Incarnation of Jesus and the Annunciation of her dignity of mother of God; her Visitation and three months' stay with her cousin, St. Elizabeth; her journey from Nazareth to Bethlehem; the birth of her divine Child; the flight into Egypt and her sojourn there with the Child Jesus and St. Joseph; her return from Egypt and hidden life in Nazareth with her Son Jesus, until he attained the age of thirty years; all the journeys she shared with her Son Jesus, following Him everywhere throughout His public ministry; her martyrdom at the foot of the Cross; her joy in the Resurrection and Ascension of her Son; the close of her life on earth, from the Ascension until her own Assumption; the holy Communions she received during that time; her most happy death; her Assumption in triumph; her glorious enthronement at the right hand of her Son, her coronation as Queen of heaven and earth; and her most blessed life in heaven since the Assumption.

### XIII. Prayer Honoring Jesus Christ in His Blessed Mother.

O Jesus, Only Son of God, Only Son of Mary, I adore Thee in one general act of adoration in all Thou art and in all that Thou hast ever brought about in Thy most holy Mother. And I adore Thee particularly and love and glorify Thee in all that Thou art and all that Thou hast brought about in her Conception, Nativity, Presentation, and the other mysteries of her life.

O my Jesus, I take infinite joy in contemplating Thee so great, so admirable, so glorified, and so loved in Thy Blessed Mother.

With my whole heart I thank Thee for all the glory Thou hast ever given and ever shalt give Thyself in her perpetually.

I beg Thee to forgive me, O my Saviour, for all the failings of which I have been guilty with respect to the honor due to Thy most honorable Mother, and for everything I have ever done in my life that was displeasing to her. May it please Thee to atone for my defects, and render to her on my behalf all the honor I should have given her during my whole life.

O Jesus, I refer to Thee all the effects of sanctity and love which Thou hast ever produced in Thy lovable Mother, and I offer Thee all the glory and love that was ever given Thee in her and by her.

O Good Jesus, I give myself all to Thee. Destroy in me everything that is displeasing to Thy holy Mother. Give me entirely to her. Grant that all my life and actions may be consecrated to the honor of her admirable life. Grant me to share in Thy love and zeal for her glory, or rather for Thy glory through her, as well as in her most pure and shining love for Thee, her burning zeal for Thy glory, her humility and her other virtues. Finally, deign to make use of me, O Jesus my Lord, to glorify Thee, and cause Thee to be glorified in her, in every way that shall please Thy holy will.

### XIV. Prayer to the Blessed Virgin, Applicable to any Mystery of Her Life.

O Holy Virgin, with all the powers of my being, I adore and honor thy Son Jesus in thee. I honor and reverence thee according to what thou art in Him and by Him, particularly in the mystery of thy Immaculate Conception, Nativity, etc. I honor all the sentiments and dispositions of thy holy soul, and all that took place in thee in this mystery.

Blessed be thou, O Holy Virgin, for all the glory Thou hast given God in this most precious mystery and in thy whole life.

I beg thee to forgive me, O Mother of Mercy, for all the lapses and sins I have committed against thee and they Dear Son. To satisfy for these I offer thee all the honor and praises that have ever been accorded thee in heaven and on earth.

O Mother of Jesus, I give myself all to thee, imploring thy sweet mercy to give me to thy Son and to destroy in me by thy merits and prayers all that displeases Him. Grant me to share in thy most pure love, thy humility and all thy myriad, resplendent virtues.

Grant that my whole life and each of my acts may be consecrated to the honor of the life and actions of thy Dear Son. Unite me to all the ardent love and perfect glory thou dost and wilt give Him forever. Take my being, my life and all that is in me, and employ me as a creature that is entirely thine, in order to glorify Him in every way thou mayest wish.

# DEVOTION TO THE SAINTS

XV. MANNER OF HONORING JESUS IN THE SAINTS AND THE SAINTS IN JESUS.

You ought to cultivate devotion to all the saints and angels, especially to your guardian angel and your patron saint, to the saints who knew Our Lord on earth, to the order of angels and saints with whom you are to be associated in heaven, and to the angels and saints who are charged to watch over the places where you live or travel, and protect your circle of friends.

You should honor them because Jesus Christ loves and honors them: *Quicumque glorificaverit me, glorificabo eum.* "Whosoever shall glorify me, him will I glorify" (I Kings 2, 30). And He adds that the Eternal Father honors those who serve His Son: "If any man minister to me," says the Son of God, "him will my Father honor" (John 12, 26). Likewise because they love and honor Jesus, they are His friends, His servants, His children, His members, and, as it were, part of Himself. Finally, to honor them is to honor Him because He is everything in them.

Therefore, you ought to venerate the relics of the saints as a portion of Jesus and part of His members. You should carry relics upon your person in union with the love with which He preserves all the saints, from all eternity, in His Sacred Heart, in order to unite yourself with the love and praises of each of the saints, whose relics you carry with you or honor at their shrines.

To honor the saints in a fitting manner:

1. You should adore Jesus in them, for in them He is everything: *omnia in omnibus* (Eph. 1, 23). He is their being, their life, their sanctity, their joy and their glory. You should thank Him for the praise and glory rendered to Himself in them and by them, and thank Him more for this than for the graces He imparted to them, or imparted to you through them, because God's interests should be dearer to you than your own. You ought to offer Him all the honor and love

that His saints ever rendered to Him, asking His infinite bounty to make you participate in their ardent love and all their other eminent virtues.

Thus, when you go on a pilgrimage, or receive Holy Communion, or celebrate Holy Mass, or perform any devout action in honor of any saint, you should offer it to Jesus, for the above intentions, in the following manner:

"O Jesus, I offer Thee this journey, this Communion, this Mass, or this act, in honor of all that Thou art in this saint; in thanksgiving for all the glory that Thou hast given to Thyself in him and by him; for the increase of his glory, or rather the increase of Thy glory in him; for the accomplishment of all the designs which Thou hast in regard to him, and that Thou mayest grant me through his prayers and intercession, Thy holy love and all the other graces necessary for me to serve Thee perfectly."

2. When you have recourse to the saints, you ought to be humble, considering yourself most unworthy even to think of them, or to be thought of by them. You should thank the saints for the service and glory they have given to Our Lord and offer yourself to them, asking them to offer you to Jesus, to beg Him to destroy in you everything that displeases Him and to cause you to share in the wealth of graces imparted to them. You should further implore them to honor and love Him for you, and to render to Him a hundred times over all the love and glory you should have given Him. Offer yourself to the saints to be used to honor and glorify Him in any way they see fit.

3. Every city, town and village has its heavenly guardians, so when you are travelling or reach a destination where you intend to spend a little time, you should greet the angels and saints who watch over that place. You should beg your good angel to salute them on your behalf, and you should ask their permission, as lords of that place, to pass through or stop over. Remember that they might in all justice forbid you to enter or pass through, because you are sinners, unworthy to walk on the face of the earth, and because your sins might perhaps draw down some just punishment of God upon the places where you dwell, or through which you pass. All these considerations give you good reason to imitate St. Dominic, who, when he entered any town,

begged God not to annihilate it on account of his sins. So it is good to pray to the angels and saints who protect the places we live in or visit, to glorify and love Our Lord for you, and to make up for the faults you may commit while you are in these places.

When you enter upon any kind of transaction with other people, you should always invoke their guardian angels and patron saints, praying that they may dispose them to do whatever tends more to the glory of God in the business you are transacting with them.

It is also an excellent practice to select a special order of saints on All Saints' day, and a particular choir of angels on St. Michael's day, choosing to honor them, or rather Jesus in them, in a more particular manner during that year, as has been explained. A practical application will be given below.

The choirs of angels are as follows:

The Angels, Archangels, Thrones, Dominations, Virtues of Heaven, Powers, Principalities, Seraphim, and Cherubim.

The orders of Saints are:

The Patriarchs, Prophets, Apostles, Martyrs, Priests, Confessors, Virgins, Widows and the Holy Innocents.

Now in order to render it a simple matter for you to honor Jesus in the saints and the saints in Jesus, I shall put it in practical form in the two following prayers. I shall apply them to St. John the Evangelist, and you may address similar prayers to any saint in particular.

## XVI. Prayer to Our Lord, Honoring Him in St. John the Evangelist.

O Jesus, I adore Thee in all that Thou art and all that Thou hast ever accomplished in all Thy saints, especially in the blessed Apostle and Evangelist St. John. O Great Jesus, Thou art in all things, and I desire to see and to honor Thee only in all things, especially in the saints, and in Thy beloved disciple St. John. Thou are everything in Him; Thou art his being, his sanctity, his joy, and his glory. How admirable art Thou, my Jesus, in all Thy saints and particularly St. John! How beloved and glorified art Thou in him! How I rejoice, my Saviour, and how I bless Thee for all the glory Thou dost give to Thyself through this great apostle!

O Good Jesus, I offer Thee all the honor and love ever accorded Thee by this divine evangelist. I give myself all to Thee; annihilate in me everything that displeases Thee and grant me a share in the graces Thou hast given to the great St. John, especially his humility, his specially tender love for Thee, his boundless charity towards his neighbor, and all his other virtues.

## XVII. PRAYER TO ST. JOHN THE EVANGELIST.

O blessed Apostle and Evangelist St. John, I adore and honor Jesus in thee, and I honor and venerate thee in Jesus with all the powers of my soul. I thank thee with my whole heart for the ardent love and faithful service thou didst render to my Saviour. I offer myself to thee; give me forever to Jesus. By thy prayers and merits destroy in me all that is contrary to His glory. Use me, if it please thee, as a creature completely at thy disposal, to glorify and love Him as thou dost see fit. Grant that I may share in thy most pure love for Him and in all thy remarkable virtues. Love Him and glorify Him for me. Make up for all the failings of which I have been guilty and may yet be guilty, in His love and His service, and give Him a hundredfold return for all the love and honor I ought to give Him. Include my love in all the loving praises thou hast ever given and shalt give to Him forever. Pray to Him for me, that I may no longer live except to love Him, that I might die a thousand times, were it possible, rather than offend Him, and obtain for me the favor that everything in me, past, present and future, may be transformed into praise and love for Him. Finally, obtain for me the grace to die in the practice of His most pure love.

# ANNUAL RETREATS AND SOME OTHER
# SPIRITUAL EXERCISES

## XVIII. EXCELLENCE AND PRACTICE OF ANNUAL RETREATS.

It is a most holy and most important thing, the usefulness of which cannot be perfectly known except to those who try it out, to devote a little time each year entirely to God, and to give oneself to spiritual exercises and prayer with exceptional care. Just as people in the world occasionally have banquets, over and above their daily meals, and enjoy themselves heartily at these festive gatherings, so, too, it is very appropriate for all Christians, who profess to live a holy life, to add to their ordinary exercises of devotion some exceptional feasting and rejoicing of the spirit, by applying themselves to God and busying themselves with loving and glorifying Him with more affection and fervor than usual. It is indeed in this that perfect joy and true delight consist, namely, in association and conversation with God by means of holy prayer.

To this St. Paul exhorts not only the religious, but all Christians, married or unmarried, advising them to depart, for a certain space, from the mutual practices and obligations of their state, and devote themselves exclusively to prayer.

This custom has been practised in the Church of God down through the ages. We read of many saints and prelates of the Church who, putting aside the cares of their normal activities and domestic affairs, frequently withdrew for a few days into solitary places, to concentrate on the contemplation, love, and glory of God.

This is what I call an annual retreat, as it takes place every year in all religious communities. It is also practised by many people in the world, who each year set aside three or four days in which they bid farewell entirely to all cares for earthly things, and withdraw into a religious house to devote themselves to exercises of piety and divine love.

You should not fail to give yourself to the practice of prayer and the love of God with more care and fervor during days of retreat in the way prescribed for you by your spiritual directors.

Your retreat ought to be made with these chief ends in view:

1. To continue and honor the various retreats of Jesus, for example, His retreat from all eternity in the bosom of His Father; His retreat for nine months in the bosom of His Mother; His retreat in the stable at Bethlehem for forty days; in Egypt for seven years; at Nazareth for the whole extent of His hidden life, which lasted until He was thirty years old; for forty days in the desert; in heaven and in the glory of the Father, ever since the Ascension; and in the Blessed Sacrament, where He is, as it were, always in retreat, in the hidden Eucharistic life, and so shall be until the end of time. Also offer it in honor of the retreats made by the Blessed Virgin, and her part in the retreats of her Son. So, the first aim, the first and foremost intention of your retreat ought to be to love and glorify Jesus and His most holy Mother, and to unite yourself always more and more to both Mother and Son.

2. To atone, during the time of the retreat, for the negligences and faults you have committed during the year, against the love and glory of Jesus and Mary.

3. To renew your desires and your strength, to dispose yourself for the reception of fresh graces, in order to walk more courageously in the ways of divine love, and destroy more completely all the obstacles encountered as we advance along the road to Paradise, our eternal retreat.

You ought to regard your annual retreat as a foretaste of heaven, and the time thus spent as a small portion of eternity. You should strive during this time to reproduce what is accomplished in heaven and in eternity, beginning here below the life and activities that are to be your everlasting occupation in heaven, to contemplate, love and glorify God as He is contemplated, loved and glorified without interruption in heaven. You should also employ the time spent in retreat as if you had no more time remaining to love and glorify Jesus, and atone for the faults you have committed against His glory and love. You should above all affirm before Him that you desire to devote yourself to these holy exercises, not for your own particular consolation, merit and interest, but only for His pleasure and for His pure glory.

As members of religious communities customarily renew their vows at the time of their retreat, I shall here set down a prayer to Jesus to foster the proper dispositions for this important renewal.

## XIX. Prayer to Jesus for the Renewal of the Three Vows of Religion.

O Jesus, my Lord, I adore, love and glorify Thee in Thy holy poverty, Thy divine purity and Thy most perfect obedience. I adore and glorify Thee in the eternal design Thou hast for all the souls who ever have made or shall make vows of poverty, chastity and obedience; and especially Thy holy design for my own soul.

I give Thee infinite thanks, O Good Jesus, for all the glory Thou hast rendered to the Almighty Father and Thyself by Thy poverty, chastity and obedience, as well as by the poverty, chastity and obedience of Thy Blessed Mother and all holy religious souls. I most humbly beg Thee to make up for my faults, and to restore unto Thyself a full measure of all the honor I ought to have given Thee by my three vows. I offer myself to Thee to do and suffer anything that may please Thee.

O Dearest Jesus, once again I offer to Thee the three vows I have made, of poverty, chastity and obedience, and I protest before heaven and earth that I desire to keep them perfectly right up to my last breath, in homage to Thy divine poverty, chastity and obedience, in honor of the vows of Thy holy Mother.

I give myself to Thee, O Jesus; may it please Thee to destroy in me all that is contrary to these three virtues and give me grace to keep these three vows with all the perfection Thou dost ask of me.

O Mother of Jesus, angels and saints of Jesus, implore Him to annihilate in me all that displeases Him and to establish in me a participation and image of His poverty, chastity and obedience, that I may ever advance in the continual imitation and adoration of His poor, chaste and obedient life on earth.

## XX. Exercise of Reparation.

The Son of God employs every resource of His divine wisdom to devise with holy ingenuity new ways of giving Himself to you, and of demonstrating His unfailing love for you; therefore, you ought also to seek out with holy ingenuity new ways to consecrate and devote the span of your life to His glory and love.

Inasmuch as you have been his enemies in the first few months of your life and since then have often been unfaithful to Him, you ought surely to make use of every kind of means of reparation for your infidelities and faults, to the full extent of your ability aided by His grace.

To make reparation, the following practice is recommended. Every year, set aside one day for each year of your life on earth; then, having profoundly humbled yourself before Our Lord, in view of the sins and ingratitude of your past life, having begged His forgiveness and implored Him to obliterate your sins in His Precious Blood and consume them in the fire of His divine love, take a firm stand in the unshakable resolution to enter upon a new life, and to begin to love and honor Jesus as though you were only now starting to live.

Stir up a strong desire to use these precious days of recollection as if they were the first days of your life, or as though they were to be the last you would ever have, to love and glorify Jesus on earth. Strive to do all you should have done in each year of your life. Strive to make such holy use of this time and to conduct yourself so perfectly in all your doings and activities, that you may to some extent make reparation for the failings of your past life.

Here is your plan of action for each day.

Devote the first day to reparation for the deficiencies of the first year of your life. This should be done in the following manner:

1. Adore Jesus in the sublime events of the first year of His life. Accuse yourself before Him, and beg His forgiveness for all the dishonor you gave Him by the state of original sin in which you were for a part of the first year of your life. To make satisfaction for this, offer to the Eternal Father all the honor His Son Jesus gave Him in the first year of His life on earth, and offer to Jesus all the honor

given Him by His Blessed Mother in the first year of his earthly life.

2. Offer to the Eternal Father everything that occurred in the first year of your life, and implore Him, by His most burning love and exceeding great zeal for the glory of His Divine Son, to transform all that you suffered, and all that occurred both outwardly and inwardly in you during your first year of life, into praise, glory and love for His Son, and for all the events, both outward and inward, of the first year of His life in this world.

Repeat to Jesus the prayer just offered to the Eternal Father and beg to consecrate all that you suffered, in body and soul, every use you made of the limbs, senses and faculties of your body and soul during that first year of your life, to the honor of His sufferings in body and soul, in union with the operations of His limbs, senses, and faculties of body and soul during the first year of His divine Infancy.

Say this prayer also to the Holy Ghost, similarly to the Blessed Virgin and to the angels and saints, that by their merits and glory they may now transform the first year of your life into eternal homage and glory to the mysteries of the first year of the life of Jesus Christ.

3. Offer to Jesus all the acts to be performed on the first day of your retreat and the love, praise and acts of adoration you shall give Him in union with the love, glory, and praises that were accorded Him in the first year of His life by His Eternal Father, by Himself, by the Holy Spirit, by His Blessed Mother, His angels and all His saints, to make Him a hundredfold return for all the glory and love you should have given Him in the first year of your life, if you had enjoyed the use of reason.

On the second day, corresponding to your second year, and on each of the other days, corresponding to each of the years of your life, you shall practise the same exercises as on the first day. Make exception, of course, for the fact that on the days corresponding to your childhood years, in which you remained in the state of baptismal grace, it will not be necessary to ask pardon for sins committed, since during that time you were incapable of sin. But you will indeed have to humble yourself greatly for having gone so long a time without really knowing God, and for having carried about within you, all that time, the principal and source of all sin, namely, the remains of the corruption of original sin, which corruption is the source of all sin.

If your years outnumber those of the temporal life of Jesus, you might carry on the same exercises with reference to the years of the glorious life of Jesus in heaven. Although it is true that the duration of this glorious and eternal life of Jesus is not counted by years in heaven, because there is no passage of time nor years in eternity, nevertheless, on earth, and with respect to us, that life may be measured by years. At present you may calculate the glorious life of Jesus, since His Resurrection, at about nineteen hundred years.

Consequently, if you are over thirty-four, you shall, on the thirty-fourth day of this pious exercise, adore Jesus in the first year of His glorified life in heaven. The next day, take the second year, and so on, performing the same exercise with respect to the years of the glorious life of Jesus as were proposed for the years of His temporal life.

You may perform this exercise not only on your own account, but also on behalf of other souls with whom you have some special bond, or to whom you are in any way obligated, uniting the years of their lives with your own, and performing the exercise for them as well as for yourself. Yet do all of this not for yourself nor for them, but for Jesus, for His glory and for His most pure love.

You might wish, during this exercise, to recite the Rosary of Jesus in glory—as follows:

## XXI. Rosary of the Glory of Jesus.

This rosary is made up of three decades and four beads, a total of thirty-four small beads, in honor of the thirty-four years of Christ's life on earth.

First, you repeat three times *Veni Domine Jesu,* "Come Lord Jesus" (Apoc. 22, 20), the inviting words with which St. John ends his Apocalypse, and you say them to invoke Jesus and draw Him into your soul, your mind and your heart, imploring Him to enter into you and annihilate everything in you that displeases Him, and to fill you with His grace, His spirit and His pure love. It is also a good thing to recite these same words with the same intention at the beginning of your other prayers and acts.

On each small bead say: *Gloria tibi, Domine Jesu, qui natus es de Virgine, cum Patre et Sancto Spiritu in sempiterna saecula.*

As you repeat this invocation you should offer to Jesus all the glory given to Him in each year of His life by His Father, His Holy Spirit and His Blessed Mother, and all His angels and saints, by way of satisfaction for your faults against Him in each year of your life, imploring Him to consecrate all that ever occurred in your life to the honor of all that took place in each year of His own.

For example, at the first bead, as you say *Gloria tibi Domine Jesu,* etc. . . . , you should offer to Jesus all the glory of the first year of His life in satisfaction for your deficiencies in honoring Him during the first year of your life. So too you should offer Him your first year, imploring Him to cause all that occurred in it to be consecrated to the honor of all that occurred in the first year of His life.

At the second bead, you should offer Him all the glory given Him in the second year of His life by His Father, etc., while also offering Him the second year of your own life, imploring Him, etc. And so on, with the other beads.

On the large beads, you say the *Gloria Patri,* and as you do so, offer to the Holy Trinity all the glory that Jesus ever gave or ever shall give to the Three Divine Persons, by way of satisfaction for your faults against the Blessed Trinity.

## XXII. ADDITIONAL SPIRITUAL EXERCISES TO BE PERFORMED EACH YEAR.

It is also a very holy practice to set aside a little time each year to acquit yourself before God of the duties you should have been obliged to pay Him at the hour of your birth and baptism, if you had possessed the use of reason. You should do the same with regard to your future obligations towards Him at the hour of death, thus using this means to prepare yourself for death. I shall, however, reserve the exercises appropriate to such matters for the last part of this book.

## XXIII. PREPARATION TO GAIN INDULGENCES

At frequent intervals during the course of the year, rich opportunities for gaining indulgences are available; yet most Christians are satisfied to seek nothing more on such occasions than exemption from the punishment due to their sins, having practically no other end in view but their own interest. This very fact prevents many from gaining the desired indulgences, and robs God of the glory which constitutes the purpose for which He offered them to you. It will consequently be very much to the point if I give you some idea of the intentions and dispositions you ought to have, if you are to gain indulgences worthily for the pure glory of God. Hence, when you wish to gain an indulgence, prepare yourself accordingly.

1. Adore the very great love which prompts God to grant you these indulgences. His burning love for you gives Him a very great desire to behold you soon united with Him; and as He well knows that the punishments you have deserved by your sins will defer the fulfillment of His desires, by detaining you in purgatory, unless wiped out in this world, He wills to give you indulgences, which are the shortest and easiest way of wiping out your deserved punishment. Give yourself to Him, in order to gain a wealth of precious indulgences not so much out of consideration for your own interests, as to fulfill His constant desire to bring you nearer to Him. Carry out everything prescribed for gaining the indulgences, in honor of and in union with the most pure love that prompts God to give them to you.

2. Adore the exceeding great love of Jesus, by which He acquired these indulgences. You must see them as fruits of the Cross and Passion of Christ, as graces which cost Him dearly indeed, since He purchased them at the price of His blood and death. Hence, you should desire to gain indulgences so that the Son of God may not be cheated of the fruits and effects of His Cross, and in order that what cost Him so dearly may not be lost, nor become vain and fruitless so far as you are concerned.

3. Adore God's justice, before which you are accountable for the penalties due to your sins, and cultivate an active desire to gain indulgences, not to escape those penalties, but to satisfy and glorify God's justice.

4. It is also good to adore God's universal design for your souls from all eternity. For from all eternity God designs to establish you in a high degree of grace on earth and of glory in heaven. But by your sins, you have put many obstacles in the way of the fulfillment of His

eternal plan. Even though the guilt of your sins may have been forgiven by a good confession, you have, nevertheless, made yourself unworthy to receive many of the graces God designed to give you, if you had not prevented Him by your sins. Now, He desires by indulgences to wipe out these iniquities and remove from your heart the obstacles raised by sin against the fulfilment of His plans. He wishes to make you capable and worthy to receive the graces planned for you in accomplishment of His infinite designs. Desire, therefore, to gain these indulgences not to escape the sufferings of purgatory, but that God may avoid being disappointed in the designs He deigns to entertain in your regard.

5. Desire to gain indulgences so that your souls may be perfectly cleansed of many evil effects left by sin, which prevent you from loving God perfectly, thus you may become able to love Him with a more pure and ardent love. To do this, each time some opportunity of gaining an indulgence arises, address the Son of God as follows:

"O Jesus, I give myself to Thee to do all that Thou dost desire me to do in order to gain this indulgence, in honor of and in union with the very great love with which Thou didst acquire it for me with Thy Precious Blood, in homage to Thy divine justice, to bring about the fulfilment of Thy designs in my regard, so that I may love and glorify Thee ever more perfectly."

## XXIV. Annual Confession.

Once you have made a good general confession, you should no longer think of your past sins, that is, not consider and examine them in detail any more, but be satisfied to detest them in general and humble yourself before God for them. It is, however, a very profitable thing, and a most important one, to make an annual confession, to review the chief faults you have committed during each year. For it is much to be feared that you may have frequently been remiss in your ordinary confessions, by having failed to approach the tribunal with the necessary preparation, contrition and other dispositions demanded by the sacrament of Penance. You cannot be too careful or diligent in a matter so important as the salvation of a soul created to love and glorify God forever.

Yearly confession has become a frequent practice among all Christians who desire to please God and to guarantee their salvation for the glory of God. There are many, indeed, who review their confessions every six months, and still others at even shorter intervals.

Adopt this holy practice at least at the end of each year, so that you may to some extent repair your failings during the year, and dispose yourself to serve and love God more perfectly the next year. If you do not do this at the end of the year, make your review of your confessions at some other time, according to the advice of your confessor, but in any case, perform it with an unusual amount of preparation, self-abasement and contrition.

And above all, make a point of protesting to Our Lord that you do not wish to make this exercise for the unburdening and satisfaction of your soul, nor for your own merit or interest, but solely for His pleasure and pure glory.

## XXV. Ending the Year With Jesus.

To end each year of your life with Jesus, you ought to close it just as Jesus ended His mortal, human life on earth. You ought to set aside a little time at the end of each year to acquit yourself of your obligations and offer fitting homage to Jesus as the following prayer suggests.

## XXVI. Prayer of Praise and Gratitude for the Close of the Year.

O Jesus, my Lord, I adore, love and glorify Thee in the last day, the last hour and last minute of Thy mortal life on earth. I adore all that happened both inwardly and outwardly on that last day, I mean, Thy last thoughts, acts, words and sufferings, Thy final use of the senses of Thy sacred body, and the last dispositions of Thy holy soul, to which I desire to unite myself now, with a view to the closing moment of my own life.

O Divine Jesus, by the light of faith I behold Thee on that last day of Thy life, adoring and loving Thy Father infinitely. Thou dost give Him fitting thanks for all the graces imparted to Thee and, through Thee, to the whole world during the time of Thy sojourn on earth. Thou dost ask His pardon for all the sins of men, offering Thyself to Him to suffer the penance due to them. Thou dost think of me with love exceeding great, with a most ardent desire to draw me to Thyself. Finally Thou dost sacrifice Thy Precious Blood and Thy most noble life, for the glory of the Heavenly Father and for love of us. Blessed be Thou infinitely for all these inestimable graces.

O Good Jesus, in honor of and in union with the love, humility, and other holy dispositions with which Thou didst perform all the last actions of Thy life, I give Thee infinite thanks for all the glory Thou didst give the Eternal Father during Thy life on earth, for all the graces Thou hast bestowed upon me and all men this year and always, as well as for the graces Thou wouldst have lavished on me, if I had not stood in Thy way.

I most humbly beg Thy forgiveness for all the outrages and indignities Thou didst suffer on earth because of me, and for all the offenses I have committed against Thee this year. In satisfaction, I offer Thee all the honor and glory rendered to Thee, during Thy time on earth and during the past year, by Thy Eternal Father, the Holy Spirit, Thy holy Mother, and by all the angels and saints. So, too, I offer myself to Thee to bear all the penance Thou mayest ordain for me in this world and in the next.

O Jesus, most worthy of love, I adore Thy infinite thoughts and designs for me on the last day of Thy most precious life; and I give myself to Thee to do and suffer all Thou dost desire of me, for the fulfilment of these unfathomable designs. Grant that I may die a thousand times rather than hinder the operation of Thy loving Providence.

O Good Jesus, I offer to Thee the last day, the last hour and the last moment of my life and everything that may happen to me outwardly and inwardly then. I mean, my last thoughts, words, actions and sufferings, as well as the last use of my bodily senses and of the powers of my soul.

May it please Thee to grant that all these things may be consecrated to the honor of the last day, the last hour and last moment of Thy life. May I die loving Thee with Thy holy love. May my being and my life be sacrificed and consumed for Thy glory, and may my last breath be an act of pure love of Thee. This is my intention, my desire, my expectation. O my Dear Jesus, relying as I do upon the excess of Thy infinite love, may it please Thee to grant, by Thy great mercy, that this may be so.

## XXVII. Prayer to the Blessed Virgin, at the End of the Year.

O Mother of Jesus, Mother of the Eternal and Immortal God made Man, I honor and venerate thee in the last hour and moment of thy life. I honor thy last thoughts, words and acts, and the last use made of the senses of thy immaculate body and of the powers of thy glorious soul. Especially I wish to honor the last act of love made by thy mother's heart for thy Most Beloved Son.

With all my heart I bless and thank thee, O holy Virgin, for all the glory thou didst render to God during thy spotless life, and for all the graces thou didst ever obtain from His bounty for me and for all men, especially during this year.

I beg thy forgiveness, O Mother of Mercy, for all the offenses thou didst suffer on earth, as well as for those I have committed this year against thee. To make satisfaction for these, I offer thee all the honor that has ever been accorded thee in heaven and on earth.

O Mother of Fair Love, I offer thee the last day, the last hour and moment of my life, and all that shall take place in me at that last moment, in honor of the last moment, hour and day of thy life, and of all that occurred in thee on that day. Unite me, if it please thee, with all the holy and divine dispositions of thy maternal heart and thy pure soul. Grant that, by thy merits and prayers, my last thoughts, words, acts and breaths may be consecrated to the honor of the last thought, words, acts and breaths, both of thy Son and of thyself. Grant that I may die loving Him with His holy love, and that I may be utterly consumed and sacrificed to His glory, and that my life may end with a last act of most pure love for Him.

O Angels and Saints of Christ, pray that He may consummate all this in me, by His exceeding great mercy and for love of Him.

## PART SEVEN

*Devotional Exercises for the Anniversary of Your Birth and of Your Baptism and for the Preparation of Your Soul for a Holy and Christian Death*

*DEVOTIONAL EXERCISES FOR THE ANNIVERSARY
OF YOUR BIRTH AND OF YOUR BAPTISM AND
FOR THE PREPARATION OF YOUR SOUL
FOR A HOLY AND CHRISTIAN DEATH*

## DEVOTIONS FOR THE ANNIVERSARY OF YOUR BIRTH

I. CONCERNING THE RIGHTFUL HOMAGE YOU OUGHT TO HAVE REN-
DERED TO GOD AT THE MOMENT OF YOUR BIRTH IF YOU HAD THE
USE OF REASON.

I can never tell you enough, nor should you grow tired of hearing
and considering (so important is it) that Jesus Christ, who is your
Head and whose members you are, passed through all the stages
of human life, through which you are passing. He did almost all
the things that you do, and performed not only His outward acts
but also all His interior actions for Himself and for you. Therefore,
Christian sanctity and perfection consist in ceaselessly uniting yourself to Him as His members, and in continuing to do what He did,
as He did it, to the best of your ability, uniting yourself with His
dispositions and intentions. It likewise consists in consenting and
adhering to what He did for you in the presence of His Father and
in ratifying it. So, too, it consists in performing all your inward actions
not only for yourself, but also for the whole world, in imitation of
the Son of God, and especially for those with whom you have some
special connection with respect to God. This Christian devotion inspires similar acts of union and imitation proportionately, towards the
Blessed Virgin, never separating the Mother from the Son. But you

will gain a clearer idea of this from reflecting upon the devotion you
should have paid Him from the very first moment of your life and
at the instant of your birth on earth, if you had enjoyed the use of
reason.

## II. Prayer to Jesus for the Anniversary of Your Birth.

1. O Jesus, I adore Thee in Thy eternal birth and Thy divine dwelling for all eternity in the bosom of Thy Father. I also adore Thee
in Thy temporal conception, and in Thy presence in the sacred womb
of Thy most pure Mother, for the space of nine months, and in Thy
birth into this world at the end of that time. I adore and revere
the great and admirable occurrence of all these mysteries. I adore
and honor the holy dispositions of Thy Divine Person and Thy holy
soul in these mysteries. With my whole heart I adore, love and bless
all the acts of adoration, love, oblation Thou didst render to the
Eternal Father, and all the other divine acts and practices offered Him
in these mysteries.

2. Again I adore and glorify Thee, O Good Jesus, as performing
all these things for Thyself, for me and for everyone in the world.
On this anniversary of my birth I give myself to Thee, O my Dear
Jesus, that I may now repeat the acts Thou didst perfect while dwelling from all eternity in the bosom of the Father, and for nine months
in the bosom of Thy Mother. I unite myself to Thee to perform this
duty as Thou didst perform it, in union with the love, humility,
purity, and other holy dispositions of Thy adorable soul. Since Thou
didst perform this act for Thyself and for me and for all men in the
world, I also desire to exercise this present devotion, not only for
myself, but for all the men in the world.

I now desire, O my Saviour, to render unto Thee as far as I can,
with the help of Thy grace, all the rightful homage I should have
paid Thee if I had been gifted with the use of reason, from the first
moment of my life. So, too, I desire to pay Thee all the due need of
adoration, praise, and love, which should have been given to Thee
at that same time by all my friends, and by all people who ever were,
are, or shall be in the world; and even that which should have been
rendered to Thee by the evil angels at the moment of their creation.

I give myself again to Thee, my Lord Jesus. Enter into me, and unite me to Thyself in order that in and by Thee I may fulfil these desires for Thy pure glory and satisfaction.

3. In union, therefore, with the devotion, love, humility, purity and sanctity, and all the other sublime dispositions with which Thou didst honor, bless, love and glorify the Eternal Father in Thy eternal and temporal birth, and in Thy dwelling from all eternity in the bosom of Thy Father, and during nine months in the bosom of Thy Mother: I acclaim Thee; I adore, love, bless, and glorify Thee together with the Father and the Holy Spirit as my God, my Creator, and Sovereign Lord. I adore, love, and glorify Thee also on behalf of all creatures—angels, men, animals, plants and inanimate things. I wish I could possess in myself the totality of their being, all their strength and all their actual or potential capacity to glorify and love Thee, that I might now use it all in paying Thee this homage for myself and for them, especially those for whom, before Thee, I have both the obligation and desire to pray with special zeal.

4. I give Thee infinite thanks, O my God, on behalf of myself, all creatures, and especially my particular friends, for the gift of life, and the capacity to know and love Thee. I thank Thee for having preserved our existence and allowed us to be born alive to receive Holy Baptism. If we had died before being delivered from original sin by the grace of Holy Baptism, which has been the misfortune of many souls, we should never have seen Thy divine face, and we should have been deprived forever of Thy holy love. May all the angels and saints bless Thee forever for this most special favor Thou hast accorded us.

5. Omnipotent Creator, Thou didst give me being and life solely that I might employ them in Thy love and service. Therefore, I offer my life to Thee. I consecrate and sacrifice it altogether to Thee, together with the being and life of all the angels, all men and all creatures, in testimony that I desire no longer to live save to serve Thee with all the perfection Thou dost ask of me.

6. O my God, what a source of humiliation and pain it is for me to think that, during the first months of my life, I was Thy enemy and under the power of Satan, in a continual state of sin that infinitely

displeased and dishonored Thee! For this I most humbly beg Thy forgiveness, O my Lord, and in satisfaction for the dishonor I gave Thee while I remained in the state of original sin, I offer Thee, O Father of Jesus, all the glory given Thee by Thy immaculate Mother during the time she dwelt in the blessed womb of St. Anne, her mother.

7. O my Jesus, in honor of and in union with the love with which Thou didst accept and bear all the crosses and sufferings that were permitted by the Heavenly Father to attend Thy temporal birth, I offer Thee all the trials and afflictions I have suffered since my birth, and those remaining for me to suffer until the end of my life, accepting and loving them for love of Thee, and begging Thee to consecrate them to the homage of Thy own sufferings.

8. O Most Kind Jesus, I offer Thee all the circumstances of my birth, and I implore Thee by Thy very great mercy to wipe out all that displeases Thee in the first part of my life. Deign to make up for my faults, giving to Thy Father and to Thyself all the honor I ought to have given Thee at that time, if I had been capable of honoring Thee; and mayest Thou grant that the earliest phase of my life may render an undying homage and glory to the divine state of Thy dwelling in the bosom of Thy Father and in the womb of Thy Mother, and to Thy eternal and temporal birth.

9. Such, O my Lord, is the rightful homage I ought to have rendered to Thee, had I been able, at the moment of my birth, and indeed from the first moment of my life, that I now endeavor to render to Thee, although very tardily and imperfectly. But what gives me infinite consolation, O my Dear Jesus, is that I know Thou didst atone for my deficiencies by Thy temporal birth. Then Thou didst render all this just homage to God the Father, performing in a most holy and divine manner all these acts and devotions for Thyself and for me. Thou didst refer and consecrate to His glory all Thy being and Thy entire life, present and to come, and together with it all my being and every state of my life, and of all creatures that ever were, are, or shall be, all the past, present, and future state of created things being just as vividly present to Thee then as now. Thou didst look upon every life as Thine own, as something given to Thee by

the Father, according to Thy blessed words: *Omnia mihi tradita sunt a Patre meo* (Matt. 11, 27). Thou wast consequently obliged, by thy profound love for Him and Thy zeal for His honor, to refer and give and sacrifice everything to Him. And this Thou didst do most excellently.

Thou didst also offer to Thy Father the holy and divine state of Thy dwelling in the sacred womb of the Virgin, all filled with glory and love for Him, in satisfaction for the dishonor that was to be rendered to Him by myself in the state of original sin. And at the same moment when Thou didst accept and offer to Thy Father all the crosses and sufferings of Thy whole life, Thou didst offer Him also all the past, present, and future trials and afflictions of all Thy members: for it is the function of the head to act for himself and on behalf of all his members, because the head and the members are but one, and also because all that pertains to the members belongs to the head, and conversely all the attributes of the head belong to the members.

And so, O divine Head, Thou hast turned my whole being and the whole condition of my life to meritorious purpose. In Thy temporal birth, Thou didst render for me to Thy Father all the rightful homage I should have rendered Him at my own birth, and Thou didst then practise all the acts and exercises of devotion that I should have practised. Be Thou blessed for ever! How willingly I consent and adhere to all that Thou didst do at that time for me! Indeed I ratify it with my whole will, and would gladly sign that ratification with the last drop of my blood. I also endorse all Thou didst do for me in all the other phases or actions of Thy life, to compensate for the faults Thou didst know I was going to commit.

In imitation of Thee, O my Jesus, in honor of and in union with the same love which led Thee thus to accomplish all things for Thyself and for all Thy brothers, members, and children, and for all creatures, I henceforth desire in all my functions and activities to render to Thee all the honor and glory I can, for myself and for all Christians, who are my brothers, and members of the same Head and Body. I desire to honor Thee on behalf of all men and all other creatures that are unworthy or incapable of loving Thee, as if all of them put together had entrusted me with their duties and obligations towards Thee, and had charged me to love and honor Thee on their behalf.

### III. Prayer to the Most Blessed Virgin.

O Mother of Jesus, I honor thee, as far as I am able, in the moment of thy holy conception, and in the instant of thy birth into the world. I honor all the love, all the adoration, praise, oblations, and blessings thou didst offer to God at that time. In union with thy love, purity, and humility as thou didst adore, love and glorify Him, and didst refer thy being and thy life to Him, I adore, bless, and love my God, with thee, my Mother, with my whole heart. I consecrate and sacrifice to Him forever my life, my being, and my whole self.

So also, acclaiming thee, O Blessed Virgin, as Mother of God and consequently as my Sovereign Lady, I refer to thee, after God, the whole state of my being and my life. I implore thee most humbly to offer to God, for me, all the love, the glory, and rightful homage thou didst render to Him at thy birth, by way of satisfaction for my faults, and to cause, by thy prayers and merits, all the phases, actions, and sufferings of my life to pay undying homage to all the phases, actions, and sufferings of thy Son's life and thine own.

### IV. Prayer to the Angels and Saints Whom You Were in Duty Bound to Honor at the Time of Your Birth.

Having acquitted yourself in the above manner of your rightful tribute of homage to Our Lord and His Blessed Mother, you should offer your salutations and pay your respects to the holy guardian angel assigned to you by God when you were born; to the guardian angels of your father and mother, of the house, the place, and the diocese where you were born; to the order of angels with whom God plans to associate you in heaven; also to the saints of the day, the place, and the district where you were born. You should thank them for their helpful favors, offer yourself to their honor all your life long according to God's holy will. You should ask them to offer you to Our Lord, to use you as an instrument for His glory, and to render to Him all the due tribute of homage you should have paid Him at your birth. Invoke these devoted guardians frequently to obtain by their prayers fresh grace and new strength for you to begin a new life, which may be totally consecrated to their glory and the glory of the God of angels and saints.

# EXERCISE FOR THE ANNIVERSARY OF YOUR BAPTISM

### V. Concerning the Rightful Tribute That You Should Have Paid to God on the Day of Your Baptism.

Holy Baptism is the beginning of your true life, that is, your life in Jesus Christ, and it is the origin of all happiness. Therefore, it is certain that you would have been obliged to render a very special tribute to your Heavenly Father on the occasion of your baptism. But you were incapable of fulfilling your obligation then because you did not have the use of reason. It is logical that you should each year set apart a little interval near the anniversary of your baptism, or else some other time, to devote yourself to prayer and thanksgiving for this priceless sacrament.

### VI. Obligations to Our Lord Jesus Christ Who Instituted and Merited Baptism for You.

The author of the holy Sacrament of Baptism is Jesus Christ our Lord. He is the source of all its graces, acquired and merited by His Incarnation, by His Baptism in the River Jordan, by His Passion and Death. He applied these infinite merits to you by virtue of His Resurrection, out of His exceeding great love. All those invaluable blessings require you to pay Him the tribute of respect expressed in the following prayer.

### VII. Prayer.

O Jesus, I adore Thee as divine Author of the holy Sacrament of Baptism, which Thou didst institute for my salvation. Thou didst also acquire and merit the grace contained in that Sacrament, by Thy Incarnation, Thy Baptism in the River Jordan and by Thy holy death.

I adore the exceeding great love with which Thou didst merit and institute this same Sacrament.

I adore all the designs which Thou didst cherish in its institution, for the whole Church and for myself in particular.

I thank Thee countless times for all the glory Thou hast given to Thyself and for all the graces Thou hast transmitted to Thy Church, and to me in particular, by this Sacrament.

I offer Thee all that glory and all the graces Thou hast produced in Thy Holy Church by this means.

I beg Thee to forgive me for neglecting to take advantage of the grace Thou didst give me in holy Baptism, and for having made it valueless by my cowardice and infidelities in Thy service, and for having even destroyed it entirely in my soul, by my sins.

I give myself to Thee, O Good Jesus; renew in me the treasure of baptismal grace, and accomplish in me, by Thy very great mercy, all the plans of Thy Providence on my behalf in the divine Sacrament of Baptism.

O Jesus, I adore Thee in the mystery of Thy Incarnation, Passion, and Death, as meriting the grace of the Sacrament of Baptism; but especially do I adore Thee in the mystery of Thy holy Baptism in the River Jordan. I adore all the dispositions of Thy divine soul in this mystery, and all the designs Thou didst then deign to have in my regard. How different was Thy Baptism, Lord, from ours! In Thy Baptism Thou didst take upon Thyself our sins, to make satisfaction and do penance for them before the Father of heaven, in the desert and on the Cross, while in our baptism Thou didst lift from us the burden of our sins, washing and effacing them in Thy Precious Blood. Baptize me with the Baptism of the Holy Ghost and of fire, even as Thy blessed precursor, St. John the Baptist, assures us Thou dost baptize, that is, consume all my sins in the fire of Thy holy love, and by the power of Thy divine spirit.

VIII. The Eternal and Temporal Birth of Jesus, and His Death, Burial and Resurrection Are the Exemplar of Baptism.

All things outside of God have their idea, their exemplar, and their prototype in God; so also Sacramental Baptism has for prototype and exemplar four great mysteries, namely:

1. The mystery of His eternal birth, because His Father, by eternal generation, imparted to Him being, life and all the divine perfections, by reason of which He is the Son of God and the perfect image of

His Father. Likewise, by Baptism He imparted to you the celestial and divine life He received from His Father; He implanted in you a living image of Himself, and He made you children of His Own Heavenly Father.

2. The mystery of His temporal birth, because at the moment of His Incarnation and birth in the Virgin, He united our nature with His and His essence with our nature, and filled it with Himself and clad Himself in it as in a garment; similarly in the holy Sacrament of Baptism He united Himself with you and incorporated you with Him; He formed Himself and, as it were, took flesh in you. He clothed and filled you with Himself, according to these words of St. Paul: "As many of you as have been baptized in Christ have put on Christ" (Gal. 3, 27).

3. The mystery of His death and burial, for St. Paul also tells us that "All we, who are baptized in Christ Jesus, are baptized in his death" (Rom. 6, 3), and that "we are buried together with him by baptism into death" (Rom. 6, 4). This means precisely the same as the thought expressed by the same Apostle in other words: "You are dead: and your life is hid with Christ in God" (Col. 3, 3), that is, you have entered by baptism into a state which obliges you to die to yourself and to the world, and to live no longer except with Jesus Christ, by a totally holy and divine life, hidden and absorbed in God, resembling the life of Jesus Christ.

4. The mystery of the Resurrection, because by His Resurrection the Son of God entered into a new life, totally heavenly and spiritual, entirely separated from the earth. And so St. Paul instructs the faithful: "We are buried together with him by baptism into death; that as Christ is risen from the dead by the glory of the Father, so we also may walk in newness of life" (Rom. 6, 4).

For these reasons, then, we owe our Saviour a great tribute of homage and should lift up our minds and hearts to Him.

## IX. Prayer to Jesus.

O Jesus, Son of God and at the same time Son of man, I adore Thee in Thy temporal and eternal birth. I give Thee infinite thanks for all the glory Thou didst thus render to Thy Father. I adore the thoughts and designs Thou didst then deign to have for me, thinking of me from the very first, O Good Jesus: Thou didst love me and didst plan to make in me a living image of Thyself, of Thy birth and Thy life. Just as Thy Father communicates to Thee His divine and immortal life, and just as Thou art consequently His Son and His most perfect image, so also Thou didst plan to transmit to me by Baptism Thy holy and celestial life, and to make me a living image of Thyself, and to transform me by grace into what Thou art by nature, that is, a child of God, and by participation and resemblance, God and another Jesus Christ. Who could ever thank Thee for such great favors! How culpable I am for having, by my sins, so often impeded the perfect fulfilment of Thy divine plan! Forgive me, my Saviour, with all my heart I beg Thee to forgive me, and I give myself to Thee so that Thou mayest make amends for my faults and renew in me that image of Thyself, of Thy birth and of Thy life. Separate me from myself and from all that is not Thee, in order to unite and incorporate me with Thee. Empty me of myself and of all things, destroy me utterly, in order to fill me with Thyself and to form and establish Thyself in me. Cause me henceforth to be a perfect image of Thyself, just as Thou art a most perfect image of Thy Father. Grant that I may share in Thy filial love for Him, since He is my Father as He is Thine; enable me to live by Thy life, that is, a holy and perfect life, truly worthy of God, since Thou hast made me God by participation; and, finally, invest me so fully with Thy qualities, perfections, virtues and dispositions, and so transform me into Thee that men may see only Jesus in me, only His life, His humility, His meekness, His charity, His love, His spirit, and His other virtues and qualities, since Thou dost will me to be Thy other self on earth.

O Jesus, I adore Thee in the mystery of Thy holy death, Thy burial and Resurrection. I give Thee thanks for the glory Thou didst give Thy Father in these mysteries, and for the thoughts and plans Thou didst have in them for me. For Thou didst always think of me in all these mysteries, and at every moment of Thy life, and Thou didst always have a special plan for me. Thy special Providence was to imprint on my soul, by holy Baptism, an image of Thy death, burial and Resurrection, causing me to die to myself and to the world, hiding me in Thyself, and with Thee in the bosom of the Eternal Father, and raising me up again and causing me to live like Thee a new life, altogether celestial and divine. For this, be Thou blessed forever. Alas, by my sins I have destroyed in myself the great effects produced by Thy goodness, and for this I beg Thee, with all humility and contrition, to forgive me. I give myself to Thee, O Good Jesus, I surrender myself to the spirit and the power of the mystery of Thy death, burial and Resurrection, that Thou mayest cause me to die again to all things; that Thou mayest hide me in Thyself and with Thyself in the bosom of Thy Father; that Thou mayest dissolve my mind in Thy mind, my heart in Thy Heart, my soul in Thy soul, my life in Thy life; and that Thou mayest establish in me the new life into which Thou didst enter by Thy Resurrection, so that I may no longer live, save in Thee, for Thee, and by Thee.

## X. Jesus Christ, in the Person of the Priest, Baptizes Each Christian.

All the Holy Fathers teach us that our Lord Jesus Christ, Himself, by the power of His holy spirit, confers all the Sacraments in the person of the priest, who represents Him and acts in His Name and by His authority. It is He who consecrates in Holy Mass and gives us absolution in the Sacrament of Penance; also He baptizes us, with various symbolic ceremonies, inspired by His Spirt in Holy Mother Church and filled with mysteries that signify great graces that are conferred upon us in holy Baptism. We should, therefore, pay Him homage in this connection.

## XI. Prayer to Jesus Christ Who Baptized You.

O my Most Beloved Jesus, I adore and recognize Thee as the One who baptized me, in the person of the priest, whom Thou didst use as a living instrument to confer this grace upon me. Alas, Lord, I knew Thee not at that time: I did not think of Thee, I did not love Thee, nor did I appreciate the very great favor conferred upon me. Yet this did not deter Thee from loving me, and receiving me among the number of Thy children, and even of Thy members, by the sanctifying grace of Baptism. O my adorable Saviour, I desire with all my heart to bring back that holy time, that happy moment in which Thou didst baptize me, in order that I may adore, bless, love and glorify Thee infinitely, imploring Thy Eternal Father, Thy Holy Spirit, Thy Blessed Mother, all the angels and saints and all creatures to love, bless and thank Thee for me forever.

O Jesus, I adore Thee as the One who, by Thy Holy Spirit, didst institute and inspire in Thy Church all the ceremonies which accompany the solemn administration of Sacramental Baptism. I adore all Thy admirable designs in their institution. I give myself to Thee that Thou mayest effect them in my person, and that by Thy great mercy Thou mayest produce in me the great and holy effects signified by these symbolic ceremonies.

O Jesus, cast out the evil spirit from me forever and fill me with Thy Divine Spirit. Give me a lively and perfect faith. Fortify my bodily senses and my spiritual faculties against every kind of temptation by the virtue of Thy holy Cross and consecrate them to Thy glory. Fill my soul with Thy divine wisdom, that is, with Thyself; excite in me the most avid hunger, thirst and desire of Thee, the principal and only food of my soul, so that I may no longer find any savor or relish in anything save Thee alone. Keep me safe in Thy Church, as in the bosom of a mother, apart from whom there is no life or salvation, and give me the grace to honor her in all her observances, as in customs taught and inspired by Thee. Give me the grace to obey all her laws and commandments, as those of a mother most worthy of honor who commands me nothing save in Thy Name. In all things and everywhere teach me to follow the maxims and guidance of her Spirit, which is entirely Thine own.

O Good Jesus, open my ears to Thy word and Thy voice, as Thou didst open the ears of man possessed by the deaf and dumb spirit, by the application of Thy sacred spittle, and close them altogether to the voice of the world and of Satan. Anoint me with the oil of Thy grace so that I may spread abroad, as it were, the divine odor of Thee in every place. Give me a firm and lasting peace with Thee and with every kind of creature. Clothe me in the white robe of Thy holy innocence and divine purity, both bodily and spiritual. Dispel the shadows of my darkness, filling me with Thy heavenly radiance. Set me on fire with Thy sacred love and cause me to be a shining and a burning light, to illumine and enkindle all my associates with the light of Thy knowledge and the fire of Thy love. Finally, if I was a source of joy to all the citizens of heaven, to the Blessed Virgin, the Eternal Father, Thyself, and the Holy Spirit, when by Baptism I was delivered from the power of Satan and admitted into the divine company of angels and saints, and even of the Three Divine and Eternal Persons, and if in token of this joy the church bells were rung after I was baptized, cause me now to live henceforth in such a way as to continue to be a source of joy and satisfaction to the court of heaven, the Queen of Angels and the Most Blessed Trinity. Grant also that I may find all my satisfaction and joy in serving and loving Thee.

## XII. Solemn Profession Made by All Christians at Baptism.

I have in another place explained the nature of the solemn and public profession made by all Christians at Baptism. For that reason I need not repeat what has already been said; but it would be worth your while to refer to it again in "Part One" of this book. I shall confine myself now to recommending a prayer to Jesus Christ in renewal of the profession made to Him at Baptism, and as a repetition in your own person of the Christian vows pronounced on your behalf then by your sponsors.

## XIII. Renewal of Baptismal Vows.

O Jesus, my Lord and my God, I adore Thee as the mystical Head whom I must follow and imitate in all things, according to my solemn and public profession made at Baptism. I promised, through my sponsors, before heaven and earth, to renounce Satan utterly with all his works and his pomps, that is, sin and the world, and to adhere to Thee as my Head, and to give and consecrate myself altogether to Thee, to dwell in Thee forever. Great indeed are this promise and profession, which oblige me, as a Christian, to practise great perfection and sanctity. To profess to dwell in Thee and to adhere to Thee as my Head is to profess to be one with Thee, as the members are one with their head; it is to promise to have but one life, one mind, one heart, one soul, one will and one thought, one devotion and disposition with Thee. It means to profess not merely poverty, chastity and obedience, but to profess Thy very self, that is, Thy life, spirit, humility, charity, purity, poverty, obedience and all other virtues. In a word, it is to make the very profession Thou didst make before the Eternal Father at the moment of the Incarnation, a profession perfectly fulfilled throughout Thy life. It means to make profession never to follow one's own will, but to seek all happiness in doing everything willed by God, to remain in a state of perpetual subjection to God, and submissive to men for the love of God. It means existing always as a host and victim continually sacrificed to the pure glory of God.

Such is the vow I made at Baptism, O Jesus my Lord. How holy and divine is that profession! How far is my life from this sanctity and perfection! How often have I failed in every respect to live up to so sacred a promise! Forgive me, most merciful Lord, forgive me. O divine Redeemer, I implore Thee to repair all my failings, and in satisfaction for them, to offer to Thy Father the inestimable honor Thou didst accord Him all Thy life long, by carrying out perfectly the profession made to Him at the Incarnation.

O my Jesus, in honor of and in union with the very great love and holy dispositions of Thy profession, I now desire to enact in my own person what I promised through others at my baptism, that is, I will to renew the profession then made by my godparents. Therefore, in the virtue and might of Thy Spirit and Thy love, I forever renounce Satan, sin, the world and myself. I give myself to Thee, O Jesus, to adhere to Thee, to remain in Thee, to be but one with Thee in heart, mind, spirit and life. I offer myself to Thee, never to do my own will, but to seek all my happiness in doing everything commanded by Thy holy will. I sacrifice myself to Thee as a host and victim to be immolated to Thy pure glory in any way that may be pleasing to Thee. O Most Compassionate Jesus, I implore Thee by Thy great mercy, grant me the grace to carry out this holy profession perfectly. Do Thou fulfil it Thyself in me and for me, or rather for Thyself and for Thy own good pleasure, in all the perfection Thou dost desire; for I offer myself to Thee to do and suffer whatever pleases Thee for this intention.

## XIV. Baptismal Tribute to the Holy Trinity.

As has been said, it is our Lord Jesus Christ who baptizes the faithful; but each soul is baptized in the Name and by the power of the Most Holy Trinity. The Three Divine Persons are present at holy Baptism in a particular manner. The Father is present generating His Son in the soul and imparting to it a new being and new life in His Son. The Son is present, being born and receiving life in the soul, transmitting His divine sonship, by which the neophyte becomes a child of God, just as He is Son of God. The Holy Spirit is present, forming Jesus in each soul even as He was formed in the bosom of The Virgin. The Father, Son and Holy Ghost are present, separating the new-born Christian from all things, taking possession of him and consecrating him specially to Themselves, imprinting Their divine character and image on his soul and establishing in his being (as in Their living temple, Their sacred tabernacle, or Their holy throne and heaven) the dwelling-place of the Blessed Trinity, Their glory, kingdom and life. And consequently, if only sin did not stand in the way, the Three Eternal Persons would dwell always in each Christian heart in a particular and ineffable manner; They would most wonderfully glorify one another by living in the soul a most holy and divine life. So, too, it follows that we belong to God as creatures entirely consecrated to Him and we must consequently pursue no other purpose in life save His glory and service. In this connection it would be well to pay the following tribute of praise to the Holy Trinity.

## XV. Prayer to the Blessed Trinity.

O Holy and Adorable Trinity, I adore Thy divine essence and Thy Three Eternal Persons; I adore Thee for having been present at my baptism; I adore all the designs of Thy Providence for me. I beg Thee to forgive me for impeding their fulfilment and in satisfaction I offer Thee the life, actions and sufferings of my Lord Jesus Christ and of His most holy Mother. I give myself to Thee, O Divine Trinity, for the accomplishment of those same designs. O Eternal Father, O Thou the Only Son of God, O Holy Spirit of the Father and the Son, enter into me; enter into my heart and my soul; separate me from all that is not Thyself, draw me to Thyself, live and reign in me, destroy in me all that displeases Thee, and cause my being and my life to be completely consecrated to Thy pure glory.

## XVI. Rosary of the Blessed Trinity.

During the time devoted to the commemoration of the day of your baptism in the Name of the Most Holy Trinity, it would be a good thing to pay particular honor to that great mystery by saying the Rosary of the most Holy Trinity, which is made up of three decades and three beads in honor of the Three Divine Persons.

First, say three times the words: *Veni Sancta Trinitas* "Come, Holy Trinity," to invoke in your memory, understanding and will the Father, Son and Holy Ghost, to give yourself to Them, that They may glorify Themselves in you as They will.

On each small bead, say the *Gloria Patri,* offering to the Father, Son and Holy Ghost all the glory that has been rendered to Them from all eternity by Their own Divinity and all that shall be rendered to Them for all eternity in heaven and on earth, by way of satisfaction for the faults you have committed against Their honor.

On the large beads, say, with the same intention, the words: *Tibi laus, tibi gloria, tibi amor, O beata Trinitas,* "Praise be to Thee, glory to Thee, love to Thee, O Blessed Trinity."

## XVII. Conclusion.

To conclude the exercise on holy Baptism, thank Our Lord for the graces He has imparted during this exercise, asking Him to forgive you for the faults you have committed in it. Offer yourself to the Blessed Virgin, to your guardian angel, to the holy angels who were present at your baptism, to the saint whose name you were given, and to all the other angels and saints. Ask them to offer you to Jesus, to thank Him for you, to pay Him on your behalf all the rightful tribute of homage you would have rendered Him at the time of your Baptism if you had had the use of reason. Invoke their generous intercession to obtain from Him the grace to carry out perfectly all the holy desires and resolutions Our Lord has inspired in your heart during this exercise.

# EXERCISE OF PREPARATION FOR DEATH

### XVIII. Preparation for a Happy Death.

Death is usually preceded by such violent throes or intense weakness that the dying person is unable to direct his thoughts to God and cannot pay Him the homage owed to His divine majesty at that crucial time. Therefore, it is extremely advisable to anticipate this disability by setting aside a few days each year to carry out now what one ought rightfully to render to God at the hour of death. St. Gertrude tells us that when she had once performed this exercise, Our Lord revealed that it was most pleasing to Him, and He promised to set aside her preparation and keep it for the day of her death. You should be confident that in His goodness He will give this grace to you also, if you make use of the same exercise. For this purpose it would be well to devote ten days to a series of ten meditations and spiritual exercises in preparation for a Christian and holy death. I now present them in due order, showing how they are to be carried out.

### First Day

### XIX. Meditation on Submission to the Divine Will.

1. O my Lord Jesus, behold me prostrate at Thy feet, adoring my Judge and Sovereign, as Thou dost pronounce on me the sentence of death, pronounced to Adam and in his person to all sinners, by Thy words: "Dust thou art, and into dust thou shalt return" (Gen. 3, 19). In honor of Thy exceeding great love and most profound humility as, prostrate upon the ground at Pilate's feet, Thou didst hear and accept the sentence of death, spoken by the Roman Governor but willed by Thy Eternal Father, in honor of and in homage to His divine justice, I submit with my whole heart to the sentence of death Thou didst pass upon me even at the beginning of the world, recognizing that I have deserved it not only by original sin, but each time I have committed sin.

2. O my God, I recognize that even if I were guilty of no sin, whether original or actual, nevertheless, by Thy absolute sovereignty and power over me Thou couldst in all holiness take away my life, annihilate me and do with me as Thou wilt.

And so in honor of the very great love and in union with the deep submission with which the Blessed Virgin, Thy Mother, accepted death even though she was not obliged to die, by reason of any sin, original or actual, I, too, accept death in homage to Thy sovereignty, abandoning myself entirely into Thy hands, that Thou mayest dispose of me in time and in eternity, according to Thy holy will, for Thy greater glory.

3. O Jesus, Thou art eternal and immortal; Thou art the source of all life, and yet Thou dost will to die on the Cross the most cruel and ignominious of all deaths in homage to the justice and sovereignty, the divine and eternal life of Thy Father, and to give me a token of Thy love. And so, my Saviour, even if I were not obliged to die on account of my sins, and even if (to suppose the impossible) I depended in no way upon Thy sovereignty, and even indeed if Thou hadst not died for me in particular, I ought not only to accept death, but even to desire to die, in order to honor Thy holy death, which is so exalted and worthy of honor that all living creatures ought to subject themselves to death voluntarily even if they were not already obliged to die, in homage to the death of their Creator made Man.

But even if Thou hadst not died, O my God, all living things ought most willingly to sacrifice their very existence to pay homage to Thy supreme and eternal being, and to bear witness by this sacrifice that Thou alone art worthy to live, and that no other being or life has any right to show itself, but should be annihilated in Thy presence as the stars of heaven are extinguished in the light of the sun.

Thy death is so worthy of honor and homage, Thy life is most worthy to be adored. With excessive love Thou didst will to die, not only to satisfy the justice of Thy Father and to honor His sovereignty, but also to sacrifice Thy human and temporal life for the glory of the divine and eternal life with Thy Father and Holy Spirit. By this sacrifice Thou didst bear witness before heaven and earth, that there is none but the divine life alone that is worthy of existence, and all other created life, however noble and excellent, should be extinguished in the sight and in the presence of this supreme and uncreated life. Therefore, in honor of Thy death, in homage to Thy life, in union with the infinite love with which Thou didst thus will to die, for such great and divine intentions, and also in honor of the burning love with which Thy Blessed Mother and all Thy saints, especially Thy holy martyrs, embraced death with a very ready will for the same intentions, I accept and embrace death with my whole heart, in whatever form it may please Thee to send it to me, that is, in the place, time, manner, and under all the circumstances it shall please Thee to decree.

And so if Thou dost order me to die a painful or even a shameful death, or that I be left desolate and abandoned by all human help, or if I am to be deprived of the use of my senses and reason, provided Thou art always with me, Thy holy will be done. I desire to accept and embrace all this in honor of Thy most sorrowful and ignominious death, in honor of the unspeakable desolation Thou didst suffer on the Cross, abandoned even by the All-loving Father. I accept it in homage to the surrender of Thy senses Thou didst make in earliest childhood. I honor Thee in the humiliation Thou didst suffer, being treated as a madman by Thy own people, at the beginning of the preaching of the Holy Gospel, and by Herod and his court during Thy Passion.

Finally, my Dear Jesus, I place myself entirely in Thy hands. I abandon myself so completely to Thy good pleasure that I no longer desire to have any other will or desire, save to let Thee will, desire and choose for me, in this and in everything else. Thou dost possess infinite wisdom and power and Thou hast a far greater knowledge and power and will to further Thy glory than I ever could have. One thing alone I beg of Thee, and it is that, since Thou didst die in love, by love and for love, if I am not worthy to die for Thy love or by that love, at least Thou mayest permit me to die in Thy dear love.

4. O my Jesus, I implore that, just as Thou didst perform all Thy actions and functions for Thyself and for all men, especially for Thy children and friends, I may be permitted, in honor of and in union with Thy love, to perform all these actions and render unto Thee all

due homage not only for myself but for all men, especially for all those for whom Thou knowest that I am both bound and anxious to pray with particular fervor.

O Mother of Jesus, surely it would seem that thou shouldst not have died, since thou art the Mother of the Eternal and Immortal Son of God, who is life itself! Yet thou didst willingly submit to death, in homage to the most adorable death of thy Son. Thus, thy death is so exalted and worthy of honor that all creatures ought to subject themselves to death by their own free will, in order to honor the death of their Sovereign Lady, the Mother of their Creator. Therefore, O holy Virgin, even if I were not obliged to die, I should, nevertheless, wish to accept death freely, and offer it to thee together with the death of each one who is dear to me, and of all mankind, in homage to thy most holy death. I most humbly implore thee, O Mother of Life, to unite my death to thine in honor of the death of thy Son and to obtain from Him the grace to die in His favor and in His love.

### Second Day

XX. THANKSGIVING FOR ALL THE BENEFITS OF YOUR WHOLE LIFE.

After you have made the solemn act of acceptance, you should prepare for a holy death, first by thanking Our Lord for all the favors you have received from Him in your whole lifetime. And it is very wise to devote a day to this exercise as follows:

1. O Jesus, I contemplate and adore Thee as the principle and source of all good things and all temporal and eternal graces past, present and future, in heaven and on earth, especially those I have received from Thee. I refer all these graces to Thee, for Thou art their source and Thy glory is their destiny. O Good Jesus, who could ever describe all the favors Thou hast done me? They are numberless and I am utterly incapable of thanking Thee for them as Thou dost deserve. O dearest Lord, may all that ever was, is, or shall be in me, may all earthly and heavenly creatures, all the angels and saints, Thy Holy Mother, Thy Holy Spirit, Thy Eternal Father, all the powers of Thy divinity and humanity, and all the graces and

mercies which emanated from Thee, may all these be employed in praising Thee forever. May they be entirely transformed into everlasting praise of Thee, of all that Thou art together with Thy Father, Thyself and Thy Holy Spirit, and of all the graces Thou didst ever impart to Thy sacred humanity, Thy Blessed Mother, the angels and saints, and all creatures, and especially the graces Thou hast given me, or would have given me if I had not stood in Thy way.

O Father of Jesus, Holy Spirit of Jesus, Mother of Jesus, angels of Jesus, Saints of Jesus, and all creatures of Jesus, bless and give thanks to Him for me forever. O Divine Jesus, do Thou glorify Thyself for me and return to Thyself a hundredfold all the thanks I ought to render to Thee.

2. O Good Jesus, Thou knowest how many favors and benefits I have received from Thy Blessed Mother, the angels and saints in heaven, and from many persons on earth. Thou knowest also how incapable I am of acknowledging them and giving thanks for them as I ought. And so I have recourse to Thee, imploring Thee most humbly to make up for my deficiencies and to give, on my behalf, to all those souls, both in heaven and on earth, all that I ought to render to them for the benefits I have received at their hands.

3. O Mother of Grace, Mother of my God, it is through thy intercession that I have received all the graces ever bestowed on me from heaven. May heaven and earth bless thee for them all, on behalf of myself and of all the thoughtless persons who have received favors from thee and give thee no thanks whatever.

### Third Day

## XXI. Confession and Satisfaction.

Having set aside one day to thank God for all the graces He has given you in your lifetime, it is most necessary that you devote another day to ask forgiveness for your sins and to make satisfaction to Him. To that end, you ought on this day to make a good confession, either an extraordinary confession or one marked by unusual contrition and self-abasement, with as much care and preparation as if it were to be your last confession. The acts of contrition and other exercises for confession in "Part Two" will serve your purpose here also. Besides doing this, you would do well to set aside a little time during the day to meditate on this matter, in the presence of God, in the following way:

1. O Most Lovable Jesus, infinitely worthy of all service and love, to whom I owe debts without number, Thou didst create me only to love and serve Thee. Yet I have done scarcely anything but offend Thee by thought, word and deed, by all my bodily senses and spiritual faculties, by my misuse of Thy creatures, against all Thy commandments, in countless different ways. O what sins! What ingratitude! What betrayals! Lord Jesus, I cast all my offenses upon Thy divine love, into the abyss of Thy mercies. Grant that I may be utterly changed into sorrow and contrition, with tears of blood to detest and wipe out the sins I have committed against that immense Goodness, so deserving of love and honor! My God, what is there that I could ever do to make reparation for my sins? But even if I were to suffer all the torments and martyrdom in the world, I still could not of myself alone repair the insult given Thee by even the least of my faults.

2. O Good Jesus, I offer Thee instead all the glory, love and service given Thee by all the saints and Thy most Blessed Mother, by their holy thoughts, words and actions, by holy use of their bodily senses and their spiritual powers, by their eminent virtues and sufferings, in satisfaction for the failures of my lifetime. I offer Thee likewise all the honor given Thee forever by all the angels, by the Holy Spirit, by Thyself, and by the Eternal Father, in reparation for the dishonor I have given Thee all my life.

3. O Heavenly Father, O Holy Spirit, O ye angels and saints, offer up for me, to my Saviour, all the love and glory you ever gave Him, in satisfaction for the wrong I have done Him by my offenses.

4. Miserable sinner that I am, by offending my God I have offended all things. I have offended the Father, the Son, the Holy Ghost, the Mother of God, all the angels and saints, and all creation, for all are concerned and offended in offense to their Creator. How, O my God, how can I make reparation for so many offenses, make satisfaction

to so many persons and pay off so many debts? I know what I will do: I have my Jesus who is in Himself an infinite wealth of virtues, merits and good works. He has been given me to be my riches, my virtue, my sanctification, my redemption and reparation. I shall offer Him to the Eternal Father, to the Holy Ghost, to the Blessed Virgin, to all the angels and all the saints in reparation and satisfaction for all the faults I have committed. O Holy Father, O Divine Spirit, I offer all the love and honor that my Jesus gave you by all His divine thoughts, words and actions, by His divine employment of all the members of His body and of His soul, by all His glorious virtues and heroic sufferings, in satisfaction for all the offenses I have committed against you all my life long.

O holy Virgin, O holy angels, O blessed saints, I offer you my treasure and my all, my Saviour Jesus Christ. I conjure you to draw upon His infinite storehouse of merit whatever you require in payment and satisfaction for all the debts I owe you, by reason of my sins and negligences.

5. O my Jesus, my divine Redeemer, do Thou make reparation for all my faults, and by Thy very great mercy atone for all my sins committed against the Eternal Father, Thyself the Son, the Holy Spirit, Thy most Blessed Mother, the angels and saints and all persons I have offended. I give myself to Thee to do and suffer in atonement whatsoever may be pleasing to Thy holy will, accepting now all the sufferings of body or spirit that I may have to bear, whether in this world or in the next, in satisfaction for my sins.

6. O most holy Virgin, I have so many obligations to serve and venerate thee; yet I have so little honored and so greatly offended thee by offending thy Son! I beg thy forgiveness, O Mother of Mercy, and I offer Thee in satisfaction all the honor ever accorded thee in heaven and on earth. I implore all the angels and saints, the Holy Ghost, thy Son, and the Eternal Father to supply for my deficiencies, and fill up the measure of glory I ought to have rendered to thee all my life long.

## Fourth Day

### XXII. HOLY COMMUNION.

Holy Communion is the most precious and effective means given you by God to render to Him all the honor and service you owe to Him. To prepare for a holy death, you should make a point of taking one day of this exercise to dispose yourself for an exceptionally well-prepared Communion, marked by extraordinary devotion and approached with as much care and recollection as if it were to be your last. The exercise I drew up for Holy Communion, in "Part Two" of this book, will prove sufficient for this purpose, provided you use it profitably.

Let me merely tell you that you should offer this special Communion to Our Lord: 1. in honor of all that He is in Himself and towards you; 2. in thanksgiving for all the effects of His love for His Father and for all creatures, but especially for you; 3. in satisfaction for all the dishonor and pain given Him by all the sins of the world, especially by your own; and 4. for the fulfilment of the plans of His Divine Providence for all men, especially for you.

Offer yourself to the Eternal Father, begging Him to unite you with the surpassing love of His paternal heart when He received His Son Jesus Christ into His bosom on the day of the Ascension. Give yourself to Jesus and beg Him to unite you with the most ardent love and profound humility with which He instituted the Holy Sacrament of the Altar, on the eve of His death. Offer yourself to the Blessed Virgin, to St. John the Evangelist, to St. Mary Magdalen and St. Mary of Egypt, and all the other saints, praying that they may cause you to participate in the love and fervor, the humility, purity and sanctity with which they received Holy Viaticum.

After you have received Communion and made the usual thanksgiving to Our Lord with unusual fervor, adore His divine plans from all eternity for you. Beg Him to forgive all the obstructions you have ever placed in the way of their operation. Fervently beg Him not to let you die until He has completed the plans of His goodness and the work of His grace in your soul. Give yourself to Him with a great

## Sixth Day

### XXIV. Christ's Last Will and Testament, and the Will You Should Make in Its Honor.

On this day you should prepare to make a will, in imitation and honor of the final testament of Jesus Christ on earth. In the presence of God you should meditate on the infinitely adorable legacy left by Christ and consider how to make your own will in the same spirit with similar dispositions. This may be done in the following manner:

O Jesus, I adore Thee in the last days of Thy life. I adore every aspect and event of these last days, but especially Thy divine Testament pronounced in the Cenacle, on Mount Olivet and from the Cross. I adore, bless and glorify the supreme love for Thy Father, the most burning charity towards us and all the other holy dispositions of Thy last Testament to mankind.

In Thy last will there are five bequests:

The *first* bequest is to Thine enemies, for, O wonder of wonders, O immensity of goodness, Thy first word and first prayer on the Cross is for Thine enemies, begging the Father to pardon them, in the very hour when they were crucifying Thee.

The *second* bequest is to the Heavenly Father, the final gift of Thy holy soul with these words: "Father, into thy hands I commend my spirit" (Luke 23, 46). These words were uttered not only with reference to Thy deified soul, but to my soul and to the souls of all who belong to Thee, which were all at that moment before Thy sight, and Thou didst look upon them as Thy own possession, forming all together but one soul with Thine, by virtue of their most intimate union. When Thou didst say to the Father: *Pater, in manus tuas commendo spiritum meum,* Thou didst speak for Thyself and for me; Thou didst commend my soul together with Thine into the hands of Thy Father, adddressing this prayer to Him who is at once Thy Father and mine, in Thy Name and my own, against the hour when my soul shall leave my body. And Thou didst make the offering of my soul with the same love with which Thou didst say *Pater* or *Father* in general, not *My Father* in particular, to show that Thou didst regard Him not only as Thy own Special Father, but as the common and universal Father of all Thy brethren and members. Thou didst pray to Him not only for Thyself in particular, but also in general for all who belong to Thee, with filial confidence and love, as much for Thyself as for them, for which mayst Thou be loved and blessed forever.

The *third* bequest in Thy will concerns the Blessed Mother, to whom Thou didst give that which was most dear to Thee after herself, the beloved disciple, St. John the Evangelist. At the same time there were represented in the person of St. John all the other disciples and children, until the end of time. When Thou didst say to Mary the words, "Woman, behold thy son" (John 19, 26), Thou didst give her not only St. John, but all other Christians to be her children. Reciprocally, in saying to St. John the words "Behold thy Mother" (John 19, 27), Thou didst give to him and also to all Christians, represented in his person, Thy most precious possession in the order of created beings, namely, Thy most Blessed Mother. Thou didst give her to them to be their Mother just as she was Thy Mother, imparting to them Thy precious relationship and character with her. That was the reason Thou didst call her no longer Thy Mother, but *Mulier,* "woman," to show the transfer to us of Thy relationship to her as Son, and the gift to us, as Mother, of her who was about to cease to be Thy Mother for a time by reason of her Son's death. And so, good Jesus, Thou didst bequeath me in Thy will to Thy Blessed Mother, not only as a servant and subject, but actually as a son: *Mulier, ecce filius tuus.* Thou didst give her to me not only as my Queen and Lady, but in the most honorable and lovable character there is—that of a Mother. O love! O excess of goodness! May the whole world be transformed into love for so great a goodness!

The *fourth* bequest in Thy will is particularly ours and concerns us so diversely that it seems to have been made for us alone.

1. During Thy last days on earth, O Jesus, Thou didst express a surpassing and extraordinary love, assuring us that Thy Father loves us as He loves Thee (John 17, 23), and that Thou lovest us as Thy Father loves Thee (John 15, 9). And Thou dost consequently urge us to love one another as Thou hast loved us (John 13, 34).

2. Thou didst likewise commend us with most particular affection

to the most exalted and powerful persons most dear to Thee, by whom Thou art most loved in heaven and on earth—that is, Thy Eternal Father and Thy divine Mother. To the Father just before setting out on the road to Calvary, Thou didst address a beautiful prayer: "Holy Father, keep them in thy name whom Thou hast given me. Not for them only do I pray but for them who through their word shall believe in me" (John 17, 11-20). While hanging on the Cross, Thou didst place our souls in His hands together with Thine own, as has been said. Thou didst also commend us to Thy divine Mother.

3. We share in Thy will because in Thy last, solemn and public prayer, Thou didst obtain from the Heavenly Father the greatest favors that could have been asked of Him, or that He could have given us. Here are the prayers Thou didst address to Him for us: "Father, I will that where I am, they also whom thou hast given me may be with me" (John 17, 24), that is, that they should have their dwelling and take their rest with Me forever in Thy bosom and Thy Fatherly Heart. "Just Father, may the love wherewith Thou hast loved me, be in them" (John 17, 25-26), that is to say: love them as Thou lovest Me, love them with the greatest, the most burning and most divine love that could ever possibly exist. Look upon them as Thou dost regard Me; love them with the very heart with which Thou lovest Me; treat them as Thou dost treat Me; give them all that Thou givest Me. "That they may be one, as thou, Father, in me and I in thee; that they also may be one in us . . . I in them, and thou in me: that they may be made perfect in one" (John 17, 21-23). O dearest Lord, what love! What more couldst Thou ask the Father for us?

4. We share in Thy will because Thou didst give us the most rare and precious gift, Thy Eternal Father to be our Father, praying Him to love us as He loves Thee, as His children with sublime paternal love. Thou didst give us Thy Blessed Mother to be our Mother. Thou didst give us Thy most Holy Body in the Eucharist, Thy holy soul on the Cross in death with the words: "I lay down my life for my sheep" (John 10, 15). Thou didst give Thy Precious Blood to the very last drop, Thy life, merits, sufferings, humanity and divinity, as

expressed in these words: "The glory which thou hast given me, I have given to them" (John 17, 22). Thou didst give up all without reserve. O dearest Lord, how admirable is Thy goodness, poured forth for us in the very hour when we were causing Thee to suffer so many evils! How can we love Thee so little and think so seldom of Thee? How can so great a love be held so cheap and be so despised by those whom Thou so lovest?

The *fifth* and last bequest in Thy will was made on Mount Olivet when, departing from the apostles and ascending into heaven, Thou didst give them Thy holy blessing. We share in this bequest also, for in imparting Thy blessing to the holy apostles and disciples Thou didst bless all of us, each one in particular, for we were all just as much present in Thy sight then as we are now. May heaven and earth bless Thee, O Author of all gifts, and may all things in heaven and earth be transformed into eternal blessings of Thee.

Such, good Jesus, are the five clauses of Thy admirable will, in honor of which I desire, if it please Thee, to draw up my own testament as follows:

## XXV. LAST SPIRITUAL WILL AND TESTAMENT.

1. O Most Kind Jesus, in honor of and in union with the love with which Thou didst shed Thy Blood and die for Thy enemies and pray to Thy Father to pardon those who crucified Thee, with my whole heart I fully forgive all those who have ever offended or injured me, and I implore Thee to grant them full pardon. I offer myself to Thee to do and suffer whatever may please Thee for their sake, even to shed my blood and die for them, if necessary. So, too, in all the humility I can muster, I beg all whom I have ever offended or displeased in my whole life to forgive me, and I give myself to Thee to make whatever satisfaction to them Thou mayest desire.

2. In honor of and in union with the exceeding great love, the most perfect confidence and all the other dispositions with which Thou didst commend Thy soul and all the souls that belong to Thee into the hands of Thy Father, I surrender my soul, with the souls of all those for whom I am bound to have special concern, into the gentle hands and the most loving heart of the Divine Father, who is my

God, my Creator and my Most Lovable Father, that He may dispose of them according to His good pleasure. I trust that His infinite goodness will place them with Thy soul, good Jesus, in His Fatherly Bosom, there to love and bless Him eternally with Thee, according to the desire of Thy soul, expressed in the words: *"Father, I will that where I am, they also whom thou hast given me may be with me"* (John 17, 24).

3. In honor of and in union with Thy great charity in giving all Thy friends and children to Thy most Blessed Mother, I resign into her hands all those entrusted to my care, imploring Thee, Good Jesus, to commend them Thyself to Thy Virgin Mother. I implore her with my whole heart, by Thy very great love for her and hers for Thee, and by the same love with which Thou didst give her Thy friends and children, to look upon them henceforth as her children in a more special way, and to be their Mother.

4. In honor of and in union with the exceedingly powerful love whereby Thou didst commend me to Thy Father on Thy last day, and didst beg Him, on my behalf, for such great favors, giving me all that was most dear to Thee, with such extraordinary tokens of that love, urging me also to love my neighbor as Thou didst love me: I commend to Thee all those whom Thou knowest I should commend particularly to Thee, and I beg Thee on their behalf for all that Thou didst ask for me from Thy Eternal Father on Good Friday. I abandon myself to Thee to love Thee as Thou lovest the Father and as the Father loves Thee. I give myself also to Thee to love my neighbor as Thou didst love me, and to shed my blood and give my life for him, if it is Thy holy will.

5. O Jesus, God of all blessings, I adore Thee in the last moment of Thy sojourn on earth, upon Mount Olivet, as Thou didst leave the earth to ascend into heaven. I adore Thee giving Thy most holy blessing to Thy Blessed Mother, Thy apostles and disciples; I adore the exceeding great love and all the other dispositions which filled Thy divine soul when Thou didst impart this supreme blessing as is related in the Holy Gospel (Luke 24, 50).

O Good Jesus, behold me prostrate at Thy feet, in union with the humility and the other holy dispositions of the Blessed Mother and the holy apostles and disciples as they received Thy blessing. I most humbly implore Thee, by all Thy love for them, and theirs for Thee, to give now to me and to all I have commended to Thee, Thy most holy blessing, so that by the power of that divine blessing all that displeases Thee in me may be destroyed and I may be altogether transformed into everlasting praise, love and benediction of Thee.

*Seventh Day*

## XXVI. THE AGONY AND THE MOMENT OF DEATH.

You shall consider this day as if it were to be your last. You must strive to spend it with as much care and devotion as if you had only this one day in which to love God. For this purpose, you should apply yourself to the contemplation and adoration of Our Lord in the last day of His life on earth, and to do everything in union with the holy and divine dispositions of His last actions. With the last day of your life in view, you should implore Jesus to unite you to his dispositions and foster them in your heart, that you may be of the number of those of whom it is said: *"Blessed are the dead who die in the Lord"* (Apoc. 14, 13) that is, who die in the dispositions of the death of our Lord Jesus Christ.

Similarly you should consider and honor the Blessed Virgin on the last day of her life, uniting yourself to her dispositions, offering her the last day of your life. The prayers addressed to Jesus Christ and His Blessed Mother for the end of the year should also serve your purpose here.

I may also add at this point that it is a good thing on this day to adore Jesus and honor His most holy Mother in their agony and death, offering your agony and death in union with theirs, imploring them to bless and sanctify your death by their own. It is also most beneficial to adore the infinite power of the divine love that caused the death of Jesus and of His most holy Mother, for they both died of love and by love. You should implore that divine love to cause you to die with Jesus and His divine Mother, and to consume and sacrifice your life in its sacred flames.

You should also honor the holy martyrs and all saints in their agony and death; offer them your agony and death, in union with their own, begging them to unite you with their holy dispositions as they prepared for death. Implore them specially to associate you with all the love and glory they gave to Our Lord on the last day of their life and at the moment they died for Him.

You should pray specially to St. John the Evangelist, St. Mary Magdalen and the good thief who died with Jesus, and all the other saints who were present at the death of the Son of God, that through the merits of their privilege in being near Him in death, they may give you special assistance at the hour of your own death.

On this same day it would be most advisable to read the Passion of Our Lord, the seventeenth chapter of St. John, containing His last words and prayers before setting forth to be crucified, as well as the prayers of Holy Mother Church for the agonizing soul, which are to be found at the end of the Breviary. For you do not know whether you will be in a fit state on the last day of your life to complete these preparations for a holy death. Hence, it is a good thing to anticipate that day, and to read the Passion of Our Lord and the above-mentioned prayers with all the devotion you would wish to put into them at the hour of death, and all the devotion with which they have ever been read by the whole Church.

But above all, when you read the seventeenth chapter of St. John, which contains the last words and prayers of Jesus, give yourself to Him in a sincere effort to pronounce these words and prayers in union with His love, dispositions and intentions when He spoke them, imploring Him to foster in your heart these sublime dispositions in preparation for the last day of your life and to produce the effects of these holy words.

Finally, cast yourself down at the feet of Jesus and His most holy Mother, to implore them to give you their most holy blessing. "O Jesus, O Mother of Jesus, give me your holy blessing for the last moment of my life. By your great goodness, grant that the last moment of my life may be consecrated to the glory of the last moment of yours, and that my last breath may be an act of most pure love for you."

## Eighth Day

### XXVII. The Particular Judgment.

It is a most holy practice, when present at a deathbed, to kneel down at the moment the person dies, to adore the advent of the Son of God, who comes to judge that soul right there in the body, where it remains until it is consigned elsewhere by His judgment. It would be quite easy to prove that the Son of God thus comes to judge the soul at the hour of death, because several passages of Holy Scripture clearly speak of it. This is not, however, the place to do so. All I have to say for the present is that if it is beneficial to adore the Son of God in the exercise of His judgment upon others at the hour of death, how much more should you adore Him in His coming for you and His judgment at the hour of your death. Therefore, you must render to Him now, freely and out of love, the honor that shall be obligatory when your end comes. Hence, this day shall be spent in this exercise, performed as follows:

1. O Jesus, Thou art the Saint of saints and Sanctity Itself, infinitely above all sin and imperfection. Yet, I behold Thee prostrate with Thy face to the earth at the feet of the All-just Father in the Garden of Olives, and the following day at the feet of Pilate, where the Eternal Father contemplates Thee as the Victim who has taken upon Himself all the sins of the world, giving Himself without reserve for the ransom of mankind. Thou hast taken the place of all sinners and borne the heavy judgment of our sins by dying on the Cross for our salvation. Thou dost accept that judgment with most perfect submission, most profound humility and most ardent love for Thy Father and for us. O Jesus, I adore and glorify Thee in this judgment and in all the holy dispositions of humiliation, contrition, submission and love with which Thou didst suffer to be judged and condemned to save us.

2. In honor of and in union with these dispositions, behold me prostrate at Thy feet, great Jesus, adoring Thee as my sovereign judge. I most willingly submit myself to Thy supreme power. I infinitely rejoice that Thou hast sovereign power over me and over all men and

angels. A thousand times I bless the Eternal Father for having given Thee this power. I affirm sincerely that if, to imagine the impossible, Thou didst not have this power, and I did have it, I would want to strip myself of it to give it to Thee; if I were not subject to Thy power to judge me, I should wish to subject myself voluntarily to that power, out of homage to Thy divine justice and to the condemnation Thou didst undergo from Thy Father during Thy holy Passion.

3. O Jesus, I adore Thee in Thy coming at the hour of my death and at the moment of Thy judgment of my soul. I adore now every aspect and detail of my particular judgment. May it please Thee to grant me now some measure of the divine light by which Thou wilt clearly show me every event of my whole life, compelling me to give an account of everything. Grant me a share in the zeal for justice with which Thou wilt be avenged for my offenses, so that I may from now on see my sins clearly and make reparation by perfect contrition, horror and detestation for these same sins.

4. O my God, how many sins I have committed against Thee all my life, by thought, word and deed, in every way! They can not be numbered, I confess; and I accuse myself before Thee, Thy Blessed Mother, before all the angels and saints, and, if it be Thy holy will, before the whole world. I accuse myself of my sins just as they are in Thy sight, as Thou knowest them. If only I could see my offenses as Thou seest them! If only I knew myself as Thou knowest me, and as I shall see and know myself in Thy light at the moment of judgment! How I shall be confounded and humiliated then by the realization of what I am! What horror my crimes will awaken in me! What regret, what anguish at having so little loved and so greatly offended so transcendent a goodness as Thine! How quickly will I then accuse and condemn my own self! Indeed there will be no need of any other judge, for I shall be the first to pass sentence upon my own misdeeds and ignominy.

5. But why wait until that final hour? Lord, at this very moment I surrender myself to the zeal of Thy divine justice and to the spirit of Thy just hatred and righteous horror for sin. In honor of and in union with Thy extreme hatred of sin, I hate and detest all my sins; I hold them in abhorrence; I renounce them forever; I offer myself to Thee

to suffer for them all the penance Thou shalt order. Casting myself down before Thy face, in the ultimate depths of abjection, to which, O great God, I have deserved to be reduced by my sins, I pronounce against myself, in the presence of heaven and earth, that final sentence. Since I, who am nothing but a worm of the earth, a handful of ashes and mere nothingness, have in so many ways offended so exalted and great a majesty, there are no tortures, either on earth, in purgatory or in hell, capable of worthily expiating my sin, without the intervention of Thy mercy and the power of Thy Precious Blood. For all these torments are finite, while the offense of my sins is infinite, since they offend an infinite majesty, and consequently deserve an infinite punishment.

So, my sovereign Judge, falling down once more at Thy feet, and in the nethermost depths of the bottomless pit of my sins, I adore and bless and love Thee with my whole heart, as pronouncing the sentence that Thou shalt pronounce at the hour of my death, and I voluntarily, with all the love possible to me, submit to this sentence, whatever it may be, telling Thee with the Royal Prophet, with all the power of my will: "Thou art just, O Lord, and thy judgment is right" (Ps. 118, 137). And I most obediently accept anything it may please Thee to ordain in my regard, in time and eternity, giving myself to Thee to bear not only all the sufferings of Purgatory, in homage to Thy divine justice, but any other penalty Thou mayest impose upon me. I take no thought of what is to become of me nor of what is to be done to me in time and eternity, provided only that the wrong and dishonor I have done Thee may be made good, no matter what the cost.

And yet, O God of mercy, do not permit that I should be numbered among those who will never love Thee. O most merciful Lord, what am I that Thou deignest to open Thy blessed eyes to look upon me, to summon me into Thy presence in judgment and to exercise Thy justice upon me? It is all too true that I deserve Thy mercy far less than Thy justice. But, O Thou Saviour of my soul, remember that Thou didst will to be judged for me, and that Thou art most worthy that my sins should be forgiven in Thee, since Thou didst ask the All-merciful Father to pardon them for me. And yet, Lord, enter not into judgment with Thy miserable and unworthy servant, but offer for me to Thy Father the judgment Thou didst sustain for my sins, and pray that His divine forgiveness be granted, not to me but to Thee.

O Father of Mercy, I confess that I have deserved to bear the stern weight of Thy judgments, and that I am not worthy that Thou shouldst give me the least grace, nor that Thou shouldst pardon the very smallest of my sins. I offer Thee the terrible judgment Thy Son sustained for my faults, and I implore Thee to pardon them, not to me, but to Thy Beloved Son, who begs Thy forgiveness on my behalf, and to give Him, also, all the graces I need for Thy service. All possible punishments in the world, visited upon me, are incapable of giving Thee fitting satisfaction for the very least of my crimes. Thy Son alone can make perfect reparation for the dishonor I have given Thee. And so I offer to Thee, and I implore Him to offer with me, all that He did and suffered in His whole life, and all the honor He ever rendered to Thee, whether by Himself or through His Blessed Mother, His angels and all His saints.

O Mother of Mercy, Mother of Jesus, O angels and saints of Jesus, offer to God all your merits and works on my behalf and all the glory you ever gave Him, in satisfaction for my offenses and implore Him to treat me not according to the rigor of His justice, but the multitude of His mercies, in order that I may love and bless Him with you forever.

### Ninth Day

XXVIII. Death and Burial.

Since Jesus Christ, our Lord, willed to pass through all the phases of human life, in order to honor His Eternal Father and to bless and sanctify them for you, you should also have a holy zeal for honoring Him particularly in each of the phases of His life, and to consecrate all the states, in which you have been and are to be, to the honor of each aspect of His mortal life. Following this teaching, after you have adored Him in the last moment of His life, dedicating to Him your own last moment, it is now very appropriate to adore Him in the state of death, in which He remained for three days, and to consecrate to Him the condition of death in which you are to be from the last moment of your life until the day of the general resurrection, as follows:

1. O Jesus, Thou art eternal life and the source of all life, yet I behold Thee cold in the darkness and shadow of death. I see Thee bid farewell, for a little while, to Thy most lovable Mother, to Thy dearly beloved apostles and disciples, and to all Thy friends left bathed in tears, in the greatest mourning and lamentation of all time. I contemplate Thy holy soul separated from Thy divine Body, with which it had so holy, so close and so sublime a union. I see this same Body, more holy and sacred than all the heavenly bodies (I mean than all those in all the heavens, and more than the empyrean heaven itself), lying in a sepulchre, among the rocks in the dust. O my Jesus, I adore, praise and glorify Thee thus. I offer Thee all the honor rendered to Thee in this state by Thy holy Mother, by St. Mary Magdalen, by the holy apostles and disciples, by the angels, by the holy souls Thou didst free from Limbo and by the whole Church, with all the glory Thy Father gave Thee, and which Thou now enjoyest in heaven, in recompense for that humiliation Thou didst bear on earth. I offer Thee the state of death which will one day be mine, in honor of that state of death in which Thou didst remain before the Resurrection. I offer Thee the separation from the company of my friends and relatives that I shall one day have to bear, in honor of the most bitter separation which Thou didst suffer, torn from the most sweet company of Thy dearest Mother, of Thy dearly beloved apostles and disciples. I offer Thee all the sorrow and the tears of my relatives and friends in honor of the sorrow and tears of Thy harrowed Mother and sorrowing apostles. I offer Thee the separation of my soul from Thy sacred body. I offer Thee all the states of my soul, until its reunion with its body, whatever they may be, in homage to the state in which Thy holy soul existed during the time it was separated from Thy body. I offer Thee the burial of my body and all the actions that shall be done in performing this burial, in honor of the burial of Thy holy body. In honor of and in union with the same love with which Thou, O good Jesus, didst will that Thy sacred body should lie upon the dust within

a hollow rock, and by which Thou hast so often given me this same body in Holy Communion, although I am nothing but a worm of the earth, I most willingly surrender my body to the ground and to the worms. I consent to be reduced to ashes and dust, but only on condition, O crucified Saviour, that all the grains of dust into which my flesh and bones shall crumble, may be so many voices praising and glorifying without interruption the adorable mystery of Thy burial, and that I may thus sing with the holy psalmist: *Omnia ossa mea dicent, Domine quis similis tibi?* "All my bones shall say: Lord, who is like to thee?" (Ps. 34, 10).

2. O Divine Jesus, even though Thy body and soul were separated, nevertheless they are continually united to Thy divinity. Thus, they never ceased to be worthy of infinite honor and adoration. Therefore, I adore Thy holy soul in its descent into Limbo. I adore all that happened in Thy soul and all the efforts produced in the souls of the Holy Patriarchs in Limbo. I also adore Thy body in the tomb, in all its members, for there is no part of it that is not infinitely adorable. I adore you, O most holy eyes of my Saviour's body. I adore you, O sacred ears of my God. I adore and praise you, O most blessed mouth and tongue of Him who is the Word and eternal utterance of the Father. I adore and bless you, O most divine hands and feet of my Lord. I adore and love you, O most amiable Heart of Jesus.

Alas, my Beloved, Thy perfect body is lifeless because of my sins! Those sacred eyes, that by their sweet aspect gave joy to all who came in contact with Thee, are now darkened by the shadow of death. Those holy ears, always open to hear the cries and prayers of all unhappy creatures, are now closed and hear no more. Those divine lips, which pronounced the words of life, have become mute and speak no words. Those blessed hands that wrought so many miracles are lifeless and still. Those holy feet, so often wearied for the salvation of the world, are no longer able to walk. But above all, the most loving Heart of my Jesus, the most exalted and noble throne of divine love, is without life or feeling. Ah, my Dear Jesus, who has brought Thee to this pitiable state? My sins and Thy love! Cursed and detestable sin, how I abhor you! O love of my Saviour, may I love you, may I bless you without ceasing!

3. O Good Jesus, I surrender myself completely to the power of Thy holy love. I implore Thee by that love, to reduce me now into a state of death that may imitate and honor Thy state of death. Utterly extinguish in me the life of sin and of the old Adam. Cause me to die to the world, to myself and to all that is not Thee. Mortify my eyes, ears, tongue, hands, feet, heart and all the other powers of my body and soul, so that I may no longer be able to see, nor hear, speak, taste, act, walk, love, think, will, nor make any other use of all the parts of my body or the faculties of my soul, save in accordance with Thy good pleasure, led by the guidance of Thy divine spirit.

4. O my Well-beloved Jesus, I give myself to Thee to derive the benefits of these words of Thy apostle: "You are dead: and your life is hid with Christ in God" (Col. 3, 3). Hide me utterly with Thee in God. Bury my mind, my heart, my will and my being, so that I may no longer have any thoughts, desires, or affections, any sentiments and dispositions other than Thine own. And just as the earth changes and transforms into itself the bodies buried within it, do Thou change and transform me completely into Thyself. Bury my pride in Thy humility, my coldness and tepidity in the fervor of Thy divine love, and all my other vices and imperfections into Thy holy virtues and perfections so that, just as the earth consumes all the corruption of the body buried in it, so all the corruption of my soul may be consumed and annihilated in Thy divine perfections.

5. O Mother of Jesus, I honor and revere thee in the state of thy death and burial. I offer thee all the honor then given thee by the angels and holy apostles. I thank thee for all the glory thou didst give to the death and burial of Thy Son by thine own. I offer thee my own death and burial, imploring thee to obtain for me, by thy holy prayers, the grace that every aspect of my earthly end may pay everlasting homage to the death and burial of thy spotless self and of thy beloved Son, our Saviour.

### Tenth Day

## XXIX. Entrance of the Soul Into Heaven and Undying Life.

Even though we are most unworthy to see the face of God and to be admitted into the blessed company of the citizens of heaven, it is, nevertheless, most certain that the Father, the Son, the Holy Spirit, the Blessed Virgin, all the angels and all the saints eagerly desire to behold you soon joined with them, to be overwhelmed as they are in the torrents of the heavenly and unspeakable delights of divine love which reigns with fulness in heaven. And we ought to have great trust that, in the goodness of God, this will one day be realized for us. Our greatest consolation in this world ought to be the thought and expectation of that day when we shall begin to love and glorify God in all perfection. What rejoicings we should voice with the Royal Prophet, at the vision and thought of that blessed day: *Laetatus sum in his quae dicta sunt mihi, in domum Domini ibimus:* "I rejoiced at the things that were said to me: We shall go into the house of the Lord" (Ps. 121, 1). "Blessed are they who dwell in thy house, O Lord: they shall praise thee forever and ever." (Ps. 83, 5).

Surely if you celebrate the day of your birth into the life of grace by holy Baptism, how much more should you celebrate the feast of your entrance into heaven and your birth into the life of glory! Anticipate that day, and begin now to celebrate that feast by means of the following exercises:

1. O Jesus, I adore, praise and glorify Thee countless times at the moment of Thy triumphant entrance into heaven. I offer Thee all the glory, love and praises that were given to Thee in welcome by the Father, the Holy Spirit, Thy Blessed Mother and all the angels. I also honor Thy Blessed Mother in the moment of her assumption into Paradise. I offer her all the glory and praises that were given her by the Omnipotent Father, by her Beloved Son, Thyself, Thy Holy Spirit, all the angels and all the saints. I offer to Thee and to Thy glorious Mother, my own entrance into Paradise, which, I hope, by Thy great mercy, to make one day, in honor of the glorious and triumphant entry of Thy ascension and her assumption. O my Most Adorable

Jesus, I desire to consecrate everything that ever was, is and shall be in me, in time and in eternity, to the honor and homage of Thee and Thy most holy Mother.

2. O Most Admirable and Most Adorable Trinity, I adore, bless and magnify Thee infinitely for all that Thou art in Thy manifold works of mercy and justice toward me and to all Thy creatures, in heaven, on earth and in hell. I offer Thee all the adoration, love, glory, praise and benediction accorded Thee forever. O my God, how I rejoice to behold Thee so full of greatness, of marvels, of glory and joy! It is enough. I desire no other glory, felicity or happiness in eternity save to behold the incomprehensible glory, felicity and happiness of Him whom I love more than myself. O my glory and my love, may all heaven and earth be transformed into glory and love for Thee! Finally, I sacrifice myself all to Thee to be sacredly annihilated and consumed forever in the most pure fire of Thy divine love.

3. O Jesus, Thou only object of my love, with what love, with what praises can I ever repay Thee for all that Thou art in Thyself, and for all the innumerable effects of Thy goodness towards all Thy creatures, myself in particular? Lord, may all Thy creatures, all Thy angels and saints, Thy Blessed Mother, and all the powers of Thy divinity and humanity be employed in blessing and loving Thee forever.

4. O Mother of God, O holy angels, O blessed saints, I hail, honor and thank you all in general, and each one in particular, especially those to whom I owe some special obligation and with whom I am to be most closely associated in eternity. In thanksgiving for all the favors I have received from you, and much more for all the glory and services you have rendered to my God, I offer to each one of you the most amiable Heart of my Jesus, source of all joy, all glory and all praise. I give you my mind and my heart; unite them with your minds and hearts and associate me in your constant chorus of praise to Him who created me, that I may praise and love Him eternally with you. Pray ardently that I may bless and love Him through you, while awaiting the day when it may please Him to unite me with you to love and glorify Him to perfection.

5. O blessed day, when I shall begin to love most purely and perfectly my Lord and Saviour who is infinitely amiable! O thousand

times happy day in which I shall begin to be all love for him who is all love for me! O Jesus, my sweet love, how consoled I am when I think that I shall love and bless Thee eternally! My eyes dissolve in tears and my heart melts with joy at the sweetness of the thought that some day I shall be completely transformed into praise and love for Thee. But, alas, when will it come, this day, so longed for and a thousand times desired? Will it yet delay for long? *Heu mihi quia incolatus meus prolongatus est!* "Woe is me, that my sojourning is prolonged" (Ps. 119, 5). *Usquequo, Domine, oblivisceris me in finem, usqueque avertis faciem tuam a me?* "How long, O Lord, wilt thou forget me unto the end? How long dost thou turn away thy face from me" (Ps. 12, 1)? *Quaemadmodum desiderat cervus ad fontes aquarum ita desiderat anima mea ad te, Deus* (Ps. 41, 2).

No more the hunted stag desires,
Fleeing in woe and weariness,
Waters to quench his burning thirst,
Than my poor heart with sadness pressed
Sighs after Thee, O Lord, my rest.

My heart is driven nigh to death
By cruel desires, merciless,
And longs for Thee, Lord, Mighty God,
And in its longing, cries apace:
When shall my eyes behold Thy face?

When, ah, when will come that day
To take my earthly woes away
And bring me home at last to Thee?

While waiting for that day, I desire, O my Saviour, to realize in myself St. Paul's words: "Our conversation is in heaven" (Phil. 3, 20), as well as Thy words of reassurance and guidance: "The kingdom of God is within you" (Luke 17, 21). I desire to live on earth as though I were not here, but living by my heart and spirit in heaven. I desire to concentrate all my powers on the establishment of the kingdom of

Thy glory and holy love within myself. But Thou knowest, Lord, that of myself I can do nothing; therefore, I give myself to Thee, that Thou mayest destroy every obstacle and perfectly establish the kingdom of Thy pure love in my body, in my soul, and in all my thoughts, words and actions.

## XXX. Conclusion of the Exercise.

At the end of these exercises on the subject of death, you should thank Our Lord for the graces He has given you through them, and beg Him to forgive the faults you have committed in their performance. Ask Him to compensate for your deficiencies, and to accomplish in you the fulfilment of His words: "Blesseed is that servant, whom when his lord shall come he shall find so doing. Amen I say to you: he shall place him over all his goods" (Matt. 24, 46-47). Pray that He may ever watch within you and for you, lest you be taken by surprise. Beg Him to keep these exercises and preparations in store for you against the hour of your death and to be Himself your disposition and preparation.

Follow the same procedure proportionately, invoking the Blessed Virgin, the angels and saints, especially the saints on whose feast day the Lord knows you are going to die.

## XXXI. Some Other Points of Advice and Necessary Dispositions for a Holy Death.

I shall here add a few other suggestions and practices which may prove useful to you, when you sense that your life is approaching its end.

The chief thing for you to do, when you feel that you are nearing the end of your life, is to devote yourself as much as possible to acts of love of Jesus, ever uniting humility with love. There is no more powerful and effective means of quickly wiping out our sins, advancing with great strides along the road to God, and giving Him pleasure than the divine exercise of active love.

If you are worried by the fear of death or by qualms of mistrust by reason of your past sins, ask some kind person to read to you the passages about confidence contained in "Part One" of this book.

If you are not too sick to listen to reading aloud, ask some kind friend to read to you, from time to time, the foregoing meditations on death, and the exercises of praise and glorification of Jesus which are to be found in "Part Five" of this book.

Let him also read passages from the Lives of the Saints or some other book of devotion, but particularly the Passion of Jesus Christ, the seventeenth chapter of the Gospel of St. John and the prayers for the agonizing soul, as on the seventh day of the "Exercise of Preparations for Death."

Do not forget, when you are at the end of your life, to remind one of your friends to gain a plenary indulgence for you, not in your own interest but for the pure glory of God, according to the method suggested in "Part Six," where indulgences are discussed.

Frequently clasp the Crucifix in your hands, so that you may from time to time make acts of love while kissing the Cross and the Five Wounds, as I explain in "Part Five."

Let the Holy Names of Jesus and Mary be ever in your heart and frequently on your lips. Renew the desire to pronounce them with the intentions recommended for the Rosary of Jesus and Mary in "Part Three."

Pray with St. Francis: "Lord, release my soul from the prison of this body that I may praise Thy Holy Name with all the just who await me in heaven."

Constantly invoke the Blessed Virgin, using the words of Holy Church: *Maria Mater gratiae, Mater misericordiae, tu nos ab hoste protege et hora mortis suscipe:* "O Mary, Mother of Grace, Mother of Mercy protect us from the enemy and receive us at the hour of death."

O Mother of Jesus, be a mother to my soul. *Monstra te esse Matrem.* "Show thyself my Mother." *Monstra to esse Matrem Jesu.* "Show that thou art the Mother of Jesus," by destroying in me, by thy prayers and merits, all that is contrary to the glory of thy Son Jesus, and causing Him to be loved and glorified perfectly in me.

Repeat with St. Stephen: *Domine Jesu suscipe spiritum meum:* "Lord Jesus, receive my spirit" (Acts 7, 58).

As you say all these words, ever unite yourself with the devotion, the love and the other holy dispositions with which they were first pronounced.

Accept your suffering in union with Jesus, in agony in the garden of Olives: *Pater, non mea voluntas sed tua fiat:* "Father, not my will but thine be done" (Luke 22, 42). And again with Jesus agonizing on the Cross, say: *Pater, in manus tuas commendo spiritum meum.* "Father, into thy hands I commend my spirit" (Luke 23, 46).

Constantly lift up your heart to Jesus, saying to Him with the beloved disciple St. John: *Veni Domine Jesu:* "Come, Lord Jesus" (Apoc. 22, 20).

Repeat with St. Peter: *Domine, tu scis quia amo te.* "Lord, thou knowest that I love thee" (John 21, 16).

Say with the good thief: *Memento mei, Domine, dum veneris in regnum tuum:* "Lord, remember me when thou shalt come into Thy Kingdom" (Luke 23, 42). And as you pronounce these words, unite yourself with the heartfelt contrition of the good thief, contrition so deep and moving that he merited the infinite grace to hear from the lips of the Son of God: "Amen I say to thee: this day thou shalt be with me in paradise" (Luke 23, 43).

Humbly repeat with the poor publican in the Gospel: *Deus propitius esto mihi peccatori.* "O God, be merciful to me a sinner" (Luke 18, 13).

Let your heart chant with King David: *Miserere mei Deus, secundum magnam misericordiam tuam:* "Have mercy on me, O God, according to thy great mercy" (Ps. 50, 3). *Suscipe me secundum eloquium tuum et vivam, et non confundas me ab expectatione mea:* "Uphold me according to thy word, and I shall live: and let me not be confounded in my expectation" (Ps. 118, 116). *In te Domine speravi, non confundar in aeternum:* "In thee, O Lord, have I hoped, let me never be confounded" (Ps. 30, 1).

You may also make use of these little aspirations: "O Jesus, love Thy Father and Thy Holy Spirit for me." "O Father of Jesus, O Holy Spirit of Jesus, O Mother of Jesus, O angels of Jesus, O saints of Jesus, love Jesus for me."

*Volo Domine Jesu te regnare super me:* "Lord Jesus, I will to have Thee reign over me."

*Dominare in medio inimicorum tuorum:* "Lord Jesus, reign over me in the midst of all Thy enemies."

"O my Dear Jesus, be Jesus to me; O my all, be all to me, for the past, present and future."

*Unum necessarium, unum volo, unum amo, unum quaero:* "One thing alone is necessary. Farewell to all things else; speak of them no more to me. I desire but one thing, I seek but one thing, I love but one thing, which is all to me, and all else is nothing to me. It is my sweetest Jesus Whom I desire, my Dearest Jesus whom I seek. Him I love and Him I long to love with all the love in heaven and on earth."

*Jesus meus et omnia:* "My Jesus is all to me. Once more, farewell to all that is not Jesus. My Jesus is sufficient for me. I desire nought but Him in heaven and on earth." *Veni Domine Jesu:* "Come Lord Jesus, enter into me, there to love Thyself to perfection."

"O Jesus, my all, be Thou my preparation for my death. O Jesus, I give myself to Thee to die with Thee, in Thee and by Thee."

"O Jesus, I give myself to Thee to unite myself, at the moment of death, with all the dispositions of love and sanctity which ennobled the death of Thy divine humanity, Thy holy martyrs and all the other saints."

"O Jesus, O Mary, Mother of Jesus, I implore you to give me your holy blessing."

Finally, try to make your last word be the Holy Name of Jesus and the sweet name of Mary: *Jesus, Mary!* or else, *Live Jesus!* or *Jesus, be Jesus to me!*

Thus, you may converse with Our Lord with profound devotion and consoling ease by means of frequent ejaculations. But if you wish Him to give you the grace to make these loving aspirations at the hour of your death, you must develop the habit of saying these words and pronouncing these ejaculations frequently during your life, especially at night, lying in bed before falling asleep, using now one, now another, according to the inspiration of the spirit of God.

It would also be well to ask those present around to assist you during your last sickness, to read and reread frequently the above prayers. And if by chance you should lose the power of speech, let them diligently continue to make these acts on your behalf, particularly if it should happen that you lose the use of your senses or your reason. Once you have made the request and expressed to your friends that it is your will for them to make acts of love in your name and for you, Our Lord will accept these precious acts as if you yourself were making them, since they are made at your request and on your behalf.

Pray also to the Blessed Virgin and your special angels and saints to carry out all these things for you, together with everything else they know God expects of you on the last day of your life. But above all, supplicate Jesus Himself to do this for you, and put great trust in His infinite goodness, that He will be your all, and will do on your behalf everything that is required of you for a holy and happy death. And I pray you to note this last point well.

Even though you should prepare yourself for death with all possible care and devotion, by means of these exercises, none the less, after having done all that has been suggested, you should not rely or rest upon your own acts, exercises and preparations, but rather place all your reliance and trust in the pure goodness and mercy of our Lord Jesus Christ, ever imploring Him to be your preparation, your virtue, your sanctification and your all.

For after all is said and done, to Jesus Christ alone does it belong to be all and accomplish all, in all men and all things that He may have the glory of all, according to the divine words of St. Paul, with which I began this book, and by which I wish to finish it: *Omnia in omnibus Christus:* "Christ is all and in all" (Col. 3, 11). Oh, Let Him then be all, in time and in eternity!

O Jesus, be all, be all on earth as Thou art in heaven: be all in all men and things. Be all in this little book. Everything it has of good is all from Thee. It speaks but of Thee and for Thee; it aims only at forming and establishing Thee in the souls of those who use it. Let its readers see in it nothing but Jesus, seek in it nothing but Jesus, and learn from it nothing but to love and glorify Jesus. Be all to him who has written this book and to those who shall read it; for Thou knowest, O Jesus, my dear all, that it is my will never, in life or in death, to have any other object or desire but to see Thee live and reign in all men and all things. Live then, Jesus, live and reign in us. The wretched Jews cried: *Nolumus hunc regnare super nos:* "We will not have this man to reign over us." We, on the contrary, desire to proclaim in the face of heaven and on earth: *Volumus, Domine Jesu, te regnare super nos.* "We want Thee, Lord Jesus, to reign over us." Reign, therefore, O King of Souls, dwell perfectly and absolutely in thy Kingdom in our hearts that we may forever sing the divine canticle: *Omnia in omnibus Jesu:* "Jesus is all in all things!" Live Jesus! Live Thou great all! Live great Jesus, Who art all! Live this great all, which is Jesus! Live Jesus! Live Jesus!

**LIVE JESUS AND MARY**

# INDEX